Lecture Notes in Information Systems and Organisation

Volume 55

Lecture Notes in Information Systems and Organization—LNISO—is a series of scientific books that explore the current scenario of information systems, in particular IS and organization. The focus on the relationship between IT, IS and organization is the common thread of this collection, which aspires to provide scholars across the world with a point of reference and comparison in the study and research of information systems and organization. LNISO is the publication forum for the community of scholars investigating behavioral and design aspects of IS and organization. The series offers an integrated publication platform for high-quality conferences, symposia and workshops in this field. Materials are published upon a strictly controlled double blind peer review evaluation made by selected reviewers.

LNISO is abstracted/indexed in Scopus

More information about this series at https://link.springer.com/bookseries/11237

Emilio Insfran · Fernando González ·
Silvia Abrahão · Marta Fernández · Chris Barry ·
Michael Lang · Henry Linger · Christoph Schneider
Editors

Advances in Information Systems Development

Crossing Boundaries Between Development and Operations in Information Systems

Springer

Editors
Emilio Insfran
Department of Computer Systems and Computation
Universitat Politècnica de València
Valencia, Spain

Silvia Abrahão
Department of Computer Systems and Computation
Universitat Politècnica de València
Valencia, Spain

Chris Barry
Cairnes School of Business & Economics
National University of Ireland Galway
Galway, Ireland

Henry Linger
Faculty of Information Technology
Monash University
Melbourne, VIC, Australia

Fernando González
Department of Business and Economics
Universitat Politècnica de València
Valencia, Spain

Marta Fernández
Department of Business and Economics
Universitat Politècnica de València
Valencia, Spain

Michael Lang
Cairnes School of Business & Economics
National University of Ireland Galway
Galway, Ireland

Christoph Schneider
IESE Business School
University of Navarra
Barcelona, Spain

ISSN 2195-4968 ISSN 2195-4976 (electronic)
Lecture Notes in Information Systems and Organisation
ISBN 978-3-030-95353-9 ISBN 978-3-030-95354-6 (eBook)
https://doi.org/10.1007/978-3-030-95354-6

This Springer imprint is published by the registered company Springer Nature Switzerland AG
The registered company address is: Gewerbestrasse 11, 6330 Cham, Switzerland

Conference Organization

Conference Chairs

Emilio Insfran, IUMTI—DSIC, Universitat Politècnica de València, Spain
Fernando González, DOE, Universitat Politècnica de València, Spain

Program Chairs

Silvia Abrahão, IUMTI—DSIC, Universitat Politècnica de València, Spain
Marta Fernández, DOE, Universitat Politècnica de València, Spain

Virtualization Chair

Abel Gómez, Universitat Oberta de Catalunya, Spain

International Steering Committee

Chris Barry, National University of Ireland Galway, Ireland
Michael Lang, National University of Ireland Galway, Ireland
Henry Linger, Monash University, Australia
Christoph Schneider, IESE Business School, Spain

Track Chairs

Managing IS Development and Operations

Ana Moreira, Universidade Nova de Lisboa, Portugal
João Araújo, Universidade Nova de Lisboa, Portugal

IS Methodologies and Education

Alfred Zimmermann, Reutlingen University, Germany
Giuseppe Scanniello, University of Basilicata, Italy

Security, Privacy and Trust in IS

Alberto Rodrigues da Silva, University of Lisbon, Portugal
Daniela Cruzes, Norwegian University of Science and Technology, Norway

Incorporating Human-Computer Interaction into IS

Jean Vanderdonckt, Université Catholique de Louvain, Belgium
Mikko Rajanen, University of Oulu, Finland

Green and Sustainable IS

Coral Calero, Universidad Castilla-La Mancha, Spain
Dorina Rajanen, University of Oulu, Finland

Current Topics in IS Development

Malgorzata Pankowska, University of Economics Katowice, Poland
Vaclav Repa, University of Economics in Prague, Czech Republic

Program Committee Members

Track: Managing IS Development and Operations

Dominique Blouin
Markus Borg
Dominik Bork
Nelly Condori Fernández
Maya Daneva
Jose Luis de la Vara
Ilias Gerostathopoulos
Abel Gómez
Jane Hayes
Eric Knauss
Seok-Won Lee
Grischa Liebel
Mariana Maia Peixoto
Beatriz Marin
Miguel Mira-da-Silva
Barbara Paech
Claudia Pons
Paulo Rupino-Da-Cunha
Mehrdad Sabetzadeh
Kurt Schneider
Christopher Vendome
Colin Venters

Track: IS Methodologies & Education

João Barata
Danilo Caivano
Oscar Diaz
Jānis Grabis
Carmine Gravino
Björn Johansson
Birger Lantow
Yoshimasa Masuda
Elena Navarro
Ovidiu Noran
Malgorzata Pankowska
Iris Reinhartz-Berger

Kurt Sandkuhl
Julio Sandobalín
Marco Santorum
Rainer Schmidt
Monique Snoeck
Karen Stendal
Janis Stirna
Ann Svensson
Torben Tambo

Track: Security, Privacy & Trust in IS

Chris Barry
Karin Bernsmed
Achim Brucker
Danilo Caivano
Ana Cavalli
Miguel Correia
Christophe Feltus
Martin Gilje Jaatun
Tim Majchrzak
Andreas Poller
Sven Türpe

Track: Incorporating Human-Computer Interaction into IS

José Creissac Campos
Netta Iivari
Marianne Kinnula
Yann Laurillau
Sophie Lepreux
Pedro J. Molina
Norbert Pataki
Jorge Luis Pérez Medina
Costin Pribeanu
Philippe Renevier
Ahmed Seffah
Marco Winckler

Track: Green and Sustainable IS

Elina Annanperä
Ruzanna Chitchyan
Felix Garcia
Patricia Lago
David Langley
Irene Lizeth Manotas Gutiérrez
Mª Ángeles Moraga
Stefan Naumann

Track: Current Topics in ISD

Cheuk-Hang Au
Peter Bernus
Tomáš Bruckner
Alena Buchalcevova
Justin Filippou
Ahmad Ghazawneh
Mairéad Hogan
Henry Linger
Nearchos Paspallis
Dijana Plantak Vukovac
Marios Raspopoulos
Karel Richta
Artur Strzelecki
Oleg Svatoš

Additional Reviewers

Vita Barletta
Alejandro Catala
Shalini Chakraborty
Hyo Cheol Lee
Sangeeta Dey
Umberto Fiaccadori
Vinh Hoa La
Michael Lang
Rakshit Mittal
Lorraine Morgan

Huu Nghia Nguyen
Sihn Hye Park
Valentina Kirinic
Dijana Oreški
Joanna Palonka
Jaroslav Pokorný
Victoria Paulsson
Martin Potančok
Mariia Rizun
Paulina Rutecka
Irish Singh
Anna Soltysik-Piorunkiewicz
Zlatko Stapić
Filip Vencovsky
Mariusz Żytniewski

Preface

The **International Conference on Information Systems Development** (ISD) is an academic conference where researchers and practitioners share their knowledge and expertise in the field of information systems development. As an Affiliated Conference of the Association for Information Systems (AIS), the ISD conference complements the international network of general IS conferences (ICIS, ECIS, AMCIS, PACIS, HICSS). The ISD conference continues the tradition started with the first Polish-Scandinavian Seminar on Current Trends in Information Systems Development Methodologies, held in Gdansk, Poland in 1988. This seminar has evolved into the International Conference on Information Systems Development.

Throughout its history, the conference has focused on different aspects, ranging from methodological, infrastructural, and educational challenges in the ISD field to bridging the gaps between industry, academia, and society. Advancements in information systems foster technological developments. The deployment of the resulting technologies in all areas of society, including in the public and private sector, the community, and in the home is greatly beneficial. ISD has always promoted a close interaction between theory and practice, setting a human-centered agenda focused on advancing the methods, tools and management of IS.

This volume is a selection of papers from ISD2021, the 29th Information Systems Development conference hosted by Universitat Politècnica de València, and held in Valencia, Spain on September 8–10, 2021.

All accepted papers have been published in the AIS eLibrary, which is accessible at https://aisel.aisnet.org/isd2014/proceedings2021. This volume contains extended versions of the best papers, as selected by the ISD2021 Proceedings Editors.

The theme of the conference was *Crossing Boundaries between Development and Operations (DevOps) in Information Systems*. It focused on the latest developments in ISD and particularly on emerging concepts, novel approaches and ideas that are likely to shape information systems research and practice in the next years.

The ISD2021 conference attracted contributions in the general area of information systems development, management, and education, as well as in more specialized topics including Security, Privacy and Trust in IS, Green and Sustainable IS and Incorporating Human-Computer Interaction into IS. ISD2021 focused on these and associated topics in order to promote research into theoretical and methodological issues and ways in which these advances enable better synergies between theory and practice.

We believe that the innovative papers assembled in these lecture notes will inform the reader of important contributions in this regard.

Valencia, Spain	Emilio Insfran
Valencia, Spain	Fernando González
Valencia, Spain	Silvia Abrahão
Valencia, Spain	Marta Fernández
Melbourne, Australia	Henry Linger
Galway, Ireland	Chris Barry
Galway, Ireland	Michael Lang
Barcelona, Spain	Christoph Schneider

Contents

A Data-Driven Optimization Computational Tool Design for Bike-Sharing Station Distribution in Small to Medium-Sized Cities: A Case Study for Cuenca, Ecuador

Fernando Cueva, Pengcheng Shi, and Priscila Cedillo

Abstract Faced with heavy vehicular traffic at present, the strategic implementation of Bike Sharing Systems (BSSs) in cities as an alternative means of transport for users is increasingly being adopted. These solutions reduce the environmental burden posed by other means of transportation, decrease costs for citizens, improves people's health due to physical activity, among other advantages. However, aspects such as the definition of bike stations' locations represent a challenge when these solutions are being implemented. Therefore, this paper presents a software tool design that supports a method that defines the location and number of stations within a BSS. Also, the tool uses a data-driven optimization model to establish the location of stations. Finally, a case study carried out in Cuenca—Ecuador, demonstrates the proposal's feasibility, showing a significant concordance with the consulting firms-consortia results (70–90% of coincidence) at a lower cost.

Keywords Bike sharing system · Public bike system · Optimization · Pollutants · Data-driven

---

A prior version of this paper has been published in the ISD2021 Proceedings (http://aisel.aisnet.org/isd2014/proceedings2021).

F. Cueva (✉) · P. Shi
Rochester Institute of Technology, Rochester, USA
e-mail: wfc9474@rit.edu

P. Shi
e-mail: pengcheng.shi@rit.edu

F. Cueva · P. Cedillo
Universidad de Cuenca, Cuenca, Ecuador
e-mail: priscila.cedillo@ucuenca.edu.ec

E. Insfran Pelozo et al. (eds.), *Advances in Information Systems Development*, Lecture Notes in Information Systems and Organisation 55,
https://doi.org/10.1007/978-3-030-95354-6_1

1 Introduction

Population growth and city urbanization lead to a greater demand for different means of transport [1]. It is increasing the number of vehicles [2]. It drives congestion with direct implications on travel times and air pollution, increasing mortality and morbidity [3].

There are several alternatives to reduce the problem of traffic congestion. Among them, public transport, vehicle access limitation by ordinance [4], shared vehicle [2], alternatives to the traditional vehicle (small ones with electric batteries) [5], motorcycles, and the implementation of a Bike Sharing System (BSS) [6]. However, the first one is limited by not having access to all city points, while the second one presents logistical and political problems [7]. The shared vehicle alternative reduces traffic congestion and provides users lower costs than private vehicles [8]; however, it is not environmentally friendly. The fourth alternative is not always accessible to all users due to the cost [5]. In the case of motorcycles, it allows users' connection with their places of destination and takes up little space, but pollution is more significant than bikes.

A BSS is a public transport alternative that allows users to take a bike at one point and return it at another, either in exchange for a fee or free. These systems enable traveling through a network of stations with multimodal connections that can be point-to-point or round-trip in an urban environment. BSS is an alternative to motorized transport that reduces travel time, generating economic savings - compared to other transport systems [9, 10], energy savings, optimizing the use of space on roads, parking, and mobilization. In addition, it can be integrated with the mass transport system, friendly to the environment, and promotes livable and healthier cities [10, 11].

However, the BSS implementation's success depends on the correct location and number of stations in the urban environment that satisfy the demand and guarantee an adequate service throughout the city. Therefore, this study aims to propose a tool that supports a method that estimates the number of stations and their optimal location. The presented informatic tool design provides an affordable solution to help designers during the stations' distribution establishment without using too many resources (e.g., economic, human). Medium and small cities could start their BSSs planning from a standardized platform supported by a data-driven software tool to define stations. This tool will consider aspects related to historical information and other public means of transport. Therefore, this study can lead to the necessary support to diminish the environmental impact produced by pollutants from cars, motorcycles, and traditional means of transportation using BSS systems with reachable stations that serve citizens around cities.

Although several companies provide consulting services for locating the optimal places for implementing the BSS's stations, those solutions are expensive. Besides, most of the time, small and medium cities could not afford their prices; being necessary to have software that uses available information sourced by other public organizations (e.g., population and demographic distribution, public transportation companies, weather historical data sources) allow making decisions automatically. On the other hand, the reviewed literature indicates that data available for each city and its characteristics have defined the stations' location differently and often without a scientifically defined, replicable, and repeatable method [12, 13].

During the main method that is supported for the system of this contribution, four stages were considered, starting with (i) defining the factors for a correct distribution of the stations; (ii) preparing and preprocessing data; (iii) determining the suitability of the stations. Finally, the operational research model defines the locations, and the number of stations considering the previous models' algorithms and outputs to design a BSS from strategic planning and its respective evaluation case study.

Consequently, having a data-driven based software tool helps in a scientific and repeatable way to optimize the station distribution to design a BSS.

The solution has been used when the main method was applied to a specific case study in the city of Cuenca-Ecuador to measure precision when comparing the method's results versus the stations' empirical location [14]. Cuenca became an interesting case study because it is a city with traffic problems, declared a World Heritage Site. Furthermore, it is a medium-size city due to its number of inhabitants (i.e., half a million approximately) and its size (72 km^2) [15].

The study is organized into sections. Section 2 presents the background and related work that identifies the factors considered in implementing a BSS in other cities. Section 3 describes the main contribution of this research. Sections 4 and 5 present the main results, conclusions, and further work.

2 Background and Related Work

According to international guidelines [8, 16], the factors that influence and must be considered for an optimal distribution of the stations are (i) demographic and socioeconomic factors such as population and job density; (ii) geographic and topographic factors; (iii) climate; (iv) places of cultural and recreational attraction, public spaces and parks; and (v) infrastructure and mass transportation. Therefore, these factors should be considered general and a starting point for the design of BSS locations.

Additionally, the specific needs, objectives, and data sources must be considered, among other specific case study aspects. In this context, BSS experiences in other countries are analyzed to define the factors that could be used in determining the location of the stations [7, 14, 17, 18].

The literature available on BSS is varied. Studies related to BSS design have focused on stations, prices, bikes, balance, and service stations. A key component to the success of the BSS design is the location of the bike stations. However, from the perspective of strategic planning, very few research studies have been conducted in this regard [19], so this component is the research's starting point. Also, as far as we know, there are a lack of software tools that support methods and allow making decisions related to the location of BSS stations.

The distribution of stations must guarantee the optimum level of service for users when they require a bike. It implies covering the total demand of the area with an optimal number of stations that ensure the service's quality [12–15], allowing to minimize the costs derived from the distance traveled and considering a penalty for unmet demand [20]. Several studies have used optimization methods for this purpose [21].

Appendix summarizes the objective, methods, and factors used by a set of studies focused on bike inventory management, station capacity, and location. Despite the contributions in using models and inventory management, works such as [20, 22] do not validate the proposals with a case study. On the other hand, other studies do not consider other factors or ignore the integration with the transport system to define the stations' location, in the case of Garcia-Gutierrez et al. [16] and Romero et al. [21], respectively. In Guo et al. [23], the approach used was robust to improve the optimization model. As it can be concluded, there are not highly flexible solutions that employing a software tool can join different data sources to establish the location of the BSS stations considering real information originated in the city in which the bike system will operate.

3 Data-Driven Strategies to Determine BSS Station Distribution

This section explains the model, factors analysis, data sources, data processing, and the proposed software solution.

3.1 Models

Previous steps allow us to establish a method which is shown in Fig. 1. Also, the method needs to be supported by a tool. Both are useful for making decisions in the station distribution's strategic planning based on different data sources. As shown in Fig. 1, four main activities were stated as part of the main method. In order to be harmonic with the main method, the software tool design presented in this paper supports each of the activities, integrating them in a solution that provides as output an optimal model with the final BSS station's locations.

This approach shows the multi data-driven philosophy with the different steps carried out to deal with the stations' distribution based on the information analysis.

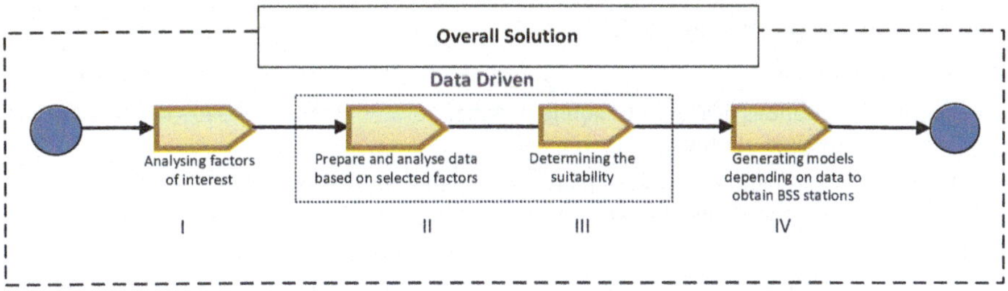

Fig. 1 Overall solution with data-driven philosophy

The different data used in the study (see Fig. 1-I) are summarized in Table 2. After handling and processing (see Fig. 1-II), these data allow obtaining the suitability areas, the cost of the pollutants (i.e., noise and NO_2) per city block (i.e., an area of the city surrounded by streets), distance matrix, and demand matrix. Finally, with the processed data, the data model is built whose objective function is to minimize the stations' costs with their penalties, distributing the stations with a number that covers the city. The final model is achieved using econometric models (i.e., hedonic prices), optimization models (i.e., set covering problem), data analytics, and machine learning algorithms (i.e., clusters) that have been proposed for data management.

This contribution constitutes a good starting point for places without resources, expertise, and a high need for a BSS, saving them time and money.

3.2 *Factor Analysis, Data Sources, and Data Processing*

This subsection explains the data-driven approach considering the impacting factors analyzed in previous studies, the data sources used in the case study, and the correlation with the general data used in other implementations. The data-driven approach allows preparing, analyzing, and determining the model's different inputs to define the station distribution.

Analyzing the factors

According to the literature review, multiple factors have been classified as low, medium, and high impact related to the level of influence on the objective (to establish the shared bike stations' location) (see Table 1). On the other hand, data on pollutants produced by automobiles, such as noise and Nitrogen Dioxide (NO_2), are used to reduce their impact on the city and its inhabitant's health, proposing an alternative transportation system. These pollutant data are analyzed with the software tool and represent an input towards searching the optimization model.

It is recommended to use at least medium and high impact factors for a good result. The factors were selected according to the application case (Cuenca city), the literature review, and the data availability in this research. High impact factors were selected: (i) demographics, (ii) bike lanes, (iii) tourist attraction, (iv) bus stops, (v)

Table 1 Factors used in the case study

Impact	Factors	Previous studies
Low impact	Stations nearby automobile parking, origin–destination matrix	[6, 17, 18, 24, 25]
Middle impact	Residential locations, recreational parks, university locations, and topography	[11, 26–33]
High impact	Job density, public transit location (bus stops), demographics (e.g., age, education, income, equity), tourist attraction, bike lanes, and land use	[6, 10, 18, 24, 34– 39]
New proposal	Pollutants and safety at both the road and city levels	

land use, and (vi) job density. Medium impact factors: (vii) the topography of the city, (viii) residential locations, (ix) parks, and (x) university locations. Low impact factors: (xi) Stations nearby automobile parking.

Additionally, new factors are proposed, such as using pollutants as penalties, traffic patterns, and safety at both road and urban levels. These factors were not present in previous studies. All these factors were used with a data-driven approach. Data were analyzed using methods that eliminate duplications, such as Principal Component Analysis (PCA), a dimensionality-reduction method used to reduce large datasets without losing representativeness. Once they were refined, they served as input for the software that allowed obtaining maps at the city block level for the city's stations' location.

Data sources

The city data are stored in different databases (public and private institutions) (see Table 2). In some cases, the information collected does not directly provide the required information but instead infers the information necessary to plan a BSS from specific data.

According to the studies analyzed in the previous sections, the data used in this research were collected to establish, on the one hand, the demand based on the factors analyzed (e.g., demographic, land use) and, on the other, the optimization of the number of stations and its distribution in the city to meet the user's needs. These data are produced in the daily activity of the city and collected by different organizations.

The data were analyzed and crossed between different sources to obtain the information used by other authors. Then other data that had not been used in previous studies were included; this allowed to obtain a better result of the station's distribution in a BSS. The data-driven approach allows establishing systematic and repeatable steps to establish the distribution of stations in countries where resources are limited.

Data processing and analysis

In this process, the data sources used and the methodologies applied are detailed according to the different factors considered for the study. Therefore, information processing was carried out to debug the data (outliers, exceptions, inconsistencies,

Table 2 Data sources

Source	Information
Commission for Environmental Management (CGA)	Noise pollution
Municipal Mobility, Transit and Transportation Company (EMOV-EP)	Nitrogen dioxide pollution
ANT (National Transit Agency)	Vehicle registration database with segmented information and information on vehicular traffic
EMOV EP	Bus database (Includes: 1. Household survey on the socio-economic conditions of the users, 2. Conditions of the bus service, and 3. Register of counts of getting on and off people)
	Tram Database: Tram stops, bus stops, and public parking lots are considered last-mile points for private vehicles
	Route of existing bike lanes
	Vehicle mobility patterns at certain times in the city
Citizen Security Council (CSC)	Accident and robbery database
A survey, database built within the doctoral thesis	Demand database. Mobility survey applied to people between 16 and 65 years old in the city of Cuenca. Reference year: 2018. Geographic coverage: City of Cuenca. The mobility survey collects sociodemographic and behavioral information on transport to characterize the user who uses a bike as a means of mobility
Internal Revenue Service (SRI)	Database of taxpayers who have economic activity in the municipality of Cuenca
ANT	Database of vehicles that pay for vehicle registration in Cuenca
Public Telecommunications, Water and Sewerage Company (ETAPA)	The database contains the telephone numbers of users throughout the Cuenca canton with a location at the property level (a)
Institute of Statistics and Censuses (INEC)	Population and housing data at the block level for the entire study area
The decentralized autonomous government of the municipality of Local government of Cuenca	The topography of the city in raster format allows obtaining the slope levels of the city
	Database of properties and their characteristics. Map of the city at the level of blocks and land use with the main activities categorized as commercial, educational, and recreational

Note (a) These data are cross-referenced with the SRI information to obtain business or business locations to establish jobs' density or other problems) and prepare it for the following phases. After debugging, that data were passed down to a block-level and then exported to an array. The array's dimensions are made up of the number of blocks in the city that were 4172 (i.e., rows), 990 bus stops, 27 tram stops, and five public parking lots defined as last-mile points (i.e., columns). In these arrays, the distances between those elements were stored (e.g., distance matrix between blocks and bus stops 4172 $\times$ 990). Another array was also created containing the components resulting from the dimensionality reduction for each city block. This process is critical as it is time-consuming, and the model's accuracy depends on this stage.

Analyzing the data

Factor analysis is carried out in order to reduce variables without loss of relevant information. The extraction method that gave the best results was the Principal Component Analysis (PCA). All the factors explain 55.28% of the variation, and a value of 0.783 was obtained in the Kaiser, Meyer, and Olkin test and Bartlett's specificity, indicating that the analysis is adequate. Intrinsic factors were grouped into three components (i) traffic factors that addressed characteristics such as bus weight, topography, parking, rush hours (traffic patterns), and accidents. (ii) Demographic factors made up of potential users, grouped into clusters and population density. Finally, (iii) component 3, composed of land use and job density. Some factors were grouped into a single layer of information called land use (i.e., university locations, tourist attractions, parks). On the other hand, pollutants were used for the hedonic price model to determine the penalty cost in the cost function.

To provide a solution to high-pollution areas through implementing a BSS, the proposed model includes a monetary penalty for the level of air pollution (NO_2) and noise. For this, the hedonic price model was used (Eq. 1) [40] to establish the value per square meter that people would pay to avoid contamination. Then, this value is multiplied for each block, obtaining the penalty per block. Thus, blocks with more contamination result in a higher value.

$$P_h = f(S_h, N_h, G_h, e_h) \quad (1)$$

Where the market price Ph of a single-family detached house with its structural (Sh) and neighborhood (Nh) characteristics, as well as environmental variables (Gh), and the error term (eh), are the standard hedonic framework. The variables used in the hedonic price model are:

1. Environmental variables of pollution: levels of nitrogen dioxide (NO_2) and noise pollution at any time of the day or night, during the day and night, measured in decibels.
2. Property features such as age, land area, length of the front, number of floors, number of bathrooms, type of floor, state of construction, the material of columns, beams, mezzanines, wall, deck, floors, doors, windows, plastered and lying.

3. External or neighborhood factors such as traffic accidents, robberies of people and houses, distance to the historic center. Other factors are if it is in front of a river if the property is a building, municipal records (RMO) for business, if the house is located in an industrial area, the services available 250 m around, type of road, and if it is located in the historic center.

The results show that the Cuenca market penalizes the property value by \$21.2 year/property per unit of NO_2 emitted in the area. The penalty values for noise pollution are lower than for NO_2 emissions. The price of the property decreases by \$3.4 on average annually for every decibel. These values make up the pollution cost penalty.

Determining origin/destination and demand arrays

In this phase, distance matrices are established between the main travel generators or origins and attractors or destinations [41], which are necessary to establish the stations' distribution. The distance matrix was calculated through the Geographic Information System (GIS). The matrix's dimensions are made up of the number of blocks in the city that were 4172 (i.e., rows), 990 bus stops, 27 tram stops, and five public parking lots defined as last-mile points (i.e., columns). It was necessary to use the distances of the central points of the blocks with each of the bus stops (4172 × 990 order matrix) and trams (4172 × 27 order matrix), parking lots (4172 × 5 order matrix), and between the blocks (square matrix of order 4172).

Determining the demand

Determining the characteristics of the potential demand for the BSS is essential to infer the leading market segments that can use the bike share system (potential users). Therefore, based on the demand database (see Table 2), a cluster analysis was first performed to find sociodemographic data patterns (e.g., age, occupation, sex, among others) of the potential demand. As a result, two clusters were obtained with adequate and almost reasonable quality (Silhouette coefficient). Cluster 1 includes private employees and people with their businesses between 20 and 55 years old, whose occupation is destined to the work environment; they are mobilized for labor issues. Cluster 2 is made up of students between the ages of 18 and 30.

Determining the suitability

In this phase, it is required to determine the areas where a station's establishment is necessary. Suitability means which blocks have the best characteristics for locating a bike station. The suitability blocks matrix makes up an input within the model. The weights obtained through the principal components' method (Analyze the data section) are taken as input and multiplied by the stations' cost to establish suitability. With this, the most suitable blocks with a lower cost were identified.

Building the model

With the previous stages, it is possible to obtain the optimal number of stations covering the city and meet the objective and the proposed restrictions. The proposed optimization model aims to maximize BSS coverage between bus stops, tram stops, last-mile points, and the city's main origins and destinations. The model is represented by an objective function, where the decision variable is the number of stations that satisfy the highest possible demand.

Here, the system provides the optimization model based on each activity of the methodology. The used metrics are part of the system and calculate the final value. The city of Cuenca is divided into 4,172 blocks. It has 990 bus stops, 27 tram stops, and 5 points in the last mile (proposed); those stations must cover within an established radius (e.g., 300, 500 m). The written model's formulation is presented using the objective function (Eq. 2) subject to the restrictions (Eqs. 3–7). The problem formulation is represented in Table 3.

Table 3 Subscripts and sets

Subscripts and sets	Input parameters	Decision variable
	D_{bb}, J_{bg},K_{bt}, L_{bm}: the distance between candidate stations and blocks, between but stops and blocks, between tram stops and blocks, between last-mile points and blocks, respectively	
	P, j, k, n: the maximum distance to cover demand in the block, the bus stops, tram stops, and last-mile points, respectively	
$b \in B$: the set of potential bike stations locations	d_{ba}, u_{bg}, w_{bt}, r_{bm}:equals 1 if the area, bus stops, tram stops, the last-mile points, respectively, can be covered by candidate station ***b*** in ***p, j, k, n*** metes, respectively, and 0 otherwise	Y_b: equals 1 if demand in area b is not covered within p distance and 0 otherwise
$g \in G$: the set of but stops	S_b: defines overall suitability of an area for candidate stations where $S_b > 0$	X_b: equals 1 if station location b is allocated and 0 otherwise
$t \in T$: the set of trams stops	h_b: is the fixed cost of setting up a station at candidate site ***b***	
$m \in M$: the set of last-mile points	δ: is the unit penalty cost for uncovered demand	
$o \in O$: the set of last-mile points	θ_{bo}: is the amount of pollutant I on site ***b***	
	v_o: cost per pollutant	
	λ: is the population to be served in area ***b***	

$$Min.\sum_{b\in B} h_b(X_b + X_b S_b) + \delta\sum_{b\in B} \lambda_b Y_b + \sum_{o\in O}\sum_{b\in B} X_b \theta_{bo} v_o \tag{2}$$

Subject to:

$$\sum_{b\in B} d_{ba} X_b \geq 1 \forall a \in A \tag{3}$$

$$\sum_{b\in B} u_{bg} X_b \geq 1 \forall g \in G \tag{4}$$

$$\sum_{b\in B} w_{bt} X_b \geq 1 \forall t \in T \tag{5}$$

$$\sum_{b\in B} r_{bm} X_b \geq 1 \forall m \in M \tag{6}$$

$$X_{b'} Y_a = \{0, 1\}, \forall a \in A, b \in B \tag{7}$$

where

Equation (2) minimizes the sum of the bike station's cost, pollution penalty costs, and unmet demand. The set of restrictions are represented by Eqs. 3–7 and ensure that residents of each defined area can access at least one station in less than p meters (3), that users can access at least one station in less of j, k, and n meters from the bus stops (4), from the tram stops (5), and the last mile points (6), respectively. Finally, the integrality constraint ensures that the decision variables take 0 or 1, Eq. (7).

3.3 *Designing a Software Solution for Station Distribution of a BSS*

Software tools play an important role when integrating a series of components to collect, store, and process data. In order to present support for the station's location in a BSS, it has been presented the architecture of a tool that shows each component necessary to support designers towards a method that allows the location of stations in small and medium cities.

Therefore, this research has included a tool that provides designers with information about station distribution in the city. Data collected and analyzed will serve as input for the provided solution to obtain the optimization model (see Fig. 2-1). The pollutants are a data source to be considered in order to obtain a hedonic price model (see Fig. 2-4), which through a proposed information system, will report the price of the pollutants (see Fig. 2-3) used, and that will be the value that people are willing to pay in order to maintain the lowest environmental impact in their living area. On the other hand, optimization models will be used based on available data to provide a data-driven approach; with these data, the city's ideal areas obtained from analyzing the different available information will be defined. The result of these models will

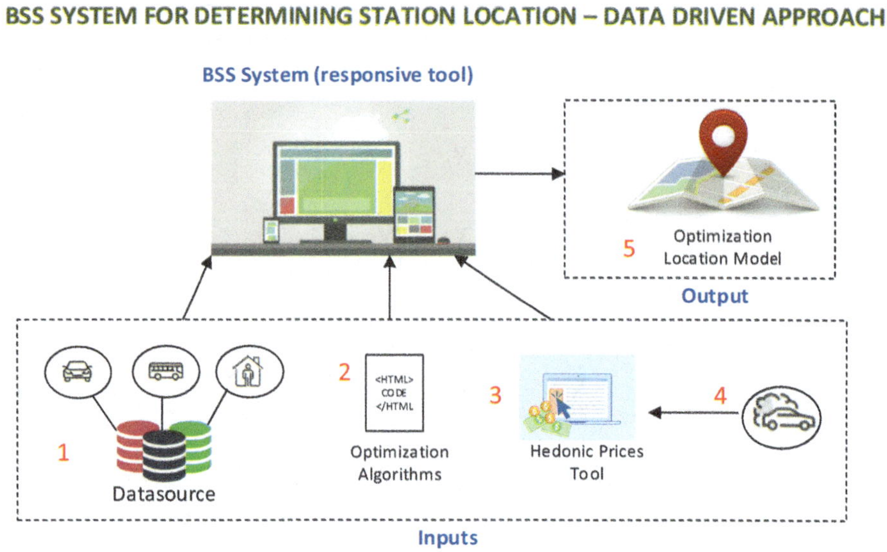

Fig. 2 BSS system for determining station's location—data-driven approach

serve as an input for the proposed system in such a way that after analyzing them, it allows the visualization on a map. This map contains the stations' distribution covering the city's different points based on citizens' demands and needs, as shown in Fig. 2-5. This software tool should be friendly and easy to use based on Web technologies. This proposed architecture is illustrated in Fig. 2.

The software has been designed to be implemented by using as backend node.js and for the front-end Angular.js. Also, several web services will be integrated into a Software Oriented Architecture (SOA), which implements a business layer that can be easily updated with new services that new data sources can feed. Also, other considerations related to event-driven patterns and asynchronous calls will be implemented. The orchestration of those services allows them to work together to implement and reach the objectives of the method.

Although the software is in an initial phase (i.e., requirements elicitation and design), a simulation of each step has been manually performed in which step by step has been followed in order to prove the feasibility of the activities when they will be implemented into the system.

4 Results

This article addresses the optimal distribution of stations (location and number) within a BSS as an alternative means of mobilization in small and medium-sized cities through an established methodological process. After applying the proposed

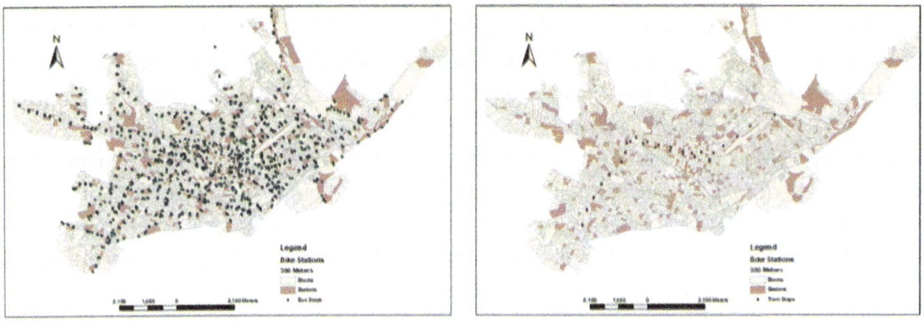

(a) (b)

Fig. 3 **a** Location of bike stations and bus stops at 300 **m.** **b** Location of bike stations and tram stops at 300 m

optimization model, the results show different stations depending on the radius used (300 or 500 m). The ideal radius is 300 m, and the maximum limit is a radius of 500 m [42]. Therefore, the ideal radius for the analysis was considered.

The model obtained by the method and supported by the system estimated 345 and 146 stations for a distance radius between 300 and 500 m, respectively. These values provide coverage to the entire city applying the restrictions established in the model. Furthermore, the maps presented reveal that the stations' location covers the bus stops (see Fig. 3a), and the tram stops see Fig. 3b, demonstrating that a BSS can be integrated with the public transport systems available in the city (i.e., buses, trams) and private cars (last mile points).

The current locations were established by the consortium formed by a Spanish company and the public mobilization company in Cuenca, named BiciCuenca [14]. The model shows high precision (70%) in comparison with the consortium. If the results are analyzed considering the contiguous blocks, the precision reaches 90% since only two existing stations' locations do not coincide with the model. The algorithms, models, and SI used in the present study provide a data-driven approach to establish the city's station distribution. Using a data-driven approach helps to design the strategic planning of a BSS used by decision-makers. This method constitutes a good starting point for places without resources, expertise, and a high need for a BSS, saving them time and money.

This research contributes to the design, improvement, or restructuring of a BSS using a method that defines the stations' distribution in a parameterizable, repeatable, and organized way, based on accepted standards.

5 Discussion, Conclusions, and Future Research

The proposed software solution design incorporates various techniques such as econometric models, data analysis, machine learning (i.e., clusters), and operations research, developing a mathematical optimization model. Several sources of information will be used, both primary (via a survey) and secondary (multiple public institutions). The model used to establish the stations' location considers a penalty for air and noise pollution, unsatisfied demand, and suitability.

Currently, the city of Cuenca has a bike-sharing system. The bike stations were located according to expert considerations (without scientific studies). The model had a precision of 70% (for exact blocks) using all the method parameters. Accuracy was 90% when contiguous blocks were included compared to existing stations in Cuenca city (prepared with expert experience).

The proposed software is computationally feasible and will work with different data types. Therefore, it will allow the station distribution's strategy step by step, which has not been explicitly done in previous studies. The implemented strategy allows a systematic flow that makes it repeatable, reliable, effective, efficient, and replicable in other similar situations in small and medium-sized cities. Furthermore, the proposal is less expensive than other studies requiring extensive or expensive human experts' participation; consequently, it saves economic, human, and time resources. In this context, the study contributes considerably to the strategic planning of a BSS related to the stations' distribution. Also, it contributes to the empirical literature on the use of pollution penalties within the model to increase the precision of station locations since no studies have been found that determine the location based on pollution data (NO_2 and noise). On the other hand, the list of factors used allows standardizing the data management approach.

Furthermore, in this article, only two pollutants were used, such as NO_2 and noise. Other pollutants such as fine particles (PM), sulfur dioxide (SO_2), and carbon monoxide (CO) could be interesting to analyze with the model in further investigations. On the other hand, other components such as bike lanes and the initial bike fleet could be considered to improve the proposed optimization model. A sensitivity analysis of the stations' optimal location can be examined in the next steps by adjusting the different penalty parameters' values and using other pollutants to identify the effect of model changes. These elements could be resolved in future research.

As a next step towards implementing the proposed solution, the structure of the data (format, type) and how data will be collected and inserted into the database will be defined. Another important aspect is the design of an optimal architecture in which the main components and their interconnections or relations will be clearly defined. In order to reach this objective, on the one hand, it will be included all the mechanisms used to clean data according to the enabled data sources by using a method (e.g., Cross-Industry Standard Process for Data Mining (CRISP)) or any other technique that allows the storing of optimal information.

Finally, the case study shows several aspects to be considered when a general method is defined. Therefore, as a first step, it can be concluded that implementing a solution that contributes to technicians in designing the best locations of bike stations can represent a powerful and cheap solution when leading the design of a BSS. This solution, therefore, represents the first approach of a tool that will support a method, which will be the next step in our research. Thus, there is expected to implement the software with the tools and languages explained in Sect. 3.

Acknowledgements This research was supported by the *Secretaría de Educación Superior, Ciencia, Tecnología e Innovación* (SENESCYT), Government of the Republic of Ecuador [grant number 704-2012]. We thank the Department of Computing and Information Sciences Ph.D. of RIT and the *Universidad de Cuenca* for the support provided to the researchers. We also thank GAD of Cuenca through their company EMOV-EP, CGA, ETAPA, SRI, INEC, CSC, who provided the necessary information for this research.

Appendices

Literature Review

Research	Objective and method
[22]	– Minimize bike stock cost, service level measured by coverage, and available bikes – Greedy heuristic for stations (open/close station until reduced cost), Dijkstra's algorithm to determine the lanes, and Palm's theorem for inventory management
[20]	– Proposed a deterministic centralized approach based on an integer non-linear program model – It manages an optimal inventory level to restock the bikes inventory where the replenishment costs and the units are minimal, and the stations do not remain unserved in the system
[43]	– Maximize the revenue for stations, bikes, and relocation. The problem was solved in several days; it means computationally intensive and with synthetic data. Based on simulations of trips by the hour, the authors defined the fleet, station capacity, and location. They proposed a mix of strategic and operational planning
[21]	Minimize the cost of private cars and public bikes with a bilevel optimization problem. The authors use the population data to determine station locations, and they integrate two means of transportation
[23]	Minimize the travel distance between stations and the overlapping between predefined clusters defining station locations at scenic spots. The optimization cluster by cluster improves computing time; it was executed in a city's specific zone
[16]	Used a bilevel optimization model to determine station location, bike number, and parking lots for bikes. They minimize the total cost of the whole transportation system (i.e., car, buses, cycling) with a study case in Mexico
[44]	Minimize travel time, consider initial bikes and parking lockers. The authors determine the dynamic demand from O/D in periods. They used an illustrative example and a mixed strategy with operational planning

References

1. Barbero, J.A., Galeota, C.: Urban transportation. Wiley Blackwell Encycl. Urban Reg. Stud., 1–12 (2019)
2. Vasconcellos, E.A.: Contribuciones a un gran impulso ambiental para América Latina y el Caribe: movilidad urbana sostenible. Santiago (2019)
3. Montero, L., García, J.: Panorama multidimensional del desarrollo urbano en América Latina y el Caribe. CEPAL, Santiago de Chile (2017)
4. Agencia Metropolitana de Tránsito: Hoy no circula. In: AMT (2016)
5. Kolk, A., Tsang, S.: Co-evolution in relation to small cars and sustainability in China. Bus Soc. (2017). https://doi.org/10.1177/0007650315584928
6. Shaheen, S.A., Martin, E.W., Cohen, A.P., et al.: Public bikesharing in North America during a period of rapid expansion: understanding business models, industry trends & user impacts. Mineta Transp. Inst. Rep. 12–29 (2014)
7. Xie, X., Tou, X., Zhang, L.: Effect analysis of air pollution control in Beijing based on an odd-and-even license plate model. J. Clean. Prod. **142**, 936–946 (2017). https://doi.org/10.1016/j.jclepro.2016.09.117
8. Qu, M., Yu, S., Yu, M.: An improved approach to evaluate car sharing options. Ecol. Indic. **72**, 686–702 (2017). https://doi.org/10.1016/j.ecolind.2016.07.018
9. Pucher, J., Buehler, R.: Making cycling irresistible: Lessons from the Netherlands, Denmark and Germany. Transp. Rev. **28**, 492–528 (2008). https://doi.org/10.1080/01441640701806612
10. Gregerson, J., Hepp-Buchanan, M., Rowe, D., et al.: SEATTLE SHARE S Bike-Share Studio Members. Seattle (2011)
11. Frade, I., Ribeiro, A.: Bicycle sharing systems demand. Procedia Soc. Behav. Sci. **111**, 518–527 (2014). https://doi.org/10.1016/j.sbspro.2014.01.085
12. Buttner, J., Petersen, T.: Optimising bike sharing in European cities: a handbook. Intell. Energy Eur. (2011)
13. Burden, A., Barth, R.: Bike-share. Opportunities in New York City. Department of City Planning, New York (2009)
14. Empresa Pública de Movilidad, Alcaldía, C.: Mapa de las Estaciones - Bici Pública Cuenca (2020)
15. Jordan, R., Simioni, D.: Ciudades intermedias de América Latina y el Caribe: propuestas para la gestión urbana. CEPAL (1998)
16. Garcia-Gutierrez, J., Romero-Torres, J., Gaytan-Iniestra, J.: Dimensioning of a Bike Sharing System (BSS): a study case in Nezahualcoyotl, Mexico. Procedia Soc. Behav. Sci. **162**, 253–262 (2014). https://doi.org/10.1016/j.sbspro.2014.12.206
17. Landrieu, M.J., Kopplin, A.: New Orleans Bike Share Feasibility Study & Business Plan Final Report (2014)
18. Tario, J.: Rochester Area Bike Sharing Program Study. Final Report. New York (State). Department of Transportation, Rochester (2015)
19. Laporte, G., Meunier, F., Wolfler Calvo, R.: Shared mobility systems. 4OR **13**, 341–360 (2015). https://doi.org/10.1007/s10288-015-0301-z
20. Lin, J.R., Yang, T.H., Chang, Y.C.: A hub location inventory model for bicycle sharing system design: formulation and solution. Comput. Ind. Eng. **65**, 77–86 (2013). https://doi.org/10.1016/j.cie.2011.12.006
21. Romero, J.P., Ibeas, A., Moura, J.L., et al.: A Simulation-optimization approach to design efficient systems of bike-sharing. Procedia Soc. Behav. Sci. **54**, 646–655 (2012). https://doi.org/10.1016/j.sbspro.2012.09.782
22. Lin, J.R., Yang Ta-Hui, T.H.: Strategic design of public bicycle sharing systems with service level constraints. Transp. Res. Part E Logist. Transp. Rev. **47**, 284–294 (2011). https://doi.org/10.1016/j.tre.2010.09.004
23. Guo, T.Y., Zhang, P., Shao, F., Liu, Y.S.: Allocation optimization of bicycle-sharing stations at scenic spots. J. Cent. South Univ. **21**, 3396–3403 (2014). https://doi.org/10.1007/s11771-014-2314-8

24. Alta Planning + Design: Cincinnati Bike Share Feasibility Study. Cincinnati Bike Share Feasibility Study (2012)
25. Alta Planning + Design: Memphis Bike Share Feasibility Study. Memphis (2013)
26. He, P., Zheng, F., Belavina, E., Girotra, K.: Customer preference and station network in the London bike-share system. Manag. Sci. **67**, 1392–1412 (2021). https://doi.org/10.1287/mnsc.2020.3620
27. Iseki, H., Tingstrom, M.: A new approach for bikeshed analysis with consideration of topography, street connectivity, and energy consumption. Comput. Environ. Urban Syst. **48**, 166–177 (2014). https://doi.org/10.1016/j.compenvurbsys.2014.07.008
28. Kabra, A., Belavina, E., Girotra, K.: Bike-share systems: accessibility and availability. Manag. Sci. **66**, 3803–3824 (2020). https://doi.org/10.1287/mnsc.2019.3407
29. Lu, W., Scott, D.M., Dalumpines, R.: Understanding bike share cyclist route choice using GPS data: comparing dominant routes and shortest paths. J. Transp. Geogr. **71**, 172–181 (2018). https://doi.org/10.1016/j.jtrangeo.2018.07.012
30. Pakdeewanich, C., Tiyarattanachai, R., Anantavrasilp, I.: Locally designed campus smart bike sharing system: lessons learned and design optimization for Thailand. In: 2020 IEEE 7th International Conference on Industrial Engineering and Applications (ICIEA), pp. 721–725. IEEE, Bangkok (2020)
31. Park, C., Young Sohn, S.: An Optimization approach for the placement of bicycle-sharing stations to reduce short car trips: an application to the city of Seoul. Transp. Res. Part A Policy Pract. **105**, 154–166 (2017). https://doi.org/10.1016/j.tra.2017.08.019
32. Peters, L., MacKenzie, D.: The death and rebirth of bikesharing in Seattle: Implications for policy and system design. Transp. Res. Part A Policy Pract. 130:208–226 (2019). https://doi.org/10.1016/j.tra.2019.09.012
33. Sun, F., Chen, P., Jiao, J.: Promoting public bike-sharing: a lesson from the unsuccessful Pronto system. Transp. Res. Part D Transp. Environ. **63**, 533–547 (2018). https://doi.org/10.1016/j.trd.2018.06.021
34. Krykewycz, G., Puchalsky, C., Rocks, J., et al.: Defining a primary market and estimating demand for major bicycle-sharing program in Philadelphia, Pennsylvania. Transp. Res. Rec. **2143**, 117–124 (2010). https://doi.org/10.3141/2143-15
35. Alta Planning + Design: Calgary Bike Share Feasibility Study City of Calgary. City of Calgari (2011)
36. Fehr & Peers, Systems E& P: Monterey County Bicycle Sharing Feasibility and Implementation Plan. Sacramento (2013)
37. Goodman, B., Handy, S.L.: Providing Equitable Access to Sacramento's Bike Share System Permalink. California (2015)
38. Maurer, L.K.: Feasibility study for a bicycle sharing program in Sacramento, California. In: TRB Committee ANF20 Bicycle Transportation (ed.) 91st Annual Meeting of the Transportation Research Board. The Road to Knowledge, Washington DC, United States, p. 14 (2012)
39. Wine, J.: Bicycle Share Feasibility Study New Orleans A Bike Easy Project With Support From New Orleans Convention and Visitors Bureau New Orleans Tourism Marketing Corporation. Bike Easy, New Orleans (2012)
40. Li, W., Kweon, B.-S., Holtan, M.T., et al.: Assessing Benefits and Costs of Urban Environmental Attributes in a Hedonic Framework: Three Southern California Case Studies. University of California, Irvine (2011)
41. Ahmed, B.: The traditional four steps transportation modeling using a simplified transport network: a case study of Dhaka City, Bangladesh. Int. J. Adv. Sci. Eng. Technol. Res. (2012)
42. García, S., Marín, A.: Covering Location Problems. In: Laporte, G., Nickel, S., da Gama, F. (eds.) Location Science, pp. 99–119. Springer International Publishing, Cham (2019)
43. Martinez, L.M., Caetano, L., Eiró, T., Cruz, F.: An optimisation algorithm to establish the location of stations of a mixed fleet biking system: an application to the city of Lisbon. Procedia Soc. Behav. Sci. **54**, 513–524 (2012). https://doi.org/10.1016/j.sbspro.2012.09.769

44. Chen, Q., Sun, T.: A model for the layout of bike stations in public bike-sharing systems. J. Adv. Transp. **49**, 884–900 (2015). https://doi.org/10.1002/atr.1311
45. Eißel, D., Peng, C.: The future of sustainable transport system for Europe. AI Soc. **29**, 387–402 (2014). https://doi.org/10.1007/s00146-013-0461-3
46. Goodman, A., Cheshire, J.: Inequalities in the London bicycle sharing system revisited: Impacts of extending the scheme to poorer areas but then doubling prices. J. Transp. Geogr. **41**, 272–279 (2014). https://doi.org/10.1016/j.jtrangeo.2014.04.004
47. García-Palomares, J.C., Gutiérrez, J., Latorre, M.: Optimizing the location of stations in bike-sharing programs: a GIS approach. Appl. Geogr. **35**, 235–246 (2012). https://doi.org/10.1016/j.apgeog.2012.07.002
48. Instituto para la Diversificación y Ahorro de la Energía: Guía metodológica para la implantación de sistemas de bicicletas públicas en España. Ministerio de Industria, Comercio y Turismo, Madrid (2007)
49. Krizek, K.J., Stonebraker, E.W.: Bicycling and transit: a marriage unrealized. Transp. Res. Rec. (2010). https://doi.org/10.3141/2144-18

A Method to Build Serious Games for Older Adults ADE2: Evaluation of User Perceptions and Threats of Validity

Priscila Cedillo, Cristina Sánchez-Zhunio, Emily Arteaga, Jefferson Arias, and Marcos Orellana

Abstract Over the years, people decrease their ability to remember certain events, which is more evident in older adults. Therefore, cognitive health professionals use tools and methods to train and assess attention and memory; among those solutions are found serious games. These games are intended to teach, while the player has fun. These games' demand an important amount of Human–Computer Interaction (HCI) characteristics, which are not formally included during their development. A previous contribution, presented a first approach of a method to build serious games, named ADE2. In those studies, we established as further work the need of perform the empirical evaluation of the solution. Therefore, this paper presents an experimental process, where the ADE2 method has been evaluated by 22 software engineers, who evaluated it by using the Method Evaluation Model (MEM). The results show that the ADE2 method can be successfully adopted by the software engineering community, and the actions performed, by following each step of the method, can be reached effectively and efficiently.

A prior version of this paper has been published in the ISD2021 Proceedings (http://aisel.aisnet.org/isd2014/proceedings2021).

P. Cedillo (✉)
Universidad de Cuenca, Universidad del Azuay, Cuenca, Ecuador
e-mail: icedillo@uazuay.edu.ec; priscila.cedillo@ucuenca.edu.ec

C. Sánchez-Zhunio · E. Arteaga · J. Arias
Universidad de Cuenca, Cuenca, Ecuador
e-mail: cristina.sanchezz@ucuenca.edu.ec

E. Arteaga
e-mail: emily.arteaga@ucuenca.edu.ec

J. Arias
e-mail: jefferson.arias@ucuenca.edu.ec

M. Orellana
Universidad del Azuay, Cuenca, Ecuador
e-mail: marore@uazuay.edu.ec

E. Insfran Pelozo et al. (eds.), *Advances in Information Systems Development*,
Lecture Notes in Information Systems and Organisation 55,
https://doi.org/10.1007/978-3-030-95354-6_2

Keywords Older adults · Serious games · Human–computer interaction · Evaluation

1 Introduction

One of the objectives of Human Computer Interaction (HCI) is to improve the individual's experience with technological software solutions interfaces [3]. There are multiple technological solutions where, the different age groups (children, youth, older adults, among others), have not been considered [14]; these solutions lack standards and usability guidelines [3, 4]. Similarly, most studies are focused on the young population, but studies are required to improve new technologies with older adults [8].

Over the years, older adults start to present problems in their daily lives, such as remembering, learning, concentrating, and making decisions on their own [4, 8, 20]. This situation requires the intervention of professionals in cognitive health [8]. Then, memory training techniques are applied, improving attention deficit problems and cognitive problems in the older people [3, 13].

Also, video games are products with the highest commercial rate worldwide. One of the reasons is, because video games implement new interaction methods and multiplayer [4, 14]. Here, serious games are also included, because they are applied in education, memory training, and improving older adults' cognitive abilities [4, 8]. Serious games are cognitive solutions, they are currently preferred because allow the integration of assistance tools, are less expensive, and more accessible [4]; unfortunately, many of those games are not adapted to the needs, characteristics, and specific preferences of older adults [4].

Moreover, Tost et al. [20] designed and implemented a game following the agile methodology, but this study does not apply standards and methodologies focused on older adults. Also, Santos et al. [19] proposed serious games using sensors, to perform physical rehabilitation and prevent falls. Moreover, several studies [10, 13, 17] have described serious game development methodologies, and their validation has been performed with older adults. Hence, there is a need to create serious games for older adults based on various techniques, to improve interaction and facilitate development. Also, it is necessary to evaluate the method through the designers and developers of software, who are the ones who build the serious games. Previously, in [6], a case study with older adults was presented; it used a serious games, which was created following the ADE2 method. To complement the evaluation, it is necessary to evaluate the method with software engineers to measure their perceptions. Therefore, this study performs an empirical evaluation of ADE2 method by using the Method Evaluation Model (MEM), which is used to evaluate methods through the constructs of perceived efficiency and current use [16].

This paper is structured as follows: Sect. 2 describes the analysis of related works; Sect. 3 briefly describes the ADE2 method. In Sect. 4, the method's evaluation is presented using the MEM method and the process for experiments proposed by

Wohlin [21]. Section 5 presents the analysis of the threats that could put the validation experiment of the ADE2 method at risk. Finally, Sect. 6 presents the conclusions and future work.

2 Related Work

Many authors have discussed about the perceptions that an older adult as an end-user has about serious games. Some of them, which combine the players' physical and mental abilities have been implemented [10, 13, 17]. In this context, Lin et al. [13] explore the user experience of software used in a casual and social environments. With a game, called GuessMyCaption, it was possible to identify that the use of natural interfaces and family memories or movements facilitate the adoption of serious games in older adults.

Similarly, Cornejo et al. [10] focus on stimulating older adults' physical and cognitive functions by proposing a game that involves hand–eye coordination. For this, the authors created a serious game with a modular design, for which three scenarios were developed. In this game, data were collected and subsequently analyzed, indicating that serious games are very attractive for older adults and are something that can be applied in their daily life.

Pesántez et al. [17] focus on a model that includes and evaluates accessibility characteristics of serious games built using model driven approaches. Said study deals with older adults who have difficulties in mitigating age-related cognitive problems. For this, they created a method called Evaluation Method of Accessibility for Serious Games (EMASG). After the evaluation, it can be observed that, to develop a serious game that has accessibility, it is necessary to start with the interest of the end-user from the beginning, also use accessibility criteria for each function.

The aforementioned contributions present the reactions of older adults when they use serious game built with a specific methodology, and how friendly they are when these games are used by end-users. However, none of them present how challenging it is for developers, engineers, and experts in the domain to create serious games efficient, which in turn meet the required accessibility criteria.

In a previous study, it was presented the creation of a methodology (ADE2), alongside a brief explanation of its use through a case study with the participation of older adults. It consisted on the creation of serious games focused on attention and memory for the elderly people. Therefore, this article aims to evaluate the effectiveness and efficiency of methodology ADE2 when it is applied by software engineers, to create serious games focused on supporting and training the older adults' attention and memory.

3 ADE2: A Brief Review About the Method

Serious games are solutions that aim to amuse or entertain participants through mental or physical tests [7]. This is why these games can involve different types of participants (e.g., children, young people, elderly people). Then, to provide games that provide the best experience for an older adult, a method to create serious games for older adults (ADE2) was proposed. To clarify the main activities of ADE2, this section provides a brief explanation of each activity. ADE2 presents the necessary steps to create serious games to reinforce the areas of attention and memory in an older adult [6].

The ADE2 method is divided into six main activities (see Fig. 1). Each activity includes its input and output artifacts and guidelines. The first activity is "*Analyzing the Situation*", this activity contains geriatric protocols and standards, which are

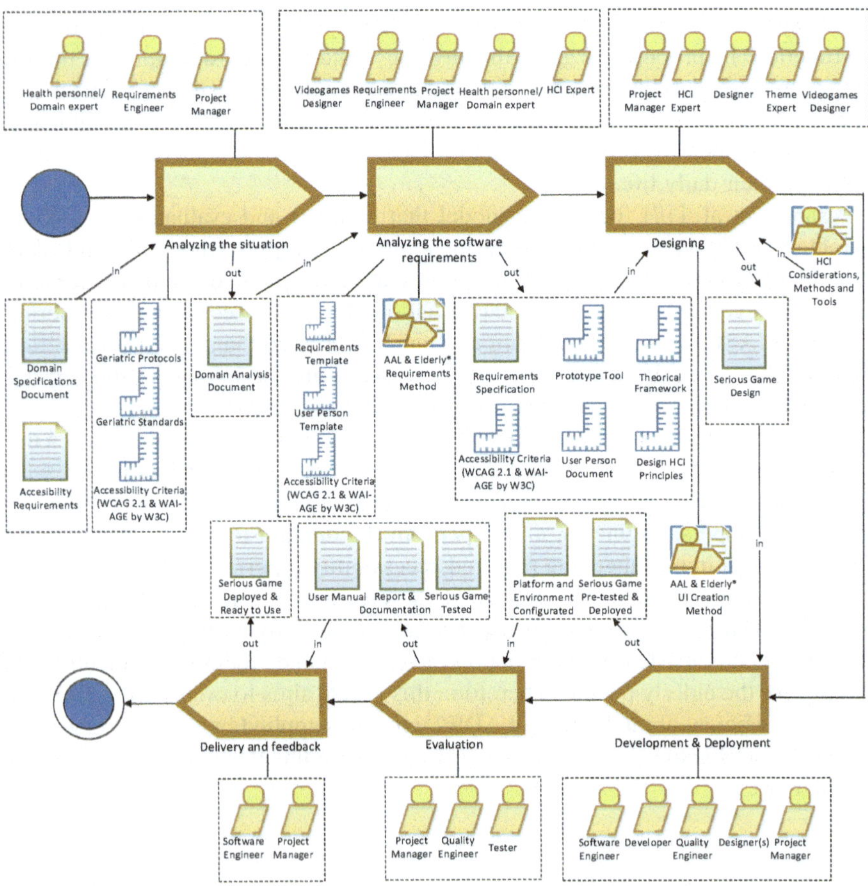

Fig. 1 ADE2 method

used during software requirements elicitation. As result of this activity, the Domain Expert and Requirements Engineer, create the Domain Analysis Document, using the Domain specifications document.

The second activity "*Analyzing the Software Requirements*", collects all the requirements to be included in the serious game. Here, the Video Games Designer, Health Personnel and HCI Expert participate. Then, there is the "*Designing*" activity, it considers accessibility criteria from the W3C and HCI design principles oriented to older adults [5, 18] to provide a game that is easy to understand and to use.

Moreover, the "Development & Deployment" activity consists of creating the user interface focused on older adults, using the AAL &Elderly* UI creation method and the serious game design. Then, the Quality Engineer and Developer implement the game. The other activity is "Evaluation", here, the Tester and the Quality Engineer try the serious game, then in the Report & Documentation, report the changes and improvements in the software. The final result is the user manual for the game. Finally, in the "Delivery and Feedback" activity, the Software Engineer and the Project Manager approve releasing the cognitive solution for use with older adults.

4 ADE2 Method Evaluation

4.1 Evaluation Method

In Cedillo et al. [6] a prototype was presented and evaluated with older adults. Then, to evaluate the acceptance and the performance in the method ADE2, the Method Evaluation Model (MEM) proposed by Moody [16] was applied. The main focus of the MEM is the evaluation of the effectiveness of the created method; therefore, it is necessary to take into consideration the following:

- Measure the effort required to apply the method and its quality in terms of the results obtained.
- The current efficiency, which is the user's effort to understand and apply the method, it can be assessed on the situation in which the MEM is applied.
- The effectiveness, which is the quality of the method, in many cases can be a measure that is determined by the user's ability to perform a certain activity and taking into account its success or failure.

The MEM constructs are based on the Technology Acceptance Model (TAM) proposed by Davis [11]. TAM is a widely used theoretical model, it allows measurement of perceptions to determine the intention to use new creative technology in the future. The constructs to measure the performance and the perceptions are presented in Fig. 2.

- Perceived Ease of Use (PEOU): Degree to which a user believes that using a system will relieve stress.

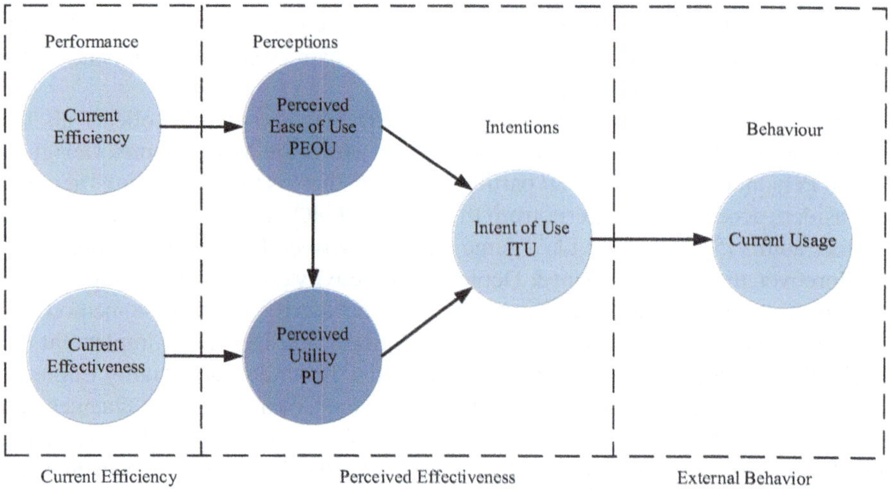

Fig. 2 Method Evaluation Model (MEM) [16]

- Perceived Utility (PU): Degree to which a user believes that using a system will highlight the work.
- Intent to Use (ITU): The extent to which the user is interested in using a particular system.

4.2 ADE2 Evaluation

This section details how the MEM was applied [16], the criteria, variables and questions which were considered during the execution and analysis of the experiment. To apply the MEM [16], it is necessary to specify the user requirements, depending on the problem's domain to resolved; in this case; the requirements are oriented to the older people. Then, the evaluation of the proposed method aimed at designing user interfaces will be performed. The following objectives arise (i) Design application interfaces that include accessibility criteria for older adults, (ii) Create easy, intuitive and user-friendly user interfaces, (iii) Design an interface to meet the user's functional requirements, (iv) Create an interface that provides the best user experience to the older people.

The method proposed by Wohlin et al. [21] has been applied to perform the quasi-experiment; this method presents the following phases: (i) Definition of the scope, (ii) Planning of the quasi-experiment, (iii) Operation, (iv) Analysis and interpretation, and (v) Presentation and reporting [16]. These phases are described below.

Table 1 Scope definition with GQM

GQM variable	Response
Evaluate	ADE2 Method
With the purpose of	Evaluate the method concerning perceived efficacy, intended future use, and perceived ease of use
From the viewpoint of	Software Engineer
In the context of	A group of professionals in the technical area (Computer Science and related careers)

Scope Definition

Authors of [2] mention the Goal-Question Metric (GQM) to define a project's goal; this approach was applied to perform the quasi-experiment. Analysis is presented on Table 1.

Then, the following research questions were defined; RQ1: Is the ADE2 method perceived as easy to use and useful? If so, are users' perceptions the result of their performance when using the method to develop serious games? and RQ2: Is there an intention to use the ADE2 method in the future? If so, are those usage intentions the result of the participants' perceptions?

Finally, to answer question RQ1, the hypotheses H1, H2, H4, and, H5 have been defined, and to answer RQ2, the hypotheses have been defined: H3, H6, H7, and H8; they are described below:

- $H1_0$: The design phase of the ADE2 method is perceived as difficult to use $\neg H1_{1.}$
- $H2_0$: The design phase of the ADE2 method is not perceived as useful $\neg H2_0$
- $H3_0$: There is no intention to use the design phase of the ADE2 method in the future. $\neg H3_0$
- $H4_0$: Perceived ease of use cannot be determined by efficiency. Efficiency is based on current efficiency performance and perceived ease of use is based on perception. $\neg H4_0$
- $H5_0$: The perception of utility is not determined by effectiveness. This hypothesis is given since, the effectiveness is based on the performance and the perceived utility is based on the perception of the effectiveness. $\neg H5_0$
- $H6_0$: Perceived utility is not determined by perceived ease of use. The perceived ease of use is found to have no influence on the perceived usefulness. This hypothesis is taken from the TAM. $\neg H6_0$
- $H7_0$: Intent to use is not determined by perceived ease of use. The perceived ease of use influences the intention to use, described in the TAM. $\neg H7_0$
- $H8_0$: Intent to use is not determined by perceived utility. The perceived utility has an influence on the intention to use, described by TAM. $\neg H8_{0.}$

Based on the aforementioned, Table 2 presents a questionnaire of 14 questions, which were used to measure the variables. The questionnaire items were formulated using a 5-point Likert scale [12], with the opposite statement question format. Several items within the same construct group were randomized to avoid systemic response

Table 2 Questions to assess user perceptions

Question	Statement positive (5 points)
PEOU1	The design phase of the ADE2 methodology is simple and easy to follow
PEOU2	In general, the design phase of the methodology is easy to understand
PEOU3	The steps of the design phase of the methodology are clear and easy to understand
PEOU4	The design phase of the methodology is easy to learn
PEOU5	I think it would be easy to master the design phase of the ADE2 methodology
PU1	I believe that the design phase of the ADE2 methodology could reduce the time and effort required
PU2	I consider that the design phase of the methodology is useful
PU3	I consider that the design phase is useful to improve the design of interfaces that relate to older adults
PU4	I think that the design phase of the methodology is expressive enough to define interfaces oriented to older adults
PU5	The use of this design phase could improve the performance of creating technological solutions focused on older adults
PU6	In general, I think that this design phase of ADE2 can be used to help develop technological applications focused on older adults
ITU1	If you need to design a technology application focused on older adults, would you consider the design phase of the ADE2 methodology
ITU2	If necessary, I would use the ADE2 design phase in the future
ITU3	I would recommend using the design phase of ADE2

bias. The PEOU is measured through the use of five questions in the survey, the PU is measured with six questions, and the ITU is measured with three questions in the survey.

Planning of the quasi-experiment

A pilot experiment was conducted with a small number of participants, to determine the following: (i) if the guides and videos proposed are adequate and easily understood by the participants, (ii) obtain feedback from the participants before experimenting with a larger number of users, (iii) determine if the pilot experiment was successful or failed, to obtain possible improvements.

Once the observations of the pilot experiment have been obtained, the experiment was planned with a greater number of participants. In this experiment, a problem is described for both the training session and the experimentation session to evaluate the ADE2 method. Additionally, three videos were made to transmit the same knowledge to the participants during the experiment. These videos were: (i) presentation of the method, (ii) guide for applying the method, and (iii) guide exercise. The videos, guides, presentations and exercises can be found at the following link: https://bit.ly/3CkzNU0.

The proposed exercise refers to making a prototype of a puzzle game, this game is focused on the design phase of the ADE2 method and must meet certain design

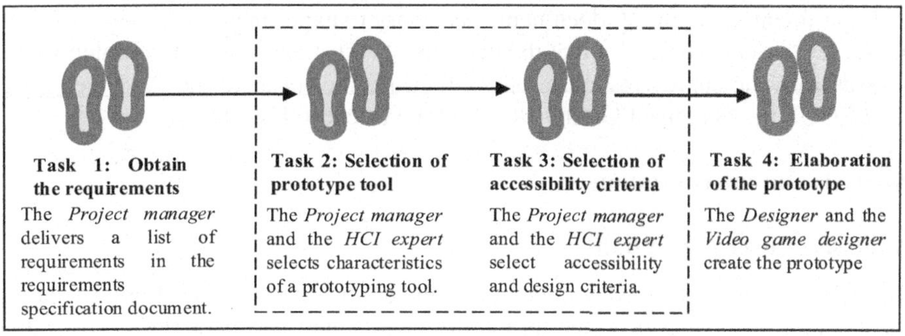

Fig. 3 Quasi-experiment tasks

requirements aimed at an older adult. Also, the tasks associated with the exercise are defined in Fig. 3 and explained below:

Task 1: Obtain the requirements based on a statement that describes the problem to be solved. This means that the software engineers receive a list of requirements, from these requirements, it must be determined whether the requirement is included or excluded according to the problem raised.
Task 2: Identify the tool that will be used to prototype the application. In this task, software engineers must select the characteristics that a prototyping tool must meet to satisfy the proposed problem.
Task 3: Select the accessibility criteria. In this task, the appropriate accessibility criteria for the application are chosen, which must meet certain requirements at the graphical user interface level. These accessibility criteria are proposed by WCAG 2.1 and WAI-AGE by W3C in [1].
Task 4: Make a prototype that meets: (i) the design criteria, (ii) accessibility criteria, and (iii) the requirements selected in the previous tasks. This activity was proposed with the aim of covering all the tasks previously proposed and, based on this, creating a robust prototype in design and easy to use for an older adult.

Operation

The training was performed online, using the Zoom platform to experiment. Twenty-two engineers (eight women and fourteen men) corresponding to technical areas participated, selected according to the skills and knowledge they possess to evaluate the ADE2 method. To experiment, four-points were defined:

- Define a web page: a simple web page was created to observe the parameters that must be met in the evaluation, with a training, experiment, survey, and video tab. The web page is found at the following link: https://bit.ly/3CkzNU0.
- Training: documents related to the application guide, the phases of the methodology, what is accomplished in each one of them, and how the flow is going.

- Experiment: contains all documents necessary to experiment.
- Survey: is a questionnaire that the participants must answer after completing the exercise. The survey response matrix will used to measure the Perceived Ease (PEOU), the Perceived Utility (PU), and the Intent to Use (ITU).

Analysis and interpretation

Analysis of user perceptions

The analysis was performed with box plots and descriptive statistics. Figure 4 shows the box plot; the values obtained for the PEOU, PU, and ITU variables have a value greater than the neutral value (3) of the Likert scale.

The Shapiro–Wilk test was performed to determine if the data has a normal distribution, then a test was selected to accept or reject the hypothesis H1, H2, and H3. It was obtained that the variables PEOU, PU, and ITU do not have a normal distribution with $p < 0.05$ (see Table 3); here, the Wilcoxon test was applied. The results allow

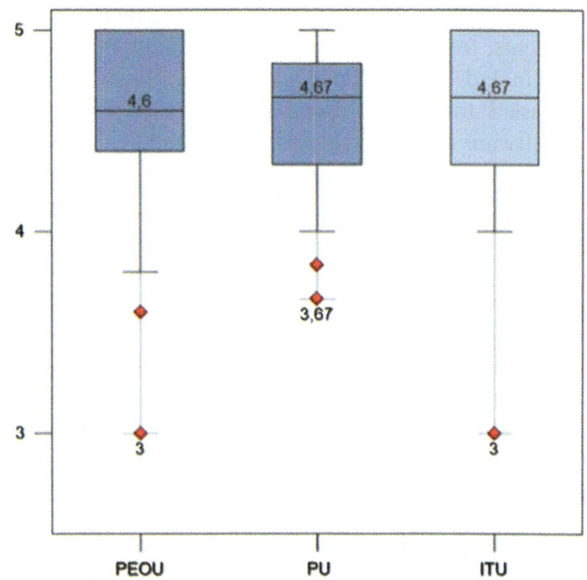

Fig. 4 Box plot for perception variables PEOU, PU and ITU

Table 3 Shapiro–Wilk test for the perception-based variables

Variable	Min	Max	Media	Std. E	Shapiro–Wilk test p-value
PEOU	3.6	5	4.7	0.42	0.000
PU	3.66	5	4.61	0.36	0.017
ITU	3.66	5	4.73	0.37	0.000

Table 4 Performance analysis

Variable	Min	Max	Media	Std. Dev
Efficiency	16	29	20.71	3.49
Effectivity	0.59	1	0.9	0.10

knowing that the hypothesis H10, H20, and H30 were rejected. Thus, the alternative hypothesis H11, H21, and H31 were accepted.

Performance analysis

User performance data is obtained from the tasks performed by the participants. Equation 1 shows the calculation of the efficiency, and Eq. 2 shows the calculation of the effectiveness in the design phase of the ADE2 method. The results obtained are shown in Table 4. On the one hand, the efficiency has a mean value of 20.71 min; the minimum value is 16; the maximum value is 29. On the other hand, the effectiveness has a mean value of 0.9 which means that the design phase provides great effectiveness (90%) because the answers to the proposed solutions were correct.

$$efficiency = \sum_{i=1}^{n} Time\ per\ activity \tag{1}$$

$$effectiveness = \sum_{i=1}^{n} \frac{Number\ of\ tasks\ completed\ successfull}{Total\ number\ of\ tasks} \tag{2}$$

Analysis of causal relationships

MEM's structure has been analyzed, that is, the causal relationships between perception variables and performance variables. The regression analysis was performed, and to determine the level of significance of the regression model, the levels suggested in [15] were applied. Table 5 shows the results obtained, and the analysis for each causal relationship is presented below:

- In causal relationship between Efficiency and PEOU, the regression model is not significant, with $p > 0.1$. R2 represents 0.02% of the variance in PEOU. As a result, the current efficiency of the participants does not influence their perceptions of ease of use. This allows corroborating which hypothesis H40 is accepted, that is to say, Efficiency does not determine the Perceived Ease of Use.
- In causal relationship between Effectivity and PU, the regression model is not significant, with $p > 0.1$. R2 represents 0% of the variance in PEOU. As a result, the current effectiveness of the participants does not influence their perceptions of perceived utility. This allows corroborating that hypothesis $H5_0$ is accepted, that is, effectiveness does not determine utility.
- In causal relationship between PEOU and PU, the regression model was found to be of medium significance with $p < 0.05$. R2 shows that the PEOU variable

Table 5 Simple regression casual relationships

Reg. element	Coef(b)	Std. E	Std. Coef	t	Sig(p)	R	R^2
Simple regression between Efficiency and PEOU							
Constant	4.601	0.582	–	7.909	0	–	–
Efficiency	0.005	0.028	0.042	0.182	0.858	0.042	0.002
Simple regression between Effectivity and PU							
Constant	4.67	0.756	–	6.169	0	–	–
Effectivity	– 0.05	0.832	– 0.015	-0.063	0.95	0.015	0
Simple regression between PEOU and PU							
Constant	2	0.782	–	3.033	0.007	–	–
PEOU	0	0.166	0.552	2.884	0.01	0.552	0.304
Simple regression between ITU and PU							
Constant	2.989	1.012	–	2.954	0.008	–	–
PU	0.377	0.218	0.368	1.725	0.101	0.368	0.135
Simple regression between ITU and PEOU							
Constant	3.069	0.881	–	3.484	0.002	–	–
PEOU	0.353	0.187	0.398	1.893	0.074	0.398	0.159

is capable of explaining 30% of the variance in PU. As a result, the number of perceptions regarding PU is not determined by PEOU. This makes it possible to reject hypothesis $H6_0$, that is, PEOU determines PU.

- In causal relationship between ITU and PU, the regression model is not significant, with $p > 0.1$. The R2 shows that the PU variable is capable of explaining 13% of the variance in ITU. As a result, the number of perceptions regarding ITU is determined by PU. This allows the $H7_0$ hypothesis to be accepted, that is, the intention to use is not determined by the perceived ease of use.
- In causal relationship between ITU and PEOU, the regression model was found to be of low significance with $p < 0.1$. The R2 shows that the PEOU variable is capable of explaining 15% of the variance in ITU. As a result, some of the perceptions regarding ITU is determined by PEOU. This allows the $H8_0$ hypothesis to be rejected, that is, the intention to use is determined by the perceived utility.

Presentation and report

Within the results report and based on results shown in Table 6, each research question will be analysed.

RQ1: Is the ADE2 method perceived as easy to use and useful? If so, are users' perceptions the result of their performance when using the method to develop serious games? Here, most participants perceived the design phase of the method ADE2 as easy to use and useful. This is because hypotheses $H1_0$ and $H2_0$ have been rejected and their alternatives $H1_1$ and $H2_1$ have been accepted. Besides, by accepting hypothesis $H4_0$ and $H5_0$, it was known that ease of use is not determined by efficiency,

Table 6 Evaluation Summary

Hypothesis	Range	Significance	Action	Results
$H1_0$	–	–	Rejected	ADE2 is easy to use
$H2_0$	–	–	Rejected	ADE2is perceived as useful
$H3_0$	–	–	Rejected	There is an intention to use ADE2
$H4_0$	$p > 0.1$	Not significant	Accepted	PEOU is not determinate by efficiency
$H5_0$	$p > 0.1$	Not significant	Accepted	PU is not determinate by effectivity
$H6_0$	$p < 0.05$	Medium significance	Rejected	PEOU is determine by PU
$H7_0$	$p > 0.1$	Not significant	Accepted	ITU is not determine by PEOU
$H8_0$	$p < 0.1$	Low significance	Rejected	ITU is determine by PU

and utility is not determined by effectiveness either. On the one hand, most participants completed the tasks correctly; this is evident because the effectiveness is 90%. However, several participants had problems when applying accessibility criteria for the prototype, also, the efficiency was altered because some participants had internet connection problems. The average time to complete the tasks was 16 min.

Finally, to RQ2: Is there an intention to use the ADE2 method in the future? If so, are those usage intentions the result of the participants' perceptions? The hypothesis $H3_0$ was rejected, and with this, it was determined that the participants intend to use it in the future. Then, hypothesis $H6_0$ was rejected, this means that the perceived utility is determined by the perceived ease of use with a 30.4% variance; hypothesis $H7_0$ was accepted, this means that the perceived ease of use does not determine the intention of use; moreover, hypothesis H80 was rejected with a 15.9% variance, and this means that the perceived utility determines the intention to use. These data are represented in Fig. 5.

5 Threats of Validity

This section presents the main problems that can jeopardize the validity of the experiment. Cook and Campell [9] consider four types of validity: conclusion, internal, construct and external.

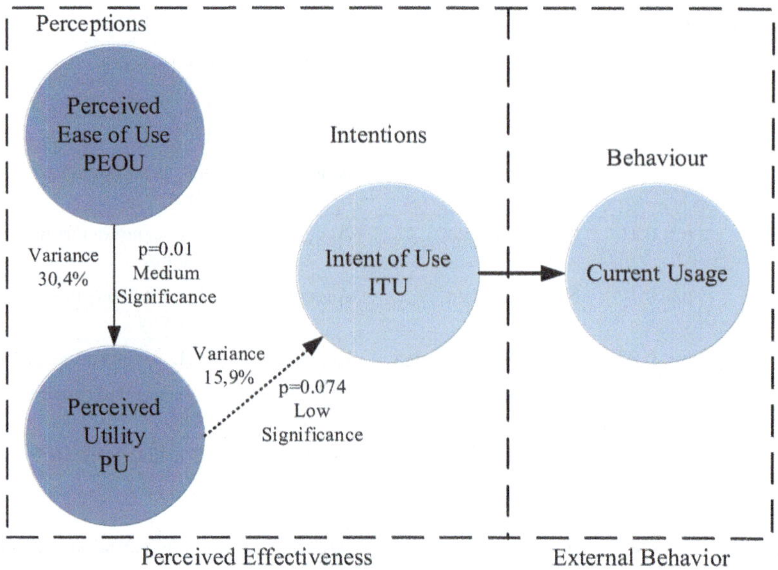

Fig. 5 Conclusion of the application of MEM to the ADE2 method

5.1 *Internal Validity*

The threat to internal validity was influenced by the quality of the internet used by the participants, in addition to the use of virtual platforms. However, the participants present in the quasi-experiment decided to participate voluntarily in a virtual way, for which, a letter with the invitation was sent via email and the entire training process was recorded. Also, a web page was prepared to carry out the quasi-experiment, a presentation video of the ADE2 method to avoid bias.

5.2 *External Validity*

External validity refers to the results generated in different contexts, and its main threat was the current COVID-19 pandemic; the quasi-experiment cannot be applied in person. A training session and a pilot test were conducted to avoid internet connection problems to reduce this threat. This allowed the participants to perform the assessment tasks with ease.

5.3 *Validity of the Construct*

The main threat to the validity of the construct is the reliability of the questionnaire. To increase reliability, the Cronbach's alpha test of questions related to each subjective variable was performed. The minimum accepted threshold being $\alpha = 0.70$, then, the following results were obtained for the PEOU variables $\alpha = 0.76$, in PU $\alpha = 0.79$ and in ITU $\alpha = 0.77$. These values have been obtained by conducting a pilot study with 5 software engineers. It was determined that the questionnaire is reliable and can be applied to evaluate the ADE2 method.

5.4 *Conclusion Validity*

The sample size and selection are made up of 22 participants belonging to professionals in the technical area; this amount may reflect a problem of the validity of the conclusion. However, the results are very satisfactory since the participants managed to develop correctly the steps established in the quasi-experiment exercise. For future work, an experiment with differentiation has been proposed to validate the ADE2 methodology with a larger sample.

6 Conclusions and Future Work

ADE2 is a method that allows to create serious games for older adults. This method contains phases, roles, guides, and artifacts that contribute to improving users' interaction with serious games. This paper presented the evaluation of software engineers of the ADE2 method. Here, the method evaluation model (MEM) was applied, evaluating user perceptions based on their performance. The method is easy to use, useful, and intended by engineers to use in the future to build serious games, and threats that may put the quasi-experiment at risk have been analyzed.

As future work, it is sought to extend the experiment to different groups of software engineers with a bigger sample, with it will present a family of experiments to corroborate the hypotheses tested in this work and to provide more accurate results. It is also intended to create other serious games by applying ADE2 in the research group. This contributes to the cognitive improvement of older adults who live at home and in care and assistance centers.

Acknowledgements This work is part of the following research projects: "Fog Computing applied to monitor devices used in assisted living environments; case study: platform for the elderly people" and "Design of architectures and interaction models for assisted living environments aimed at older adults. Case study: ludic and social environments". Therefore, we thank DIUC of Universidad de Cuenca for its support. Also, we thank "Laboratorio de Investigación y Desarrollo en Informática (LIDI) - Universidad del Azuay" for its academic support.

References

1. Arch, A.: WAI Guidelines and Older Web Users: Findings from a Literature Review (2008)
2. Basili, V.R., Agresti, W.W.: The experimental paradigm in software engineering. Lect. Notes Comput. Sci. (including Subser. Lect. Notes Artif. Intell. Lect. Notes Bioinformatics) **706**, 33–37 (1993)
3. Blasko, D.G., Lum, H.C., Harris, M., Blasko Drabik, H., Halse, S.: Spatial perception orientation task (SPOT). In: Proceedings of the Extended Abstracts of the 32nd Annual ACM Conference on Human Factors in Computing Systems—CHI EA '14, pp. 1753–1758. ACM Press, New York, New York, USA (2014)
4. Bouchard, B., Imbeault, F., Bouzouane, A., Menelas, B.-A.J.: Developing Serious Games Specifically Adapted to People Suffering from Alzheimer (2012)
5. Cedillo Orellana, I.P., Beltrán, P., Rodríguez, P., Serrano, F., Bermeo, A.: MOOCEP: Un método para construir cursos masivos para Adultos Mayores: Usando una creación MOOCEP. Enfoque UTE **9**(1), 25–33 (2018)
6. Cedillo, P., Arias, J., Arteaga, E., Sánchez-Zhunio, C., Prado-Cabrera, D.: ADE2: Towards a method for implementing serious games for older people's memory training. In: Proceedings of the 7th International Conference on Information and Communication Technologies for Ageing Well and e-Health, pp. 46–56. SCITEPRESS—Science and Technology Publications (2021)
7. Charsky, D.: From edutainment to serious games: a change in the use of game characteristics. Games Cult. **5**(2), 177–198 (2010)
8. Chi, H., Agama, E., Prodanoff, Z.G.: Developing serious games to promote cognitive abilities for the elderly. In: 2017 IEEE 5th International Conference on Serious Games Applications and Health SeGAH 2017 (2017)
9. Cook, T.D., Campell, D.T.: Quasi-Experimentation Design and Analysis Issues for Field Settings. USA Hought. Mifflin Co. (1979)
10. Cornejo, R., Hernandez, D., Tentori, M., Favela, J.: Casual gaming to encourage active ageing. IEEE Lat. Am. Trans. **13**(6), 1940–1950 (2015)
11. Davis, F.D.: A technology acceptance model for empirically testing new end-user information systems: theory and results. Management (1985)
12. Hartwick, J., Barki, H.: Hypothesis testing and hypothesis generating research: an example from the user participation literature. Inf. Syst. Res. **5**(4), 446–449 (1994)
13. Lin, Y.H., Mao, H.F., Tsai, Y.C., Chou, J.J.: Developing a serious game for the elderly to do physical and cognitive hybrid activities. In: 2018 IEEE 6th International Conference on Serious Games Applications and Health SeGAH 2018, pp. 1–8 (2018)
14. Meftah, C., Retbi, A., Bennani, S., Idrissi, M.K.: Mobile serious game design using user experience: modeling of software product line variability. Int. J. Emerg. Technol. Learn. **14**(23), 55 (2019)
15. Moody, D.L.: A Practical Method for Representing Large Entity Relationship Models (2001)
16. Moody, D.L.: The method evaluation model: a theoretical model for validating information systems design Methods. Inf. Syst. J. 1327–1336 (2003)
17. Pesantez-Cabrera, P., Acosta, M.I., Jimbo, V., Sinchi, P., Cedillo, P.: Towards an evaluation method of how accessible serious games are to older adults. In: 2020 IEEE 8th International Conference on Serious Games and Applications for Health (SeGAH), pp. 1–8. IEEE (2020)
18. Sanchez-Gordon, S., Luján-Mora, S.: Web accessibility of MOOCs for elderly students. In: 2013 12th International Conference on Information Technology Based Higher Education Training, ITHET 2013 (2013)
19. Santos, A., Guimaraes, V., Matos, N., Cevada, J., Ferreira, C., Sousa, I.: Multi-sensor exercise-based interactive games for fall prevention and rehabilitation. In: Proceedings of 2015 9th International Conference on Pervasive Computing Technology Healcare PervasiveHealth 2015, pp. 65–71 (2015)
20. Tost, D., von Barnekow, A., Felix, E., Pazzi, S., Puricelli, S., Bottiroli, S.: SmartAgeing: a 3D serious game for early detection of mild cognitive impairments. In: Proceedings of the 8th

International Conference on Pervasive Computing Technologies for Healthcare, pp. 294–297. ICST (2014)
21. Wohlin, C., Runeson, P., Höst, M., Ohlsson, M.C., Regnell, B., Wesslén, A.: Experimentation in software engineering. Exp. Softw. Eng. **9783642290**, 1–236 (2012)

Accessibility of Digital Content in Europe: Users' Perspective

Inés López Baldominos, Vera Pospelova, Luis Fernández Sanz, and Ana Castillo-Martínez

Abstract European Union has decided to impulse accessibility of digital contents through several directives, which include all types of digital information and files. As technicians cannot curate and supervise all the contents of information systems, now accountability has expanded to include users who create or add contents to information systems. This paper presents the results of a survey to 525 persons in several countries of EU to check awareness and general knowledge of users on digital accessibility. Results suggest the need of much more effort to ensure the digital accessibility out of the technical aspects managed by IT professionals.

Keywords Digital accessibility · EU Directive · Users · Survey

1 Introduction

Digital services, products and information are already part of the daily lives of virtually the entire Society. We have examples of information systems supporting online banking and commerce, the use of public online services, communication with family and friends, etc. Digital accessibility is therefore not just a matter of technical standards, but also of political will and moral obligation towards equality, as seen during these times of global pandemic reality. As laws have been passed to force public

A prior version of this paper has been published in the ISD2021 Proceedings (http://aisel.aisnet.org/isd2014/proceedings2021).

I. López Baldominos (✉) · V. Pospelova · L. Fernández Sanz · A. Castillo-Martínez
Universidad de Alcala, Alcala de Henares, Spain
e-mail: ines.lopezb@edu.uah.es

V. Pospelova
e-mail: vera.pospelova@uah.es

L. Fernández Sanz
e-mail: luis.fernandez.sanz@uah.es

A. Castillo-Martínez
e-mail: ana.castillo@uah.es

E. Insfran Pelozo et al. (eds.), *Advances in Information Systems Development*,
Lecture Notes in Information Systems and Organisation 55,
https://doi.org/10.1007/978-3-030-95354-6_3

and private spaces to incorporate good physical accessibility practices, the European Union has promoted specific legal measures for digital accessibility. Digital accessibility is a right for all citizens, as stated in the European Union (EU) Directive 2016/2102 [1], which defines digital accessibility as the "principles and techniques to be observed when designing, constructing, maintaining, and updating websites and mobile applications to make them more accessible to users, in particular persons with disabilities". As a result, public sector websites, intranets, extranets, published documents, multimedia files and mobile applications must guarantee digital accessibility. This legal act of EU affects all public administration bodies, publicly funded projects, educational centers, and those private companies that develop their activity for the public sector.

Political continues to drive digital accessibility. The EU has gone even further with the publication of the new Directive 2019/882 [2], which imposes digital accessibility also on websites, apps and digital content of essential services as transportation, online banking or e-commerce, for public and private operators, with entry into force in 2025.

Prior to these legislative acts, some EU countries already had legislation regulating digital accessibility in specific and more technical cases, e.g., web accessibility. This is the case of Spain through RD 1494/2007 [3]. Nevertheless, as stated in the EU Directive, now every digital resource or service must meet accessibility criteria and consequently the responsibility has migrated from just "technicians" or "experts" to every user who creates or manages digital information, documents, and multimedia files. Traditionally, technicians have been the ones in charge of ensuring accessibility. Usability and user experience experts and development technicians are motivated and aware of making the systems accessible but they reported time and cost constraints and lack of training [4]. Now, IT professionals would have an unbearable amount of work if they had to review every document, link or multimedia file uploaded to a system. For example, a big municipality website hosts 58,700 PDF documents, a ministry around 19,800 or a medium university 12,000, according to Google Advanced search. Therefore, ICT users will need digital accessibility competences and skills at the same time they are increasing awareness of their contribution. The general situation is one of appropriate compliance on websites but it is not rare to find failures in digital files: authors have confirmed this in several contracts with public authorities to fix their accessibility problems. Evidence taken from experiences with libraries websites in the US shows that documents are a particularly hard element that cause difficulties to blind users when they are posted on a website without respecting accessibility guidelines [5]. Another research [6] concluded similar points when evaluating accessibility in university websites and the documents hosted on it. Non-accessible office application files pose additional problems for users with special needs [7].

Digital accessibility requires the involvement of more and more agents and education is one of the contexts present from the beginning of this process. From teachers and students to managers and e-learning platforms developers, every stakeholder is essential in the process of making digital information accessible. The most used e-learning platforms, as Moodle or Blackboard, include accessibility in their systems.

However, these are not closed platforms and administrators and teachers should follow good accessibility practices in their role of content creators and managers. The sustainable way to achieve this goal is a cultural change and increasing awareness of these large groups [8]. Universities should provide as much training as possible accompanied by incentives to faculty and staff during periods of relative normalcy to be ready during the periods of stress [9]. Additionally, universities are currently training the future developers, consultants, and managers, so information technology programs should include accessibility in their curriculum. However, all these actions clash with the reality and observation confirms that the goal is far from being achieved [10]. Albeit the implication of higher education has grown in the last years, there is still a lack of policies to settle correct procedures, roles and responsibilities [11].

Budget is a limitation, but digital accessibility should be approached as a business opportunity that brings both tangible and intangible benefits to organizations [12]. On one hand, in a similar way as happens in software quality, the earlier you introduce accessibility requirements and verification in your processes, the fewer economic impact of possible issues. The return on investment in accessibility is achieved with an intelligent and appropriate allocation of resources [13]. On the other hand, digital accessibility directly relates to usability and universal design, which imply that systems have a higher number of potential users independently of their age, gender, capacities or needs as every user can actually benefit from digital accessibility.

Other authors point to the institutional context as an additional barrier to digital accessibility. To the extent that accessibility involves multiple parties and requires effort and involvement of diverse stakeholders, the way organizations are able to coordinate all actors and share goals, agendas, and efforts greatly influences the achievement of the requirements needed to comply with standards [14].

This paper is divided into five sections: Sect. 2 describes the data collection process while Sect. 3 presents the analysis of data and results. Section 4, describes the main accessibility issues found in real cases and, finally, Sect. 5 summarizes conclusions and depicts future lines of work.

2 Information Gathering

This research pursues several objectives. Firstly, we want to determine the degree of awareness, motivation and existing knowledge about digital accessibility among different groups of people, vocational education and training (VET), public institutions and small and medium enterprises (SME). These groups are those most affected by the obligation to meet the principles of digital accessibility. VET professionals and managers, including higher education teachers, are involved in lifelong learning to disseminate the concepts and skills needed for digital accessibility. Accessibility is mandatory for public digital information so employees and managers of public institutions are directly impacted. Employees and managers of SMEs are also obliged to ensure accessibility to work with the public sector and in publicly funded projects.

Secondly, we want to analyze the relations between them and other factors such as the age, professional experience, gender or country to determine where it is most beneficial to impulse training and awareness actions.

We have used an online survey on the EU Survey platform to gather information from the above-mentioned groups of stakeholders with both qualitative and quantitative data based on closed questions.

2.1 Sample Description

The survey had 525 participants from different countries within the European Union. Most of them came from Spain (50.1%), Italy (16.4%), Hungary (15.6%), Sweden (8%) and Ireland (6.3%) (see Fig. 1). These countries can be separated into two groups, Italy and Spain had regulation on digital accessibility before the European Directive of 2016, and Sweden, Ireland and Hungary did not. We also reached a significant participation of every professional group, especially of public administration workers (44.4%) while VET and HE professionals represent 37.9% and SME 17.7%. Age shows a bell-shaped pattern. The vast majority of the participants (83.8%) were between 30 and 60 years old. Participants indicated professional experience of more than 20 years (32%) or between 10 and 20 years (24%), shaping a good representation (see Fig. 2). Regarding gender, there is a slight majority of female respondents (60%).

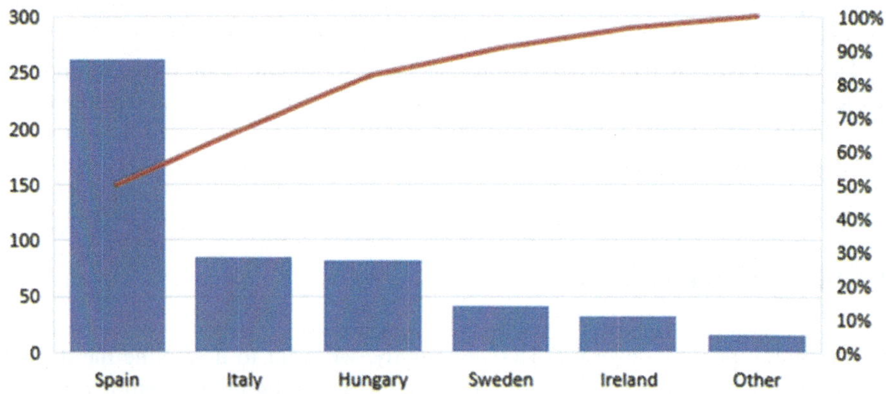

Fig. 1 Distribution of the sample by country

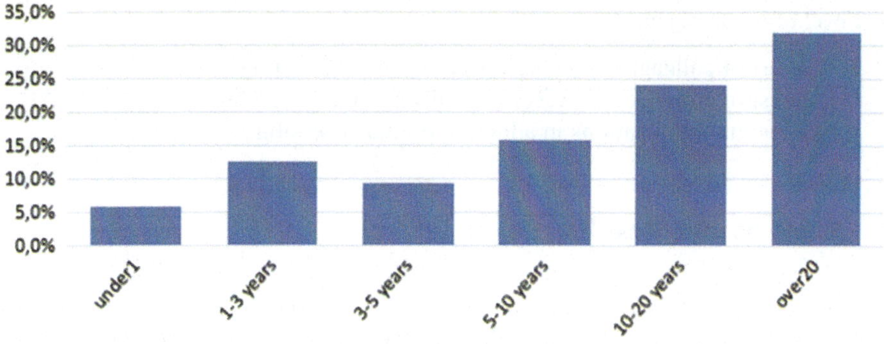

Fig. 2 Distribution of the sample by professional experience

2.2 *Survey Description*

The survey had several objectives. Firstly, checking the degree of knowledge about existing legislation. Secondly, checking if the participants really understand the concept of accessibility or if they are incurring in some of the most widespread myths. Finally, knowing the degree of involvement they would have, both personally and in their respective organizations to promote digital accessibility and to participate in training activities. Consequently, we designed a set of questions grouped in five different areas.

- Respondent profile
  - Personal data, including country, stakeholder, years of working experience, age and gender
  - Self-assessment of skills in internet navigation, word processing tools, presentations tools, PDF, and media files
  - Training received to achieve those skills
- Knowledge about digital accessibility
  - Self-rate the level of awareness on the topic
  - Correct definition of digital accessibility
  - Elements that should be enhanced by good digital accessibility
- Applicable regulation
  - Knowledge about the existence of national regulation, in the European Union and in the own organization
- Motivation and responsibility
  - Worth the effort/money
  - Best reasons to support the effort
  - Profile of the users accountable for the task

- Level of involvement
  - Interest of colleagues and organizations in contributing
  - Interest of employees in receiving information or training
  - Interest of organizations in adopting digital accessibility.

3 Analysis and Results

We intend to study the relationship among factors based on the responses to questions in the survey. Firstly, we will check the influence of the categories used to describe the sample (country, age, gender, profession and experience) and the questions areas, which are level of awareness, knowledge on accessibility and regulation, motivation and knowledge on individual accountability regarding digital accessibility. Secondly, we will analyze the relationships among the different areas to see whether the answers given in each question have an influence on the rest.

3.1 General Knowledge on Digital Accessibility

Awareness is one of the main aspects when talking about accessibility. Data revealed that only the 18.1% declare to know what accessibility is and have worked in the field. This number rises to 47.6%, who are the ones that affirm knowing what it is although they have never worked with it (details in Fig. 3).

Initially, one could think that age or experience might affect the level of awareness, in one way or another. Nevertheless, we have found out that neither age nor experience nor gender influence awareness. When focusing in the different countries, there are two differentiated groups regarding the existence of regulation before de EU Directive. Awareness is higher in Spain and Italy than in the rest of the countries where there is generally more lack of knowledge (details in Fig. 4).

Awareness itself is not enough to implement good practices on digital accessibility. It should be accompanied by adequate and coherent knowledge. Data shows

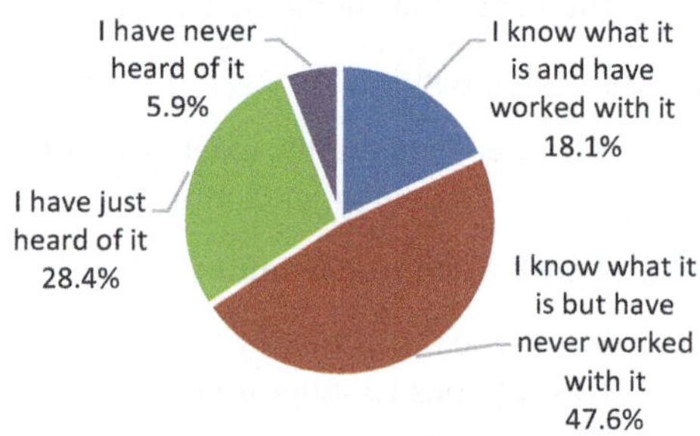

Fig. 3 Digital accessibility awareness

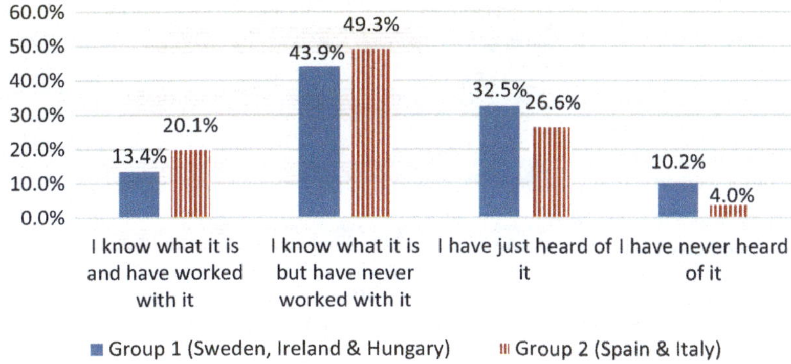

Fig. 4 Level of awareness depending on the country

that this is still a point to be improved. Participants were asked to decide which definition best matched their understanding of digital accessibility among four possible answers. These definitions were chosen in order to incorporate some of the main myths regarding digital accessibility. In the following list, only definition 2 is correct:

- Definition 1: Ease of access to information on computers/digital devices and ease of their interconnection irrespective of the different data formats, operating systems, technologies, etc.
- Definition 2: Digital content presented and formatted to allow everyone to access information and services, irrespective of their personal capacities and needs.
- Definition 3: Absence of barriers to allow open and transparent access to public data.

Contrary to natural intuition, the correct definition is the most chosen among all groups except those who say they know and have worked with digital accessibility. Even more, the most accurate group are those who said they had never heard of the concept of accessibility (58%). This value is not high enough considering that we are talking about a mandatory and reportable element. 45.8% of the participants who affirm knowing what accessibility is do not choose the correct option. The main problem relates to the wrong assumption of ease of access with the concept of accessibility, possibility of accessing and understanding content irrespectively of users' special needs. This misunderstanding is clearer as the level of awareness increases. Nearly half of the ones who have worked with digital accessibility (48.4%) chose definition 1. This is very remarkable, and may be influenced by the fact that the previous legislation focused on the more technical aspects and the changes introduced with the new European directives have not yet caught on among professionals and the general population (complete data in Fig. 5).

When analyzing data on knowledge (see Fig. 6) segmented by country, we see that the existence of previous regulations (as happens in group 2 of countries) does

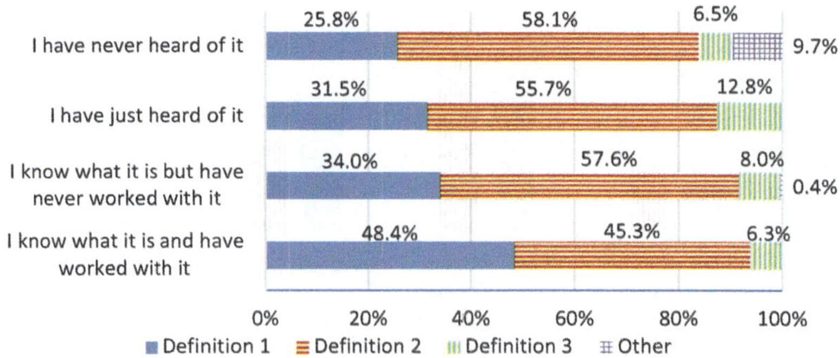

Fig. 5 Definitions chosen depending on the awareness declared

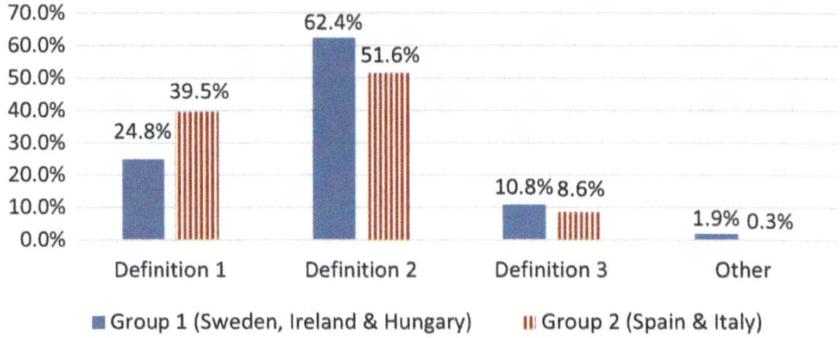

Fig. 6 Definition chosen depending on the country

not necessarily led to a more accurate concept of accessibility and the same misconception arises again. The correct definition is chosen by 62.4% of group 1 and 51.6% of group 2. By contrast, 39.5% chose definition 1 of group 2 and 24.8% of group 1.

A single definition may not be enough to determine whether people have a correct concept of digital accessibility, so participants were also asked about the elements to be enhanced by good digital accessibility practices. The options were website design, mobile app design, databases, office files, media files and other. They could select the combination of options they consider best, being the most accurate website design, mobile app design, office files and media files. Digital accessibility definitely does not affect databases and "other" option might be included or not depending on each one's interpretation. Results are clear, only 2.1% of the sample chose the correct combination and just 28.6% include office files and 27.8% media files in contrast to 34.3% that chose databases (see Fig. 7). Website and mobile app design are elements that people tend to associate more to digital accessibility. Users are more aware that accessibility is necessary in web and apps but not in the elements mentioned by the EU directives such as files.

Level of awareness and identifying the elements affected by accessibility are not directly related. The number of people selecting each element, decreases as the level

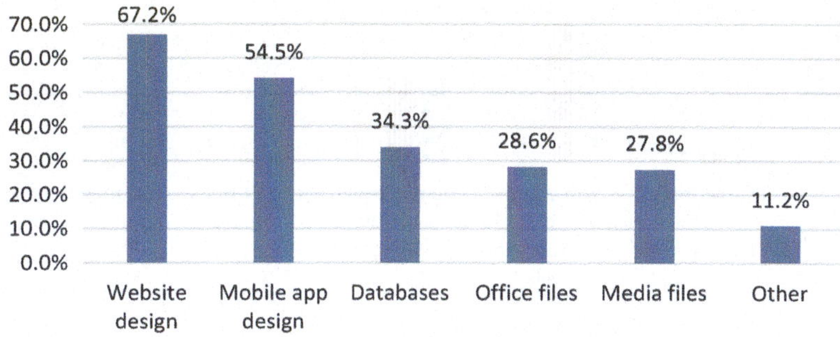

Fig. 7 Elements that should be enhanced by good digital accessibility practices

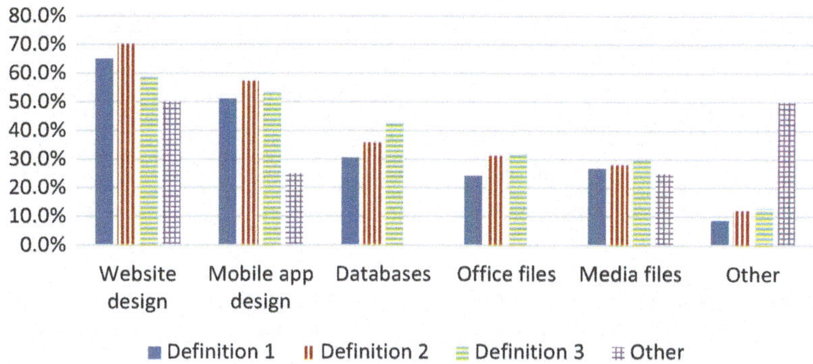

Fig. 8 Relation between the definition chosen and the elements declared as affected by digital accessibility

of awareness decreases, this includes databases. As show data in Fig. 8, a better knowledge of digital accessibility does not translate in knowing which elements are affected. In fact, people who do not select the correct definition mostly select office and media files. There is a general lack of awareness of accessibility requirements in these new items, even among those who know the term.

We have not found evidence of the relation between other factors such as age, experience or gender to greater awareness or better knowledge on the topic, as there are misconceptions and lack of understanding in every category independently of the group.

3.2 Applicable Regulation

There is legislation regulating the accessibility of digital information both at the European level and in each of the member countries of the European Union, at least

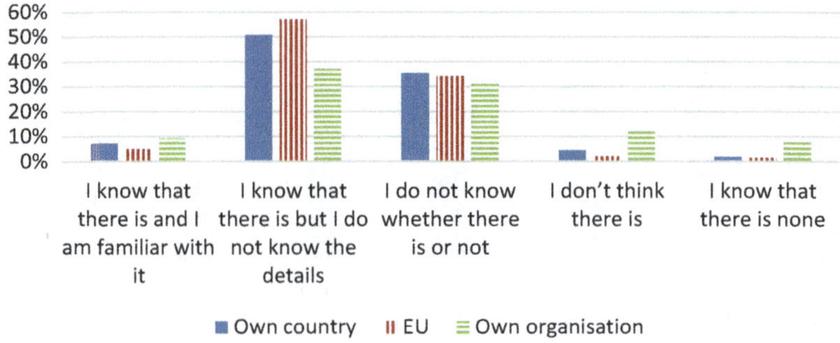

Fig. 9 Knowledge about the existence of regulation about digital accessibility in different levels

Table 1 Correlation coefficients (r) between awareness on digital accessibility and knowledge about the existence of regulation

		Awareness on the term digital accessibility (%)
Awareness on regulation	European level	34.7
	National level	32.1
	Organization level	22.2

since 2018 was the deadline date for countries to adapt their legal framework to EU Directive 2016/2102. In addition, companies are gradually incorporating initiatives to improve accessibility, as they are obliged to guarantee it by law or by market.

Participants were asked whether they are aware of the existence of regulation on digital accessibility at these different levels, in the EU, in their country and in their organization. The results (see Fig. 9) show that the general situation is of ignorance and people seem to see the directives as something that exist but with no need to go in-depth as there are no implications in their daily life. In none of the three levels, the percentage of people being familiar with regulations reach 10%.

Logic may lead us to think that a higher knowledge about regulation might imply that participant is more aware on what accessibility is. Awareness on the term accessibility and knowledge about the existence of regulation seem to be interrelated thus, the correlation coefficient is no high enough to stablish a positive correlation in none of the legislation levels. Values do not rise above 35% (see Table 1).

The factors used to define the sample do not have influence with awareness on regulation, in a neither positive nor negative way.

3.3 Motivation and Responsibility

The predisposition shown by the participants towards digital accessibility is favorable. When asked if achieving digital accessibility is worth the effort and money, a

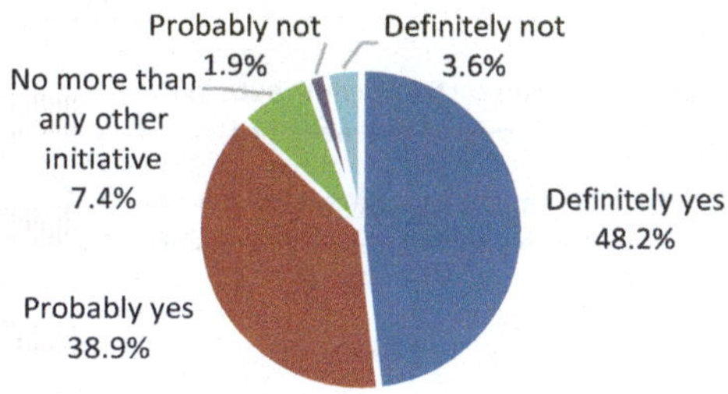

Fig. 10 Worthwhile (effort/money) of adapting digital services and information

majority (48.2%) stated that definitely yes, followed by 38.9% that answered probably yes (see Fig. 10). The main reason for implementing digital accessibility is that it prevents isolation and discrimination, and facilitates an integrated and equal society (44.8%). It is also relevant that benefits everybody, not only people with disabilities (31%) and that it is something necessary for equity and justice for all (18.9%). The fact that it is a compulsory element mandated by law is the main reason for only a 4.2% of the respondents.

In general, the high level of motivation is accompanied by an intention to take individual responsibility for ensuring accessibility. More than the 60% stated that users can certainly contribute in their daily activities, 31.4% said the users can contribute but only under professional supervision and only 6.7% referred to experts as the only capable of implementing it. As show data in Fig. 11, as participants become aware of the worthiness of implementing digital accessibility, they also become more willing to take responsibility for their daily tasks. It also happens that there are responses in the category "Other", as if digital accessibility would need the involvement of a third agent apart from users and IT professionals. This agent can be a person to make an

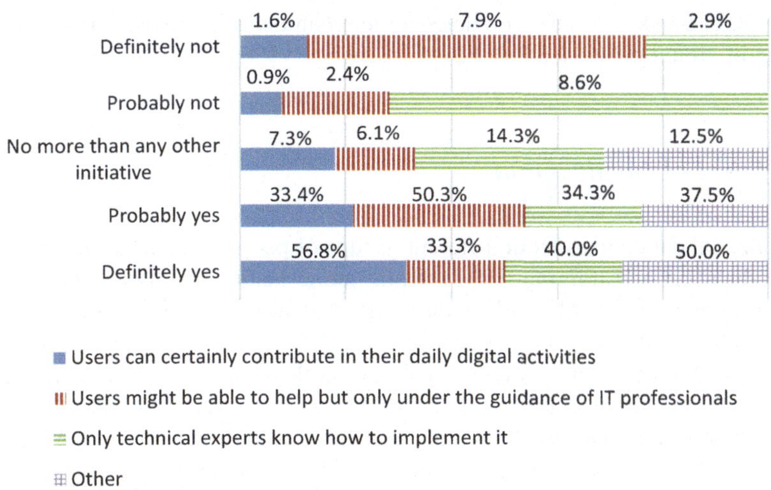

Fig. 11 Motivation impact on assuming the responsibility of digital accessibility

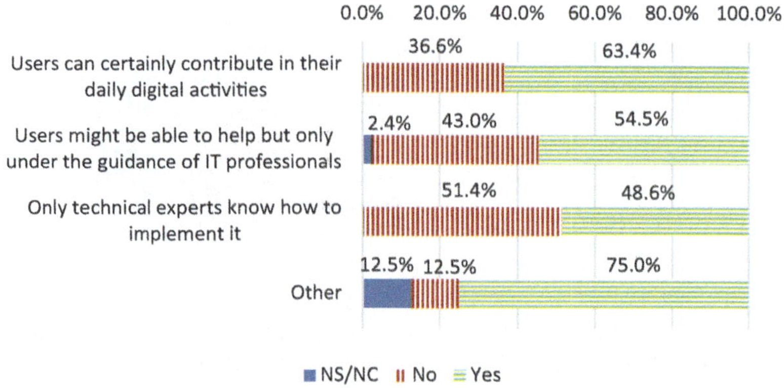

Fig. 12 Impact of training on the assumption of responsibilities

ongoing follow-up assessment, to check compliance with the regulations or a legal figure.

Data show that knowing that it is everyone's responsibility does not imply knowing the correct definition of accessibility. There is no relation between being more motivated to implement accessibility and assume the responsibilities with selecting the correct definition. Even more, although when asked directly participants tend to say that every user can contribute, the reality is that they selected the "technical elements" (websites, apps and databases) as the ones that should be enhanced by good digital accessibility (see Fig. 7).

An important factor that influence the implication on the process is amount of specific training. On one hand, people with training in digital skills show more inclination to assume that they can contribute to accessibility in their daily tasks. On the other hand, the ones who delegate in technicians are mostly people with no training in digital skills (see Fig. 12).

3.4 *Level of Involvement*

The collected data comes from different groups of people such as those from vocational education and training (VET), from public institutions and from small and medium enterprises (SME), all of them affected in some way by the mandatory nature of the legislation.

We asked participants whether if their colleagues would have interest in contributing to digital accessibility. The majority answers "Probably yes" (see Fig. 13). Only less than the 20% think that there would be a strong commitment. The general trend is that people from public administrations are more willing to get involved, while those from small and medium enterprises show less interest unless

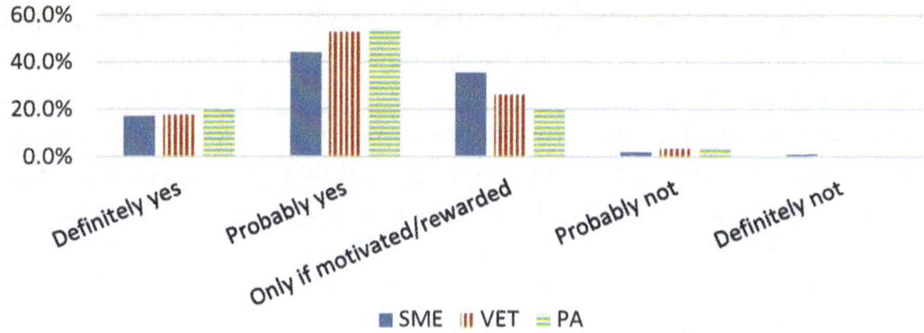

Fig. 13 Participants' colleagues' interest in contributing to digital accessibility

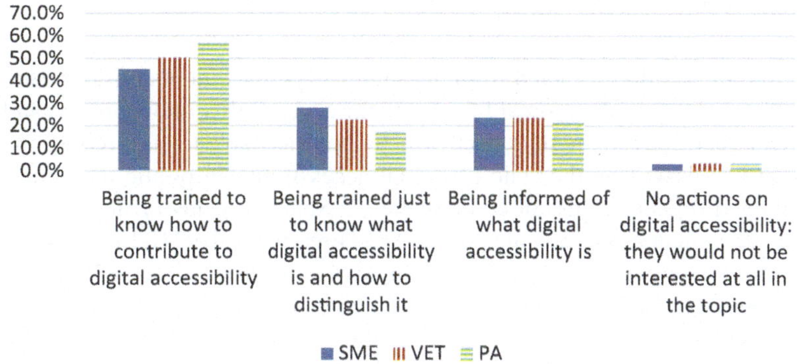

Fig. 14 Level of involvement that participants would have in digital accessibility training

there is any kind of reward. When asked whether if their organizations would be interested, the tendencies are the same. Commitment but with remarks, as the majority say that probably yes. In addition, the most motivated are the public administrations followed by the VET centers. SMEs are the ones that would have more interest if rewarded.

Involvement can take place at different levels, data in Fig. 14 show that a majority of participants from each group would prefer a deeper training approach that allows them to contribute. Once more, the ones that show a higher level of involvement are those from public administrations, followed by VET centers. SME employees are more focused on results and may see accessibility as something that does not produce as many benefits.

3.5 Limitations of the Study

This study presents logical limitations according to the adopted approach. The first one is the sample for the survey. It could include more people and better balance so that every segment is equally represented, especially more countries. However, it is probably the largest study in terms of countries and people related to digital accessibility as far as we know.

Other limitation are the questions based in self-rating or self-assessment, e.g. the cases of digital skills or awareness on accessibility and legislation. Accuracy do not used to be always good but the sample size mitigates this risk. Questions on professional profile are limited to the identification of general group not capturing the specific role. This led to categorize them by areas and not by profile, e.g., technicians and administrative profiles.

4 Additional Observations from Real Cases

Apart from the results extracted from the survey, it is relevant to consider additional observations of the implication of IT users in the accessibility of documents and files.

Present year 2021 is the date from which countries have to start reporting to the European Comission on the state of digital accessibility in public institutions and other obliged organizations. In consequence, a Spanish Ministry in the process of adapting documentations and files to the EU Directive 2016/2102 [1] requested us services for making files accessible: the job involved more than 180 PDF documents (rather homogeneous in format and type of content) as well as templates and a big report in PDF with more than 250 pages. All these files included 51 graphs, 76 tables, 5 complex diagrams, structured lists, links, formulas, etc.

After completing all the work, we observed the following facts and problems among many others:

- Some pages were scanned as images and included directly in the document
- Use of blank spaces and line breaks for formatting and widen spacing
- Use of simulated lists without structure marks
- Tables, graphs and links included as images, without preserving the editable original files
- Use of an incoherent title structure
- Use of inappropriate font types and sizes
- Use of color to convey information.

The first four do not directly relate to accessibility, but to digital skills. For example, the fact that public employees use blank spaces and line breaks reveals a lack of strong digital skills when creating and managing office files. This digital skills deficit is widespread across all age and gender groups as revealed data from ICDL [15]. This study suggests that basic digital skills will not naturally improve in the future without formal training. So government and public administration should consider more intense effort to ensure digital skills in public employees, not only for the general interest of productivity and effectiveness in the new digital administration but also to support the role of IT users in the generation and management of accessible digital information and contents. Measure may not only include classical training activities but also requiring widely accepted certifications of digital skills for entering the public service. In general, there is huge room for improvement in the training of public employees to ensure that digital contents and documents could be compliant with the EU accessibility regulation.

5 Conclusions and Future Work

Digital accessibility is an element that has not been developed enough in organizations, even if it is mandatory in many cases. Europe has made an effort in promoting it, through the directives, but further effort still needs to be made to raise awareness among the population. Moreover, results from this study show that there is a lack of coherent knowledge. Misconceptions are widespread, and people tend to overrate their knowledge on digital accessibility. This does not only refer to know what accessibility is but also to be aware that it is not just a technical issue. Everyone who develop or manage digital information has responsibility in the whole process, as just one non-accessible file on a web would ruin accessibility, no matter how many standards that site meets.

This is the reason why training activities are needed. There is no clear relationship between age and experience either favoring accessibility or harming it. Young people do not show better knowledge, even if considered as "digital natives". We cannot expect a demographic trend will solve the problems. We need to train all those involved.

Training does not involve a great difficulty. Authors had performed training activities involving 34 secondary and higher education teachers with clear results: all the participants ranked their previous digital skills almost as "enough to learn how to develop accessible documents and content" and the difficulty of the course was "normal" for 79%. Digital skills and difficulty are not an obstacle but there is a lack of training in accessibility for teachers in universities and institutions. However, training itself is not enough for digital accessibility, both public and private organizations need to raise awareness among employees to be compliant with European directives fostering a training and awareness-raising plan to promote digital accessibility.

While digital accessibility is an element that has been actively promoted at the legislative level by the EU, there is hardly any mention to it in the Digital Competence Framework for Citizens, DigComp 2.1 [16]. The new version 2.2 is now being developed and we are leading the working group which analyzes the areas where digital accessibility needs to be considered as well as the necessary competences, attitudes and skills for users. This has also encouraged the design of a certification in digital accessibility. This would provide users with a solid basis for applying accessibility principles in their daily tasks and would reduce the control that managers and technicians would have to exercise.

Although there are automatic tools for checking accessibility of web pages through HTML analysis, when it comes to PDF documents hosted on them, the analysis has to be done one by one. We are also working in the development of a tool to automate the accessibility analysis of PDF documents of a whole website starting from its home URL.

References

1. European Parliament and Council of the European Union: Directive (EU) 2016/2102 of The European Parliament and of the Council of 26 October 2016 on the accessibility of the websites and mobile applications of public sector bodies. October 26, 2016. https://eur-lex.europa.eu/legal-content/EN/TXT/?uri=CELEX:32016L2102 (2016)
2. European Parliament and Council of the European Union: Directive (EU) 2019/882 of The European Parliament and of the Council of 17 April 2019 on the accessibility requirements for products and services. April 17, 2019. https://eur-lex.europa.eu/legal-content/EN/TXT/?uri=CELEX:32019L0882 (2019)
3. de la Presidencia, M.: Real Decreto 1494/2007 de 12 de noviembre por el que se aprueba el Reglamento sobre las condiciones básicas para el acceso de las personas con discapacidad a las tecnologías, productos y servicios relacionados con la sociedad de la información y medios de comunicación social. BOE, 2007. https://www.boe.es/boe/dias/2007/11/21/pdfs/A47567-47572.pdf (2007)
4. Inal, Y., Guribye, F., Rajanen, D., Rajanen, M., Rost, M.: Perspectives and practices of digital accessibility: a survey of user experience professionals in Nordic countries. Assoc. Comput. Mach. (2020). https://doi.org/10.1145/3419249.3420119
5. Wentz, B., Lazar, J.: Inclusive design of a web-based resource to assist public librarians with providing government information to library patrons in the United States. In: Inclusive Designing, Cham, pp 259–268 (2014)
6. Alahmadi, T., Drew, S.: Accessibility evaluation of top-ranking university websites in world, Oceania, and Arab categories for home, admission, and course description webpages. J. Open Flex. Distance Learn. **21**(1), 7–24 (2017)
7. Lazar, J., Goldstein, D. F., Taylor, A.: Ensuring Digital Accessibility Through Process and Policy. Morgan Kaufmann (2015)
8. Reis, A., Barroso, J., Gonçalves, R.: Supporting Accessibility in Higher Education Information Systems, pp. 250–255 (2013)
9. Lazar, J.: Managing digital accessibility at universities during the COVID-19 pandemic. Univ. Access Inf. Soc. (2021). https://doi.org/10.1007/s10209-021-00792-5
10. Lazar, J.: Integrating accessibility into the information systems curriculum. In: Proceedings of the International Association for Computer Information Systems, pp. 373–379 (2002)
11. Mancilla, R., Frey, B.: Administrative Supports for Digital Accessibility: Policies and Processes. Quality Matters, 2020. https://www.qualitymatters.org/sites/default/files/research-docs-pdfs/QM-Digital-Accessibility-Policy-Process-WP.pdf (2020)
12. Rush, S. (ed): Contributors: Shawn Lawton Henry, Eric Eggert, Brent Bakken, Vicki Menezes Miller, Laura Keen. "The Business Case for Digital Accessibility." Education and Outreach Working Group, 2018. https://www.w3.org/WAI/business-case/ (2018)
13. Horton, S., Sloan, D.: Accessibility for business and pleasure. Assoc. Comput. Mach. **23**(1) (2015). https://doi.org/10.1145/2843590
14. Kulkarni, M.: Digital accessibility: challenges and opportunities. IIMB Manag. Rev. **23**(1), 91–98 (2019). https://doi.org/10.1016/j.iimb.2018.05.009
15. López Baldominos, I., Fernández Sanz, L., Pospelova, V.: Análisis de las competencias digitales básicas en Europa y en España. JENUI **5**, 77–84 (2020)
16. Carretero, S., Vuorikari, R., Punie, Y.: DigComp 2.1 The Digital Competence Framework for Citizens. Joint Research Centre, 2017. http://publications.jrc.ec.europa.eu/repository/bitstream/JRC106281/web-digcomp2.1pdf_(online).pdf (2047)

Authentic Learning for Groupwork Skills: A Comparison Between a Physical and a Virtual Experience

Mairéad Hogan

Abstract Development of teamwork skills is a stated goal of many group assignments in university settings. However, the challenges associated with the effective design of assignments to achieve this goal have been well-documented. Students regularly circumvent the process by dividing the work and completing it separately. The difficulties inherent in a normal academic environment have been compounded by the restrictions and difficulties placed on lecturers and students during a global pandemic. This paper discusses the use of an authentic learning approach in 'normal' times and an authentic learning approach adapted to a virtual environment during Covid-19 and whether they impact on the development of teamwork skills in a post-graduate user experience design (UXD) module. Using the Groupwork Skills Questionnaire (GSQ), analysis shows the 'live' version of the learning experience resulted in improved task-based teamwork skills while the virtual event had no impact.

Keywords Teamwork · Authentic learning · Hackathon · User experience

1 Introduction

Students frequently participate in group work at university level. There are many benefits of this to them, including social support, improvements in self-esteem, development of critical analysis skills, enhanced learning, enhanced motivation, and students taking ownership of the process of learning [1–6]. Students may also develop skills (e.g. communication and other collaborative skills) that will be of use to them in the workplace [7–9].

Unfortunately, research indicates that students do not, in many instances, enhance their collaborative or teamwork skills when engaging in group work. Some of the

A prior version of this paper has been published in the ISD2021 Proceedings (http://aisel.aisnet.org/isd2014/proceedings2021).

M. Hogan (✉)
National University of Ireland Galway, Galway, Ireland
e-mail: mairead.hogan@nuigalway.ie

E. Insfran Pelozo et al. (eds.), *Advances in Information Systems Development*, Lecture Notes in Information Systems and Organisation 55,
https://doi.org/10.1007/978-3-030-95354-6_4

issues identified include disparity in workload, students working separately on individual elements without collaboration, students reluctantly accepting a majority viewpoint in order to avoid conflict, and lack of identification of students who do not do their fair share of work [2, 10–13].

Additional problems can be encountered when students are working in virtual teams. While courses in the past may have planned a virtual element to their course to enhance virtual teamwork [1, 14, 15] during the Covid-19 pandemic many lecturers found themselves in the difficult position of suddenly converting to online teaching and virtual group assignments as a way of dealing with the restrictions placed on daily life.

This study focuses on the adaptation to a virtual format of an authentic learning approach that had been used successfully in previous years and examines its impact on teamwork skills. It also compares the impact on teamwork skills of the live event and the virtual event.

1.1 Student Group Work

Students can work individually or in groups in order to complete coursework. It is important to determine which is the most appropriate for a given task. Working in groups is of most benefit for complex problems which are poorly defined, and for which there is no clear-cut solution [16]. While the majority of research has examined benefits to students (see Sect. 1), group work can also benefit the tutor through a reduction in workload, increased efficiency and the ability to vary assessment methods [17, 18].

Group assignments must be carefully designed to realise the benefits of group work. The task must be relevant and of sufficient complexity for collaboration. It is also important to consider how the team will work together and how individuals will be held accountable [1, 4, 10, 17, 19].

1.2 Virtual Teamwork

Virtual assignments had become more commonplace in third level institutions with the increase in online learning pre-Covid-19 [20]. During Covid-19, many more courses were forced to move to an entirely online environment for teaching and assessment. Virtual assignments can be beneficial to all students as the skills acquired can translate to the workplace where virtual teams are commonplace [14, 21, 22].

While many of the challenges inherent to any form of groupwork apply to virtual groups, there are additional challenges in a virtual environment. Students can be reluctant to participate due to technical inexperience with the tools, a desire to meet face-to-face and prior negative experience of group work generally, leading to concern about managing those issues in a virtual environment [15]. Frequently, team members do not interact with one another in any significant way, often due to uncertainty in how to engage or a lack of understanding of expectations and thus fail to develop as groups [16, 20]. Overall, issues with communication, team management and technology are some of the main problems encountered in virtual teams [14, 22, 23], often leading to a focus on the task, rather than the socio-emotional elements of groupwork [20]. Many of these challenges can be addressed by ensuring students have an opportunity to get to know one another and ensuring roles are clearly defined [20].

Additional challenges experienced in an academic setting include equity issues in terms of contribution, whether by low-performing members not contributing, or domineering members over-contributing [15, 20]. Peer evaluation and clarity regarding contribution expectations can be used to mitigate these.

While challenges are common in virtual group assignments, there are benefits over and above traditional group work. In particular, students who may be reluctant to participate in a physical classroom setting are often more likely to participate virtually [15]. Students can improve their ability to track communications, and can develop empathy and teamwork skills [15, 20]. Many students also believe the experience of being on a virtual team helps them gain useful professional skills [15].

1.3 Authentic Learning

A key trend in higher education that can be used to realise many of the benefits of groupwork is assessment for learning, rather than assessment of learning [24]. Assessment for learning can be defined as 'any assessment for which the first priority in its design and practice is to serve the purpose of promoting students' learning' [25]. This focus on 'learning by doing' has been used in the training of apprentices for generations and is a successful method of developing competence and knowledge through practice rather than limiting learning to the classroom [26]. The authentic learning environment may be simulated to replicate the conditions of the realistic environment in which the tasks would normally take place. The tasks must be true to reality and have relevance to the goals. In order to realise the benefits of the process, the environment must allow interaction and socialisation; facilitation and guidance must be effective; students must be encouraged to own the process and reflect on their learning [7, 13, 27, 28]. Authentic learning has been shown to improve critical thinking, communication, and problem-solving skills [27], to motivate students, and to facilitate their ability to apply classroom learnings [28].

Challenge-based Learning (CBL) is an authentic learning approach where students and teachers collaborate to solve real problems [29]. It can be used to develop a variety of skills such as problem solving, leadership and critical thinking. Student learning engagement is improved, and it is an efficient and effective approach of teaching [30].

1.4 Hackathons in Education

Hackathons can be used as a method of authentic learning. A hackathon is an event where participants with a variety of skills collaborate in teams with the aim of solving a particular problem in a short period of time [31]. Using effective communication, participants organise themselves and develop projects [32]. Hackathons have been shown to help with personal development, improve skills, increase critical thinking and creativity, result in innovations, and provide opportunities for networking [31, 33, 34].

In an educational setting, the participants develop knowledge and skills by engaging with a specific problem. The learning is experiential because of the social and contextual elements of the event [35]. Peer learning is a major benefit of the hackathon [35, 36]. Hackathons are used extensively for educational purposes, particularly in computer science. However, they can be used in other areas such as science, user experience design (UXD) and marketing [35–38].

In order to achieve the envisaged educational benefits, the hackathon should be designed appropriately. CBL is an effective approach to structuring a hackathon [35]. This requires 3 distinct phases: Engagement, where the Big Idea is explored and defined in order to identify an essential question; Investigation, where the challenge is researched using guidance questions; and Act, where a real-world solution is implemented. Other issues to consider include various practicalities, such as ensuring participants have access to wall space for discussion purposes and to display ideas, ensuring the focus at the early stages is on non-technological approaches, ensuring guidance is available for team formation and to determine progress [37].

2 The UX Assignment

The assignments discussed in this paper were completed by students of the Interactive Systems Design module on an MSc in Information Systems Management (ISM) programme and the Human Computer Interaction module on an MA in Digital Media (DM) programme in an Irish university. The students on both programmes came from a variety of undergraduate backgrounds, with some having worked for a number of years prior to returning to education. Both modules are designed to develop user-centred design techniques including:

- User research to understand user needs.
- Design skills.
- Evaluation skills to assess and improve design.

Previous students on the MSc ISM participated in a live hackathon event in prior years. The aim of this was to provide an assignment that required students to fully engage with the subject and to provide additional psychological, social and academic benefits that can be achieved with authentic group work (see Sect. 1). Due to Covid-19, a physical event was not possible in 2020 so it was decided to run a virtual event with similar aims. The MSc ISM and the MA DM students participated in this virtual event.

The live event in 2018 and 2019 was a UX Hackathon (Empathy Jam Galway). It was a full-day event, with mentors and judges from industry and academia. The inclusion of industry partners was an important element of the authentic learning experience for students. The virtual event in 2020 was a half-day UX hackathon (Design Jam Galway) where groups of students worked on a design challenge with support from mentors from academia and industry. While Design Jam provided an authentic learning environment, it was not possible to include some of the more sophisticated elements of Empathy Jam, such as involvement of the public to act as potential end-users.

This study seeks to extend previous research by assessing and comparing the impact of a live challenge-based group assignment and a virtual challenge-based group assignment on groupwork skills. Therefore, the following hypotheses are proposed:

- H1: Participation in a live UX hackathon leads to improved groupwork skills.
- H2: Participation in a virtual UX hackathon leads to improved groupwork skills.
- H3: Participation in a live UX hackathon leads to better groupwork skills than participation in a virtual UX hackathon.

3 Methodology

Both assignments were designed to help students develop user-centred design skills. An additional aim was that, by working in teams in an authentic learning environment, they would also develop teamwork skills of benefit to them in the workplace.

Empathy Jam Galway was designed to follow the real interactions and tasks that are part of a user-centred design process. Design Jam Galway was designed to emulate the design process of a UX team working virtually. The effect of the assessment methods on teamwork skills was assessed using the Groupwork Skills Questionnaire [39].

3.1 Empathy Jam Galway

Empathy Jam Galway was a UX hackathon that provided an authentic learning experience to students in the area of user-centred design [40]. The first Empathy Jam (https://www.empathyjam.com), took place in 2016 in New York using the tagline 'Empathize, collaborate, and design a better New York'. Participants practiced user research techniques with the public. They then designed and tested their proposed solution with members of the public.

The event in Galway was designed following the guidelines of Herrington and Herrington [41] regarding authentic learning environments. The main considerations were that the challenges be designed in a way that required collaboration; participants should realistically engage with potential users; coaching and structure should be provided by mentors; and participants should have opportunities to articulate potential solutions and for reflection on learnings.

The day was structured so that it followed a CBL layout. The students *Engaged* with the challenge, followed by an *Investigation* phase where they interacted with members of the public, who were potential users. During the *Act* phase, using the result of their user research, they created paper prototypes and conducted tests with members of the public.

3.2 Design Jam Galway

Due to Covid-19 restrictions, a live event could not take place in 2020. The event was structured so that it followed a CBL layout, where participants *Engaged* with the challenge in a brainstorming session. They then *Investigated*, using electronic resources, and finally *Acted*, by creating a prototype. Support and guidance were provided by mentors from academia and industry to ensure they stayed on track and made the best use of the resources available to them. They used Miro, an online collaborative whiteboard, to develop their ideas.

3.3 Assessment

Empathy Jam required a video submission, while Design Jam required creation of an infographic. It was believed that creation of a video describing the experience would be problematic due to Covid-19 restrictions. Those who attended Empathy Jam produced a 7-min-long video demonstrating what they did and learned on the day. Students who attended Design Jam created an infographic detailing their experience of the event.

Students were provided with resources, such as tutorials, physical equipment and software they could use to create the videos and infographic. They were also provided with links to examples that could be used for inspiration.

3.4 Groupwork Skills Questionnaire

Both team and task elements are important for teamwork to be effective. However, students have a tendency to focus their efforts on task elements, whilst ignoring interpersonal or team elements [10]. Cumming, Woodcock et al. [39] developed a groupwork skills questionnaire (GSQ) that assesses interpersonal and task related groupwork skills. Its purpose is to examine whether a group assignment improves teamwork skills. They [39] use the term groupwork skills to 'describe the set of skills that individuals employ to enhance group functioning'. The GSQ focuses on skills used by group members in academic and work settings. It has been validated in a variety of settings [42–44].

GSQ assesses both task and interpersonal skills. The task skills are those that contribute to management of the project and the group (e.g. determining strategy, schedules) while the interpersonal skills are those that relate to the dynamics within the group (e.g. considering the feelings of other group members). The two types of skills are evaluated separately, which is seen as a strength of this tool over other instruments that measure groupwork skills.

Each student completed two questionnaires, one at the beginning of the semester, which evaluated their usual approach to groupwork and the second after the assignment was completed and which assessed their behaviours on the current assignment. This approach was used for two reason: (1) to assess changes in individual behaviours; and (2) to address a potential limitation of using a self-report measure, namely, the potential for exaggeration when reporting on behaviours [45]. Comparing pre- and post- behaviours can mitigate against this limitation.

The GSQ assesses the respondent's perception of their groupwork skills. There are 10 questions in total, 5 of which relate to task skills and 5 of which relate to interpersonal skills (see Table 1). The pre-assignment questionnaire used the stem 'When working in groups I tend to…' and asked them to rate each of the questions on a scale of 1–5 (never to always). The post-assignment questionnaire used the stem 'When working in this group I…'. Average scores were calculated for task and interpersonal scales, both pre-assignment and post-assignment.

Table 1 Groupwork skills questionnaire

Task questions	Interpersonal questions
1. Remind the group how important it is to stick to schedules	1. Provide emotional support to my group members1
2. Construct strategies from ideas that have been raised	2. Be sensitive to the feelings of other people
3. Clearly define the roles of each group member	3. Show that I care about my group members
4. Move the group's ideas forward towards a strategy	4. Be open and supportive when communicating with others
5. Evaluate how well the group is progressing towards agreed goals	5. Be there for other group members when they need me

Table 2 Groupwork scores

Assignment	Pre-interpersonal	Pre-task	Post-Interpersonal	Post-task
Empathy Jam (n = 62)	4.1065	3.9935	4.2645	4.4129
Design Jam (n = 24)	4.0500	3.8833	4.1167	3.7750

4 Results

Empathy Jam was held in 2018 and 2019 and had 62 participants in total. Design Jam was held in 2020 and had 24 participants. The pre- and post-assignment questionnaires were completed by all participants.

The scores from the pre-assignment questionnaire (see Table 2) were initially compared to determine whether the groups differed in their starting position. There was no significant difference between the two cohorts in either interpersonal or task behaviours when working on assignments previously.

To determine whether participation in either of the events impacted on groupwork behaviours, paired t-tests were conducted. For Empathy Jam, while no significant difference was evident for the interpersonal behaviours, a significant difference, with a moderate effect, was noted for task related behaviours ($t = 5.068$, $df = 61$, $p < 0.001$, $d = 0.647$). Thus, H1 (Participation in a live UX hackathon leads to improved groupwork skills) can be partially accepted.

For Design Jam, no significant difference was evident for the interpersonal or task related behaviours, suggesting participation in Design Jam did not improve groupwork skills. Thus, H2 (Participation in a virtual UX hackathon leads to improved groupwork skills) was rejected.

The post-assignment groupwork behaviours of participants in both events were then compared using t-tests. No significant difference was observed between the groups for interpersonal behaviours. However, the rating for task behaviours was higher for those who participated in Empathy Jam than for those who participated in Design Jam (4.4129 vs 3.7750). The ratings were compared using t-test which showed a significant difference ($t = 4.922$, $df = 84$, $p < 0.001$, $d = 1.183$), with the value for Cohen's d indicating a large effect, therefore suggesting Empathy Jam is a more effective approach to developing task related groupwork behaviours than Design Jam. Thus, H3 (Participation in a live UX hackathon leads to better groupwork skills than participation in a virtual UX hackathon) was partially accepted.

5 Discussion

The baseline scores were quite high for interpersonal ($m = 4.0907$, s.d. $= 0.64034$) and task ($m = 3.9628$, s.d. $= 0.60392$) related behaviours, with no significant difference evident between the two cohorts. Both assignments used an authentic learning approach, with Empathy Jam being a 'live' event that incorporated interaction with potential users to design a potential solution. In contrast, Design Jam was a virtual event and focussed only on the design aspects of development. While Empathy Jam appeared to improve the task related skills of participants, Design Jam improved neither. In fact, while there was no significant difference pre- and post-assignment in task related behaviours, the mean value post-assignment was lower than pre-assignment for Design Jam, suggesting that participants were less effective in their task-related teamwork behaviours in a virtual environment than they had been for prior group activities.

Neither event impacted on interpersonal groupwork skills. This may be due to a number of factors. The mean baseline for interpersonal behaviours was high ($m = 4.0907$, $s.d. = 0.64034$) and so, improving them significantly would be difficult. This may be due to the fact the students were post-graduate students, many of whom had previous work experience which may have enhanced their interpersonal groupwork behaviours. An alternative explanation may be due to the complex nature of interpersonal behaviour and the individual differences in these [46]. Developing effective interpersonal skills is complex and requires effort and time. Therefore, multiple interventions may be required to show an improvement.

Task related groupwork behaviours improved for participants of Empathy Jam, while Design Jam did not significantly affect them. In addition, those who participated in Empathy Jam reported better task related behaviours than those who participated in Design Jam. The biggest difference between the two events was the fact Empathy Jam was 'live', while Design Jam was virtual. There were other differences, such as the submission medium (video vs infographic) and the fact user research formed part of Empathy Jam. However, the design approach and the interaction with mentors was similar for both events.

The results of this study provide evidence that the 'live' authentic learning event was more successful at improving task-related groupwork behaviours than the virtual event. According to Angelo and McCarthy [1], groupwork should be designed in a way that facilitates the development of students' groupwork skills. The authentic learning approach used in Empathy Jam appears to do so for task related behaviours. In contrast, a virtual event, while also following an authentic learning approach, did not appear to improve groupwork behaviours.

6 Conclusion

Development of teamwork skills is frequently seen as a desirable outcome of assignment work on university courses. An authentic learning approach has been shown to be effective in developing these skills in a 'live' setting [47]. However, the restrictions placed on universities with the advent of Covid-19 limited the options available for developing these skills and necessitated the use of virtual approaches.

A virtual hackathon, following the recommendations of Herrington and Herrington [41], was designed to provide an authentic leaning experience. This included industry involvement, mentors to provide guidance, and provision of appropriate resources, such as talks and training in the use of tools. Despite this, the event did not improve groupwork behaviours for the participants. Participants were asked for feedback in a post-event survey on what helped, and what hindered, the teamwork elements of the event. Some of the main issues identified included: connectivity issues; not knowing one another before the event; not being able to see one another (e.g. when using the whiteboard they could not see faces, those with poor connectivity turned off their camera); lack of leadership within the group; lack of clarity regarding roles within the project. However, participants were positive about the event overall, and felt that the main benefits included support from the mentors, the use of collaborative tools and the commitment of team members.

Based on the feedback, it would appear that more careful design of the virtual event is required to enable development of groupwork skills. While little can be done to improve individuals' wi-fi connectivity, many of the other issues can be addressed. For example, groups could be formed in advance and tasked with some ice-breaker activities to enable them to get to know one another better; clear definition of roles within the project would help to resolve the issues regarding leadership and roles; when using whiteboards, where possible, they should not use full screen to ensure they can see others' faces.

While the virtual nature of Design Jam came about because of restrictions due to Covid-19, it provided benefits to students. They generally felt it was a useful event that helped to improve their design skills and their use of virtual collaborative and design tools. Future events of this nature should build on the positives, whilst learning from the feedback regarding the limitations encountered, with the aim of creating a virtual event that can enhance subject matter learnings and build teamwork skills.

7 Limitations

Self-reported data, as was used in this study, has the potential for social desirability and participant bias, and may result in over-reporting of positive behaviours. While this was mitigated by comparison of measures, the use of an objective measure of groupwork skills in future research would give a more comprehensive view of behaviours.

The generalisability of the results may be affected by the fact participants self-selected into the assignment and were not randomly allocated to groups. Additionally, while the two modules are similar in terms of content and student background, none of the MA in DM participated in empathy Jam.

References

1. Angelo, R., McCarthy, R.: Group assignments as a class element to promote performance in virtual groups. Inf. Syst. Educ. J. **16**(4), 4–12 (2018)
2. Burke, A.: Group Work: how to use groups effectively. J. Effect. Teach. **11**(2), 87–95 (2011)
3. Hwang, M.I.: Relationship between teamwork and team performance: experiences from an Erpsim competition. J. Inf. Syst. Educ. **29**(3), 157–168 (2018)
4. Knapper, C.: Changing teaching practice: strategies and barriers. In: Taking Stock: Symposium on Teaching and Learning Research in Higher Education. University of Guelph, Ontario (2008)
5. Laal, M., Ghodsi, S.M.: Benefits of collaborative learning. Procedia. Soc. Behav. Sci. **31**, 486–490 (2012)
6. Masika, R., Jones, J.: Building student belonging and engagement: insights into higher education students' experiences of participating and learning together. Teach. High. Educ. **21**(2), 138–150 (2015)
7. Ashford-Rowe, K., Herrington, J., Brown, C.: Establishing the critical elements that determine authentic assessment. Assess. Eval. High. Educ. **39**(2), 205–222 (2013)
8. Brown, R., Zuo, N., Shockley, J., Buck, S.: An Authentic learning approach to group assignments: an analysis of student attitudes. Appl. Econ. Teach. Resour. **1**(2), 1–13 (2019)
9. Giuliodori, M.J., Lujan, H.L., DiCarlo, S.E.: Collaborative group testing benefits high- and low-performing students. Adv. Physiol. Educ. **32**(4), 274–278 (2008)
10. Fransen, J., Kirschner, P.A., Erkens, G.: Mediating team effectiveness in the context of collaborative learning: the importance of team and task awareness. Comput. Hum. Behav. **27**(3), 1103–1113 (2011)
11. LaBeouf, J.P., Griffith, J.C., Roberts, D.L.: Faculty and student issues with group work: what is problematic with college group assignments and why? J. Educ. Hum. Dev. **5**(1), 13–23 (2016)
12. Lejk, M., Wyvill, M., Farrow, S.: Group assessment in systems analysis and design: a comparison of the performance of streamed and mixed-ability groups. Assess. Eval. High. Educ. **24**(1), 5–14 (2006)
13. Wilson, B.G.: Constructivism for active, authentic learning. In: Reiser, B., Dempsey, J. (eds.) Trends in Instructional Design and Technology, pp. 61–67. Pearson, Boston, MA (2017)
14. Cleary, Y., Slattery, D.M., Flammia, M., Minacori, P.: Developing strategies for success in a cross-disciplinary global virtual team project: collaboration among student writers and translators. J. Tech. Writ. Commun. **49**(3), 309–337 (2019)
15. Olson-Buchanan, J.B., Rechner, P.L., Sanchez, R.J., Schmidtke, J.M.: Utilizing virtual teams in a management principles course. Education + Training. **49**(5), 408–423 (2007)
16. Wilson, K.J., Brickman, P., Brame, C.J.: Group work. CBE Life Sci. Educ. **17**(1) (2018)
17. De Hei, M.S.A., Strijbos, J.-W., Sjoer, E., Admiraal, W.: Collaborative learning in higher education: lecturers' practices and beliefs. Res. Pap. Educ. **30**(2), 232–247 (2014)
18. Strauss, P., Alice, U.: Group assessments: dilemmas facing lecturers in multicultural tertiary classrooms. High. Educ. Res. Dev. **26**(2), 147–161 (2007)
19. Scager, K., Boonstra, J., Peeters, T., Vulperhorst, J., Wiegant, F.: Collaborative learning in Higher Education: Evoking Positive Interdependence. CBE Life Sci. Educ. **15**(4) (2016)
20. Loh, J., Smyth, R.: Understanding students' online learning experiences in virtual teams. MERLOT J. Online Learn. Teach. **6**(2), 335–342 (2010)
21. Lee, S.-H., Bonk, C.J., Magjuka, R.J., Su, B., Liu, X.: Understanding the dimensions of virtual teams. Int. J. eLearn. **5**(4), 507–523 (2006)
22. Lohle, M.F., Terrell, S.: Knowledge management using student feedback: a study of online students lived experiences on virtual teams. Issues Inf. Syst. **17**(4), 260–265 (2016)
23. Davison, R.M., Panteli, N., Hardin, A.M., Fuller, M.A.: Establishing effective global virtual student teams. IEEE Trans. Prof. Commun. **60**(3) (2017)
24. Brown, S.: A review of contemporary trends in higher education assessment. @tic. revista d'innovació educativa **60**(14), 317–323 (2015)

25. Black, P., Harrison, C., Lee, C., Marshall, B., William, D.: Working inside the black box: assessment for learning in the classroom. Phi Delta Kappan. **86**(1), 8–21 (2004)
26. Black, P., William, D.: Inside the black box: raising standards through classroom assessment. Phi Delta Kappan. **80**(2), 139–144 (1998)
27. Fox, J., Freeman, S., Hughes, N., Murphy, V.: "Keeping It Real": a review of the benefits, challenges and steps towards implementing authentic assessment. Irel. J. Teach. Learn. High. Educ. **9**(3) (2017)
28. Mejías, E., Monereo, C.: As life itself: authentic teaching and evaluation of professional consulting competencies in a psychology course. In: Cano, E., Ion, G. (eds.) Innovative Practices for Higher Education Assessment and Measurement. IGI Global (2017)
29. Apple: Challenge Based Learning a Classroom Guide. Apple Inc (2011)
30. Johnson, L., Adams, S.: Challenge Based Learning: The Report from the Implementation Project. The New Media Consortium (2011)
31. Calco, M., Veeck, A.: The Markathon: adapting the Hackathon model for an introductory marketing class project. Mark. Educ. Rev. **25**(1), 33–38 (2015)
32. Duhring, J.: Hackathon pedagogies as educational technology. In: Open, the Annual Conference of National Collegiate Inventors and Innovators Alliance (2014)
33. Groen, D., Calderhead, B.: Cutting edge: science hackathons for developing interdisciplinary research and collaborations. eLife **4**, e09944 (2015)
34. Komssi, M., Pichlis, D., Raatikainen, M., Kindström, K., Järvinen, J.: What are Hackathons for? IEEE Softw. **32**(5), 60–67 (2015)
35. Gama, K., Alencar, B., Calegario, F., Neves, A., Alessio, P.: A Hackathon methodology for undergraduate course projects. In: IEEE Frontiers in Education Conference, San Jose, CA, USA (2018)
36. Kienzler, H., Fontanesi, C.: Learning through Inquiry: a global health hackathon. Teach. High. Educ. **22**(2), 129–142 (2016)
37. Page, F., Sweeney, S., Buruce, F., Baxter, S.: The use of the "Hackathon". In: Design education: an opportunistic exploration in international conference on engineering and product design education. Aalborg, Denmark (2016)
38. Richard, G.T., Kafai, Y.B., Adleberg, B., Telhan, O.: Stitchfest. In: Proceedings of the 46th ACM Technical Symposium on Computer Science Education—SIGCSE '15, pp. 114–119 (2015)
39. Cumming, J., Woodcock, C., Cooley, S.J., Holland, M.J.G., Burns, V.E.: Development and validation of the Groupwork Skills Questionnaire (Gsq) for higher education. Assess. Eval. High. Educ. **40**(7), 988–1001 (2015)
40. Hogan, M.: From time square to Eyre square: hackathons as authentic learning for information systems students. In: Sixth International Conference on Higher Education Advances, Valencia, Spain (2020)
41. Herrington, A., Herrington, J.: What is an authentic learning environment? In: Tomei, L.A. (eds.) Online and Distance Learning: Concepts, Methodologies, Tools, and Applications Information Science Reference, Hershey, PA, pp. 68–77 (2007)
42. Cooley, S.J., Cumming, J.: outdoor education increases students' groupwork skills, attitudes and self-efficacy during higher education. In: The Sixth International Outdoor Education Research Conference—Future Faces: Outdoor Education Research Innovations and Visions, Otago, New Zealand (2013)
43. Cooley, S.J., Burns, V.E., Cumming, J.: Using outdoor adventure education to develop students' groupwork skills. J. Expe Educ. **39**(4), 329–354 (2016)
44. Cooley, S.J., Eves, F.F., Cumming, J., Burns, V.E.: "Hitting the Ground Running": preparing groups for outdoor learning using a theoretically-based video. J. Adv. Educ. Outdoor Learn. **20**(1), 30–48 (2018)

45. Kormos, C., Gifford, R.: The validity of self-report measures of proenvironmental behavior: a meta-analytic review. J. Environ. Psychol. **40**, 359–371 (2014)
46. Bedwell, W.L., Fiore, S.M., Salas, E.: Developing the 21st century (and beyond) workforce: a review of interpersonal skills & measurement strategies. In: NRC Workshop on Assessing 21st Century Skills (2011)
47. Hogan, M., Young, K.: Designing group assignments to develop groupwork skills. J. Inf. Syst. Educ. (Pending)

Business-IT Alignment Anti-patterns

A Thought from an Empirical Point of View

Jean-Philippe Gouigoux and Dalila Tamzalit

Abstract This preliminary work aims to formalizes observed recurring bad business-IT alignment scenarios. This observation has been conducted subsequently to a 6-years empirical experience of audits of about thirty companies. It considers two research questions: (1) are there recuring BITA problems independently of the business domains? (2) how to formalize them? 14 BITA anti-patterns have been identified. A visual representation and an identity card are proposed to formalize them and illustrated on the 4 most encountered BITA anti-patterns. A first milestone is thus proposed towards a common base of BITA anti-patterns and open the discussion with BITA experts among researchers and practitioners, to pooling our efforts and identify research tracks. In fact, BITA is steel a crucial challenge for companies to have a good alignment between business and software. Moreover, handling misalignments is becoming much more sensitive for companies to move towards adoption of new digital capabilities in Digital Transformation challenges.

Keywords Antipatterns · Business-IT alignment · Information systems governance · Digital transformation · Reuse

1 Introduction

While several companies and industries conduct their Digital Transformation (DT), misalignments and bad dependencies between business processes and their supporting software systems are discovered and become much more sensitive and

---

A prior version of this paper has been published in the ISD2021 Proceedings (http://aisel.aisnet.org/isd2014/proceedings2021).

J.-P. Gouigoux
SALVIA Développement, Aubervilliers, France
e-mail: jp.gouigoux@salviadeveloppement.com

D. Tamzalit (✉)
Université de Nantes, Nantes, France
e-mail: Dalila.Tamzalit@univ-nantes.fr

E. Insfran Pelozo et al. (eds.), *Advances in Information Systems Development*, Lecture Notes in Information Systems and Organisation 55,
https://doi.org/10.1007/978-3-030-95354-6_5

even increase in highly-dynamic contexts of digital strategy. Most companies for now have been considering IT as an aside specialty and almost all of them have a dedicated direction or service for IT, with an average 72% of the budget being burnt in maintenance only [1], whereas investment in evolutions towards Business-IT alignment should represent the higher part of budget [2]. Business-IT alignment (BITA) represents a crucial issue for information systems. It is among the top concerns for Information Technology (IT) leaders [3]. By Business-IT alignment, we mean the dynamic ability of a business organization to use, in an efficient and coherent way, Information Technology (IT) to achieve business objectives and improve its competitiveness [4–7]. BITA aims at maximizing the value created by a company by aligning its digital strategy with its business strategy. As Information Technology (IT) is skimming competition among companies, it is becoming the strongest asset of companies and their main differentiator, especially in the context of Digital Transformation (DT) that attracts lot of enthusiasm this last couple of years [2, 8–13]. By considering the new trend of digitalization and regarding its complexity, several authors argue that it's time to shift the paradigm for a better understanding on how to meet the challenges of IT in its several layers (like hardware, virtualization, management tools, automation tools, operating systems or software applications) in the issue of BITA [2, 13–16]. According to Kahre et al. [13], 48% of the CIOs in US firms spend most of their time attempting to align their IT strategies with the overall organizational objectives. The scope of BITA is large. We do not address strategic alignment (e.g., how to use IT do obtain competitive advantages) but we explicitly focus on the operational nature of Business-IT alignment. We focus on the software part of IT, namely the business applications and the alignment between the business functions layer and the supporting software layer. We leant on the results, based on a six-years industrial experience, of previous audits and advices of about thirty of IT systems in France. We formalize the observations we made by identifying recurring bad business-IT alignment scenarios. Our article is addressed to BITA experts, both researchers and practitioners, as a material to work on, to improve, to complete. It represents the first milestone towards a common base of BITA anti-patterns. We identified 14 BITA anti-patterns, but for reasons of space, we detail one anti-pattern, the most frequent in our experience, and we summarize 3 other anti-patterns that are also strongly present in the studied information systems.

The paper is organized as follows: after this introduction, Section 2 presents the exploratory research methodology, the context of the work and the two addressed research questions. Section 3 addresses issues and challenges of Business/IT alignment between the four considered layers of an information system. Section 4 presents the visual recognition and documentation, via the identity card, of BITA anti-patterns. Section 5 illustrate in a detailed way our approach through the most important anti-pattern and presents a discussion about the main causes, impacts and possible solutions to address it. Section 6 present a summary of three other important anti-patterns. Section 7 addresses related work, while Section 8 discuss the limitations of our work and opens future research directions before concluding in Section 9.

2 Exploratory Research Methodology

The starting point of this work came from a brainstorming about how to bring together academia and business in closer collaboration. Among different domains, the Business-IT alignment concern was quickly identified. In fact, BITA problems have not yet been solved. They are always weighing heavily on Information Systems of companies and industries, exacerbated with the Digital Transformation trend. We took a step back and analyzed different Information Systems previously audited by the practitioner author and we leant on the software architecture experience of the academic author to identify, aggregate and formalize our observations.

2.1 Context: The Observed Information Systems

The practitioner author audited and advised 29 companies during 6 years, from 2014 to 2019 when he was the CTO of MGDIS,[1] a French software development and vendor applications that targets public collectivities.

Though it is not possible to explicitly identify the advised companies for confidentiality reasons, the following list (Table 1) gives an overview of their characteristics. These organizations include public agencies, like ministries, regional and departmental councils mainly in France, as well as some large cities and some mid-sized private enterprises. From 2014 to 2018, organizations that have been advised for information system alignment projects were similar (Table 1– Left side). They were all public organizations with the almost same business domain and following same regulation. So, recurring alignment issues appeared to us to be just normal. In 2018, new different categories of companies (public as well private) started to be advised (Table 1—Right side). The same recurring alignments issues were noticed. The experience of the first phase (2014–2018) helped to clearly and quickly identify recurring misalignment scenarios in the second phase (2018–2019) and to answer them. By analyzing afterwards, in 2020, the results of the conducted audits of these about thirty different information systems, we identified a couple of same recurring problems, like bad smells: whatever was their number of users (from 40 to 8000), the technologies used and the business domains, all companies encountered a couple of similar misalignment scenarios.

2.2 Research Questions

It was interesting to try to detect the cause/consequence connections for each recurring problem and potential similarities. The post-analysis conducted on all the information systems encountering a given problem established the presence of the same

[1] http://www.mgdis.fr.

Table 1 Observed information systems

20 observed organizations (2014–2018)				9 observed organizations (2018–2019)			
Index type	Year	# users	Domain	Index type	Year	# users	Domain
1 Regional Council	2014	450	Complete map	21 Agriculture	2018	1200	Complete map
2 Departmental Council	2014	200	Persons + Finance	22 Pollutants management	2018	200	Complete map
3 Regional Council	2014	300	IAM + Persons	23 Lawyers	2018	200	IAM + Persons
4 Regional Council	2014	500	Persons	24 News Industry	2018	1500	Geographical
5 Regional Council	2014	450	Persons + Finance	25 Agriculture	2019	4300	Persons
6 Regional Council	2014	300	Persons	26 Food transformation	2019	1000	Data ontology
7 Software Editor	2014	130	Business Intelligence	27 Software Editor	2019	800	Persons
8 Equipment Industry	2014	8000	Complete map	28 Software Editor	2019	40	Persons
9 Regional Council	2015	400	Persons	29 Government agency	2019	80	Data ontology
10 Regional Council	2015	650	Persons + EDM + IAM				
11 Regional Council	2015	200	Complete map				
12 Chamber of Commerce	2015	300	Professional training				
13 Departmental Council	2016	80	Complete map				
14 Regional Council	2016	800	IAM				
15 Regional Council	2016	300	Complete map				
16 Equipment Industry	2016	1200	IAM				
17 Software Editor	2016	170	Planning + Persons				
18 City	2017	120	Persons				
19 Chemical Industry	2017	200	Finance + BI				
20 Reginal Council	2018	650	IAM + Persons				

obvious, but wrong, solutions. We noticed that these solutions are commonly (re)used but are usually ineffective and risks being highly counterproductive [17]. We can formalize our objective through two main research questions:

1. RQ1: "When faced with recurring alignment problems in different information systems, is there a same common wrong solution? Are there independent of the business domain?"
2. RQ2: "What are their characteristics? How to formalize them, in order to classify them and populate a dedicated base?"

The use of the "anti-pattern" expression came from the GOF book [18]: an anti-pattern distinguishes itself "from a bad habit, bad practice, or bad idea, by being a commonly-used process, structure of pattern of action that, despite initially appearing to be an appropriate and effective response to a problem, has more bad consequences than good ones". This definition, coupled to our observations and our research questions lead us to use the expression "Business-IT Alignment anti-patterns" or, for short, "BITA anti-pattern". We identified 14 BITA anti-patterns in the considered information systems, and behind each of them, we identified the same recurring bad scenario. We propose to formalize the cause/consequence connections and suggest an identity card to document identified BITA anti-patterns. Before explaining our findings, we first present issues and challenges of BITA.

3 Issues and Challenges of Business-IT Alignment in Information Systems

In the context of BITA's challenges [6, 7, 19], the main encountered issue is inappropriate and bad coupling between business and IT, mainly:

1. When modifications are directed by IT changes, several side effects are introduced (e.g., prohibitive costs, high failure risks or strong coupling).
2. When the business strategy changes, the underlying changes at the IT layer are hindered because the business is often, especially in legacy systems, embodied in the IT.

It is of importance that the business strategy should not be guided by IT changes: it is of importance to have loose coupling between business and its underlying IT solutions to cope more easily with changes. To position our claims, we consider the following layers of an IS.

3.1 Business and IT: The 4 Layers of an Information System and Their Relationships

We lean on a four-layer diagram, as often seen in Enterprise Architecture [20–23], to articulate issues and pitfalls of Business/IT alignment (BITA). The considered

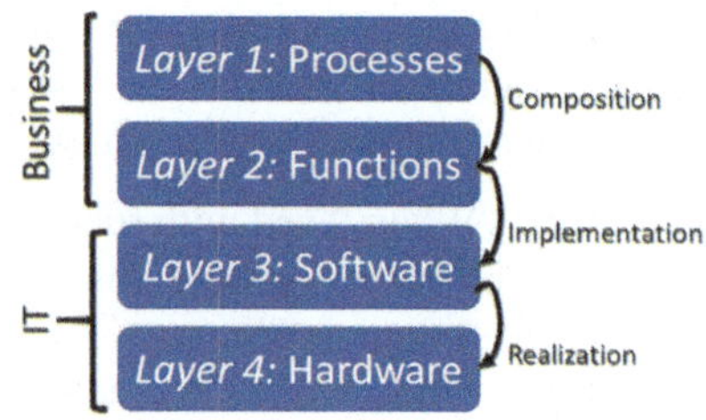

Fig. 1 Four-layers diagram of an information system

framework is the four-layer representation of the CIGREF, a network of major digital French companies and public administrations. This representation (Fig. 1) is widely accepted in by all French CIOs. This diagram is used to represent information systems by separating their content in four layers, each relying on the following one:

- **Layer 1—Business processes**: this layer presents the value definition of the enterprise, through chained activities to perform the business, like the Business Process Models. It is the layer where the digital transformation happens.
- **Layer 2—Business functions**: is the catalogue of all business functions, generally classified in five domains: Business, Master Data Management, Collaborative, Common tools and Business Intelligence.
- **Layer 3—Software:** represents the applications owned or used by the company. Not all business functions have corresponding software, as some operations may be entirely manual.
- **Layer 4—Hardware**: namely hardware and infrastructure supporting the software.

The relationships between the layers have different semantics: Layer 2 exposes business functions used for the composition of business process of Layer 1. Layer 3 is an implementation of function of Layer 2 and Layer 4 is the realization of the Layer 3.

3.2 BITA Issues on the Four Layers

Lack of alignment between the two business layers (layers 1 and 2) or between the two technical layers (layers 3 and 4) is not a critical issue. On layers 1 and 2, only the business is concerned. Adjustment can be made on processes or functions without generally involving the IT department. Conversely, adjusting the software (Layer 3) and hardware (Layer 4) to each other is a pure IT problem and the business is not supposed to be concerned about how many machines are used or which version of the OS is exploited, as long as business functions are correctly exposed. The Achilles heel of Business-IT alignment is at the interface between Business and IT, so between Layers 2 and 3: daily-concerns of functional and IT people are often non-convergent and their background and skills avec different while both have to work together towards the same global business objective of the company.

3.3 BITA Challenges

A utopic IT system would have a perfect alignment with the business it supports, thus, between layers 2 and 3. Each business function (element of layer 2) is realized by one, and only one, software component (element of layer 3), as illustrated in Fig. 2. Of course, this one-to-one relation is not about number of runtime application processes: there may be as many as needed provided since they are all based on the same component/version. A more realistic example of a good alignment is illustrated in Fig. 3. It is a picture of a real company's organization (details are omitted for confidentiality reasons). The links between layers are of interest since they show the underlying degree of coupling and dependencies.

The main point to notice in Fig. 3 is that a few business functions (layer 2) point towards the same instance of software (layer 3). In addition, there is no sharing of software across business domains (the highest-level grouping inside layer 2): the only sharing is between functions that are operated by the same organizational direction, or for software that implements the processes themselves (ERP, middleware or orchestration software for instance), which is acceptable as it does not convey unwanted coupling. As we can see in Figs. 2 and 3, graphical representation helps to propose and understand a global overview of a complex situation by focusing on points of interest. Graphical summaries have often been used to concisely explain a pattern (like for Object-Oriented Programming [18] or for Enterprise Integration Patterns [24]).

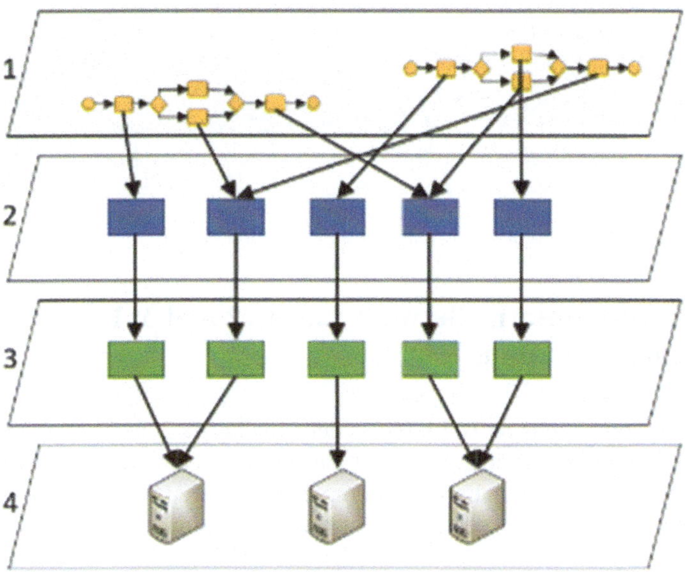

Fig. 2 Ideal alignment for simplistic and elementary information systems

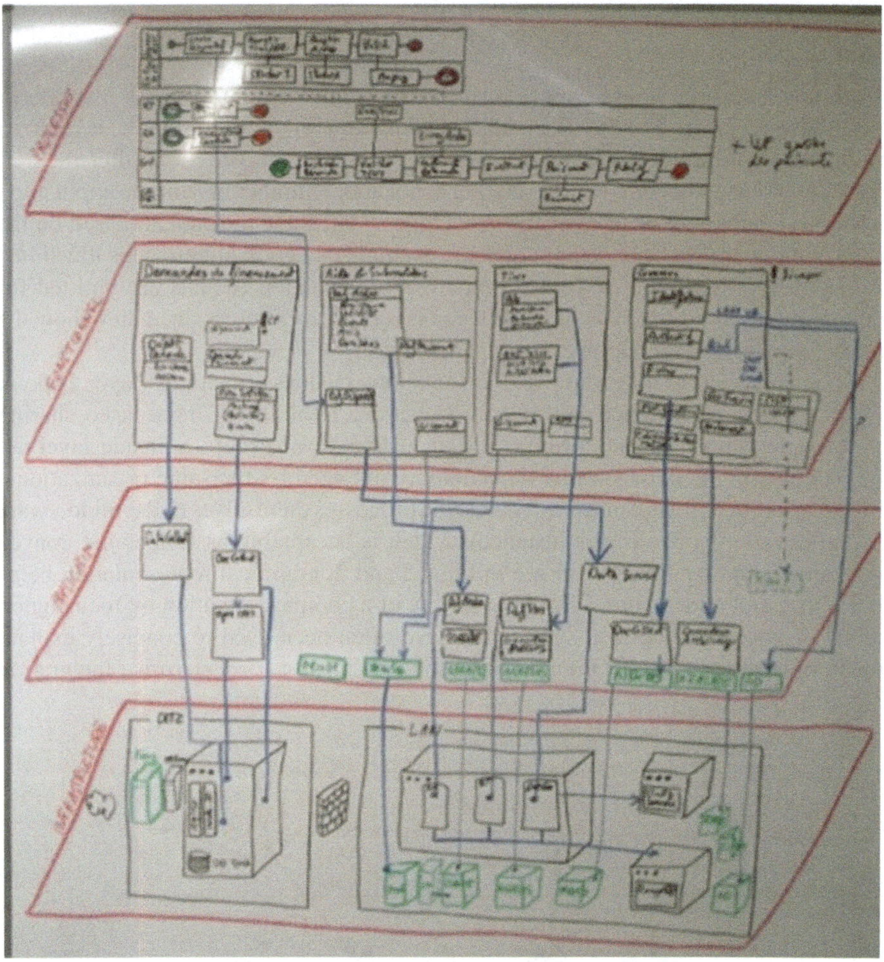

Fig. 3 Correct alignment for a simple real-world information system

4 BITA Anti-patterns Between Layers 2 and 3: Recognition and Documentation

We remind that we focus on BITA issues between layers 2 and 3 of an information system. Before presenting identified anti-patterns between these two layers, it is of interest to first highlight the alignment complexity between business functions (layer 2) and software (layer 3), especially during the integration.

4.1 Alignment Complexity Between Layers 2 and 3

When a function (layer 2) is realized by a software artefact (layer 3), there is more than just align[2]ing the identifiers. A service means a name, a way to be called (including address, protocol and formats) and a contract. This contract itself being often much more than a technical one but including, for example, Service Level Agreement details or conditions of use. The contract, according to us, is the main mean of alignment between business and IT. Links between layer 2 and layer 3 can be bidirectional: items from layer 2 can be realized by item(s) of layer 3 and item(s) from layer 3 can depend on item(s) from layer 2. Let's illustrate, in Fig. 4, how these links had impacts on the information systems of the advised companies.

- *Bad situation: Technical coupling (left part of* Fig. 4*):* cooperation is done at the IT layer, between two pieces of software. This technical coupling is difficult and risky to evolve. An evolution in the software layer may break the equivalent functional dependency in Layer 2.
- *Good situation: Correct indirection (right part of* Fig. 4*):* integration of two functions is indirect: a function is realized by a software and this last implements the integration by pointing to the needed other function, which is in its turn realized by another piece of software. This indirection generates low coupling, and the caller can be changed without impact on the called piece of software and the implementation can be changed without any impact for the applications that call the function itself, since the contract protects them.

4.2 Identity Card for the Antipatterns

To characterize the bad BITA situations, we propose the identity card to document the BITA antipatterns. This identity card (Fig. 5) has different properties, spread out in three main parts:

1. A general presentation (Visualization, Short name, Description and Typical cause),
2. Four indicators for effects and recovery efforts (Effect on evolution, Effect on usability, Ease of recovery, Time to recover), with different possible values.

Technical coupling	Correct indirection
IT overused (directs the business) 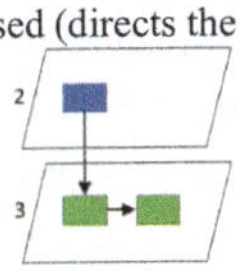	Good balance through the use of contract interface. 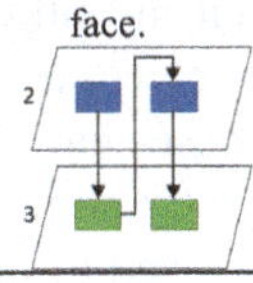

Fig. 4 The two integration scenarios between layer 2 and layer 3

<table>
<tr><td rowspan="5">Visualization:
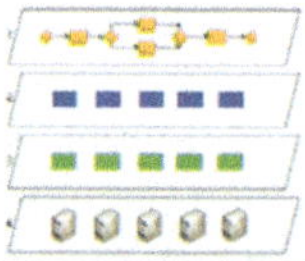</td><td colspan="2">Short name</td></tr>
<tr><td rowspan="2">Description:</td><td>Effect on evolution:</td></tr>
<tr><td>Effect on usability:</td></tr>
<tr><td rowspan="2">Typical cause:</td><td>Ease of recovery:</td></tr>
<tr><td>Time to recover:</td></tr>
<tr><td colspan="3">Characterization:</td></tr>
<tr><td colspan="3">Consequences:</td></tr>
<tr><td colspan="3">Additional hints:</td></tr>
</table>

Fig. 5 Business-IT alignment antipatterns identity card

3. Additional information (Characterization, Consequences, Additional hints)
4. These properties (explained in Table 2) have been identified from the industry standard on backup recovery, using Recovery Point Objective (how much is lost/has coupling problem) and Recovery Time Objective (how long does it take to go back to normal/to align the system).

5 Illustration with the Antipattern #1

5.1 Description

This antipattern "Business evolution implemented through a completely technical integration", is the most important one in terms of frequency of occurrence within the audited systems, of impacts on the information system and its complexity of recovery. It is first described via its identity card then illustrated through examples before presenting its main causes, the difficulties it causes and possible solutions to address it.

5.2 Examples

A well-known example of this antipattern is when Extract Transform Load Process (ETL) or Enterprise Application Integration (EAI) is used to connect directly two databases. From far, the most-often seen example of this antipattern is, the use of an ETL to try and integrate the different functions that have to be coordinated. Of course, there is a need for a technical link somewhere but the right way to create it is definitely not to do so without any indirection level, like advised in the right part of Fig. 4. Direct links between two pieces of software in layer 3 (Fig. 6) results in dangerous technical coupling. Lot of cases have been observed by the authors at customers' sites where the ETL was directly connecting two databases without any indirection. Whereas this action is supposed to make the IT system better by exploiting the richness of interconnecting business, interconnecting only on the technical layer causes even

Table 2 Explanations of the identity card of the BITA anti-patterns

Visualization quick visual identity to the antipattern	**Short name:** the name should be consensual for documentation and classification	
	Description: explains the visual appearance (**visualization**) of the pattern, mainly the dependencies between the layers	**Effect on evolution:** – *None*: the antipattern does not hinder the system's ability to evolve. Its impact is on other aspects (e.g., performance, ease of use) – *Weak*: business evolutions can be implemented, but not as easy as it could ideally be – *Medium*: evolution of the system is possible but requires some planning and analysis – *Strong*: the system is blocked or severely constrained by the antipattern
		Effect on usability: – *Non-noticeable:* the antipattern has no impact on the business users' day-to-day work – *Low*: the users perceive the problem in some situations, with limited impact – *Medium*: the situation has a significant impact on the business – *High*: the IT system is difficult to use; workarounds are common and/or errors arise in it that can have a measurable impact on the business
	Typical cause: a short description of the main reason why the antipattern may appear in an IT system	**Ease of recovery:** – *Easy*: multi-step, well-documented methods exist to reduce and suppress the antipattern, with limited or virtually inexistent impact on the users – *Average*: the antipattern can be reduced or removed with low impact providing a careful analysis is realized beforehand – *Complex*: removing the antipattern from the system requires an important analysis effort, while still not being able to ensure that users will not be impacted
		Time to recover: – *Quick*: the recovery method can be applied with expected results in days or weeks – *Medium*: the recovery method needs a few months/sprints to be functional – *Long*: the effort to recover will be measured in years (including stabilization of the business uses after detecting unexpected impacts)
Characterization: a more thorough description of the antipattern		
Consequences: lists the most known problems and their effect on the system		
Additional hints: indicates symptoms that are often associated with the antipattern		

<table>
<tr><td rowspan="5">Visualization:
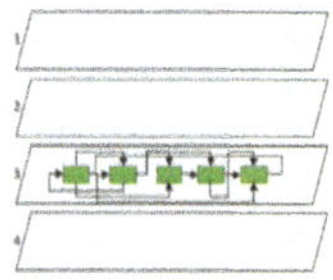</td><td colspan="2">Short name: Pure technical integration</td></tr>
<tr><td rowspan="2">Description: many items in 3 depends on several items in 3</td><td>Effect on evolution: strong</td></tr>
<tr><td>Effect on usability: none</td></tr>
<tr><td rowspan="2">Typical cause: IT system organization led by technical needs instead of functional</td><td>Ease of recovery: complex</td></tr>
<tr><td>Time to recover: medium</td></tr>
<tr><td colspan="3">Characterization: software applications call each other directly or through the use of other software, without any level of indirection or contracting.</td></tr>
<tr><td colspan="3">Consequences: this causes high degree of coupling, since modifying a given application may have impact on many others, and thus many other functions or workflows depending on them. The system gets rigid and fragile to any evolution.</td></tr>
<tr><td colspan="3">Additional hints: coupling is typically caused by direct software calls to APIs, PL/SQL methods, COM functions, use of triggers. Middleware, when used inappropriately, also causes coupling, only displacing it in another software process.</td></tr>
</table>

Fig. 6 Pure technical integration anti-pattern

greater problems. The link will fail for every non-compatible modification on either side of it. It is important to notice that this anti-pattern occurs in systems with poorly designed coupling.

5.3 Main Causes

This antipattern may be the mother of all business/IT alignment ones we identified. Pure technical integration affects basically all studied IT systems. The problem typically comes from the fact that technicians have been trusted to implement interactions between business functions. However, how competent and willing they were, they created technical coupling, simply because they worked on their own layer of competence (layers 3 and 4).

5.4 Difficulties Caused by the Pattern

An ETL alone makes it for some technical coupling but as far as there is the associated amount of maintenance, the situation is acceptable. The real difficulties, which have been observed many times, happen when several ETL tasks are active in sequence (or even worse, without synchronization) while their chaining is not anymore controlled. It is the case for systems with poor IT implementation. On a particular occurrence, a departmental council synchronizing at night five different applications containing data about individuals and legal entities came to a point where duplications, conflicts and roundtrips made the whole process collapse. Complete recovery of the process could not be achieved and several months passed until the situation was cleared. This

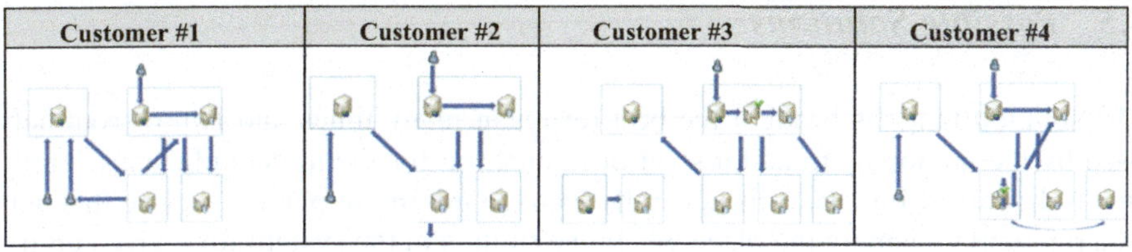

Fig. 7 Simple customer's data streams

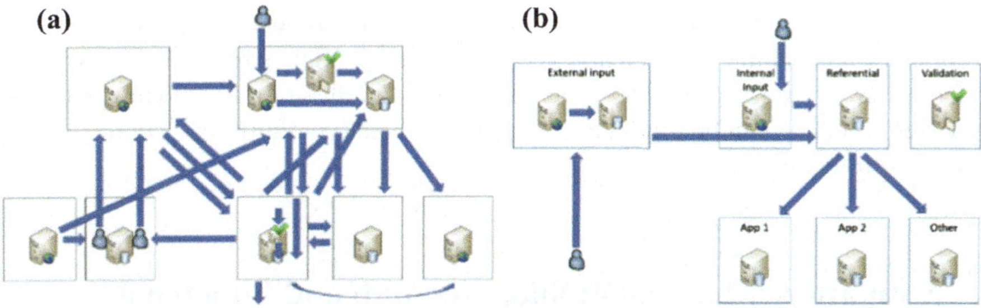

Fig. 8 **a** Real data streams for all the customers **b** data streams with a referential

is the typical difficulty for banks for instance, of having a process that is completely embedded in the software and for which knowledge has been lost. In the end, the business rules are in COBOL and we can no longer rewrite them. Other examples have been observed where the complexity was not so high in the different information systems, but still caused problem.

The diagram in Fig. 7 shows the GDPR-related streams for four different customers. Each of these sets of streams can be managed independently without too much maintenance effort, but the difficulty came from the fact that one given piece of software was supposed to accommodate all these situations. Superimposition of schemas is illustrated in Fig. 8a.

In such a network of data streams, it is particularly difficult to ensure robustness of the integration, non-occurrence of defaults and non-regression of features. Fig. 8b shows how the complete system that has been streamlined into well-aligned, contract-based, generic data exchanges, following a multi-year effort.

5.5 *Possible Solutions*

The solution that has brought the best results at many times and is now routinely used by the authors is to add a level of indirection for the targeted business entity (the right part of Fig. 4). This generally leads to putting in place a service that acts as a referential, namely the place where the truth is in the system for a given entity. This service is both functional and software, in the spirit of a nice alignment. This approach gave the diagram (b) in Fig. 8 of personal data streams after reorganization around a "person" referential.

A more technical view of the solution is where the orchestration, mediation and proprietary levels have been clearly separated (Fig. 9). The stream of data shows a much better control and this design can be made GDPR-compliant. Thus, the right to be dereferenced can be implemented quite easily and without risk, contrary to the former architecture.

6 Antipatterns 2, 3 and 4: Silo, Monolith and Functional Multiple Implementation

In this section we summarize the 3 other most important antipatterns that occurred frequently in audited information systems.

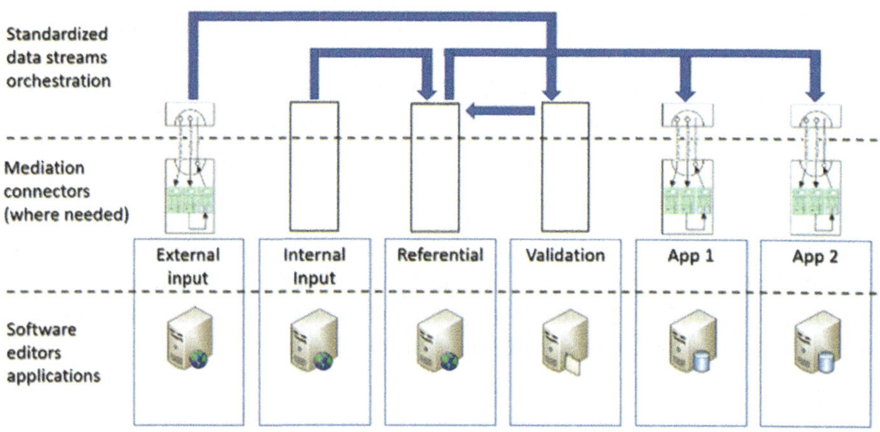

Fig. 9 Technical view of the reorganization

6.1 Antipattern #2: "The Functional Silo Dedicated IT Subsystem"

Description

Visualization	Dedicated silo	
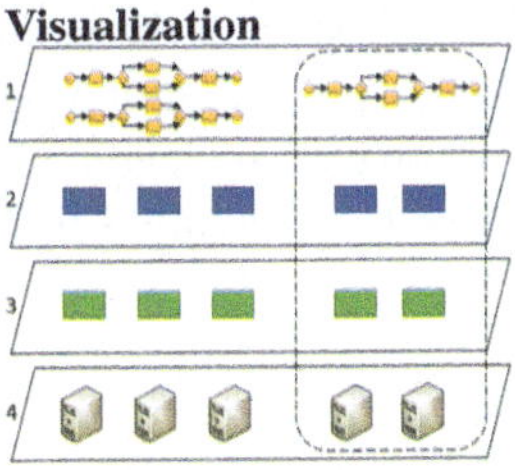	**Description**: related sets of items on layers 1, 2, 3 and 4 appear to be completely separated from the rest of the map	**Effect on evolution:** medium **Effect on usability:** low
	Typical cause: the use of a dedicated software suite has made difficult to interoperate with the rest of the Information System	**Ease of recovery:** easy **Time to recover:** quick
Characterization: a part of the IT system appears to be completely isolated from the rest. This may be the desired goal in some strong regulatory contexts, but this can also lead to duplicate business functions in other software		
Consequences: the separation of software and hardware resources gives a false impression of autonomy of functions and processes. However, the mere fact that the silos belong to the same organization almost always carries a coupling, which one day will become active and cause unexpected coupling		
Additional hints: a first sign of trouble may be that the whole appears as a silo, but the detailed map shows unassumed technical links between applications or databases. That means that the silo is still viewed as a separate system whereas, in practice, it has already started to be linked to the rest of the IT system, without these links being led—let alone known—from the business point of view		

Example

In a fusion or acquisition of a company by another, the capacity to quickly merge human resources, including salary, vacation, calendars, etc. is essential. The HRIS (Human Resource Information System), and more generally the HR domain, has a good maturity in Business/IT alignment, generally because the owners already tried to accommodate all functions inside a single piece of software. The antipattern happens when the HR thinks it can operate in IT system independently from the rest of the company's business domains, while employees represent entities highly used in other parts of the IT system: employees have accounts, they connect to the stock application or they are associated to customer relationships. It is mainly a lack of IT culture when HR think they are completely separated from the other parts of the IT system.

Main causes

The main source of this kind of situation is a lack of IT culture and the belief that separating software can result in separating functions. Customers avoiding this pattern are actually rare and the case only happens when the CEO or CTO has a strong IT background.

Difficulties caused by the pattern

The problem is that, in this example, HR think they are completely separated from the other parts of the IT system. And indeed, they are, as far as the business functions are concerned: salary has no direct relation to material stocks, just like interns training is not linked to the products catalogue. But the devil lies in the details, as usual: the persons who get the salary are the same that operate the software storing the stock figures and the training may be part of the products catalogue. Thus, changing the version of the product catalogue may cause a problem in the employees' management, hence a coupling that is not expected. This can be even worse than having a little stronger but well-known coupling.

Possible solutions

The solution to this solution is first to acknowledge the problem, which might use a lot of explanation to the stakeholders. Once the situation is clarified and the links are shown, traditional approaches to align IT to business can be used.

6.2 *Antipattern #3: "Monolith Application"*

Description

<table>
<tr><td>Visualization</td><td colspan="2">Monolith</td></tr>
<tr><td rowspan="4">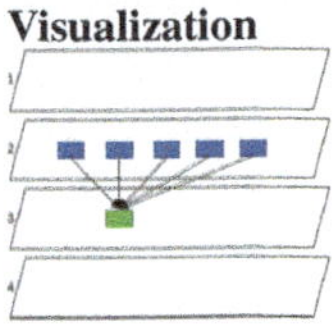</td><td rowspan="2">Description: many items in level 2 point towards a unique item in level 3</td><td>Effect on evolution: strong</td></tr>
<tr><td>Effect on usability: low</td></tr>
<tr><td rowspan="2">Typical cause: dependence on external software editors</td><td>Ease of recovery: easy</td></tr>
<tr><td>Time to recover: long</td></tr>
<tr><td colspan="3">Characterization: multiple (unrelated) business functions are implemented via the same software</td></tr>
<tr><td colspan="3">Consequences: as the software gathers many functions, it has to change to follow different business requirements, triggering other changes. The system thus becomes more and more fragile</td></tr>
<tr><td colspan="3">Additional hints: this antipattern is often accompanied with numerous technical dependencies to the concerned application. Only people with experience can make modifications to it</td></tr>
</table>

Example

An actual example coming from one of the authors' customers is shown in Fig. 10 (only levels 1–3 are shown, and the actual data is blurred for confidentiality reasons). Two software applications, out of more than twenty, gather at least a third of the data streams, representing around half of the links between items in the level 3.

After interview of users, we were able to connect these applications one-level up to at least ten functions in the level 2. Though it was not clearly visible at first, these

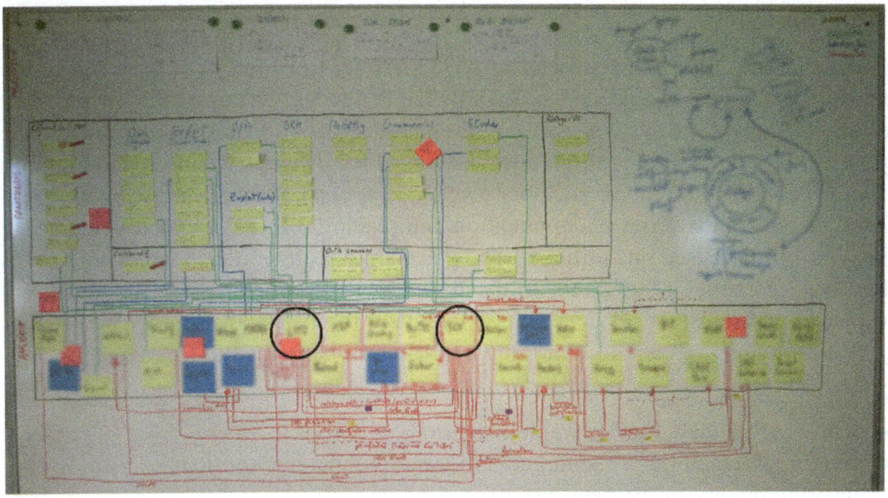

Fig. 10 Real-world example of a Monolith

applications thus constitute monoliths, as they assemble many different functional responsibilities.

Main causes

Two main causes are the precursors of this situation. The first comes from the finance, which generally thinks buying one piece of software that covers many functions will cost less than buying a dedicated software application for each function. Though the "best of breed" approaches are now well-know, this reflex still happens a lot among non-technical deciders. The second cause comes from the users, who are generally keener in using a single highly integrated software than switching from one to another. This is highly understandable, as a good GUI is a factor of productivity. However, experimented IT deciders know that this comes at a price, which is the capacity of evolution of the system, and that the decision has to be pondered depending on the context. Techniques like iframe integration may also be used to provide a seamless GUI approach on two different applications.

Difficulties caused by the pattern

Monoliths are a pain because touching them may have impact on lots of functions, sometimes in a non-predictable way. In the case of one of the authors, a 1.2 million LoC (lines of code) monolithic piece of software was so crippled that only one version could be released with a complete Quality Assurance cycle in a year; changes to a module would often affect others that had not any known functional relationship to it. The application has been modernized in the past years to a set of 60–70 microservices with an average 1000 LoC, while reducing standard debugging time for a bug by 30%. Releases are now monthly.

Possible solutions

So-called "Big Bang" approaches in the IT are almost always impossible in the industry, as the business processes are now too dependent on computers to allow for a complete halt of the system. As a consequence, solutions to antipatterns have to be progressive and possible without interruptions of the process. Removing a monolith from an IT system thus needs to apply several steps, each of them removing one functional responsibility from the application and placing it in a dedicated application. Responsibilities based on entities will be placed into "referentials", which will act as the Single Version Of the Truth" in the system, while no-persistance functions will be placed into transient services, which will naturally be stateless and scale ideally.

A traditional approach to migrating a transient function is the following:

- defining the new service API;
- deploying the new service implementation;
- pointing the method of the targeted monolith to the new service;
- ensuring quality of the new system;
- iterating on the other similar functions of the monolith (with good quality software, this step should not be necessary, as all uses of the functions should point to a single method in the source code);
- removing central method in the monolith to ensure no new uses are added.

In non-transient functions, the process is made slightly more complex by the additional steps that are necessary for the migration of the data:

- migrating the data into the new service;
- in the same time, deploying a mediation connector so that modifications in the new service are reproduced in the old monolith, thus ensuring the correct functioning of legacy code that relies on this data;
- when the monolith would send the data to other software applications (direct coupling or through middleware), ensure that a mediation connector also exists for each of these applications;
- migrate, one by one, all uses of the data from the monolith to the new service;
- once all calls have been derived, suppress the data cache from the monolith.

As these methods have been used in many cases in industrial-grade IT systems, a dedicated article may have to be written on this way of solving the antipattern.

6.3 Antipattern #4: "Functional Multiple Implementations"

Description

Visualization	Functional multiple implementations	
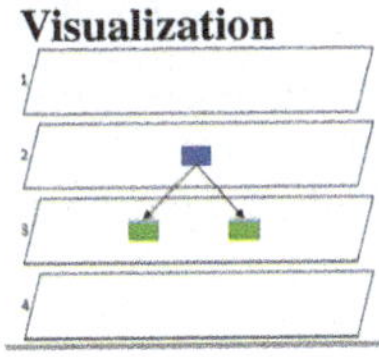	**Description**: a single item in 2 points toward several entries in 3	**Effect on evolution**: strong **Effect on usability**: medium
	Typical cause: lack of comprehension of the functional and/or business model	**Ease of recovery**: average **Time to recover**: medium
Characterization: a single business function is implemented by two (or more) distinct pieces of software		
Consequences: the implementation of a given function differs depending on the context. Business evolutions are not necessarily ported in all the implementation and the behavior of the system becomes erratic		
Additional hints: different users in different contexts observe unexpectedly different results from the same action. Business calculation like prices may differ depending on which application is consulted. Reporting has to be consolidated to find the truth in the system. Differences in functional or business behavior may also appear depending on the kind of device used to realize an action on the system		

Example

The business function colloquially called "reporting" used for electronic documents generation is used by several business functions. Dedicated applications tend to include it inside their own code, thus duplicating the software behind a single function. One of the studied IS had more than 40 different implementations. Most of the time, these applications are themselves monoliths, since they include this function as well as some others in addition to their main business responsibility.

Main causes

The main cause of this antipattern is definitely the lack of norms and standards (or of their correct and affordable implementation) behind the business functions that needs to be achieved. A few decades ago, authentication and identification tended to be implemented (and thus) duplicated in many applications that needed them. The coming of LDAP and open source implementations made it easy and inexpensive for applications to delegate these functions. Sadly, many common business functions lack this kind of standardization and are duplicated in huge quantities, although this could be done quite easily (in our document generation example, a contract with one method taking as inputs the CMIS URL of the template and the ODP URL for the data and outputting the CMIS URL of the document generated is extremely simple but already goes a long way in answering the main user stories).

Difficulties caused by the pattern

An IT system known by the authors counted more than 40 different implementations of the "document fusion" function used as an example above. This of course led to extremely long times in changing such simple things as the logo of the entity, which had to be done in all applications, sometimes even in every document templates inside the "reporting" module of a given application.

A confusion between responsibilities may also arise in this situation. Since all implementations are not exactly the same, the single function may be rendered in different ways depending on the application chosen. In our example, a single report could have a different appearance, and sometimes even a different content due to embedded business rules when it comes from one module or another, leading to potential legal issues.

Possible solutions

The possible (and in this case highly recommended) solution to this antipattern is to unify the implementations around a single standardized service contract. If no norms exist, one should be created locally to the IT system, using pivotal format and canonical entities (Domain Driven Design is a good approach). Once the contract is established, evolution towards a correct system can be realized progressively: clients of the function can each point to the new service, whereas the implementation of this service may first point to several legacy applications in order to maintain compatibility, and then reduce step by step to only one application that carries all necessary options for all uses.

Special care should be taken in this situation to ensure that what is seen as a single business function is not actually multiple in itself. For example, identification of an external account and identification of an internal account may be both implemented by an LDAP server, but that does not mean that this implementation should be unified, because the functions are actually different from the business point of view, which is more important. If an economy of resources is sought, then an LDAP server supporting multitenancy will be the best move, since it will provide separation of responsibility while using a single software engine.

7 Related Works

Surprisingly, most of research works on alignment between business and IT, and also Digital Transformation, are from the management field [8–10, 25–27] while digital strategy implies to embody IT challenges and changes at the strategic level of any company. To our knowledge, no work addressed formalization of antipatterns of Business-IT alignment by considering the four layers of an IT System. Most of antipattern existing works address a specific paradigm or context: few works addressed antipatterns to adopt SOA, which is the closest to the four-layers diagram we consider, like Brown et al. [28] that gives a list of antipatterns in a textual format but no high-level overview of them. Other works are more tied to IT risk management [29] while some works address antipatterns in Process Modeling [30–32]. More recent works use alignment antipatterns in the context of ontologies [33, 34]. A couple of research works address alignment issues through the use of norms and pivotal formats using Domain Driven Design [14, 35–37]. In [38], authors precise that the developed conceptual model that detects business-IS strategies misalignment cannot be generalized.

8 Limitations and Future Work

Limitations: one main limitation of our work is that the analysis has been conducted afterward and based on observations conducted on the results of the audit of about thirty companies in their alignment concerns. We need to push forward our findings to ensure proper generalization and general implications, answer the lack of statistics and avoid drawing inference too quickly [39, 40]. In addition, we made a couple of assumptions: the work is mainly about software serving direct business requirements where modularity and separation of concerns are assumed to be done to a reasonable degree, which is not always the case. Other facets need to be addressed, e.g., the scale, the distributed nature, the roles and stakeholder diversity, the types of alignment required (functional, legal, human factors and socio-technical considerations) or security and privacy. The overlap between these facets and also the domino effect when implementing a change need to be considered.

Future work: several future research works are envisaged. From the practitioners' side, the first objective is to map out misalignment's scenarios of companies, to define a methodology to help detection of antipatterns and filling the identity card and, then, analyze and confront the results through the proposed anti-patterns. The second objective is to see if and how we can generalize our findings. Research works like Seddon et al. [39], Wieringa et al. [40] or Yin [41] represent a good starting point for this objective. Ideally, we would also like to start to populate a BITA anti-patterns basis to make it available. We also aim to publish the 10 other anti-patterns we have identified. In addition, we would like to compare the proposed identity card with the twelve components of alignment of Luftman et al. [42]. They represent the axes on which the misalignment can be felt, and it would allow to classify the antipatterns according to the impact they have on each axis, with a radar diagram for example. In the meantime, we identified a couple of academic research tracks, starting by the state of the art. We can mention, among them: (i) *for what aims BITA antipatterns can be used and how?* For instance, reverse engineering of an IT system on the 4 layers and its comparison to the antipatterns; (ii) *for what kind of systems?* We used them on existing/legacy systems but they can be used as guidelines to avoid bad design of new IT systems; (iii) *for what kind of evolution?* They can be used to address refactoring and improvement of IT systems. Moreover, it is utopic to think that analyzing an existing system will give a set of "perfect" antipatterns. It is more likely to have a set of partial antipatterns. One will need to deal with these partial results to evolve the system. In the context of complex systems, it is important to lean on good visualization means in order to detect antipatterns (like 3D representation or augmented reality). In any case, it is of importance to keep in mind the importance of ensuring continuous and qualitative BITA and by emphasizing on the links between the Business and the IT.

9 Conclusion

Although abstraction and best practices for designing applications are now widely taught and used, stepping back for complete and complex systems are not taught at school but are learnt from practice, generally after several years. They are in addition taught for IT people and not for managers. Managers as well IT employees need more formal frameworks and tools to help them to see more clearly the current and potential future technology landscapes. BITA issues fall under this category and encounter several challenges at different levels: strategy, business processes, business functions, software and the supporting infrastructure. We focused on the software side of BITA, between the business functions and there underlying software. We considered and analyzed the results of a 6-years' experience of audit and advice of about thirty public and private French companies in their alignment concerns. We proposed the concept of *BITA antipattern*, in the spirit of software patterns and antipatterns widely adopted by companies [18, 28, 43, 44]. We also proposed an *identity card* to document antipatterns that can appear between the layers 2 and 3 of an information system. This identity card proposes a visualization of each antipattern, its attributes and descriptions with respect to effect on system evolution, effect on usability or ease of recovery. We detailed our approach on the most frequent and important antipattern we met and summarized 3 other common antipatterns. We have identified 10 additional anti-patterns left for future work. To conclude, we remind that this work is a construction-oriented research and is a retrospective rather than an in-situ exercise. It aims at proposing insights observed from industry experience and represents a first milestone for a further research objective to formalize, apply and enhance the methodology by applying it on companies, and why not of different countries, and it also aim at opening several research tracks (methodology, tools to assist the detection, misalignment management and bad dependencies between business processes and supporting software): there is definitely room for improvement in developing formalisms, approaches and tools for managers and IT deciders to help them to cope with IT changes from the strategy viewpoint.

References

1. https://www.computerworld.com/article/2486278/it-management/how-to-balance-maintenance-and-it-innovation.html
2. Yeow, A., Soh, C., Hansen, R.: Aligning with new digital strategy: a dynamic capabilities approach. J. Strateg. Inf. Syst. **27**(1), 43–58 (2018)
3. Braun, C., Winter, R.: Integration of IT service management into enterprise architecture. In Proceedings of the 2007 ACM Symposium on Applied Computing, pp. 1215–1219 (2007)
4. Horlach, B., Drews, P., Schirmer, I.: Bimodal IT: business-IT alignment in the age of digital transformation. Multikonferenz Wirtschaftsinformatik, 1417–1428. (2016)
5. Luftman, J.: Assessing business-IT alignment maturity. Strateg. Inf. Technol. Govern. **4**, 99 (2004)
6. Luftman, J., Kempaiah, R.: An update on business-IT alignment: "A Line" has been drawn. MIS Quart. Execut. **6**(3) (2007)

7. Wu, S.P.J., Straub, D.W., Liang, T.P. : How information technology governance mechanisms and strategic alignment influence organizational performance: insights from a matched survey of business and IT managers. MIS Quart., 497–518 (2015)
8. Hess, T., Matt, C., Benlian, A., Wiesböck, F.: Options for formulating a digital transformation strategy. MIS Quart. Execut. **15**(2) (2016)
9. Kane, G.C., Palmer, D., Phillips, A.N., Kiron, D., Buckley, N.: Strategy, not technology, drives digital transformation. MIT Sloan Manag. Univ. Press, 1–25 (2015)
10. Matt, C., Hess, T., Benlian, A.: Digital transformation strategies. Bus. Inf. Syst. Eng. **57**(5), 339–343 (2015)
11. Peppard, J., Ward, J.: The Strategic Management of Information Systems: Building a Digital Strategy. Wiley (2016)
12. Jonathan, G.M., Rusu, L., Perjons, E.: Business-it alignment in the era of digital transformation: Quo vadis? In: Hawaii International Conference on System Sciences (HICSS), Hawaii, USA, pp. 5563–5572 (2020)
13. Kahre, C., Hoffmann, D., Ahlemann, F.: Beyond business-IT alignment-digital business strategies as a paradigmatic shift: a review and research agenda. In: Proceedings of the 50th Hawaii International Conference on System Sciences (2017)
14. Hinkelmann, K., Gerber, A., Karagiannis, D., Thoenssen, B., Van der Merwe, A., Woitsch, R.: A new paradigm for the continuous alignment of business and IT: combining enterprise architecture modelling and enterprise ontology. Comput. Ind. **79**, 77–86 (2016)
15. Manfreda, A., Štemberger, M.I.: Establishing a partnership between top and IT managers. Information Technology & People (2019)
16. Galliers, R.D.: In celebration of diversity in information systems research. J. Inf. Technol. **26**(4), 299–301 (2011)
17. Budgen, D.: Software Design. Pearson Education (2003)
18. Gamma, E.: Design Patterns: Elements of Reusable Object-Oriented Software. Pearson Education India (1995)
19. Adomavicius, G., Bockstedt, J.C., Gupta, A., Kauffman, R.J.: Making sense of technology trends in the information technology landscape: a design science approach. MIS Quart., 779–809 (2008)
20. Chorafas, D.N.: EA and New Generation Information Systems. CRC Press (2016)
21. Khoshafian, S.: Service Oriented Enterprises. Auerbach Publications (2016)
22. Strnadl, C.F.: Aligning business and IT: the process-driven architecture model. Inf. Syst. Manag. **23**(4), 67–77 (2006)
23. Winter, R., Fischer, R.: Essential layers, artifacts, and dependencies of enterprise architecture. EDOCW'06. In: 10th IEEE International, pp. 30–30. IEEE (2006)
24. Hohpe, G., Woolf, B.: Enterprise Integration Patterns: Designing, Building, and Deploying Messaging Solutions. Addison-Wesley Professional (2004)
25. Gerow, J.E., Grover, V., Thatcher, J., Roth, P.L.: Looking toward the future of IT-business strategic alignment through the past: a meta-analysis. MIS Quart., 1159–1186 (2014)
26. Nylén, D., Holmström, J.: Digital innovation strategy: a framework for diagnosing and improving digital product &service innovation. Bus. Horiz., 57–67 (2015)
27. Renaud, A., Walsh, I., Kalika, M.: Is SAM still alive? A bibliometric and interpretive mapping of the strategic alignment research field. J. Strat. IS **25**(2), 75–103 (2016)
28. Brown, W.H., Malveau, R.C., McCormick, H.W., Mowbray, T.J.: AntiPatterns: refactoring software, architectures, and projects in crisis. JW & Sons, Inc. (1998)
29. Wiesche, M., Schermann, M., Krcmar, H.: When IT risk management produces more harm than good: the phenomenon of 'mock bureaucracy'. In: System Sciences (IEEE HICSS), 2013 46th, pp. 4502–4511. IEEE (2013)
30. Gschwind, T., Koehler, J., Wong, J.: Applying patterns during business process modeling. In: International Conference on Business Process Management, pp. 4–19. Springer, Berlin (2008)
31. Koehler, J., Vanhatalo, J.: Process anti-patterns: how to avoid the common traps of BPM. IBM WebSphere Dev. Tech. J. **10**(2), 4 (2007)

32. van Der Aalst, W.M., Ter Hofstede, A.H., Kiepuszewski, B., Barros, A.P.: Workflow patterns. Distrib. Parallel Databases **14**(1), 5–51 (2003)
33. Guedes, A., Baião, F.A., Revoredo, K.: Digging Ontology Correspondence Antipatterns. WOP (2014)
34. Silva, J., Baiao, F.A., Revoredo, K.: Interactive Ontology Alignment using Alignment Antipatterns: A First Experiment. In (28). Brazilian Computer Society (2016)
35. Evans, E.: DDD: Tackling Complexity in the Heart of Software. Addison-Wesley (2004)
36. Evans, E., Szpoton, R.: Domain-Driven Design. Helion (2015)
37. Gouigoux, J.P., Tamzalit, D.: From monolith to microservices: lessons learned on an industrial migration to a web oriented architecture. In Software Architecture Workshops 2017 IEEE, pp. 62–65 (2017)
38. El-Telbany, O., Elragal, A.: Business-information systems strategies: a focus on misalignment. Procedia Technol. **16**, 250–262 (2014)
39. Seddon, P.B., Scheepers, R.: Towards the improved treatment of generalization of knowledge claims in IS research: drawing general conclusions from samples. Eur. J. IS **21**(1), 6–21 (2012)
40. Wieringa, R., Daneva, M.: Six strategies for generalizing software engineering theories. Sci. Comput. Program. **101**, 136–152 (2015)
41. Yin, R.K.: Case Study Research and Applications: Design and Methods. Sage (2017)
42. Luftman, J., Papp, R., Brier, T.: Enablers and inhibitors of business-IT alignment. Commun. Assoc. Inf. Syst. **1**(1), 11 (1999)
43. Buschmann, F., Henney, K., Schmidt, D.C.: Past, present, and future trends in software patterns. IEEE Softw. 24(4) (2007)
44. Martin, R.C.: Agile Software Development: Principles, Patterns, and Practices. Prentice Hall (2002)

Fuzzy Personalization of Mobile Apps: A Case Study from mHealth Domain

Fabio Sartori and Lidia Lucrezia Tonelli

Abstract The growing interest in wearable devices has stimulated the development of mHealth applications: users can be monitored at different levels of granularity and their data can be exploited for recommendations about different aspects of their conditions, i.e., physical, psychological, and social. To this aim, recommendation systems should be able to profile patients to suggest them the most proper actions to promote effective behavior changes. This paper presents a solution to this challenging research topic implemented in an Android app, based on the adoption of fuzzy logic to cluster users according to quantitative and qualitative variables about their physical and psychological well-being. Four classes have been obtained from the two models developed, in accordance with previous experiments. The final aim of user profiling is promoting group physical activity among users characterized by similar behaviors.

Keyword Wearable devices · mHealth · Fuzzy logic profiling · Behavior change intervention

1 Introduction

The growing interest in smartphone and wearable devices adoption has originated great potential to develop mHealth applications. Care for elderly is one of the most promising fields. Wearable devices can be useful to reduce the need for going to the doctor's office, with many benefits in terms of lower costs and waiting times, as well as to monitor aged people living in critical conditions, characterized by

A prior version of this paper has been published in the ISD2021 Proceedings (http://aisel.aisnet.org/isd2014/proceedings2021).

F. Sartori (✉) · L. L. Tonelli
University of Milano-Bicocca, Milan, Italy
e-mail: fabio.sartori@unimib.it

L. L. Tonelli
e-mail: l.tonelli@campus.unimib.it

E. Insfran Pelozo et al. (eds.), *Advances in Information Systems Development*, Lecture Notes in Information Systems and Organisation 55,
https://doi.org/10.1007/978-3-030-95354-6_6

dependent living, fall risk, chronic disease, dementia, social isolation, depression, poor well-being and poor medication management [20].

Although fitness trackers have been mainly conceived as devices for younger people, they have become an important market for aged ones too. They are considered devices that improve the quality of life, increasing the autonomy level of elderly and supporting them to delay the negative effects of aging [37]. Wearing a device that monitors and tracks movements, possibly suggesting how and how long physical activity should be fulfilled encourages the user to be more proactive on increasing his/her activity level, from both duration and quality perspectives [37]. Wearable devices have also demonstrated their usefulness in the management of chronic diseases. Chronic diseases are often characterized by the emerging of multiple disorders. People at higher levels of risk can be continuously monitored at home. Patients suffering from heart diseases, diabetes, and so on, can collect data about their conditions and interact with doctors at distance [26, 27]. Today, patients with diabetes, one of the more important chronic illnesses worldwide [2], can wear sophisticated glucose monitors to check continuously their status [8, 19].

Despite these successful results, adoption rate of these technologies seems to be still low. Some studies, like e.g. [6], point out the need to offer more personalized experiences to users as a key issue to increase the acceptability of mHealth applications by frail people. In this paper, we reflect about this topic presenting an mHealth app designed to increase the physical activity (PA) level in sedentary people, namely MoveUp, tailored on physical and psychological characteristics of users. Physical activity is one of the most important factors to prevent or mitigate chronic diseases: incorporating behavior change theories (BCTs) into mHealth apps, meant as "observable, replicable, and irreducible component of an intervention designed to alter or redirect causal processes to regulate behavior" [25], is one of the most promising approach from the personalization point of view. The acceptance level of app for PA support has been the subject of many studies: in [36] it has been highlighted how the users' expectations towards their future developments are very high. In particular, users would be interested to see improvements from the entertainment features perspective, like e.g., comparison with peers. To this aim, the MoveUp module has been now extended with new features, so that the user has the possibility to accomplish physical activity suggested by the app joining a group of peers: a user profiling functionality has been added to MoveUp to estimate the overall level of physical and psychological well-being at the end of a week, based on fuzzy logic. This function has been exploited to implement a calendar shared between the users, to accomplish the suggested activity on their own as well as in group, being stimulated to obtain more significant results from collaborative tasks.

The rest of the paper is organized as follows: Sect. 2 provides a brief literature review about personalization of mHealth applications; Sect. 3 presents the main conceptual and computational aspect of the fuzzy method developed. Section 4 presents the experiments conducted to set-up the fuzzy profiling function of MoveUp. Section 5 shows how the fuzzy profiling has been used in the MoveUp module through the implementation of calendar shared among the users. Finally, Sect. 6 ends the paper addressing future research.

2 Related Work

According to [12], computer technology offers three ways to persuade people: adaptation, personalization, and feedback. Among them, personalization refers to the incorporation of one or more recognizable individual characteristics (e.g., the first name of a person) in a content. Personalization of mHealth apps is an important research trend; in a recent paper [35], the authors provide an exhaustive review of users' perceptions of mHealth apps. They selected 356 papers for screening, according to a plethora of criteria grouped into four main categories. Among them, the device related (mHealth apps among the others) and user (patients and physicians among them) features were considered, that are relevant for the purposes of our study. Patient's point of view is that apps should be fully customizable to meet their needs, being created to support them. They want to be free to configure main parameters [6]. Another interesting point is to increase the interactivity level between users and apps: in [7] the adoption of avatars that evolve according to users' behavior is suggested. Personalization becomes essential when mHealth apps are devoted to support people affected by more complex diseases, to tackle by means of methods varying according to variable conditions of patients [15]. Personalization can be a crucial aspect in the design of mHealth apps too: in [13] a user-centered framework is proposed, where end-users are involved to re-design an existing app for tuberculin skin test analysis. The authors point out that this approach, based on the integration of information systems research and design thinking, has allowed to identify usability requirements and limitations of the original app. They conclude that engaging end-users is crucial when developing mHealth applications.

Usability is another key issue related to personalization: its scope is to assess how a product can be exploited by specific users to achieve given goals with effectiveness, efficiency, and satisfaction with respect to a specific context. Usability of mHealth apps can be measured according to models like [38], where traditional features like efficiency, satisfaction, learnability, memorability, and errors are extended with specific issues for mobile devices, such as the mobile context, hardware limitations and data-entry challenges. A recent work [22] pointed out that satisfaction, referring to user likability, comfort and pleasure, ranked as the top attribute for mHealth apps users. According to this claim, the top three reasons to stop using mHealth apps are they are not as useful as claimed by developers, not user-friendly and affected by functioning errors.

Some authors point out how the development of persuasive system is crucial to improve their acceptance level and, consequently, a better promotion of behavior change interventions. In [33] a persuasive system is characterized by four main components: the *user context*, that involves information about the user useful to implement an opportune persuasion strategy; *use context*, that enables the user interface and data storage to adopt the persuasion strategy; *user-system interaction*, that includes means for the user to define and complete tasks and assessments, view results, and so on as well as opportune mechanisms to record and archive necessary data; *system-mediated messages*, concerning the way behavior change messages are delivered to the user. In [14], tactics are defined as generic actions that describe how to deliver persuasion to the user. Tactics could be implemented by means of messages on the smartphone screen, audio notifications, and so on, depending on the device where the system is installed and running.

Given the importance of personalization in the development of mHealth apps, and the different possibilities we must implement it, understanding which dimensions should be stressed to this aim is crucial. One of the most interesting studies is [17], where user, system functionalities, information and app properties are proposed. The first one is characterized by four indexes: user personality, user profile, need for cognition and perception of social norms. The second dimension depends on app functionalities, like reminders or self-monitoring, and gaming features, like goal setting, rewards or levels and progression. The information dimension concerns the quantity and quality of information and knowledge exchanged among users and feedback returned by the application to the user. Finally, app properties involve aesthetics and customizable features.

Many references in literature propose fuzzy logic to manage personalization within applications in many fields, such as education [34], e-commerce [28] and telecommunication [39]. In healthcare, fuzzy logic has been adopted to design and implement systems tailored on users affected by hypertension [10] and back pain [18], as well as to tune parameters of artificial pancreas controller [24] or to predict the responses to the treatment method for warts [21]. In what follows, fuzzy logic will be adopted to present our approach to personalization in mHealth app design and implementation.

3 Proposed Method

In our case study, the user exploits an Android™ application suggesting him/her how much physical activity to accomplish during the week; the evaluation is based both on quantitative, physical (e.g., how much time do you train during a week?) and on qualitative, psychological variables (e.g., how well did you feel during the training session?). From the physical point of view, the metabolic equivalent of task (MET) variable is used to estimate the amount and intensity of PA accomplished; from the psychological perspective, the MoveUp module estimates users' self-efficacy (SE) at the end of each training session.

3.1 Conceptual Model

The MET per minute of PA calculus is based on the relationships between MET and heart beat rate (HBR), given by the following formula:

$$MET_{min} = 4 * Time^{MPA} + 8 * Time^{IPA} \tag{1}$$

where $Time^{MPA}$ and $Time^{IPA}$ are the periods of time the subject is involved in *moderate* and *intense* physical activity, measured in minutes.

A PA session is defined *moderate* if the registered HBR values are in the range $\left[\frac{6*MHR}{10}, \frac{7*MHR}{10}\right]$, where $MHR = 220 - age$ is the subject *maximum heart rate*, depending on his/her age. A PA session is defined *intense* if the registered HBR values are in the range $\left(\frac{7*MHR}{10}, \frac{8*MHR}{10}\right]$. Two PA sessions per week must be accomplished by the user, who is free to distribute them according to his/her wishes. To take care of psychological well-being, the *self-efficacy* variable [3] has been considered. SE, also referred as *personal efficacy*, is the extent or strength of one's belief in his/her own ability to complete tasks and reach goals. Self-efficacy is evaluated through a collection of questions about the positive or negative conduction of training sessions; the self-efficacy of the day is given by the arithmetic mean of the provided answers:

$$SE_{day_i} = \frac{\sum_{j=1}^{n} answer_j}{n}$$

where $day_i, i \in [1, 2]$ identifies the current day of physical activity, n is the number of questions posed to the user and $answer_j$ is the value given by the user, usually an integer value in the range [1…4]. Currently, two questions are posed to the user for self-efficacy estimation: *How much do you feel able to do similar training next week, despite its duration? How much do you feel able to do similar training next week, despite its intensity?* The sum of SE_{day_i} values returns the whole self-efficacy on a week (thus,$2 \leq SE_{week} \leq 8$). Note that a user could refuse to answer to the questions: in this case, his/her SE_{week} would be set to 1 by default, to indicate that the user's psychological conditions were not so good that week regardless of the PA sessions.

The MoveUp module has been tested in a real experiment (due to the lack of space, further details about the experiment, during which 60 users, 25 female and 35 male subjects in the 35–45 age range, have been monitored for eight weeks in performing PA tasks suggested by the system. The starting point for each user was 120 MET per week (equivalent to 30 min of moderate physical activity). The wearable device to get heart beat rate was a *PulseOn*™ smartwatch. A profile for each of them was developed, combining eight values of PA (numeric values from $MET_{min} \in [120, 240, 360, 480, 600]$) and SE (numeric integer values in the range [1, 8] obtained during the test, for a total of 16 features. These features have been analyzed with experts to define the following groups of people according to the comparison with an *optimal profile* exploiting the case-based reasoning paradigm. Such profile characterizes a user capable to increase his/her goal every week, thanks to highest levels of both MET and SE variables. Such user would reach the maximum amount of MET, i.e. 600, at the 5th week of training, maintaining the goal for the last three weeks. Four classes have been determined, on the basis of similarity percentage to the optimal profile: *Static* ∈ [0%,50%); *Complicated* ∈ [50%,60%); *Slow but gradual* ∈ [60%,70%); *Capable* ∈ [70%,100%].

Further details about the conceptual model of MoveUp are out of paper scope; they can be found in [4, 5]. Here, the challenge is understanding how results obtained from the study can address useful extensions of MoveUp from the mHealth standpoint.

3.2 *Fuzzy Profiling of Users in MoveUp*

As reported above, personalization on the user characteristics is crucial for an application like MoveUp. In this sense, the possibility to determine which cluster a person belongs to could be an important parameter to increase the performance of the mobile app. To this aim, the experiment above can be considered as a starting point: given that a user demonstrates a specific behavior, that can vary dynamically week by week on the basis of both physical and psychological conditions, it is possible to think that such behavior can be quantified with respect to a suitable profile, in order to obtain better suggestions by the application (e.g. tailoring them on the current user profile in addition to the effective result of the training session) as well as proposing him/her to accomplish training sessions in group rather than being alone. In order to obtain a reliable profile for each user, a method to deal with uncertainty must be chosen in fact, classes above are separated by thin lines; in particular, complicated, and slow but gradual profiles are characterized by close values of similarity around the 55% threshold, thus a decision about them is not clear. For this reason, fuzzy logic has been adopted.

Two models have been created. As shown in Fig. 1, such models are different not only from the input data point of view, but also from the semantic perspective. The first model, namely week by week, focuses on user data week by week, the second one, namely feedback, considers the performance variation (positive, negative, or null)

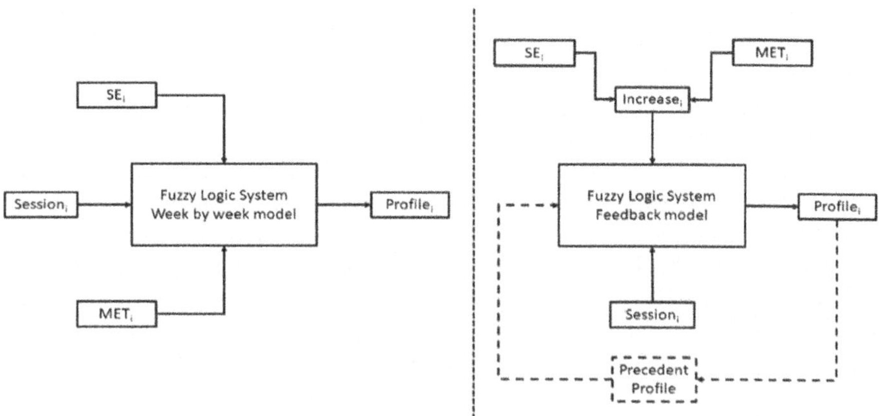

Fig. 1 On the left, a sketch of the week-by-week model; on the right, a schema of the feedback model

with respect to the past (i.e., the previous profile of the user). The *week-by-week model* aims at providing an instantaneous description of user capabilities, possibly showing sharp variations from one session to the next one; the feedback model goal is to give a more reliable estimation of the user profiling on a longer time horizon.

Input variables for the week-by-week model are MET, SE and Session, each one represented by triangular fuzzy sets, as shown in Fig. 2. The Session variable assumes crisp values, corresponding to the current week of activity, but is represented by means of a triangular fuzzy set. This choice allows using the model for different analysis too, considering training sessions belonging to distinct weeks. Also MET and SE assume crisp values, but the adoption of triangular fuzzy sets allows thinking to different uses of the model in the future. For example, it could be possible to profile a user by means of real performance in terms of MET rather than in terms of goal achieved. The membership functions values of the three sets are in [0, 1].

The output fuzzy set, namely Profile, returns a value in [0, 1] that defines the user profile calculated by the system. To design it, the thresholds determined by case-based reasoning approach have been maintained. The Profile set is depicted in

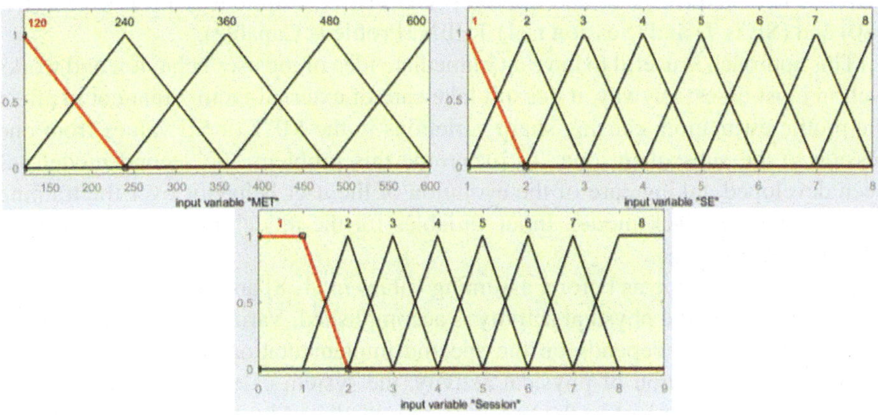

Fig. 2 Input fuzzy sets for the week-by-week model

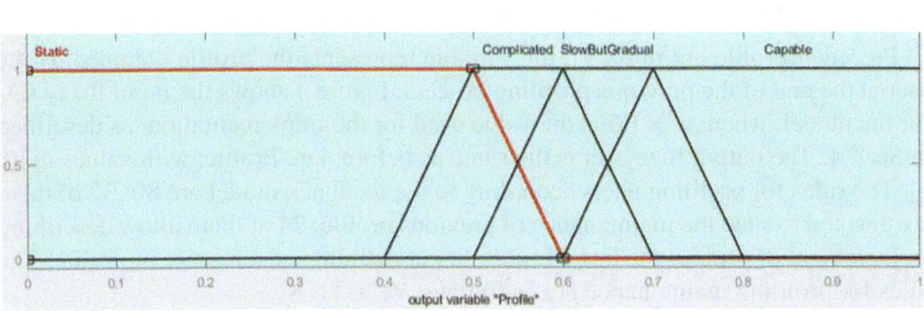

Fig. 3 Output fuzzy set for the week by week model

Fig. 3; the membership functions values are in the [0, 1] range as for the inputs. The rules for user profiling in the week-by-week model are 240, and they are as follows:

IF (MET IS met_i) and (SE IS se_i) and (Session IS i) THEN (Profile IS profile_i)

where met_i and se_i are the MET and SE values for the session i, and $profile_i$ is the output value calculated by the system. Such rules are based on clusters defined by case-based reasoning method. First of all, the input values of the optimal profile would be: Session 1: MET = 120, SE = 8; Session 2: MET = 240, SE = 8; Session 3: MET = 360, SE = 8; Session 4: MET = 480, SE = 8; Session 5: MET = 600, SE = 8; Session 6: MET = 600, SE = 8; Session 7: MET = 600, SE = 8; Session 8: MET = 600, SE = 8.

Some rules impose that if a user reaches these values, his/her profile is capable. On the contrary, in case of particularly low values, rules impose the profile is static. Complicated and slow but gradual profiles are obtained if a user reaches intermediate values, considering also the session and comparing the SE and MET values with respect to the optimal profile and the experimental results, like for example: IF (MET is 120) and (SE is 6) and (Session is 1) THEN (Profile is Complicated); IF (MET is 120) and (SE is 7) and (Session is 4) THEN (Profile is Static); IF (MET is 480) and (SE is 7) and (Session is 4) THEN (Profile is Capable).

This approach is useful to have an immediate idea of the user behavior, and works well in most cases; anyway, it doesn't take care of external factors that could affect the profile estimation, causing sharp variations in the MET or SE values from one session to the subsequent one. To overcome this problem, the second model has been developed, taking care of the evolution of the user behavior over the training sessions: the feedback model. Input variables for the model are Session, Increase and PrecedentProfile.

Session is the same as before, assuming values in [1, 8] and defining the number of the week when the physical activity is accomplished. Variable Increase is valued in [−a, a], where a depends on the specific implementation of the model; given a user, for each session of physical activity, the system calculates the increase of performance with respect to the previous one, mediated by the self-efficacy stated by the user, associating a numeric value concordant with the result (negative, if PA decreases, positive otherwise): (PA− & SE−) ⇒ −a; (PA− & SE+) ⇒ −a + 1; (PA+ & SE−) ⇒ +a − 1; (PA+ & SE+) ⇒ +a. Finally, values for variable.

PrecedentProfile are in [0, 1]; the variable represents the profile obtained by the user at the end of the previous profiling process. Figure 4 shows the input fuzzy sets for the model, where a = 1.5 is the value used for the implementation, as described in Sect. 4. The output fuzzy set is the same as before, i.e., Profile, with values in [0, 1]. The rules for profiling users according to the feedback model are 80; 32 of them are devoted to state the maintenance of previous profile; 24 of them allow describing an increment of profile; the last 24 rules aim at defining a decrement of profile. The rules for profiling maintenance are as follows, $\forall w \in [1, 8]$:

IF (Session is w) and (Increase is PA− & SE−) and (PrecedentProfile is Static).
THEN (Profile is Static);

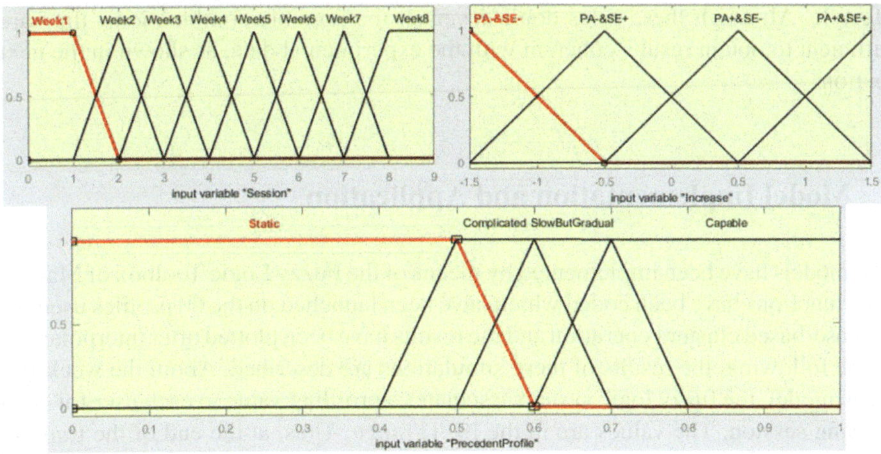

Fig. 4 Input fuzzy sets for the feedback model

IF (Session is w) and (Increase is PA− & SE+) and (PrecedentProfile is Complicated) THEN (Profile is Complicated;)

IF (Session is w) and (Increase is PA+ & SE−) and (PrecedentProfile is SlowButGradual) THEN (Profile is SlowButGradual);

IF (Session is w) and (Increase is PA+ & SE+) and (PrecedentProfile is Capable) THEN (Profile is Capable).

The rules for incrementing the profile are similar to the following ones, $\forall w \in [1, 8]$:

IF (Session is w) and (Increase is PA+ & SE+) and (PrecedentProfile is Static) THEN (Profile is Complicated);

IF (Session is w) and (Increase is PA+ & SE+) and (PrecedentProfile is Complicated) THEN (Profile is SlowButGradual);

IF (Session is w) and (Increase is PA+ & SE+) and (PrecedentProfile is SlowButGradual) THEN (Profile is Capable).

Finally, the rules for decrementing the profile are like the following ones, $\forall w \in [1, 8]$:

IF (Session is w) and (Increase is PA− & SE−) and (PrecedentProfile is Complicated) THEN (Profile is Static).

IF (Session is w) and (Increase is PA− & SE−) and (PrecedentProfile is SlowButGradual) THEN (Profile is Complicated).

IF (Session is w) and (Increase is PA− & SE−) and (PrecedentProfile is Capable) THEN (Profile is SlowButGradual).

Different from the week-by-week model, rules of the feedback model have been designed to avoid sharp variations (both negative and positive) in the performance level, trying to follow a natural and gradual behavior change intervention in the user lifestyle. Although these rules don't cover all the possible combinations, they are sufficient to obtain results coherent with the experimental data, as shown in the next section.

4 Model Implementation and Application

The models have been implemented by means of the Fuzzy Logic Toolbox of Matlab. Two functions have been coded which have been launched on the 60 profiles used for the case-based cluster generation and the results have been plotted after interpolation. In the following, the results of these simulations are described. About the week-by-week model, the fuzzy logic system associates a profiling value to each user for each training session. The values are in the [0, 1] range. Thus, at the end of the training period, each user will have a set of 8 points, each one representing his/her profile at the end of a given week of physical activity. These points have been interpolated by a polynomial function of 7th degree, finding a curve that represents the evolution of a person during the time horizon. Left part of Fig. 5 shows some examples. It is evident how some users are characterized by uniform behaviors, while others present many jumps due to unsuccessful performances; this demonstrates how the week-by-week model is not useful to derive a function for describing the behavior of MoveUp users; instead, it is good for giving an instantaneous picture of it to implement social functionalities within it. In order to find classes of functions for clustering users, the average distance between the points of two polynomials has been used: given I the set of 500 sampled points in the [1, 8] (used to draw the graphs of profiles in Matlab) and two polynomials representing the profiles of two users $p_1(x)$ and $p_2(x)$ respectively, such distance is:

$$d = \frac{\sum_{x \in I} |p_1(x) - p_2(x)|}{500}$$

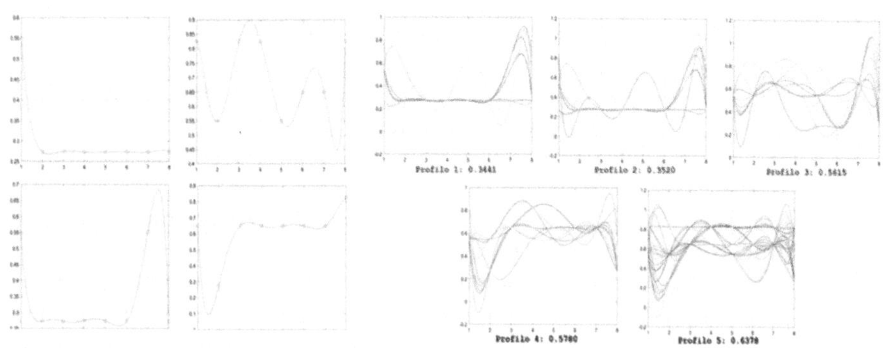

Fig. 5 On the left, some profile of users during the eight weeks of training; on the right, clusters of profiles according to the week-by-week model

The calculus has been repeated on every pair of polynomials, on every profile obtained by the system. Then, classes composed of polynomials characterized by lower values of d have been created. Right part of Fig. 5 shows the five clusters obtained. The classes are not clearly distinguishable: many profiles belong to more than one collection. Moreover, the distance among the final values of outputs calculated at the end of the last week of training is short; once again, these results demonstrate how the week-by-week model is not suitable to characterize a long-term profile of a person.

Also, in the feedback model a user profile is described by 8 values. Since this model takes care of positive/negative variations of MET/SE rather than their effective values, a logarithmic interpolation has been used to highlight the individual's increase/decrease: $f(x) = a + b\log(x)$, with $a, b \in R$. The feedback model generates both increasing and decreasing functions, being reasonable to think that profiles associated to increasing functions are comparable to capable and slow but gradual, while profiles associated to decreasing functions would have been classified as static and complicated. Looking at the complete map of profiles in left part of Fig. 6, the clustering into four classes is more evident. This classification is coherent with the one created by case-based reasoning method, as depicted in right part of Fig. 6: **Static** profiles are described by a decreasing function f i.e. $f(9) < 0.6$ (light blue lines in the figure); **Complicated** profiles are represented by a decreasing function f i.e. $f(9) \geq 0.6$ (blue lines in the figure); **Slow but gradual** profiles are described by an increasing function f i.e. $f(9) < 0.7$ (green lines in the figure); **Capable** profiles are represented by an increasing function f i.e. $f(9) \geq 0.7$ (purple lines in the figure). This model allows giving a more complete description of a profile during and/or at the end of the training time horizon with respect to the week by week one. By analyzing the behavior of the person in terms of increasing/decreasing functions it could be possible to propose corrections in the personalized training plan, in order to find the best way to support him/her. Moreover, it could be possible to have a clearer

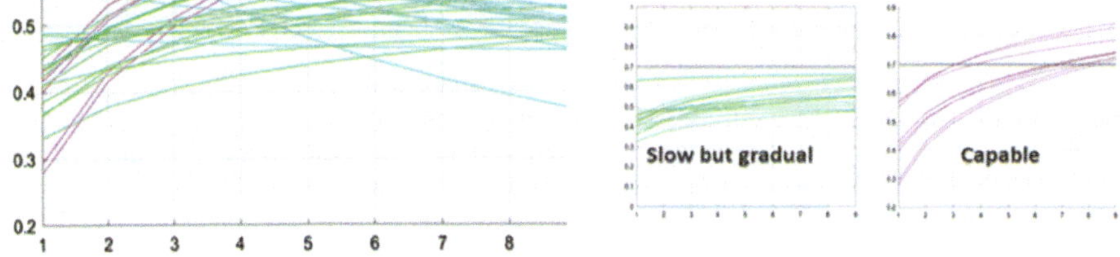

Fig. 6 On the left, the 60 profiles resulting from feedback model use; on the right, the four profiles emerging from the feedback model adoption

idea on what kinds of actions to take to implement an effective behavior change intervention, i.e., from the physical, psychological, or both perspectives.

The fuzzy logic system for user profiling has been integrated within MoveUp to enable new functionalities. First, week by week model has been exploited to give immediate feedback to the user about his/her performance: Part A) and Part B) of Fig. 7 show the dedicated GUIs. The user can select his/her expected level of performance, choosing it among four possibilities: *Turtle*, the avatar of the *static* profile; *Cat*, a representation of *complicated* profile; *Leveret*, representing the *slow but gradual* profile; *Cheetah*, the metaphor of the *capable* profile. At the end of the session, the user can ask the system to show him/her the profile variation according to the real physical and psychological data. Showing the profile is optional, since the possible decrease with respect to user expectations could have negative impact on the behavior change plan. Part C) of Fig. 7 shows the MoveUp GUI to present the result of week-by-week profiling method to the user: of course, four alternatives are possible, based on the calculus. The window also summarizes the amount of PA MET required. Second, the fuzzy logic system has been used to extend the *function* with *social* issues. *Group physical activities* are important research topics from both the physical and psychological perspectives. In [11] it is demonstrated how group physical activity is more effective than individual one to reduce fatigue in patients suffering for breast cancer. Anyway, this study also shows that most patients prefer individual activity to group one. The comparison with peers is still an important psychological barrier, that many researchers are trying to analyze. Interesting outcomes have been obtained in applying group physical activity for supporting aged people [32] to overcome barriers, like e.g., living in not safe neighborhoods. Another interesting study [16] showed that group PA positively impacts on PA levels outpatients with schizophrenia, with many benefits on their quality of life too.

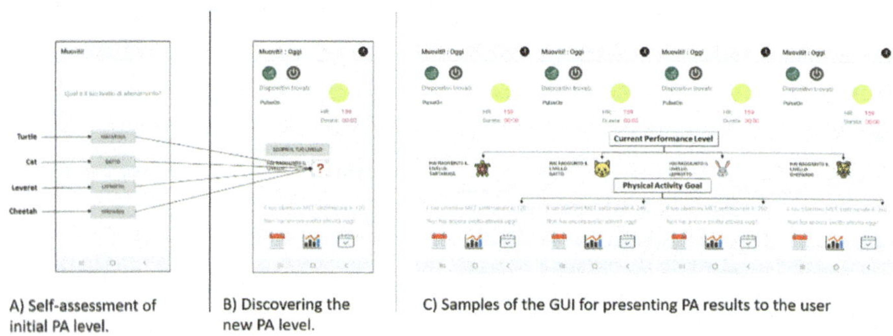

Fig. 7 On the left, the GUI for self-assessment of initial profile by the user; on the center, the GUI for discovering the user according to the fuzzy logic system evaluation; on the right, the GUI that presents to the user the results of his/her training session at the end of the week

Fig. 8 The calendar function developed in MoveUp

Following such guidelines, the user profiling in MoveUp has been exploited to implement a calendar of activities shared among a group of people. Figure 8 shows a sketch of the graphical user interface. First of all, the user has the possibility to plan a new PA session as he/she prefers. It is possible to specify the type of activity (e.g., running) and the scheduling in terms of day of the week and time. Then, the user can decide to maintain the activity *private* or to publicize it over the shared calendar to enable others to join the same session.

The calendar implemented in MoveUp is shown in the center of the figure. Red activities are private training sessions: other users will not be able to see them on their calendars. Green activities are public training sessions, inserted by the current user as well as his/her buddies. All the users will see them on their calendars; moreover, they will have the possibility to subscribe to one or more of them (see right part of the figure), receiving information about weather condition forecast and the group participants' profile (leveret in the figure), to understand if that activity could fit with his/her programs or not. While social functionalities of MoveUp are based on the week-by-week model, the feedback approach has been integrated into reporting part of the app. This function can be activated by clicking the *graph* icon in the GUI (see right part of Fig. 7) and allows presenting some information about the user performance in graphical form. In particular, the *Profile graph* depicts the logarithmic interpolation of feedback model as described above. The profile graph is useful for the analysis of the long-term behavior of the person, to understand how he/she has globally faced the challenge of behavior change as suggested by the app.

5 Discussion

The fuzzy profiling function of MoveUp is a sample of application for real-time classification of user behavior. The fuzzy models developed are not devoted to discover the lifestyle of a person, like in [29], but to derive a synthetic representation of real-time data of a person with declared, problematic lifestyle, to promote a behavior change from profitable comparison and collaboration with others. In this sense, the use of fuzzy logic to analyze quantitative and qualitative variables about, respectively, the physiological and psychological well-being is the most important innovation of the approach with respect to the state of the art. According to [14], tactic can be defined as a set of generic actions to describe how delivering persuasion to users. The implementation of fuzzy profiling of users has allowed to consider tactic in the MoveUp module: the comparison with peers could be a way to improve the interest of users in changing his/her own lifestyle. Moreover, the implementation of social support features in MoveUp is a significant improvement with respect to similar apps like [33], where this crucial persuasive feature was not considered, given that primary task support, computer human dialog support and system credibility support were already satisfied in MoveUp, thanks to the existing architectural choices [30]. Unfortunately, an evaluation of the proposed approach is not possible at the moment: it was planned to test it as done in the past to collect data, monitoring a set of target users and acquiring quantitative and qualitative information about the effectiveness of the method. This phase has been postponed due to COVID-19 pandemic, that makes difficult to schedule group physical activity in Italy. Anyway, it is possible to evaluate the fuzzy MoveUp approach from the personalization perspective discussing its features with reference to dimensions proposed in [17]. Table 1 summarizes the evaluation, where Y adjacent to a feature means the fuzzy based approach allows satisfying it.

User dimension features stated by our approach are user profile and perception of social norm. While the first one is quite clear, given the goal of the fuzzy based approach, the second feature refers to the perceived social pressure to perform or not the behavior, i.e., the suggested amount of MET compared to the peers. System functionalities features are both satisfied: given that functionalities concern the services provided to user by the application, like reminders or self-monitoring, also this feature is implicitly guaranteed by the fuzzy method goals; gaming features, like goal setting, rewards, levels, and progression, are represented by the avatars the user merits at the end of each training week. About information dimension, it is possible to say that the user profiling elaborated by MoveUp can provide useful feedbacks not only to the user but also to other roles possibly involved in his/her support, like caregivers, doctors, and other professionals. Finally, the adoption of avatars, calendar and graphical representation of user's profile has increased the app properties level from the aesthetics point of view. Thus, seven of ten indexes of mHealth apps personalization have been successfully covered thanks to the proposed approach.

With respect to the persuasion issue, it is possible to compare the MoveUp module with the RightOnTime app architectural pattern defined in [33], it is possible to notice

Table 1 Personalization level in MoveUp, according to [17]

Users		System functionalities		Information		App properties	
Personality	N	App functions	Y	Knowledge/Information	Y	Aesthetics	Y
User profile	Y	Gamification features	Y	Feedbacks	Y	App features	N
Need for cognition	N						
Social norm perception	Y						

that user context use context, user-system interaction and system-mediated messages features were already considered in previous implementations of the app. The social interaction dimension, provided by the shared calendar of physical activities is the real novelty with respect to the past. The RightOnTime app didn't implement it explicitly, despite such dimension was ideally considered in the overall information flow, being related to information about user context and use context. In MoveUp, the possibility to make group physical activity is an instance of social interaction, that is linked not only to user context and use context, but also to the user-system interaction and system-mediated messages components.

6 Conclusions and Future Works

This paper has presented a recent development of MoveUp, an mHealth app to support sedentary adults to change their behavior to avoid the arising of chronic diseases. This development concerned the integration of *social* functionalities in MoveUp: before this work, the user was invited by the system to perform the suggested amount of PA on his/her own, now he/she can choose whether to join a group of peers or to continue alone. To this aim, a fuzzy logic system to profile the user based on his/her physical and psychological state has been implemented. Two distinct models have been adopted: *week by week*, devoted to return an *instantaneous* classification of the user according to his/her performance at the end of a session of PA, and *feedback* that aims at defining a more stable and objective picture of the user behavior in a long-term period.

Future works concern both theory and practice. First of all, field test will be planned to evaluate the positive/negative perception of the MoveUp development among users. This test will allow to collect data about the impact that group PA has on behavior change in the mHealth context. It will be possible to analyze the benefits/drawbacks of making PA with people characterized by the same or different profiles, possibly extending the SE definition with new questions about the feelings of accomplishing group PA. The goal of this knowledge acquisition campaign would be the enrichment of SE definition through the estimation of *social indicators* for the users, given that group PA has been demonstrated to have positive influence on different groups of people, like adolescents [9] and aged people [23]. Another interesting issue would be to analyze the characteristic of the *virtual community* emerging from the use of the MoveUp module, thanks to introduction of group PA functionalities, adapting the SOVC metrics used in the past [31].

From the practical point of view, the possibility to adopt different shapes for fuzzy sets definition is under evaluation. Moreover, the lessons learned about the adoption of fuzzy logic in profiling users of the MoveUp module will be evaluated for the development of new modules. In particular, similar approach could be proposed for a *diet module* to profile users and develop similar social functionalities, like e.g. group dinners at home or restaurant.

References

1. Armstrong, T., Bonita, R.: Capacity building for an integrated non communicable disease risk factor surveillance system in developing countries. Ethn. Dis. **13**(2 Suppl 2), S13–S18 (2002)
2. Association, A.D., et al.: Diagnosis and classification of diabetes mellitus. Diabetes Care **37**(Supplement 1), S81–S90 (2014)
3. Bandura, A.: Self-efficacy: toward a unifying theory of behavioral change. Psychol. Rev. **84**(2), 191 (1977)
4. Baretta, D., Sartori, F., Greco, A., D'Addario, M., Melen, R., Steca, P.: Improving physical activity mhealth interventions: development of a computational model of self-efficacy theory to define adaptive goals for exercise promotion. Adv. Human-Comput. Interact. **2019** (2019)
5. Baretta, D., et al.: Wearable devices and AI techniques integration to promote physical activity. In: Proceedings of the 18th International Conference on Human-Computer Interaction with Mobile Devices and Services Adjunct, pp. 1105–1108. ACM (2016)
6. Bauer, A.M., et al.: Acceptability of mhealth augmentation of collaborative care: a mixed methods pilot study. Gen. Hosp. Psychiatr. **51**, 22–29 (2018)
7. Bendixen, R.M., et al.: A user centered approach: understanding client and caregiver needs and preferences in the development of mhealth apps for self-management. JMIR mHealth uHealth **5**(9), e141 (2017)
8. Cappon, G., et al.: Wearable continuous glucose monitoring sensors: a revolution in diabetes treatment. Electronics **6**(3), 65 (2017)
9. Chuah, M., Jakes, G., Qin, Z.: Wifi treasure hunt: a mobile social application for staying active physically. In: Proceedings of the 2012 ACM Conference on Ubiquitous Computing, pp. 631–632 (2012)
10. Das, S., Ghosh, P.K., Kar, S.: Hypertension diagnosis: a comparative study using fuzzy expert system and neuro fuzzy system. In: 2013 IEEE International Conference on Fuzzy Systems (FUZZ-IEEE), pp. 1–7. IEEE (2013)
11. Desbiens, C., Filion, M., Brien, M.C., Hogue, J.C., Laflamme, C., Lemieux, J.: Impact of physical activity in group versus individual physical activity on fatigue in patients with breast cancer: a pilot study. The Breast **35**, 8–13 (2017)
12. Dijkstra, A.: The psychology of tailoring-ingredients in computer-tailored persuasion. Soc. Pers. Psychol. Compass **2**(2), 765–784 (2008)
13. Farao, J., Malila, B., Conrad, N., Mutsvangwa, T., Rangaka, M.X., Douglas, T.S.: A user-centered design framework for mhealth. PLOS ONE **15**(8), 1–18 (08 2020)
14. Fenicio, A., Calvary, G., Laurillau, Y., Vanderdonckt, J.: Prosper: modeling the change, driving the persuasion. In: Actes de la 28ième conference francophone sur l'Interaction Homme-Machine, pp. 59–69 (2016)
15. Floch, J., et al.: User needs in the development of a health app ecosystem for self-management of cystic fibrosis: user-centered development approach. JMIR mHealth uHealth **6**(5), e113 (2018)
16. Gomes, E., et al.: Effects of a group physical activity program on physical fitness and quality of life in individuals with schizophrenia. Ment. Health Phys. Act. **7**(3), 155–162 (2014)
17. Gosetto, L., Ehrler, F., Falquet, G.: Personalization dimensions for mhealth to improve behavior change: a scoping review. Stud. Health Technol. Inf. **275**, 77–81 (2020)
18. Kadhim, M.A., Alam, M.A., Kaur, H.: Design and implementation of fuzzy expert system for back pain diagnosis. Int. J. Innov. Technol. Creat. Eng. **1**(9), 16–22 (2011)
19. Khansa, L., et al.: Health information technologies for patients with diabetes. Technol. Soc. **44**, 1–9 (2016)
20. Khosravi, P., Ghapanchi, A.H.: Investigating the effectiveness of technologies applied to assist seniors: a systematic literature review. Int. J. Med. Inf. **85**(1), 17–26 (2016)
21. Khozeimeh, F., et al.: An expert system for selecting wart treatment method. Comput. Biol. Med. **81**, 167–175 (2017)

22. Liew, M.S., Zhang, J., See, J., Ong, Y.L.: Usability challenges for health and wellness mobile apps: mixed-methods study among mhealth experts and consumers. JMIR mHealth uHealth **7**(1), e12160 (2019)
23. Maillot, P., Perrot, A., Hartley, A.: Effects of interactive physical-activity videogame training on physical and cognitive function in older adults. Psychol. Aging **27**(3), 589 (2012)
24. Mauseth, R., et al.: Proposed clinical application for tuning fuzzy logic controller of artificial pancreas utilizing a personalization factor. J. Diabetes Sci. Technol. **4**(4), 913–922 (2010)
25. Michie, S., et al.: The behavior change technique taxonomy (v1) of 93 hierarchically clustered techniques: building an international consensus for the reporting of behavior change interventions. Ann. Behav. Med. **46**(1), 81–95 (2013)
26. Milani, R.V., Bober, R.M., Lavie, C.J.: The role of technology in chronic disease care. Prog. Cardiovasc. Dis. **58**(6), 579–583 (2016)
27. Milani, R.V., Lavie, C.J.: Health care 2020: reengineering health care delivery to combat chronic disease. Am. J. Med. **128**(4), 337–343 (2015)
28. Ojokoh, B., Omisore, M., Samuel, O., Ogunniyi, T.: A fuzzy logic based personalized recommender system. Int. J. Comput. Sci. Inf. Technol. Secur. (IJCSITS) **2**(5), 1008–1015 (2012)
29. Rodriguez, N.D., et al.: Couch potato or gym addict? Semantic lifestyle profiling with wearables and knowledge graphs. In: 6th Workshop on Automated Knowledge Base Construction, AKBC@NIPS 2017, Long Beach, California, USA, December 8, 2017. OpenReview.net (2017)
30. Sartori, F., et al.: Virtual round table knights for the treatment of chronic diseases. J. Reliab. Intell. Env. **5**(3), 131–143 (2019)
31. Sartori, F., Melen, R., Pinardi, S.: Cultivating virtual communities of practice in kafka. Data Technol. Appl. **52**(1), 34–57 (2018)
32. Schutzer, K.A., Graves, B.S.: Barriers and motivations to exercise in older adults. Prev. Med. **39**(5), 1056–1061 (2004)
33. Tikka, P., Woldemicael, B., Oinas-Kukkonen, H.: Building an app for behavior change: case rightontime. In: BCSS@ PERSUASIVE, pp. 3–14 (2016)
34. Troussas, C., Krouska, A., Sgouropoulou, C.: Collaboration and fuzzy-modeled personalization for mobile game-based learning in higher education. Comput. Educ. **144**, 103698 (2020)
35. Vo, V., Auroy, L., Sarradon-Eck, A.: Patients' perceptions of mhealth apps: Meta ethnographic review of qualitative studies. JMIR Mhealth Uhealth **7**(7), e13817 (Jul 2019)
36. Woldaregay, A.Z., et al.: Motivational factors for user engagement with mhealth apps. In: pHealth, pp. 151–157 (2018)
37. Yusif, S., Soar, J., Hafeez-Baig, A.: Older people, assistive technologies, and the barriers to adoption: a systematic review. Int. J. Med. Inf. **94**, 112–116 (2016)
38. Zhang, D., Adipat, B.: Challenges, methodologies, and issues in the usability testing of mobile applications. Int. J. Human-Comput. Interact. **18**(3), 293–308 (2005)
39. Zhang, Z., Lin, H., Liu, K., Wu, D., Zhang, G., Lu, J.: A hybrid fuzzy-based personalized recommender system for telecom products/services. Inf. Sci. **235**, 117–129 (2013)

Government IT Projects: Current Evidence of Cost and Schedule Overrun and Their Antecedents

Adam Alami, Christian Østergaard Madsen, and Oliver Krancher

Abstract Although government information technology (IT) projects are often claimed to suffer from cost and schedule overrun, current valid evidence of the magnitude of the problem and its antecedents is difficult to find. To address this gap, we present a mixed-methods study based on 54 Danish government IT projects completed between 2011 and 2020. Using archival data and measures established by Flyvbjerg and colleagues, we find that cost and schedule overrun is substantially lower than reported in previous studies. Qualitative analysis based on interviews and documents in a purposefully selected sub-sample shows that projects are more likely to be completed within budget and schedule if managers actively adopt four key practices: building one team, accommodating uncertainty, rigorous project management and capitalizing on previous domain knowledge. Our findings also suggest that scope reductions may help projects complete within budget and schedule. We discuss theoretical and practical implications for IT project management.

Keywords Government IT projects · IT project performance · Cost overrun · Schedule overrun · Project management

1 Introduction

The public sector is increasingly seeking to digitalize internal and external processes. The goals of these efforts include increased efficiency and effectiveness, higher user

---

A prior version of this paper has been published in the ISD2021 Proceedings (http://aisel.aisnet.org/isd2014/proceedings2021).

A. Alami · C. Østergaard Madsen (✉) · O. Krancher
IT University of Copenhagen, Copenhagen, Denmark
e-mail: chrm@itu.dk

A. Alami
e-mail: adal@cs.aau.dk

O. Krancher
e-mail: olik@itu.dk

E. Insfran Pelozo et al. (eds.), *Advances in Information Systems Development*, Lecture Notes in Information Systems and Organisation 55,
https://doi.org/10.1007/978-3-030-95354-6_7

satisfaction and adherence to national and international laws [1, 2]. This digitalization mostly occurs in the shape of information technology (IT) projects, which we—following the project management literature—define as temporary organizations established to deliver specific IT-related outcomes (e.g., implementing a new software system) [3]. However, studies suggest that IT projects in both the public and private sector frequently experience cost and schedule overrun or fail, partially or completely, to deliver their expected benefits [4]. This is deeply problematic if we consider the importance of the IT projects and the economic loss associated with failed projects.

Significant work has been published on the empirical distributions of cost and schedule overruns in IT projects [5], but the current scientific knowledge about cost and schedule overrun in government IT projects is limited on three fronts. First, we lack current, valid evidence of government project performance. Although there is substantial evidence stemming from 1990 to 2010, it is possible that IT project performance has changed due to policy changes or to recent developments such as the agile movement. Second, while there is substantial literature on IT project failure, there are surprisingly few studies on the reasons for project success or failure in government IT projects. Yet government IT projects face peculiar challenges such as tendering processes and legitimacy pressures, which warrant specific attention on these projects. Third, although the literature has examined distinct performance dimensions such as effectiveness and efficiency [6], few studies have opened the black box of efficiency (i.e., why do projects achieve a particular performance?), seeking to explain why projects meet budget versus schedule targets. We address these three gaps through the following two research questions:

RQ1: How do government IT projects perform with regards to cost and schedule?

RQ2: Why do government IT projects achieve a particular performance outcome (i.e., over budget and over schedule, under budget and over schedule or under budget and under schedule)?

Our contribution to the body of knowledge related to public sector IT projects are the results of an empirical analysis, based on data submitted to the Danish Council for ICT, of 54 completed government IT projects. We followed established guidelines and a mandated IT project model. Our data are current and reliably sourced. We present an analysis of how the projects performed in meeting cost and schedule estimates. We followed established methods and definitions for the calculation of project cost and schedule overrun, as presented by Flyvbjerg et al. [7]. In comparison to previous studies [4, 5, 8], our findings show lower average values for both cost overrun and schedule overrun. This indicates that government organizations are becoming increasingly adept at delivering IT projects. To deepen our understanding of why government IT projects attain a particular performance outcome, we used qualitative methods to investigate six projects in our sample in depth. This phase of the study gave insights into the antecedents of cost and schedule over- and underrun.

Our contribution extends beyond an improved understanding of the cost and schedule performance of our sample. We identified a set of practices (Table 2) and conditions that influence the chances of the sampled projects to remain within cost and schedule. Our qualitative analysis shows that building one team, accommodating uncertainty, applying rigorous project management, and capitalizing on previous domain knowledge enhance the ability of the projects in our sample to achieve positive cost and schedule performance. This indicates that project managers have become aware of the importance of socially tuned practices, such as collaboration and knowledge sharing in project delivery. The significance of rigorous project management practices is not diminished; they remain the "bread and butter" of good project management.

2 Background and Related Work

2.1 IT Project Performance

Among the most cited studies on software project performance are the Standish Groups' CHAOS reports, which have received much attention both in and outside of the academic literature. However, the CHAOS reports have been criticized [8–11]. For example, critics note that the results are not consistent with other studies, and that the figures are influenced by political bias [8].

Moløkken and Jørgensen present a literature review of cost and schedule overrun in software projects [8]. They suggest several methodological issues with survey studies' approach to measuring software projects performance, such as "non-random samples, low response rates, and frequent use of data collection techniques (questionnaires) potentially leading to low data quality" [8]. They conclude that "project overruns are frequent, but most projects do not suffer from major overruns. The average cost overrun reported by Standish Group's Chaos Report (89%) is not supported by other studies. An average cost overrun of 30–40% seems to be the most common value reported" [9].

To the best of our knowledge, the most comprehensive peer-reviewed study of IT projects performance is presented by [4, 5]. They analyzed 1,471 IT projects, of which 92% were conducted in public agencies and 83% were US-based. They found that the average cost overrun was 27%, and the average schedule overrun was 55%. They also found that one in six projects were so-called "Black Swans" with an average cost overrun of 200% and an average schedule overrun of 70%. Although their work presents a very comprehensive empirical investigation, they acknowledge the potential threat of sampling bias given that they sampled projects based on data availability. Our study focuses on process performance (or project efficiency), which is the success of the development process itself (i.e., extent to which the project was delivered on schedule and within budget) [6].

The current literature mainly presents survey, interview-based data or case studies of individual projects. We found only one study includes statistical data on project performance (Taylor 2017). Taylor (2017) examines the relationship between the use of public cloud infrastructure and cost and schedule overrun. Although the paper reports sample characteristics related to cost and schedule overrun, it is difficult to infer population values of cost and schedule overrun from the data due to two difficulties. First, Taylor's sample includes multiple reports on the same project, making it difficult to disentangle the final from intermediate performance of the projects. Second, the study uses metrics of cost and schedule overrun that are difficult to compare with the metrics established by Flyvbjerg and colleagues.

2.2 *Factors Contributing to IT Project Performance*

Our search shows little work has looked at the factors influencing process performance. But there is a vast literature on the topics of project failure and determinants of projects success. This literature, however, uses mostly empirical evidence from private sector failures, despite that the often heard assertion that the likelihood of failure is higher in the public sector [12].

So far, the current literature points to ineffective project management being a significant failure factor [12, 13]. However, Flyvbjerg [14] asserts that "strategic misrepresentation" is a plausible explanation for project under performing in general. He explains that projects strategically overestimate the benefits and underestimate costs when planning projects [14]. Dongus et al. present a literature review which provides a classification of the determinants of information systems (IS) projects performance [15]. They propose six categories of determinants: Project-related characteristics, IS team characteristics, user-related characteristics, user/IS team-related characteristics, relational processes and formal processes [15]. This review shows that there is a comprehensive understanding of what influences project performance, though their analysis does not focus on process performance and on government projects. Our work explores the relations between some of these determinants and process performance in government projects. Section 6 positions our findings vis-a-vis the literature.

3 Study Design

To investigate our research questions, we opted for a mixed-methods, a combination of quantitative and qualitative studies. The underpinning rationale behind this choice is to achieve expansion and credibility [16]. *Expansion* is a methodological quality that seeks to extend the breadth and range of inquiry. *Credibility* is an enhancement of the integrity of findings [16].

We opted for an explanatory mixed-method design [16]. Explanatory sequential studies can be used to explain or to form groups. It is best used when the study is quantitatively oriented, when there is access to instruments, and there is an ability to reach participants. In this study, a quantitative data collection period is followed by a qualitative collection period (QUAN $\rightarrow$ QUAL), which is then interpreted.

A strength of the explanatory sequential study is the two-phase structure, and the straightforward method of study [16]. In addition, the second phase (i.e., QUAL) helps interpret the findings of the first phase.

3.1 Phase I: Quantitative Phase

Our quantitative data is sourced from the Division for central government ICT management (the division) reporting documents. All Danish government IT projects that have an estimated budget of at least 10 million DKK and that include software development are formally required to be risk-assessed by the division. These projects must submit reporting documentation, including the project initiation document, a business case, half-yearly status reports and final report upon completion to the ministry's division for Ministerial IT governance.

These data present a unique research opportunity for several reasons. First, the projects reporting documents provide current data, with all projects initiated in the period between 2011 and 2020. Second, relying on this data reduces sampling bias, given that reporting is mandatory for all projects above 10 million DKK. This compares favorably to other data collection approaches such as survey or analysis of archival data not stemming from mandatory reporting practices. Flyvbjerg et al. note such a potential sampling bias when acknowledging that "projects that are managed well with respect to data availability may also be managed well in other areas, resulting in better than average (i.e., non-representative) performance for such projects" [17]. Third, the use of a consistent project management model and of consistent project status indicators ensure that the figures are comparable between projects. Fourth, the validity of the data is further strengthened by the authoritative character of the projects' documentation, which is compiled and agreed on by a number of stakeholders, involving factual evidence such as project expenses according to time tracking. This leads arguably to more reliable evidence than survey studies asking one key informant per project to recall project performance indicators.

Quantitative Data. Our data is comprised of 54 completed central government IT projects. These projects were completed between 2011 and 2020. They have diverse scopes, including custom software development, software package implementations, hardware and software integration, and major enhancements of existing software. The projects in our sample used different project management (PM) methodology to execute the projects, including agile, waterfall (i.e., plan-based) and hybrid (i.e., a combination of waterfall and agile) methods. We observed two procurement strategies in these projects, fixed-price or time-and-materials.

RQ1 aims at assessing the current levels of budget and schedule adherence. To this end, we collected the projects' reports from the division and built a database to store these projects' information for the purpose of our empirical investigation. We then extracted information on budgets and schedules from the reports. To ensure accurate identification of cost and schedule estimates, we chose the data from the earliest point available in the project's lifecycle, because we wanted the data to be as close as possible to those presented "at the time of decision to build" [7]. Therefore, we collected data from the project initiation documents (PID), as first submitted to the Danish Council for ICT, rather than from the business case resubmitted to the division after the projects' risk assessment. We also collected data on the projects' realized costs and schedules from the completed projects' final reports.

We manually transferred the data to a MS Excel spreadsheet. Then, we and a representative from the division validated the data by referring to the original project documents, the bi-annual status reports, and the division's database. Finally, we adjusted the realized costs to constant prizes, choosing the project's initiation year as a baseline, to allow for the calculation of cost overrun.

Data Analysis. Once the raw data collection and validation were completed, we calculated the cost overrun following established definitions in project management literature as "actual out-turn cost minus estimated costs in percent of estimated costs" [14]. We measured the project's duration by converting start and end times to days, and calculated schedule overrun using the same formula as for cost overrun [5]. We then calculated mean and median of cost and schedule overrun and plotted them in a scatter plot.

3.2 Phase II: Qualitative Phase

When quantitative data precedes qualitative data, the aim is to investigate with a quantitative sample and then to explore in more depth with the qualitative phase [16]. We aimed to understand why the projects in our sample ended up with an over/under budget and over/under schedule performance. We selected six projects based on performance to achieve a maximum variation of the phenomena in question (i.e., RQ2). Then, we interviewed six project managers, the individuals who managed the projects to completion and an IT department manager.

We selected the six projects such that our qualitative sample included two projects with cost and schedule overrun, two with budget and schedule underrun, and two with budget overrun and schedule underrun. There were no projects with budget underrun and schedule overrun in our quantitative sample. Our selection strategy aimed at achieving purposeful sampling [18] to include projects with diverse representation. We selected cases to represent the variety found in the whole sample of projects. For example, for quadrant 2 projects, we selected one project that used agile and a second project that used a waterfall model.

Qualitative Data. We opted for semi-structured interview and documents analysis for our qualitative phase. The interviews lasted around 60 min and generated an average of 17 pages of text each when transcribed verbatim. The interview guide is available at this link.

We analyzed 20 documents of the six projects; these include business cases, project initiation documents, project closure documents, risk assessments and recommendation letters. These documents provided us with backgrounds and additional context to the projects. This analysis entails thorough examination and interpretation of the documents' content [19]. This is an iterative process consisting of thematic analysis of the content. Two authors conducted the first iteration prior to the interviews. The purpose of this iteration is to inform the questions of our interviews. The second iteration took place after the interviews to supplement the insights from the interviews.

Data Analysis. We used thematic analysis to analyse our qualitative data. Thematic analysis is an analytical technique for identifying, analyzing and reporting patterns (themes) within data [20]. Our analytical approach was inductive, our interpretation of the text was not based on existing theory but rather based on the meaning that emerges from the data. Braun and Clarke suggest six steps to conduct thematic analysis: (1) Familiarizing yourself with your data, (2) generating initial codes, (3) searching for themes, (4) reviewing themes, (5) defining and naming themes and (6) producing the report [20]. Here, we report the fundamental stages, which are (2) and (3).

To generate the initial codes, we used open coding to analyze the interviews verbatim. We used our RQ2 as a lens to qualify the codes. Using our RQ2 as an analytical lens allowed us a very tightly focused approach to identifying relevant codes in our data. Open coding refers to the interpretive process of systematically analyzing raw data line-by-line, searching and identifying concepts and finding relations between them. Each of the three authors conducted the initial coding separately. Then, we organized three consecutive sessions to discuss and compare our codes and develop a final list of codes.

The open coding exercise yielded a set of codes. Subsequently, we categorized the codes into categories by comparing codes to each other. This method enabled us to organize and group similarly coded data into categories or families when they shared similar characteristic and attributes.

4 Findings

4.1 Quantitative Phase

Table 1 presents descriptive statistics. The statistics on realized costs and realized duration give insights into the characteristics of our sample. Realized costs varied from 8.3 million DKK (or \$1.3 million) to 138.7 million DKK (\$22.0 million), with a mean of 39.6 million DKK (or \$6.3 million). Realized duration varied from 1.08 to 6.25 years, with a mean of 2.29 years.

The statistics on cost and schedule overrun address RQ1. Cost overrun ranged from −52.3 to 168.7%, with a mean of 9.3% and a median of −1.3%. Schedule

Table 1 Descriptive statistics

Variable	Mean	Median	Std. Dev	{Min; Max}	Skewness
Realized costs (in million DKK)	39.6	31.8	30.0	{8.3; 138.7}	1.67
Realized duration (in years)	2.29	2.52	1.37	{1.08; 6.25}	0.64
Cost overrun (in %)	9.3	−1.3	45.4	{−52.3; 168.7}	1.73
Schedule overrun (in %)	31.1	14.6	43.9	{−15.0; 214.0}	2.27

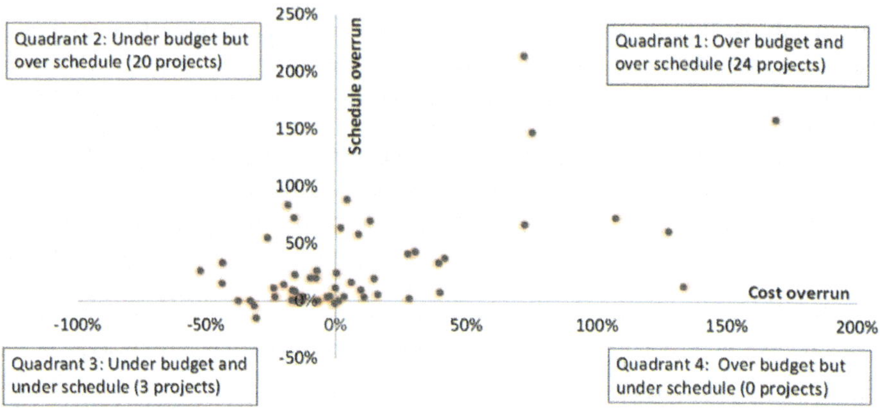

Fig. 1 Scatter plot of cost and schedule overrun

overrun ranged from −15.0 to 214.0%, with a mean of 31.1% and a median of 14.6%. The differences between mean and median are due to positive skew, which was 1.73 for cost overrun and 2.27 for schedule overrun.

Figure 1 visualizes cost and schedule overrun by means of a scatter plot, which is divided into four quadrants based on positive versus negative cost and schedule overrun. Twenty-four projects had positive budget and schedule overruns (Quadrant 1), with a few projects exceeding the planned budget and schedule by more than 100%. Twenty projects went under budget but over schedule (Quadrant 2). Three projects remained both under budget and under schedule (Quadrant 3). No project in our sample went over budget but under schedule. Seven projects do not fit into any of the quadrants because they were exactly on schedule.

4.2 *Qualitative Phase*

In RQ2, we asked why the projects in our sample ended up in a particular quadrant. In response to this question, our analysis indicates that the main drivers, experienced by our participants, for projects in our sample to conclude with a positive efficiency

Table 2 Overview of the practices and conditions influencing project's performance

Practices and conditions influencing performance	Quadrant #1	Quadrant #2	Quadrant #3
Practices			
Building one team	–	+	+
Accommodating uncertainty	–	+	+
Rigorous project management	–	+	+
Capitalizing on previous domain knowledge	–		+
Condition			
Scope change	–	+	–

(quadrant 2 or 3) is the adoption and implementation of four practices. These practices sway the projects toward a positive efficiency when adopted and fostered. Projects in quadrant 1 did not achieve a positive efficiency not for lack of trying, but mostly because they lacked the application of these practices and experienced conditions that influenced the efficiency negatively. Table 2 lists the practices and the conditions we observed in our data. The plus sign (+) indicates the adoption of the practice by the projects in the relevant quadrant. The minus sign (−) shows either the practice was not adopted or simply it was not possible due to project's circumstances. We also observed a condition which is an occurrence of something, mainly scope change that either influenced the performance positively (when the scope is reduced) or negatively (when the scope increases).

The difference between practices and conditions, in our data, is that practices are the application or use of ideas or methods to enhance the ability of the project to achieve a positive efficiency. We observed that project managers are actively taking the necessary actions to implement these practices. Conversely, conditions are the occurrence of something not within the control of the project. In this section, we will report and discuss these practices and conditions.

Building One Team. The focus on building an effective team and creating an environment that stimulates collaboration is highly visible in our interviews data. Projects, in quadrant 1 and 2, invested in building one team, which eventually has paid off. While various characteristics can lead to effective teams, we observed an emphasis on establishing a unified and consolidated team from the inception of the project. Project managers have taken effective actions to create collaborative teams.

Collaboration enhanced the chances of the projects' teams in quadrant 2 and 3 to achieve a positive efficiency. These projects demonstrated high levels of collaborative behavior despite their complexity. Some of these projects have taken the extra step to collocate with the vendor to create a unified team atmosphere and a feeling of togetherness. This project manager explains: "*So quite specifically on this project, at [the name of the project] we have a supplier, it is [the name of the supplier] at this time, we sit with them physically, we can, have the opportunity to sit with them, so that is, where we sit and can work with them, as one now works with colleagues, and it does with such a project, especially when it becomes intensive, that it becomes incredibly effective, because clarifications can be made a lot quickly.*" When team members work together openly, processes and goals become more aligned, leading the team towards achieving positive efficiency.

We also observed that lack of collaboration undermined achieving positive efficiency. Projects in quadrant 1 struggled to create a highly collaborative environment. For example, one project in quadrant 1 experienced a troubled relationship with the vendor. Eventually, they were unable to establish a one-team environment. The project manager described it as being "*two very very different cultures.*" The project selected an American vendor for a niche product. During the project execution, the relationship unfolded with problems and difficulties. The parties were not able to establish trust and each one deployed a rather divergent method to run their respective side of the project. While the American vendor used an agile method, the Danish counterpart had a preference for a sequential and gated phases approach, described by the project manager as "waterfall." The project manager explains: "*So you have such a totally agile secret organization that does projects that way and then you get that complete waterfall model in the other side, and they do not fold together very well, you could say. There are a lot of problems in it.*" These conditions were unfavorable for swaying the project to achieve a positive performance. The project manager concluded: "*So, well, it [cultural and PM methodologies differences] do not provide completely optimal conditions.*"

Collocating the project team in the same physical location is a measure taken by some project managers to enhance the collaborative aspects of the one-team approach. A project manager explains: "*In general, I think it is our experience, it is that sitting together works really well, because you can just make these clarifications quite quickly, which would otherwise require some writing or you have to time that one can meet at certain times.*"

In addition to collocating all the parties in one single location, i.e., "under the same roof", project managers also thrived to secure the commitment of key business stakeholders (e.g., product owner) to become part of the team. This project manager attributes, to some extent, the success of her team collaboration, i.e., "fantastic collaboration", to the initiative of bringing the team "under the same roof." She asserts: "We have had a fantastic collaboration." Then, she further elaborated on how this successful collaboration was achieved: "*Everyone sat physically together you could say, on the same floor, close up with each other.*" Still, the commitment of the business stakeholders to this collaboration is necessary to elevate its chance to succeed. She explained that the "presence" of the product owner has boosted the collaborative atmosphere, "*I think we were pretty good at trying to make it work too. Yes. and at [project name] the product owner was probably even more present.*"

Accommodating Uncertainty. All six projects have experienced some level of uncertainty at the time of estimation and planning. But, those who managed to accommodate it in their planning were successful at achieving a positive efficiency. Our data shows that these projects faced uncertainty in the level of business needs. We define uncertainty of business needs, as it appears in our data, as a potential deficiency in business needs at the time of the estimation has taken place, which can be characterized as inaccurate, unknown or unreliable. This condition triggers a behavior to safeguard the project from going over budget and over schedule. This takes place by generously estimating the budget and schedule. This project manager stated: "*We had an expectation that it would be quite expensive. So, therefore, it has been budgeted quite high.*"

We observed that neglecting this type of uncertainty undermines achieving a positive efficiency for projects in quadrant 1. Projects in quadrant 1 did not know how to accommodate uncertainty or it was simply not possible. Uncertainty of business needs, in both cases, stemmed from the newness and originality of what was wanted by the business stakeholders. Subsequently, this condition affected the project's ability to accurately estimate the budget, which inherently led to an over budget performance when it is not accommodated and an under budget performance when accommodated. This project manager explained: "*So the deviation [from estimated budget] is not because we estimated poorly, it was because it was not possible.*" Another project manager described the state of business need at the start of the project as "*totally unknown.*"

The projects that were successful at accommodating this type of uncertainty were those that managed to detect the degree of "unknowns" in the business requirements at the outset of the project during planning and estimation. For example, this project manager characterized the business requirements as uncertain when the planning for the project was taking place. He explains: "*So you see, you have some kind of idea of where this carries you and what it is for something you look into. And then there is something in it where you say, this is uncertain, which must we assume it may be it comes with so it we have to budget that it may be that it comes.*" To mitigate the risks of this uncertainty on the estimated budget, this project manager budgeted for a buffer to absorb potential increases in the costs, once the "unknowns" become knowns and requiring higher cost to implement.

We conclude that this measure is a project manager skill. When the condition of uncertainty is monitored and detected, some project managers react accordingly to accommodate it. Still, sometimes, it is difficult to detect, like in the case of a project in quadrant #1; the project manager explains that at the start of the project they "*did not know this [business requirements] was what we wanted, but we can see it now.*" The requirements have unfolded as the project progressed along. He explains: "*We have along the way become so much wiser that we can now say, well that was actually what we needed.*"

Rigorous Project Management. Projects in quadrant 2 and 3 had high commitment to rigorous project management practices. These are mainly tracking the budget and the schedule rigorously. This has taken place in the procedures put in place and also by assuming accountability for the budget and schedule expectations by the project managers. This project manager explains that the organization had a robust tracking mechanisms in place, which have helped the project. He said: "*I was very much on the financial management of it … We kept track of the supplier and the finances and things, the schedules … So it has been a lot of finances, supplier management,* *following up that things were reached on time.*" Another project manager implied accountability when he was asked about the project perspective on budget. He said: "*Of course we should look at the budget and in particular the Ministry of Finance, there is rarely enough money ... which is such a stricter duty, that we must try to stay within the framework, so of course there was focus on the budget.*" We also observed that projects in quadrant 2 and 3 had better stakeholders engagement. This project manager stated that he invested rigorous effort to ensure the involvement of key stakeholders. He said: "*We fought hard for our [name of department] and our [name of a second department] to take responsibility for coming and saying that what we were now trying to propose, also it was what they want, tried to get them involved in these projects.*"

Rigorous budget and schedule control have a tangible implementation complemented by the intrinsic motivation of the project manager to meet the cost and schedule expectations. Having the tools and mature processes in the organizations to track project expenditures and schedule are the necessary infrastructure that assist project managers in their pursuit to meet performance expectations. However, the presence of this infrastructure is not sufficient; tracking budget and schedule also needs the motivation of the project manager and feeling accountable towards these expectations. This project manager describes his project being "classic", i.e., typical and of the highest quality, when it comes to finances and schedule. He explains: "*I was very much on the financial management of it. You could say we were like that, shared quite classically, or quite traditionally that we had an IT department that kind of posed with the project managers, and we kept track of the supplier and the finances and that things, the schedules, and then we had a business that just kept track of the content and when in what time do you want things for? So it has been a lot of finances, supplier management, following up that things were reached on time. So this project has been such a very classic project management.*"

Capitalizing on Previous Domain Knowledge. Some project managers capitalized on their teams' knowledge and experience of the business domain, from previous projects, to achieve a positive outcome. Interestingly, this is the only practice that we observed in quadrant 3 but not in 2. However, we do not attribute the positive performance in quadrant 3 solely to this practice. It is the combination of establishing and fostering a one-team approach, accommodating uncertainty, and adopting rigorous project management practices.

Domain knowledge, as talked about in our interviews, points to the comprehension and understanding of the inner workings, processes, procedures and other key aspects of a business. Both projects in quadrant 3 have shown intimate knowledge of the business domain. Both teams have previously worked with the same organizations to deliver similar projects. They became effective at learning the business domains and able to translate that knowledge to understand business needs. This project manager explains: "*So there we had quite of dirt under our nails and knowledge of what is being demanded at institutions, where are the issues, what is what can be difficult, so there we were flagged into the team that owns the systems and had to run the re-tender, where we helped to specify requirements, and part of the requirements specification then runs over to make or have discussed, how to make an implementation plan...*".

The only measure we observed in our data to facilitate this practice is the reuse of the same team, supplier and resources to execute subsequent projects within the same organization. This does not only capitalizes on previous knowledge but also maintains the sense of togetherness, which enables better knowledge sharing. This project manager explains: "*We are not a super team on anyone must they or flawless, not at all, not at all, but the chemistry has been pretty crucial here actually and the knowledge of each other.*" Another project manager echoed similar thought: "*So they had worked together before and were happy to work together.*"

Scope change. Scope change can have either a favorable or unfavorable effect on efficiency. When a project in our sample experienced a scope increase, then the effect on its efficiency was negative. However, a scope reduction has helped a project in quadrant 2 to achieve a positive efficiency.

One project in quadrant 2 has benefited from this condition, which was translated to a lower expenditure and eventually to an under budget performance. Projects in quadrant 1 experienced a scope increase. This unfavorable condition is a manifestation of the uncertainty of the business needs. When the business needs exhibit unknowns, it is anticipated for the project to experience scope increases. This project manager explains: "*I would think that the scope changes are the primary ones. We have taken in things that we did not have in the beginning. And then there are also in some areas that we have been surprised at how much storage [storage requirements for the data].*"

In conclusion, the projects in our sample ended up in quadrant 1, mainly for their inability to handle the uncertainty of the business needs at the time of estimation. This condition had a subsequent effect on increasing the scope. Quadrant 1 projects also failed to create a highly collaborative environment, which has created sub-optimal conditions to achieve a positive efficiency. Projects in quadrant 2 and 3 have invested in establishing a one-team approach and had a strong awareness of the uncertainty of the business needs, which they accommodated for. In addition, these projects followed rigorous project management practices. The distinguishing practice that helped projects end up in quadrant 3 was the team's ability to capitalize on previous knowledge of the business domain. This quality has helped the teams to understand the business needs and mitigate potential uncertainties.

5 Limitations and Threats to Validity

We acknowledge the limitation presented by the size of our qualitative phase sample. We selected only six projects for the qualitative phase. However, our objective was not to reach saturation of coding but to explore and support our quantitative results. This limitation may have led to the identification of fewer practices than it should be or what is universally used in the broader spectrum of IT projects in order to achieve a positive performance. Another limitation of our work is that we did not account for rival theories as alternative explanations to the performance of the projects in our sample. This does not lessen the impact of our findings. To the contrary, our informants' accounts show strong inclination to praise the performance of their projects to the practices they discussed. In addition, the practices and the conditions we identified are contextual to our sample. Other practices also exert influence in IT projects performance but do not manifest in our cases.

A possible external threat to validity is the coverage of our sample. Our sample is limited to Danish government IT projects, with a minimum budget of 10 million DKK, completed in the period 2011–2020, and which have been reported to the Division for central government ICT management. This implies that we cannot generalize our findings beyond our sample. This does not undermine our findings by all means. We contribute to IT projects performance literature by using reliable and valid data.

This study's threats to internal validity are the budget size of the projects in our sample and the representation of Danish government IT projects in our sample. Our sample represents large projects. Smaller IT projects tend to perform slightly better than larger IT projects [15]. This may have influenced the quantitative analysis toward higher cost and schedule overruns. Another threat to internal validity is the projects in our sample are not a true representation of Danish public sector IT projects. The Division for central government ICT management itself has acknowledged the problem that not all eligible IT projects are reported to them. For instance, a government organization might split an IT project into several smaller projects with a budget below 10 million DKK to avoid reporting to the Danish Council for ICT.

6 Discussion and Conclusions

A key observation of our study is that cost and schedule overrun was substantially lower in our sample than in previous studies [4, 5, 8]. This finding demonstrates a positive shift in IT projects performance. Informed by the observations we made in the qualitative phase of this study, we can conclude that the projects in our sample have shown a noticeable maturity in delivering IT projects. Project managers have actively taken actions to implement practices to help them achieve positive efficiency.

We also find that our sample defies the long-held claim that cost and schedule overrun are mutually inclusive. This mutuality is not always true. Our analysis shows that projects in our sample managed to achieve a budget underrun but not a schedule overrun. Studies have often suggested close correlations between schedule and cost overruns. Few studies (e.g., [21]) advise that this correlation does not necessarily mean causality. Various factors may contribute to driving the schedule overrun but not always mean a cost overrun. This relationship is underexplored in IT projects management. Our finding suggests that the assumed mutuality is questionable, and the relation between the cost and schedule outcomes warrant further investigation.

Traditionally, the literature of project management has been preoccupied with project performance as an end state without providing the context, i.e., why projects end up with a budget and schedule overrun or underrun. Our qualitative analysis indicates that when projects actively adopt practices (Tbl. 2) to strengthen their delivery capability, they may achieve a positive efficiency. Except for rigorous project management, the other practices fit within the broader grouping of human factors. This has been pointed out previously by [22]. They studied the success factors in Norwegian public IT projects, and they suggest that "success factors tend to focus on human factors, e.g., involvement, competence and collaboration." In the remainder of this section, we discuss the practices we identified in our study in light of previous literature on the topics and we draw conclusions.

It is interesting to see project managers paying attention to building one team to achieve a positive efficiency. This quality has been accentuated in previous work on many occasions (e.g., [23]). There is significant work available on the topic of building a successful team. Several determinants' have been proposed to build a successful team, such as communication, empowerment, commitment, cohesiveness, etc. The particularity of our finding is the unified team approach adopted by the studied projects. Government IT projects often rely on outsourcing procurement models to deliver the business needs. This usually implies engaging a party outside the public sector to perform services and create products. Sometimes both parties have no prior history of working together. To mitigate the lack of familiarity, project managers can take actions to unify the parties involved to create one team atmosphere to deliver the project. Collaboration does not imply only working closely with the supplier but also engaging and involving the business stakeholders closely. Mohagheghi and Jørgensen report that involving stakeholders was an important success factor in their sample [22].

Our findings show that the projects we investigated experienced uncertainty on the business needs at the time of estimation and planning. Managing requirements uncertainty has received attention from researchers in the software engineering research (e.g., [24]). However, this literature still lacks concrete advice and strategies for project managers to accommodate requirements uncertainty during the budget estimation. For budget estimation at the planning phase, Flyvbjerg and colleagues [7, 14] suggest strategies for accommodating uncertainty by allowing for risk buffers, but there is little empirical evidence about the use of this strategy and its effects. Our data show that these strategies can indeed help to avoid cost overrun. Our finding suggests that project managers may provide an estimate that is more than its actual estimate of completion because they include some allowances for uncertainties of business needs.

The literature on projects failure has pointed out project management issues as a key factor for decades (e.g., [13]). Some of the issues we found in the literature are underestimated timeline, weak definitions of requirements and scope, inefficient risk analysis and management, unsuccessful monitoring and measurement. Our findings show that rigorous project management practices help projects achieve a positive performance, specifically the strong awareness of the need to monitor the budget and be accountable for it.

The importance of knowledge retention and transfer in project-based environment has been emphasized in the literature (e.g., [25]). Knowledge management in IT projects has some challenges; this is mainly because of the one-off nature of the work and the discontinuities in methods of organization and flows of personnel, materials and information [25]. Our findings show that project managers have become aware of this problem. Some of the projects we investigated have taken actions to re-use teams from previous projects within the same organization to capitalize on their accumulated knowledge.

Overall, the analysis of our sample data does not show a gloomy picture of the state of Danish public IT projects' performance. Our descriptive statistics values for both cost overrun and schedule overrun are relatively lower than what has been reported previously in the literature. Our qualitative analysis demonstrates that project managers are actively pursuing the implementation of particular practices to achieve positive efficiency.

There remain interesting questions for future research; for example, how the size of the projects in our sample influenced their performance and what possible performance patterns exist, i.e., the combination of various conditions in favor of a better performance. This study is a first instance with an explorative purpose. In our future work, we envisage investigating some of the abovementioned questions.

Acknowledgements The authors would like to thank the interviewees and their respective organizations for participating in this study. Further, the authors would like to thank the anonymous reviewers for their valuable feedback. Adam Alami and Christian Ø. Madsen are employed by the Research Centre for Government IT, which is a co-funded collaboration between the IT University of Copenhagen and the Danish Ministry for Finance. The ministry has provided the documentation on IT projects, but had no part in defining, guiding or performing the research. The ministry made no textual, editorial, or other contributions to the paper but has received an earlier draft version to correct possible factual errors concerning the ministry and Danish council for ICT.

References

1. Rose, J., Persson, J.S., Heeager, L.T., Irani, Z.: Managing e-Government: value positions and relationships. Inf. Syst. J. **25**, 531–571 (2015). https://doi.org/10.1111/isj.12052
2. Lindgren, I., Madsen, C.Ø., Hofmann, S., Melin, U.: Close encounters of the digital kind: a research agenda for the digitalization of public services. Gov. Inf. Q. (2019). https://doi.org/10.1016/j.giq.2019.03.002
3. Jenner, S.: Transforming Government and Public Services: Realising Benefits Through Project Portfolio Management. CRS Press (2016)
4. Flyvbjerg, B., Budzier, A.: Why your it project may be riskier than you think. Harv. Bus. Rev. **89**, 1–6 (2011). https://doi.org/10.2139/ssrn.2229735
5. Budzier, A.: Theorizing Outliers: Explaining Variation in IT Project Performance. https://ora.ox.ac.uk/objects/uuid:9fd44230-32a0-41f0-861e-4ef999aea22f (2014).
6. Wallace, L., Keil, M., Rai, A.: How software project risk affects project performance: an investigation of the dimensions of risk and an exploratory model. Decis. Sci. **35**, 289–321 (2004)
7. Flyvbjerg, B., Ansar, A., Budzier, A., Buhl, S., Cantarelli, C., Garbuio, M., Glenting, C., Holm, M.S., Lovallo, D., Lunn, D., Molin, E., Rønnest, A., Stewart, A., van Wee, B.: Five things you should know about cost overrun. Transp. Res. Part A Policy Pract. **118**, 174–190 (2018). https://doi.org/10.1016/j.tra.2018.07.013

8. Moløkken, K., Jørgensen, M.: A Review of Surveys on Software Effort Estimation, pp. 223–230 (2003)
9. Jørgensen, M., Moløkken-Østvold, K.: How large are software cost overruns? A review of the 1994 CHAOS report. Inf. Softw. Technol. **48**, 297–301 (2006). https://doi.org/10.1016/j.infsof.2005.07.002
10. Eveleens, J.L., Verhoef, C.: The rise and fall of the Chaos report figures. IEEE Softw. **27**, 30–36 (2010). https://doi.org/10.1109/MS.2009.154
11. Glass, R.L.: The standish report: does it really describe a software crisis? Commun. ACM **49**, 15–16 (2006). https://doi.org/10.1145/1145287.1145301
12. Gauld, R.: Public sector information system project failures: lessons from a New Zealand hospital organization. Gov. Inf. Q. **24**, 102–114 (2007). https://doi.org/10.1016/j.giq.2006.02.010
13. Anthopoulos, L., Reddick, C.G., Giannakidou, I., Mavridis, N.: Why e-government projects fail? An analysis of the Healthcare.gov website. Gov. Inf. Q. 33, 161–173 (2016). https://doi.org/10.1016/j.giq.2015.07.003.
14. Flyvbjerg, B.: Policy and planning for large-infrastructure projects: problems, causes, cures. Environ. Plan. B Plan. Des. **34**, 578–597 (2007). https://doi.org/10.1068/b32111
15. Dongus, K., Ebert, S., Schermann, M., Krcmar, H.: What determines information systems project performance? A narrative review and meta-analysis. Proc. Annu. Hawaii Int. Conf. Syst. Sci. 2015-March, 4483–4492 (2015). https://doi.org/10.1109/HICSS.2015.536
16. Creswell, J.W., Clark, V.L.P.: Designing and Conducting Mixed Methods Research. Sage Publications (2017)
17. Flyvbjerg, B., Holm, M.S., Buhl, S.: Underestimating costs in public works projects: error or lie? J. Am. Plan. Assoc. **68**, 279–295 (2002). https://doi.org/10.1080/01944360208976273
18. Palinkas, L.A., Horwitz, S.M., Green, C.A., Wisdom, J.P., Duan, N., Hoagwood, K.: Purposeful sampling for qualitative data collection and analysis in mixed method implementation research. Adm. Policy Ment. Heal. Ment. Heal. Serv. Res. 42, 533–544 (2015). https://doi.org/10.1007/s10488-013-0528-y
19. Bowen, G.A.: Document analysis as a qualitative research method. Qual. Res. J. **9**, 27–40 (2009). https://doi.org/10.3316/QRJ0902027
20. Braun, V., Clarke, V.: Qualitative research in psychology using thematic analysis in psychology using thematic analysis in psychology. Qual. Res. Psychol. **3**, 77–101 (2006)
21. Majerowicz, W., Shinn, S.A.: Schedule matters: Understanding the relationship between schedule delays and costs on overruns. IEEE Aerosp. Conf. Proc. 2016-June (2016). https://doi.org/10.1109/AERO.2016.7500722
22. Mohagheghi, P., Jørgensen, M.: What contributes to the success of IT projects ? An empirical study of IT projects in the Norwegian public sector. J. Softw. 12, 751–758 (2017). https://doi.org/10.17706/jsw.12.9.751-758.
23. Jetu, F.T., Riedl, R.: Determinants of information systems and information technology project team success: a literature review and a conceptual model. Commun. Assoc. Inf. Syst. 30, (2012). https://doi.org/10.17705/1cais.03027
24. Sillitti, A., Ceschi, M., Russo, B., Succi, G.: Managing uncertainty in requirements: a survey in documentation-driven and Agile companies. Proc. Int. Softw. Metrics Symp. **2005**, 10–17 (2005). https://doi.org/10.1109/METRICS.2005.29
25. Bresnen, M., Edelman, L., Newell, S., Scarbrough, H., Swan, J.: Social practices and the management of knowledge in project environments. Int. J. Proj. Manag. **21**, 157–166 (2003). https://doi.org/10.1016/S0263-7863(02)00090-X

Heat Maps from Decision Flaps—What We See and What We Think

Chris Barry, Mairéad Hogan, and Michael Lang

Abstract This research study observes how consumers are influenced by the design of decision constructs encountered during the online transactional process. The default values of decision constructs and how decisions are framed, set out the scope of the analysis. A multi-method approach is taken to examine error rates and attitudes of users when making micro-decisions. Eye tracking technology and Cued RTA interviews were used to gather both quantitative and qualitative data. Powerful techniques, namely heat maps and gaze plots, are used to visualise and inform the discussion. The study found: choice errors abound; consumers dither and vacillate during decision-making, extending dwell times; and that there are gender differences in outcomes.

Keywords IS design · Consumer choice · Eye tracking · Heat maps · Gaze plots

1 Introduction

In the short history of online retailing, there have been many cases of firms using unfair practices in respect of the presentation and design of optional extras in commercial transactions. The European Union has had to introduce legislation to regulate such practices [1]. Specifically, they have said that all optional extras must be communicated in a "clear, transparent and unambiguous way" and that they should only be accepted by the consumer on an 'opt-in' basis. There should, therefore, be an

A prior version of this paper has been published in the ISD2021 Proceedings (http://aisel.aisnet.org/isd2014/proceedings2021).

C. Barry (✉) · M. Hogan · M. Lang
National University of Ireland Galway, Galway, Ireland
e-mail: chris.barry@nuigalway.ie

M. Hogan
e-mail: mairead.hogan@nuigalway.ie

M. Lang
e-mail: michael.lang@nuigalway.ie

E. Insfran Pelozo et al. (eds.), *Advances in Information Systems Development*, Lecture Notes in Information Systems and Organisation 55,
https://doi.org/10.1007/978-3-030-95354-6_8

expectation amongst online consumers that to receive a proffered option *requires* an action.

Despite the legislation and guidance directed at 'micro-decisions' along the Business-to-Consumer (B2C) transactional process, many such decisions like purchasing insurance or speedier delivery have become time-consuming, complicated and ambiguous to users [2, 3]. The stop-start nature of online purchasing has now turned into a stressful journey as consumers flap and stutter, impatiently, towards choice.

This paper attempts to re-create and explore something of the problematic nature of consumer decision-making. In doing so it is hoped to answer questions about the influence of default values set by firms for consumer choice and the impact of how decision text wording is framed.

2 Background to the Study

2.1 Decision Constructs in the Transactional Process

Previous research by the authors into the B2C transactional process identified a taxonomy of decision constructs that can be presented to users making micro-decisions in everyday interactions [4]. Some of the construct types are straightforward and easily navigated, while others, such as the various designs of opt-out, can, due to a lack of clarity, lead to confusion and errors. This may be a result of the language used or other design elements of the construct. The main areas of confusion are in the framing of the text or in the default value for the construct (e.g. a pre-ticked or unticked checkbox). Both framing and the default value of the construct have been shown to influence user performance [4, 5].

2.2 Eye Tracking Visualisation

Eye tracking allows a researcher to follow a user's visual interaction with a stimulus and to, in effect, see what they see. Our eyes are constantly moving in order to gather useful information from within our visual field. Information is absorbed and sent to our brain for processing when our eyes stop and focus on something, known as a 'fixation'. The paths between these fixations are known as 'saccades'. In contrast to fixations, no information is processed during a saccade. Eye tracking records the order, position and duration of the fixations and the saccades between them [6]. The accumulated duration of fixations is known as user 'dwell time' and is widely used in the findings below in Sect. 5 to analyse aspects of participant interactions.

The sheer volume of data in a visual interaction makes it difficult to grasp the pattern of eye movements. Therefore, graphical representations of users' visual paths are useful in order to see the big picture. Two commonly used visualisations of the viewer's pattern of attention on a screen are heat maps and gaze plots [6–9].

Heat maps are colour-coded visual representations of the number of fixations, or the summed duration of those fixations, on different areas of a screen [8]. Red is generally used to indicate areas with high numbers, or duration, of fixations, while green indicates low numbers or duration. Areas without colour indicate the viewer may not have fixated on the area. Lack of colour does not necessarily mean the viewer did not see the area, as a peripheral viewing may not have been detected by the eye tracker. Heat maps provide effective, visual summaries of large volumes of data that would be difficult to grasp if presented numerically [10]. They show us what the viewer looked at, as well as how intensely they focussed on different areas of the stimulus [6, 9]. They are also useful tools to compare how different users view a stimulus or how a user views different stimuli [6].

When using heat maps, it is important to choose the right type, and to provide adequate information, to ensure the reader understands what they represent [10]. The most common types of heat maps use the duration of fixations, where the colours indicate summed duration of fixations, or fixation count, where differing colours indicate relative numbers of fixations, regardless of duration. They can also show duration density which illustrates duration as a percentage of trial duration; or count density, which illustrates count as a percentage of the total trial count. Heat maps can depict a single user's interaction or an aggregated view showing multiple users' interactions.

Gaze plots show the fixations and saccades over a specific time period. Dots are generally used to indicate fixations, while lines are used to indicate saccades moving from one fixation to the next [6, 8]. The size of the dot, like bubbles on a bubble chart, indicates the relative duration of the fixation. Gaze plots clearly demonstrate the visual path followed by the viewer, illustrating where the viewer directed their attention, as well the sequence in which these periods of focus occurred [6].

Both approaches add value but, as with all tools, have limitations. Gaze plots can become cluttered when there are a large number of fixations or when tracking multiple viewers, while heat maps do not show the order of the fixations [6, 7].

3 The Research Approach

This study forms part of a larger body of research examining cognitive load and information processing when interacting with micro-decisions in the B2C transactional process. It was designed to target experienced online consumers with knowledge of information systems design and development. Such candidates were, by selection, controlled for deficiencies in application knowledge, technology acuity and educational attainment. The research experiment data were collected from a convenience sample of 114 participants in 456 experiment trials. The participants were all post-graduate students taking IT-related programmes, had significant computing experience as online consumers, and worked on PC, tablet and phone platforms. The

Table 1 Opt-out decision constructs

Decision construct name	Construct type code	Default value	Framing
Un-Selected Rejection	USR	Un-selected	Rejection
Pre-Selected Rejection	PSR	Pre-selected	Rejection
Pre-Selected Neutral	PSN	Pre-selected	Neutral
Pre-Selected Acceptance	PSA	Pre-selected	Acceptance

study was made up of three dimensions: an eye tracking experiment; self-assessment evaluations (subjective cognitive load); and Cued Retrospective Think-Aloud (RTA) sessions. The Cued RTA sessions were conducted with 23 participants.

This paper focuses on a high-level analysis of the data from the 23 Cued RTA participants who took part in the experiment examining opt-out decision constructs. Table 2 identifies the four types or 'variants' of opt-outs. They are distinguished in two respects: the default value (whether the checkbox is pre-selected or un-selected) and how the decision is framed. The framing may be acceptance framing (e.g. 'I want…'), rejection framing (e.g. 'I don't want…'), or neutral framing (i.e. 'Rescue Plus') which is a simple statement of the product name. All variants of opt-out decisions were examined: Un-Selected Rejection framing; Pre-Selected Rejection framing; Pre-Selected Neutral framing; and Pre-Selected Acceptance framing (see Table 1).

This research experiment captured a mixture of qualitative and quantitative data. Much of the quantitative data was captured using eye tracking equipment and consisted of the number of eye fixations, saccades and dwell times (i.e. the summed duration of fixations). This data indicated where, for how long and in what order, the participant examined the screens presented to them. Direct measurement was also

Table 2 Decision constructs presented to participants

Construct type	Example of decision constructs as used in this trial	
USR	☐	Rescue Plus includes free car hire and travel expenses. If you would rather not purchase Rescue Plus, please tick this box
PSR	☑	Rescue Plus includes free car hire and travel expenses. If you would rather not purchase Rescue Plus, please untick this box
PSN	☑	Rescue Plus
PSA	☑	Rescue Plus includes free car hire and travel expenses. I want to purchase Rescue Plus

used to determine the accuracy of participant choice and was a critical appraisal of the individual's performance.

Qualitative, subjective data was gathered using Cued RTA sessions. In this approach to think-aloud, the participant articulates their thoughts and feelings while watching a recording of the interaction [11]. This approach is most appropriate for use with eye tracking because it does not impact on visual fixations [12] and task performance [13].

Additionally, heat maps and gaze plots were used to gain a 'big picture' view of the participants' interaction with the decision constructs. Following the guidance of Bojko [10], they were used for data visualisation. The maps used were chosen to show fixation duration rather than fixation count, as, according to Wang, Yang et al. [14], duration heat maps show where high levels of cognitive processing take place.

4 Experiment Set-Up

Participants were advised that they would be presented with four mock-up screens of webpages of consumer decisions, that each screen would have a decision point and that they would be told what to decide: i.e., whether to Buy or Don't Buy the optional product.

For each screen in each case, the decision text had a checkbox beside it. Participants were asked to examine the text of the decision and decide whether to leave the checkbox as is, or to change it. Once participants had made that decision, they clicked on the appropriate button (named Change Checkbox or Leave Checkbox) in the bar shown in Fig. 1. The order of the four screens was randomized and each participant received an equal number of Buy or Don't Buy instructions.

A timer was set from the start of the experiment and participants were advised of the parameters of the trial. They were particularly advised that as each decision screen was presented to them, to work at their normal pace, not to feel under pressure to complete it quickly or to over-analyse, and to look at, and read, whatever information they normally would digest to make the decision.

5 Findings and Analysis

5.1 Participant Decision Performance

Measuring how well consumers performed during an online interaction was an important assessment of the ease with which the purchase of an optional extra could be completed. Thus, the most essential assessment of a participant's interaction was:

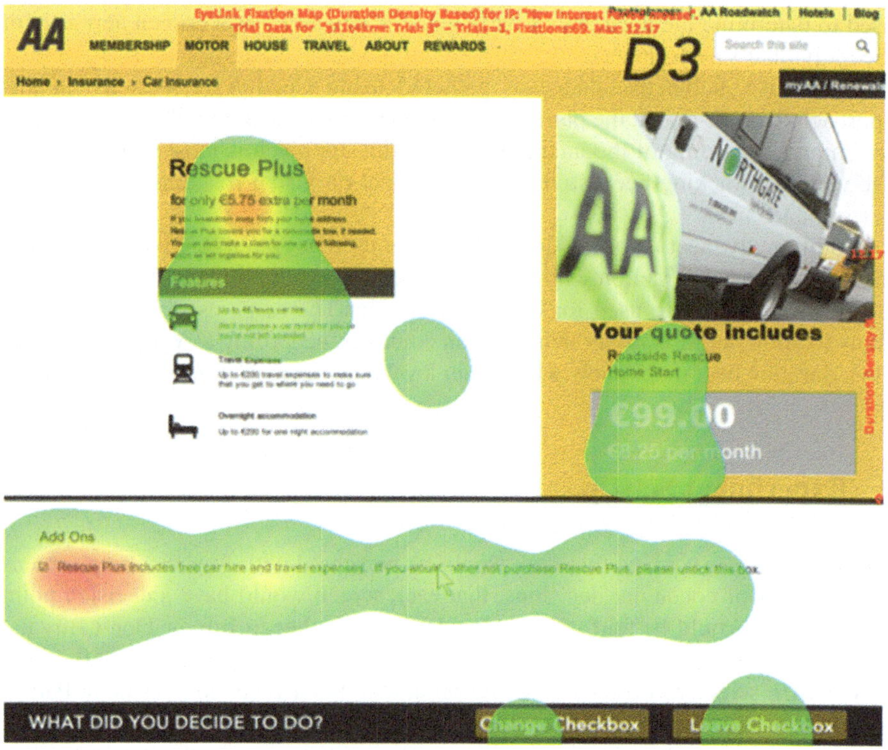

Fig. 1 An interaction typifying the worst decision-makers

did they make the correct decision? This data was captured at the end of each decision construct when participants signalled whether they would change or leave the checkbox.

The overall error rate from the study was 26% (see Table 3). That one in four intended micro-decisions made in an online transactional process could be wrong is an alarming finding. This phenomenon, and the variability in error rate between

Table 3 Error rate for construct types

Construct type	Correct	Incorrect	Total
Un-selected Rejection—USR	72 (63%)	42 (37%)	114
Pre-selected Rejection—PSR	86 (75%)	28 (25%)	114
Pre-selected Neutral—PSN	87 (76%)	27 (24%)	114
Pre-selected Acceptance—PSA	94 (82%)	20 (18%)	114
Overall	339 (74%)	117 (26%)	456

decision constructs, is laid out and discussed in previously published work [15]. The key differences in error rates between construct types are shown in Table 3.

Statistically significant differences were found in error rates depending on whether the response was pre-selected and how it was framed, i.e., as a rejection, as an acceptance or neutrally. Decisions that were presented with un-selected rejection framing (USR) resulted in a 37% error rate, while those presented with pre-selected acceptance framing (PSA) resulted in 18% incorrect selections. Thus, it was concluded that the type of decision construct a user is shown significantly influences decision performance [16]. The overall error rates for the Cued RTA participants follow a similar pattern to all participants in the study.

5.2 *Interaction Time for Cued RTA Participants*

Construct Type Dwell Times

A key part of this study was to capture and analyse the temporal dimensions of the experiment for each participant. Times were recorded for every aspect of the experiment. Reported and discussed here are times for each of the four decisions completed by each participant (called a 'trial'), and the times spent looking at a specific area of the screen (called an 'interest area', IA). Table 4 lays out these times (IA_DWELL_TIME and TRIAL_DWELL_TIME) for each decision construct for Cued RTA participants. IA_DWELL_TIME is the sum of the durations of all fixations in the interest area. TRIAL_DWELL_TIME is the sum of the duration of all fixations from the start of the interaction to the end. IA_DWELL_TIME_% is the dwell time for the interest area expressed as a percentage of the dwell time for the full interaction from start to finish. The decision constructs, from USR to PSA, are laid out broadly in order of the complexity of each construct, from most to least. The IA_DWELL_TIME_% is a particularly useful measure of how much time was directed at the main interest area of the screen.

Reflecting on the nature of micro-decisions during online transactional interactions, reveals many are short and dealt with quickly by consumers. The average dwell time participants spent on each decision was 12.38 s. However, as can be seen in

Table 4 Construct type interest area and trial dwell times for Cued RTA participants

	IA_DWELL_TIME	TRIAL_DWELL_TIME	IA_DWELL_TIME_%
Construct type	Mean (ms)	Mean (ms)	Mean (%)
USR	8407	14,079	61
PSR	8955	14,750	63
PSN	3057	9938	38
PSA	5260	10,740	54
Overall	6420	12,377	54

Table 5 Construct type dwell times by gender for Cued RTA participants

Gender	Construct type	IA_DWELL_TIME	TRIAL_DWELL_TIME	IA_DWELL_TIME_% (%)
Female	*USR*	7633	11,480	68
	PSR	10,537	13,529	78
	PSN	2788	6433	45
	PSA	4810	8014	61
	Overall	6442	9864	63
Male	*USR*	9457	15,232	58
	PSR	10,545	17,639	62
	PSN	3111	12,024	33
	PSA	5738	11,614	53
	Overall	7213	14,127	51

Table 4, considerable variation in dwell times were observed depending on the decision construct type, with PSR and USR being considerably longer than the other two. Table 5 lays out the breakdown of dwell times by gender, discussed in later sections.

When participant dwell times are examined by construct type and within dwell time bands, interesting clusters emerge. Table 6 illustrates that the more problematic and complex decisions (USR and PSR) take much longer to complete for the decision-makers. Conversely, the less difficult constructs (PSN and PSA) were completed more quickly. Table 6 also shows that there are many cases of long dwell times, more fully discussed later in the analysis.

Cued RTA Best Versus Worst Decision-Makers

A useful lens of analysis can be used in looking at the interaction activity of cohorts of the best and worst decision-makers. The best decision-makers are expressed as those choosing the correct option across all four decision constructs when instructed to purchase or not purchase the Add On product (of which there were eight participants). Conversely, the worst decision-makers were those choosing the incorrect option in two or three decision construct cases when instructed to purchase or not purchase the Add On product (of which there were four participants).

Table 6 Construct type by dwell times bands for Cued RTA participants

	Band (in ms)			
Construct type	<10,001	10,001–15,000	15,001–20,000	> 20,000
USR	9	5	4	5
PSR	8	5	3	7
PSN	14	6	1	2
PSA	13	7	0	3

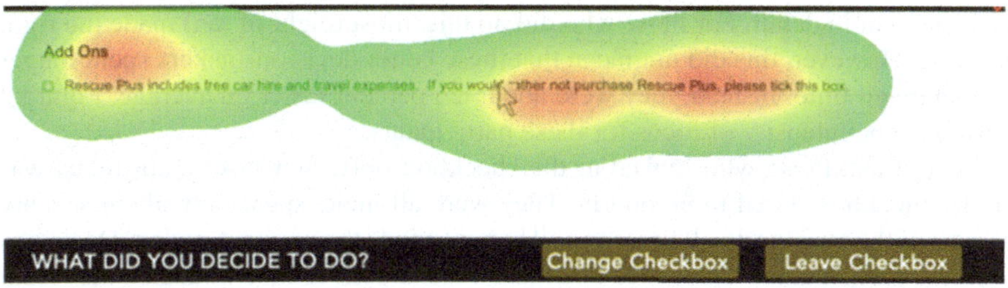

Fig. 2 Typical USR heat map for a strong gaze concentration (Add On interest area)

Dwell times were almost twice as long for the worst decision-makers than those of the best. Their times were characterised by more prevarication and a distracting focus on less relevant parts of the screen, such as detailed features of the Add On. Such an interaction is typified in Fig. 1. The best decision-makers were more focused on the Add On interest area, typified by a heat map in Fig. 2. Of the eight best decision-makers, six were female and two were male. All four of the worst decision-makers were male.

5.3 *Interaction Heat Maps for Cued RTA Participants*

As outlined previously, heat maps are a powerful technique in presenting aggregated analysis of participant fixations and gaze concentration. They may be rendered for all participants cumulatively or produced for individual participants. The heat maps reveal deep and significant insights into the short, but intense, process of participant decision-making immediately prior to choice. A series of heat maps were prepared for each individual Cued RTA participant's interaction with all four constructs and are presented and discussed below.

Heat Map Analysis—Un-Selected Rejection (USR) Construct

The USR construct is complex. The interest area contains three elements: the checkbox and two sentences (see Table 2). The checkbox is unticked and, based on comments from participants, appears to suggest to consumers that an option should require action. For example, "Why would I make a decision to choose Rescue Plus?" or "I would have to change the box to not get the add on!".

The first sentence, whilst not particularly complex, requires no action. It is merely informative and seemingly superfluous given a detailed description elsewhere on the page. It is the second sentence that explains the real function of the checkbox. If the participant does not want to buy Rescue Plus, they must return to the checkbox and tick it.

The complexity of the decision, in terms of its framing and default value (un-selected), means it should attract a comprehensive perusal of the checkbox and the second sentence, which in turn should compel participants to study and re-study each element in detail. For those who did do this, most (eight of ten) made the right decision. However, this did not mean that these better decision-makers spent longer in total dwell time. Instead, they were about ten percent faster on average. Figure 2 illustrates the intensity of focus for these participants.

In contrast, those who looked at the checkbox only, or whose main focus was on the checkbox, fared more poorly. They were all male, spent only about seventy percent of the average dwell time, and all bar one made the wrong decision. Decisions for these participants were rushed and inaccurate and most likely made on the visual appearance of the checkbox. Their interaction is typified by Fig. 3.

Others looked heavily at areas of the screen outside the interactive area and, while these areas provided information about the product offered for purchase, they did not provide any information that would help the user to decide whether to tick the checkbox or leave it as is. These individuals were mostly male (five of six), had longer dwell times and made mostly incorrect decisions. It is indicative that they were unrushed but perhaps slower to focus on the more critical task at hand.

Only three participants paid scant or no attention to the checkbox and sentences. All were male, two of whom made an incorrect choice. While all participants bar these three spent most time looking at the interest area, some participants focused their attention mainly on the sentences and in particular (or at least equally), the second sentence. These, in the view of the researchers, were the most diligent and, in outcome, the most successful.

The concentration on the buttons to leave or change the checkbox would naturally come towards the end of the interaction. While it is difficult to assign intent at this juncture, it might be expected that there would be a more concentrated focus amongst decision-makers on the button of choice, with more divided attention by those who were less sure which action to take. Of those who focused mainly on the relevant button, most made correct decisions and were representative in terms of gender. Of those whose focus was equally divided between the two buttons, half made an incorrect choice.

Heat Map Analysis—Pre-Selected Rejection (PSR) Construct

The PSR construct, on the face of it, may appear less complex than the USR since its checkbox is ticked (see the wording in Table 2 earlier). However, this is not borne out

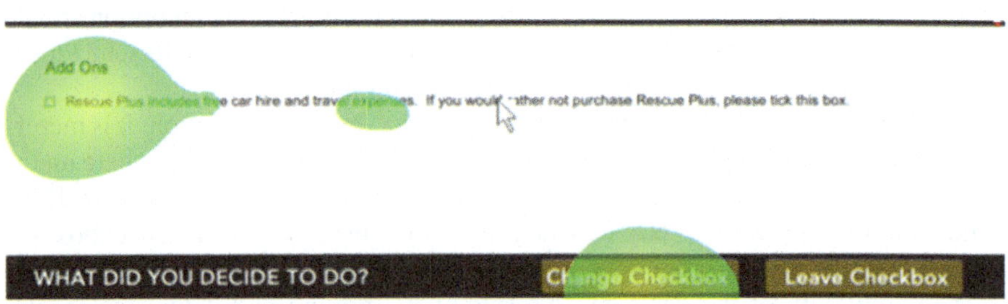

Fig. 3 Typical USR for a weak gaze concentration (Add On interest area)

Table 7 Mean dwell times for interest areas sentence 1 and 2

	IA_DWELL_TIME	
	Mean (ms)	
Construct type	Sentence 1	Sentence 2
USR	2935	4028
PSR	3073	4596
PSN	1861	–
PSA	2836	1595

in dwell times. The dwell times for PSR, as shown in Table 7, are the highest across all decision constructs for both sentences. Navigating the second sentence demands particular user vigilance—to *not* receive the option, users must *untick* the checkbox. Each of these is a form of negation and requires even more consideration for PSR than for other constructs.

Examining error rates for Cued RTA participants interacting with the PSR construct, a number of observations emerge. More so than in the case of USR, participants spent significant effort directing their focus across the PSR interest area. In the case of females, six of seven produced a solid intensity of gaze in trying to more fully understand the construct checkbox and sentences, and all made the correct decision. Most males also made solid efforts to peruse the interest area but more mistakes were made. Of those who made errors, it was possible to discern either a distracting focus on features elsewhere or considerable deliberation around the leave or change buttons.

A gaze path map for a typical PSR participant is very revealing (see Fig. 4). At a glance it shows green circles representing fixations and green lines representing saccades. The cumulative build of the gaze path across all fixations and their proximate location on the screen generates a heat map, across the total duration of a trial. In this case, it shows pronounced gaze concentration in many areas of the screen: the option features in the middle of the screen, across the interest area (checkbox, sentence 1 and sentence 2) and between the change or leave button.

Heat Map Analysis—Pre-selected Neutral (PSN) Construct

Dwell times for the PSN was significantly lower than for USR or PSR constructs. That this suggests a more easily understood construct is debatable. Firstly, there is only one sentence as part of the interest area text—'Rescue Plus' (see Table 2 earlier). Secondly, the two-word 'instruction' is no more than a declarative statement and not an instruction at all. Thus, the heat maps show greater deviation to feature text that more fully describes Rescue Plus. That participants are thrown by the neutrally-framed construct is borne out by Cued RTA transcripts where participants report seeking confirmatory signals for their interpretation of the construct.

The average dwell time of the single sentence text of 1861 ms is markedly lower than for other constructs, see Fig. 5 for a typical example. However, this belies the complexity of the construct and the 24% error rate which matches PSR. In evidence

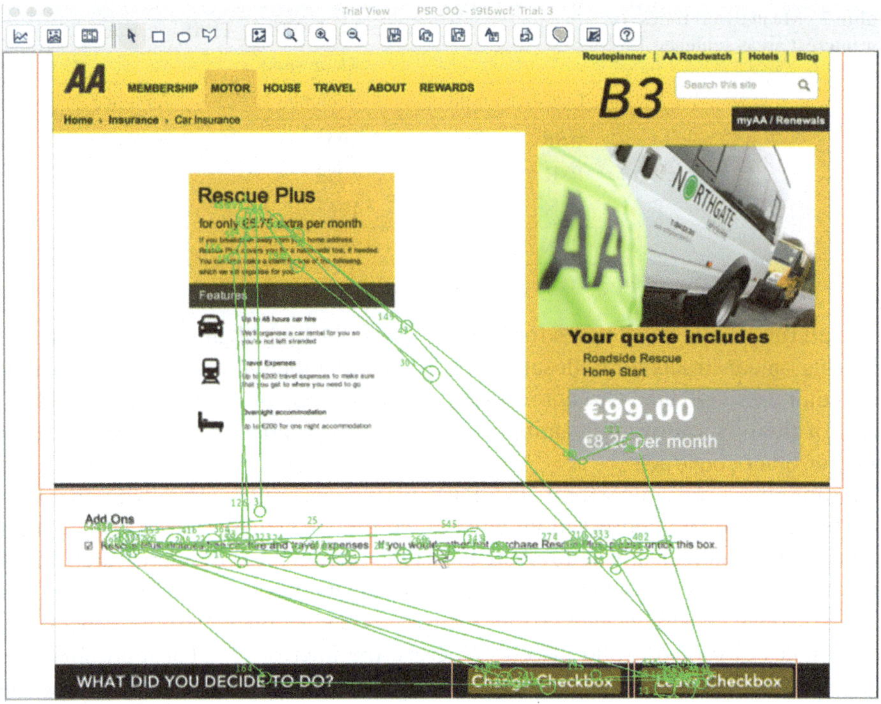

Fig. 4 Gaze plot of a typical PSR participant

Fig. 5 Typical PSN heat map

of the dwell intensity, the number of fixations (45) for two words is equal to the PSA construct and within range of the others (58–67).

That no females featured amongst the incorrect decision-makers may be explained by a general over-confidence amongst males in self-assessment evaluation carried out during trials and noted in Cued RTA recordings. The latter revealed a clash of views in responses on errors. Some liked the conciseness of the construct and thought its clarity would help avoid mistakes. Others believed errors were more likely to occur due to the very brevity of the instruction—the neutrality of the construct itself puzzling. For those, checkbox pre-selection added confusion. Thus, in the absence of instruction, errors occurred from the assumed belief that to receive an option, an action is required. Without such guidance, some participants erroneously unticked the checkbox.

Heat Map Analysis—Pre-selected Acceptance (PSA) Construct

The PSA decision construct attracted the most benign and least negative response, evidenced in the Cued RTAs and self-assessment evaluations. The experience of participants elicited unusually positive comments such as "This was a lot easier…" and "This makes more sense". The clarity of the instruction in the second sentence—'I want to purchase Rescue Plus'—meant that participants spent only about one third of the time deliberating over the second sentence than for USR and PSR. The remaining dwell time was divided around the checkbox and reading feature details of the option. The gaze activity is captured in a sample screen in Fig. 6.

Many of the participants felt the PSA pre-selected checkbox reinforced the positive declarative nature of the second sentence. For the other pre-selected checkboxes, this did not appear to be case. While the PSA construct had the lowest error rate (18%), errors arose from a predisposed belief that action was required to purchase,

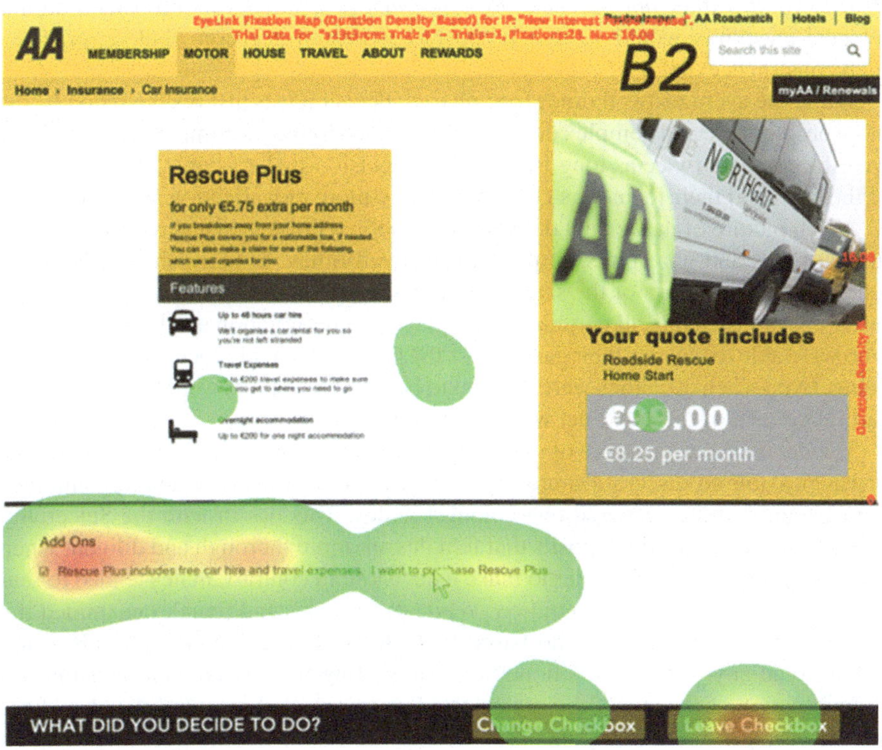

Fig. 6 PSA heat map of typical gaze activity

leading some to change the checkbox. The heat maps of these participants show some distraction with feature text, as they try to make sense of their confusion.

6 Conclusions

This study set out to test the ability of consumers to make multiple micro-decisions under laboratory conditions that were goal-oriented and time-constrained. They were placed under some pressure to make the sort of decisions that they all encounter routinely in online purchasing activities. The time-related data captured was microscopic and in millisecond detail. It made it possible to carefully assess decision performance, visual acuity and gaze patterns.

In the rush of so many non-linear information streams, participants struggled in their sensemaking. Mistakes were made in a seemingly straight-forward transactional context i.e. "do you want to buy this optional extra when buying car insurance?" Differing combinations of the default value of a simple checkbox and the framing of a question contributed to a shockingly-high error rate of more than one in four decisions. For the Un-Selected Rejection (USR) construct, to couple such a sentence (*If you would rather not purchase Rescue Plus, please tick this box*) with an unselected checkbox would seem a preposterous design decision—but, in practice, such constructs exist!

While the average dwell time spent on each decision was just twelve seconds, the more problematic and complex decisions took much longer to complete. Dwell times were found to be twice as long for the worst decision-makers compared with those of the best, and their focus was characterised by more prevarication and distraction.

A rich picture of participant deliberation emerged through visual representations, in heat maps and gaze plots, of participant dwell times. Broadly, those who spent longer examining parts of the screen more relevant to the decision made better and faster decisions. While all participants displayed some agitation and hesitancy, those who were able to balance their gaze across the page and quickly focus on choice fared better. Even when decisions were thought to be more straightforward by participants, careful perusal of the construct was required to avoid errors.

The decision performance of males versus females is notable within the findings. It was possible to discern a more deliberated pattern of decision making amongst females and a more scattered one amongst males. This ties in with the Selectivity Hypothesis [17–19], which posits that females are more thorough and diligent when processing information in order to make a decision. In contrast, males tended to rely on single, obvious cues and intuition. While most males and females examined the full text, it was only males who based their decision solely on the checkbox and did not read any of the instructional text, suggesting they based their decisions on a combination of the cue of the pre-selected or un-selected nature of the checkbox, and an intuitive belief as to what that meant, rather than a considered examination of the information available to them.

Much of the confusion around optionality was crystalised by one participant who, when looking at a USR decision construct, exclaimed it's "weird if you left a box unchecked you'd get something". Given the EU directives on optionality and societal ethical expectations of commercial online retailers, consumers should not have this to say. It is time for more rigorous enforcement of the regulations.

7 Further Data Analysis and Research

Participants' activity in choosing whether to purchase an optional extra in the study echoes the process of satisficing and heuristics in decision-making [3, 20]. Patterns of scanning and non-sequential deliberation identified in this study and visualised via gaze plots characterised participant activity. Matching and mapping this behaviour with appropriate decision-making models would merit a novel use of the data captured in this research.

Interesting findings regarding gender differences in engagement patterns warrant further analysis. This study focused on a mainly qualitative examination of the interactions of a small number of participants. Heat maps and gaze plots were used to provide 'big picture' visualisation of participants interactions. They supported the Selectivity Hypothesis showing differences in how males and females process information. A more detailed analysis, incorporating quantitative and qualitative dimensions, will be carried out to determine the impact of these differences on user performance.

References

1. European Union: Directive 2011/83/Eu of the European Parliament and of the Council of 25 October 2011 on Consumer Rights (2011)
2. Barry, C., Hogan, M., Torres, A.M.: Low-cost carriers and high-tech barriers—user views on questionable web design practices in Ireland. Ir. J. Manag. **31**(1), 43–58 (2011)
3. Bobadilla-Suarez, S., Love, B.C.: Fast or frugal, but not both: decision heuristics under time pressure. J. Exp. Psychol. Learn. Mem. Cogn. **44**(1), 24 (2017)
4. Hogan, M., Barry, C., Torres, A.M.: Theorising and testing a taxonomy of decision constructs. J. Cust. Behav. **13**(3), 171–185 (2014)
5. Lai, Y.-L., Hui, K.-L.: Internet opt-in and opt-out: investigating the roles of frames, defaults and privacy concerns. In: Proceedings of the 2006 ACM SIGMIS CPR Conference on Computer Personnel Research: Forty Four Years of Computer Personnel Research: Achievements, Challenges & the Future, pp. 253–263. ACM, Claremount, California, USA (2006)
6. Djamasbi, S.: Eye tracking and web experience. AIS Trans. Human-Comput. Interact. **6**(2), 37–54 (2014)
7. Raschke, M., Blascheck, T., Burch, M.: Visual analysis of eye tracking data. In: Huang, W. (eds.) Handbook of Human Centric Visualization (2014)
8. Schall, A., Romano Bergstrom, J.: Introduction to eye tracking. In: Bergstrom, J.R., Schall, A.J. (eds.) Eye Tracking in User Experience Design, pp. 3–26 (2014)
9. Wong, W., Bartels, M., Chrobot, N.: E-commerce websites. In: Bergstrom, J.R., Schall, A.J. (eds.) Eye Tracking in User Experience Design, pp. 187–216 (2014)

10. Bojko, A.A.: Informative or misleading? Heatmaps deconstructed. In: Jacko, J.A. (ed.) Human-Computer Interaction, pp 30–39. New Trends, Springer, Berlin, Germany (2009)
11. Ball, L.J., Eger, N., Stevens, R., Dodd, J.: Applying the peep method in usability testing. Interfaces **67**, 15–19 (2006)
12. Kim, B., Dong, Y., Kim, S., Lee, K.-P.: Development of integrated analysis system and tool of perception, recognition, and behavior for web usability test: with emphasis on eye-tracking, mouse-tracking, and retrospective think aloud. In: Usability and Internationalization. Hci and Culture, pp. 113–121. Springer, Berlin Heidelberg (2007)
13. van den Haak, M., de Jong, M., Jan Schellens, P.: Retrospective vs. concurrent think-aloud protocols: testing the usability of an online library catalogue. Behav. Inf. Technol. **22**(5), 339–351 (2003)
14. Wang, Q., Yang, S., Liu, M., Cao, Z., Ma, Q.: An eye-tracking study of website complexity from cognitive load perspective. Decis. Support Syst. **62**, 1–10 (2014)
15. Hogan, M., Barry, C.: Turning up the heat—user errors and other insights into option selection. IADIS Int. J. WWW/Internet **17**(2), 119–135 (2019)
16. Barry, C., Hogan, M.: Watching people making decisions: a gogglebox on online consumer interaction. In: 28th International Conference on Information Systems Development (ISD2019), Toulon, France (2019)
17. Meyers-Levy, J.: The influence of sex roles on judgment. J. Consum. Res. **14**(4), 522–530 (1988)
18. Meyers-Levy, J., Loken, B.: Revisiting gender differences: what we know and what lies ahead. J. Consum. Psychol. **25**(1), 129–149 (2015)
19. Meyers-Levy, J., Maheswaran, D.: Exploring differences in males' and females' processing strategies. J. Consum. Res. **18**(1), 63–70 (1991)
20. Newell, B.R., Rakow, T., Weston, N.J., Shanks, D.R.: Search strategies in decision making: the success of "Success." J. Behav. Decis. Mak. **17**(2), 117–137 (2004)

Modeling Boundary-Spanning Business Processes in Industry 4.0: Incorporating Risk-Based Design

Vítor Ribeiro, João Barata, and Paulo Rupino da Cunha

Abstract Industry 4.0 brings new challenges to the digitalization and decentralization of business processes. This paper contributes with a Business Process Modeling and Notation (BPMN) Extension that addresses the inter-organizational nature of the fourth industrial revolution and the need to address risk-by-design since the early stages of industrial collaboration. The proposal results from two design science research cycles. The extension named IOBP 4.0 provides an integrated description of (1) private/shared process elements, (2) local/distributed manufacturing stages, (3) technology incorporation strategy in the production network, and (4) risk situations. IOBP 4.0 can be useful for companies certified by the ISO 9001 quality standard that need to disclose their processes and third-party collaborations, following a risk-based approach. Moreover, incorporating risk-based process design in Industry 4.0 may improve business process resilience in manufacturing networks.

Keywords Industry 4.0 · Inter-organizational business process · Risk-based thinking · BPMN · Extension · Business process management

1 Introduction

Digital transformation requires a new logic for risk-aware business process management (BPM). The work of [1] highlights three emerging BPM priorities, namely, agile and more configurable "light touch routines," infrastructure flexibility (e.g.,

---

A prior version of this paper has been published in the ISD2021 Proceedings (http://aisel.aisnet.org/isd2014/proceedings2021).

V. Ribeiro (✉) · J. Barata · P. R. da Cunha
University of Coimbra, CISUC, Coimbra, DEI, Portugal
e-mail: vhribeiro@dei.uc.pt

J. Barata
e-mail: barata@dei.uc.pt

P. R. da Cunha
e-mail: rupino@dei.uc.pt

E. Insfran Pelozo et al. (eds.), *Advances in Information Systems Development*, Lecture Notes in Information Systems and Organisation 55,
https://doi.org/10.1007/978-3-030-95354-6_9

increasing adoption of the Internet-of-Things (IoT)), and mindful actors more prepared to make decisions in different parts of the process. Industry 4.0, the high-tech strategy introduced by the German government, is a paradigmatic example of digital transformation [2]. Manufacturing processes now rely on IoT, mobile systems, or artificial intelligence techniques to improve production flows [3]. However, modeling business processes in Industry 4.0 is challenging, requiring new approaches to represent how digitalized companies are changing their operations [4] and the possible risks involved.

Risks are a key topic in the information systems (IS) research agenda, entangled in BPM activities [5]. For the last years, the importance of risk management has grown, due to several reasons, such as (1) customer requirements; (2) regulatory pressure; (3) public image; and (4) management attitudes that are becoming more professional in integrating risks in their strategies, planning, and operations [6]. Furthermore, risk-based thinking is also a priority for modern quality management standards like ISO 9001, suggesting a process approach to management. Therefore, incorporating risks in business process models is crucial.

The new BPM logic is also extensible to the supply chain. On the one hand, creating a technological infrastructure to decentralize production provides visibility to product flows since the early stages of sourcing raw materials for product use. On the other hand, requiring more "*effectiveness of communication between actors and favoring data collection and sharing*" [7]. As a result, processes are becoming increasingly "inter-organizational," distributed, and agile, but also more challenging to manage with traditional modeling languages, such as Business Process Modeling and Notation (BPMN) [8]. For example, BPMN cannot represent all the details of Inter-Organizational Business Processes (IOBP) [8] since it lacks the semantics to describe the dependencies of the global control flow of the message exchange [9]. Additional problems are the absence of formal specification of process interfaces and support for alignment with multiple partners. Furthermore, capturing all the information required to audit risks [10] is more difficult in decentralized manufacturing contexts. However, the original BPMN cannot represent potential points of error, formal specification of risks, risk categories, risk likelihood, and impact on the process [11].

Aiming to advance the new BPM logic [1] in Industry 4.0, we conducted a design science research project in cooperation with companies in technical coatings (e.g., thermal spraying, plasma, or electrodeposition of advanced materials) and paper pulp production (e.g., eucalyptus pulp production, bioelectric energy production, forest management). This paper details the second design science research (DSR) cycle in a leading European producer in the pulp sector, being one of the most efficient producers in Europe of bleached eucalyptus pulp. Additionally, the company produces electricity from forest biomass, having several power plants. Our overall research objective at this stage was to create a BPMN extension to model inter-organizational business processes for Industry 4.0 adoption (IOBP 4.0), incorporating risk-based thinking in the process models.

The remainder of this paper is structured as follows. Section 2 presents foundational literature in Industry 4.0, IOBP, BPMN, risks and other related work. We detail the research approach in Sect. 3, and the results follow in Sect. 4. Subsequently, we demonstrate (Sect. 5) and evaluate (Sect. 6) the adoption of IOBP 4.0 in a real-world setting. The paper closes by stating conclusions, the main limitations, and future work opportunities.

2 Background

2.1 Industry 4.0

Industry 4.0 started a new digital transformation era by adopting cyber-physical systems (CPS) [12]. This global change is supported by cloud technologies and the Internet [2], integrating physical assets (e.g., machines, components) and "cyber" capabilities to improve real-time monitoring and control of advanced production processes [13].

Industry 4.0 enables companies to have more flexible manufacturing processes and analyze data in real-time, improving operational decision-making and strategic planning [2]. However, instead of being restricted to internal operations, Industry 4.0 is a boundary-spanning phenomenon that needs external information and more complex relationships with business partners. Digital transformation also extends to the redesign, coordination, and improvement of supply chains, from early manufacturing to after-sales [14].

The decentralization of manufacturing comes with an associated challenge: horizontal integration, establishing collaboration networks between companies in the supply chain, sharing resources, and exchanging increasing amounts of data [2]. In addition, moving from single to multi-site manufacturing raises the need to support decentralized decisions and orchestrate technological components (e.g., machines, enterprise systems) that can interact with each other and with workers in real-time, generating more complex data flows and activities [3].

More complex business processes in Industry 4.0 are mobilizing academia to propose process modeling approaches [15]. One of the main goals is to assist managers in moving beyond organizational borders and understand process-centric work practices that expand to different elements of supply chains [7] while keeping the process compliant, traceable, and resilient.

2.2 Inter-Organizational Business Processes

IOBP are sequential activities executed in collaboration by two or more trading entities to achieve a business objective of shared value [16]. Implementing IOBP requires a minimum level of trust between the participating organizations, guaranteed through legal contracts, which specify the responsibilities and obligations agreed by all the participating parties [17].

Currently, IOBP models are usually created independently by each partner organization, using disconnected documentation and procedures. This approach enables each business partner to focus on its internal activities. Aiming to improve this disjointed approach, [18] proposes a way to merge different process models supporting collaboration in producing components and products by creating a unified perspective of the business process. However, the design of IOBP is problematic:

- The interaction between internal business processes and IOBP requires transparency between partners [19];
- The coordination of IOBP interdependencies is challenging (e.g., equipment shared by different partners) [9];
- Partner's responsibilities across the different activities in the IOBP flow must be defined [20];
- Semantic gaps may occur, caused by each business partner having its specific internal process language and terminology [8];
- Autonomy may be required by each business partner to design, execute and improve their internal business processes and strategies, eventually leading to different paces of digital transformation. Mechanisms are needed to synchronize and reduce the degree of coupling between the external and internal interfaces of the business partners in the IOBP [9];
- Business partners may be distributed across different geographical locations, each subject to distinct compliance requirements and laws [21];
- Monitoring decentralized activities and decisions in IOBP requires deploying policies that allow traceability of metrics of the several elements (e.g., state of process execution, inventory count in each partner) [22].

The contributions for modeling IOBP are significant, but the resulting process models are often incomplete [8, 9] and difficult to share within the organizations. Therefore, new or extended notations (e.g., using BPMN) can be created to promote the design and execution of IOBP more wholly and effectively.

2.3 Risk-Based Thinking and Business Process Models

ISACA [23] defines risk management as the process of identifying the vulnerabilities and threats to the information resources used by an organization in achieving their business objectives and deciding what countermeasures, if any, to take in reducing the risks to an acceptable level, based on the value of the information resource to the organization. According to [24], a definition for risk comprehends (1) the probability that the actual outcome of an event will differ from the expected outcome and (2) the impact associated with that outcome. A report of the World Economic Forum [25] defines five essential risk categories: economic, environmental, geopolitical, societal, and technological risk.

In the context of BPM, risk management can contribute to assessing the process regarding the existing risks, adopting risk mitigation strategies, and serve as a tool to support the revision and design of the business process, at design time and at execution time.

Several risk models have been proposed in the IS field. The proposal of [26] introduces a three-level hierarchy of risks. The third level is the most exhaustive and consists of the compliance and operational risks that emerge from business processes (e.g., information security, privacy and, regulatory issues). Kaplan [26] suggests that level 3 risks can be more predictable and related to operational procedures. The second level includes strategy risks, such as environmental, human resources, and IT-related risks [26]. Finally, at level 1, global enterprise risks may occur due to the most unlikely events, usually called "black swan", which reveal the most adverse consequences for the organization's survival [26]. Nevertheless, studies incorporating risks in business process models for Industry 4.0 adoption are still nascent in the literature.

2.4 BPMN and BPMN Extension Mechanisms

Business process models are used to document business processes, enabling their understanding and analysis by domain experts with different backgrounds [27], playing a pivotal role in management activities [22].

Business Process Modeling and Notation is a popular industry standard for business process modeling. It provides an intuitive and simple notation that is readily understandable by business users [28]. It also has a well-defined language meta-model that simplifies tool integration and model exchangeability [29].

BPMN provides an "*extension by addition*" mechanism that enables the definition and integration of domain-specific concepts [30]. Moreover, BPMN allows to create extensions, while ensuring BPMN core elements' validity [31]. Finally, the development of BPMN extensions is usually less costly than developing an entirely new domain-specific modeling language from scratch [29].

According to the BPMN standard [31], the mechanisms for language extension mechanisms are organized as follows:

- Extension: Binds the extension attributes to a standard BPMN model definition;
- ExtensionDefinition: Supports the incorporation of attributes in a specific element or a new element. Composed by several ExtensionAttributeDefinition (name and type);
- ExtensionAttributeDefinition: Defines new attributes as characteristics of a customized element (e.g., string, integer, Boolean);
- ExtensionAttributeValue: Incorporates the attribute value.

The study presented by [30] suggests a methodology to create BPMN extensions. However, only a few developed BPMN extensions are designed in conformance with OMG's standard [32]. Most of them are created using meta-model and XML-schema customizations, raising problems with tool integration, comprehensibility, and model exchangeability [29].

Business process models have two elements more specific to inter-organizational process descriptions: (1) pools representing entities (e.g., organizations) that perform business processes [8], and (2) message flows depicting information exchanges between organizations. However, the standard BPMN elements cannot represent all the details from the IOBP 4.0 domain, including risks more specific to the decentralized nature of Industry 4.0. Therefore, BPMN extensions emerge as a promising solution [32].

2.5 Establishing the Link: Business Process Modeling in Industry 4.0, IOBP and Risk

Numerous BPMN extensions have been proposed for Industry 4.0 contexts. PyBPMN [4] is one of the most mentioned, presenting an approach to the specification and management of the resources associated with the business processes supporting cyber-physical systems. Further studies in this field include the modeling of industrial IoT scenarios [33], analysis of business process fragments for manufacturing activities [34], and ubiquitous business process modeling [35]. The study conducted by [36] proposes a BPMN extension for manufacturing. These authors create elements for representing manufacturing operations and resources, then present different examples for using them.

BPMN extensions are also available for IOBP. For example, the pioneer contribution presented by [37] using pools and messages. The work of [38] presents the design of a BPMN extension for collaborative business processes. The proposal focuses on concepts related to the execution of collaborative tasks, activity privacy, confidentiality, state of progress of activities, and data management. In addition, the authors propose a meta-model and a set of new graphical elements for collaborative business processes.

Risk-aware business process modeling has already captured the attention of different researchers. The work of [39] presents and evaluates a BPMN extension to represent human physical risks (e.g., heavy lifting, repetitive work) in the several stages of the business process. The contribution of [11] proposes a BPMN extension for risk handling, introducing elements such as risk handlers, risk mitigation methods, and risk factors. The study of [40] defines a BPMN extension for quantitative risk assessment by including information about the likelihood and consequences of failures, in terms of business value, in different granularities of processes fragments. The framework proposed by [6] suggests that risks and workarounds should be jointly considered to model uncertainty in organizations.

Despite these essential contributions for modeling IOBP, Industry 4.0, and risk-aware process models, an integrated approach to model manufacturing in IOBP risk-aware scenarios of digital transformation is still necessary to develop, and practical examples are scarce. Therefore, this section's related work can be integrated and extended, serving as the starting point for our research, explained in the next section.

3 Research Approach

We selected design science research (DSR) as the approach to create our extension since it is a problem-solving paradigm that relies on kernel theories to produce inventive artifacts [41]. DSR evolves iteratively, starting with the "*problem identification and motivation, define objectives of a solution, design and development, demonstration, evaluation, and communication*" [42].

Our initial DSR cycle had a problem-centered initiation [42], including contacts with industry experts and a literature review on the topics of BPMN extensions and Industry 4.0. The next step was designing the IOBP 4.0 extension and demonstrating its utility [41]. The design phase follows the approach proposed by [30] using UML profiles, later improved by [43] with the analysis of the domain and its conceptualization [43]. First, we conceptualized the IOBP 4.0 domain as an ontology, revealing the main domain concepts, relationships, and properties. Then, we conducted an equivalence check to assess if the IOBP 4.0 concepts were semantically equivalent to the standard BPMN elements (e.g., tasks, gateways, data objects).

We instantiated the artifact in different companies adopting Industry 4.0 and decentralized manufacturing. Figure 1 synthesizes our DSR.

After confirming the few contributions available for the detailed modeling of IOBP 4.0 (see left of Fig. 1, problem description), we identified a BPMN extension as the most promising solution. After its design, we tested it in a real-world case in a technical metal coatings provider adopting Industry 4.0 strategies. A new cycle was necessary to incorporate risks in IOBP 4.0 process models conducted in a large paper pulp manufacturer. The case company's mission is to produce paper pulp and develop solutions for forest management and bioelectric energy production. The case company's operations require some outsourcing, and it is investing in a new system to

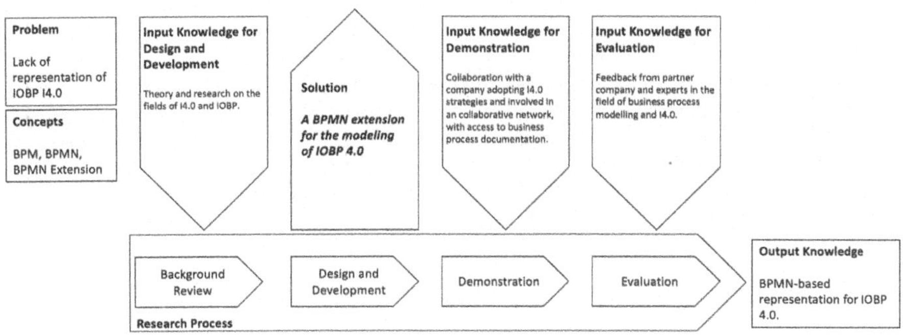

Fig. 1 DSR Grid for IOBP 4.0 (adapted from [44] and [42])

monitor the several decentralized operations (e.g., timber cutting, pulp production, bioelectric energy production). Being ISO 9001 certified, the company found our approach interesting to model processes aligned with Industry 4.0 investments. In addition, the company provided process-related documentation, which allowed us to model the process using standard BPMN notation and IOBP 4.0. Section 4 details the artifacts created during our DSR.

4 IOBP 4.0 BPMN Extension Development

Section 4.1. presents the domain ontology for IOBP 4.0. Subsequently, we describe the extension elements.

4.1 Domain Ontology

Figure 2 depicts the ontology we designed to understand the domain, concepts, and attributes. This domain's central concept is the business process involving two or more business partners (IOBP 4.0, on the top) and their process activities [8]. The five main risk categories [25] are represented below.

According to inter-organizational agreements, each business partner coordinates or acts in the process (coordinates or participates). Partners must comply with specific regulations (e.g., laws, procedures, standards, contract agreements) [21], exchange

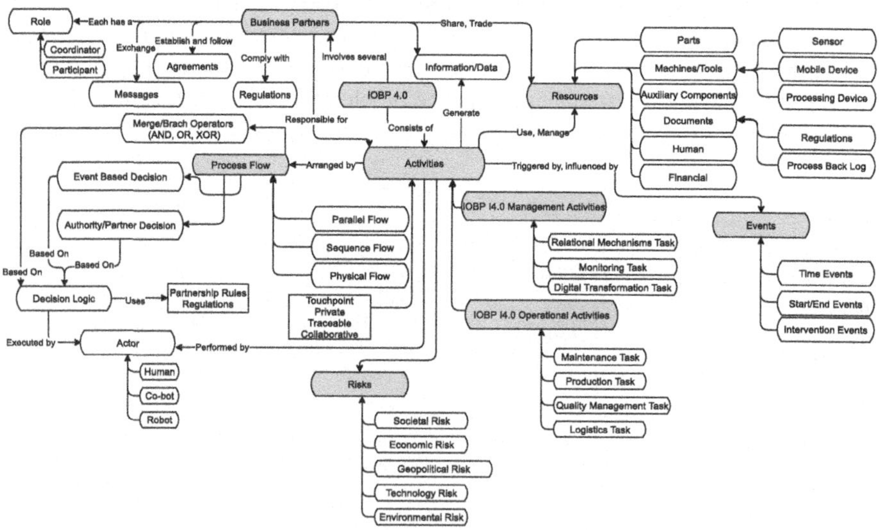

Fig. 2 Domain ontology of IOBP 4.0

data (through messages and documents) [9]. In addition, they may share resources in the manufacturing network (e.g., parts, auxiliary components) [34].

The business partners execute IOBP 4.0 management activities (e.g., relational mechanisms task, monitoring task, digital transformation task), and actors (e.g., human, co-bot, robot) perform IOBP 4.0 operational activities (e.g., maintenance task, production task, quality management task, logistics task), utilizing resources (e.g., parts, auxiliary component, machines, human, financial) [34]. There is a direct impact between activities and events (e.g., time events, start/end events, intervention events) that coexist in business processes [9]. Activities' data need to be traceable and may be public or private [22]. The activities are executed according to the process flow (e.g., parallel flow, partner flow, physical flow)- on the left side of Fig. 1. In certain parts of the flow, decisions are made (e.g., gateway, event-based decision, authority/partner decision) about the activities to be executed next, based on a decision logic (e.g., partnership rules/agreement, regulations) [9] executed by actors (e.g., human, co-bot, robot). Finally, the risks involved in process execution can be represented according to different categories.

4.2 *Graphical Representation of IOBP 4.0 BPMN Extension*

Table 1 introduces the BPMN elements identified in our domain ontology model. The design team's goal was to uniquely identify each new BPMN element while keeping BPMN consistent (e.g., task represented by a rectangle with rounded corners).

Table 1 presents thirty-one elements that compose the IOBP 4.0 extension, integrating Industry 4.0, IOBP, and risk-based thinking in process models. The table adapts elements from BPMN extensions proposed for manufacturing (e.g., production task, quality management task, logistics task, maintenance task, parts, physical flow) [34, 45], IOBP (e.g., private task, traceable task, private data, shared data) [38], and critical risk categories [25]. Our contribution adds a new group of cyber-physical elements that are pillars of Industry 4.0 (e.g., robot actor, human actor, co-bot actor, processing devices, sensor, machines, tools) and IOBP elements (e.g., partnership participant pool, partnership manager pool, partner intermediate event, partner gateway, touchpoint task, digital transformation task, relational mechanism task). Additionally, new elements represent the five essential risk categories defined by [25]: technological risk, societal risk, geopolitical risk, environmental risk, and economic risk. We developed the BPMN extension elements using Lucidchart [46] and its icon library, aiming to support the representation of the IOBP 4.0 concepts. In Sect. 5, we demonstrate the most recent version of the IOBP 4.0 extension in the selected paper pulp company.

Table 1 Graphical representation of IOBP 4.0

BPMN concept	Domain	Description	Graphical representation
Task	Manufacturing	The production task represents a sub-type of task to execute production activities (e.g., assembly, cleaning, handcraft, heat treatment)	
Task	Manufacturing	The quality management task represents a sub-type of task executing quality management activities (e.g., product testing, check non-conformities)	
Task	Manufacturing	The logistics task represents a sub-type of task related to logistics activities' execution (e.g., packaging, handling, materials' storage)	
Task	Manufacturing	The maintenance task represents a sub- type of task related to equipment, systems, and tools maintenance (e.g., machine replacement, preventive maintenance)	
Task	IOBP	The traceable task identifies that a specific task is traceable, meaning that a set of metrics is retrieved and registered to execute that task	
Task	IOBP	The private task represents that a specific task is private, meaning that no information on that task is shared with the partners, being kept confidential	
Task	IOBP	The touchpoint task means that it is a region of interest for partners. Information about the task execution/state may be shared	

(continued)

Table 1 (continued)

BPMN concept	Domain	Description	Graphical representation
Task	IOBP	The collaborative task means that a specific task is executed and managed in collaboration between several business partners	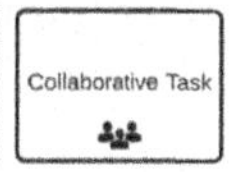
Task	IOBP	The relational mechanism task represents the activities related to managing relationships between the business partners, managing the responsibilities, authority, and capacities of each partner	
Task	IOBP	The digital transformation task represents the activities related to executing improvements in the business processes using digital technologies	
Gateway	IOBP	The partner gateway represents a moment in which a specific partner decides the "path" of the activities to be executed in the following steps	
Intermediate Event	IOBP	The partner intermediate event represents a specific partner's intervention in an activity, started by an authorized partner's decision	
Process Flow	Manufacturing	The physical flow represents the transport/movement of materials (physical objects) between one Flow Element and the next. The transport may occur within (e.g., internal logistics) or between partners	

(continued)

Table 1 (continued)

BPMN concept	Domain	Description	Graphical representation
Data Object	Manufacturing	The regulations represent the laws and standards that business partners must follow (e.g., ISO 9001)	
Data Object	IOBP	The private data object means that a given data object (or one of its children) is private, meaning that no information on that data is shared with the partners, being kept confidential	
Data Object	IOBP	The shared data object means that a given data object (or one of its children) is shared: data is accessible to other partners	
Connected to Task or Flow	Manufacturing	Parts are essential elements in industry flows (e.g., parts for assembly). They are used and exchanged between the partners and in manufacturing activities	
Connected to Task or Flow	Manufacturing	Represents the machines/tools used in several activities (e.g., production machinery)	
Connected to Task	Cyber-Physical	Processing devices are used in process tasks to record information, manage documents, execute algorithms, or analyze data	
Pool	IOBP	The partnership manager is the main responsible for the execution, monitoring, and management of the IOBP	

(continued)

Table 1 (continued)

BPMN concept	Domain	Description	Graphical representation
Pool	IOBP	The partnership participant is responsible for executing activities and reporting the agreed information to the partnership manager	
Task, gateway	Cyber-Physical	Represents the tasks and gateways that a human actor may execute	
Task, gateway	Cyber-Physical	Represents the tasks and gateways that a co-bot actor may execute	
Task, gateway	Cyber-Physical	Represents the tasks and gateways that a robot actor may execute	
Task, Gateway	Cyber-Physical	Represents sensors used in tasks or incorporated in resources, enabling the retrieval of data and traceability of elements	
Task	Risk	Represents a task in which there is an economic risk	
Task	Risk	Represents a task in which there is a risk for the society or the human actor	
Task	Risk	Represents a task in which there is a risk related to geopolitical issues	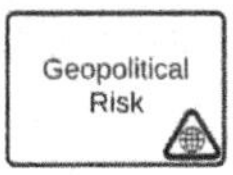
Task	Risk	Represents a task with a risk of potential harm to the environment (e.g., gas leak, oil leak)	
Task	Risk	Represents a task with a risk for the IT infrastructure (e.g., system crash)	

5 Demonstration

Figure 3 shows a partial view of the biomass business process of the case company modeled in standard BPMN.

The process is triggered when the Case Company receives the biomass from the suppliers. Then, the Case Company verifies the condition of the biomass. If the biomass is crushed, it is sent directly to the crushed biomass sections. Otherwise, the biomass is sent to the crush section and must be transformed to be in proper conditions to produce electricity. The biomass is then set for sale to bioelectric companies. When a request for biomass is received, the transport and details are scheduled. The biomass is then transported to the biomass company's facilities, along with the details of the transport and biomass. The bioelectric company receives the biomass, which is then used to produce bioelectric power.

Figure 4 shows the same process modeled with the proposed IOBP 4.0 extension.

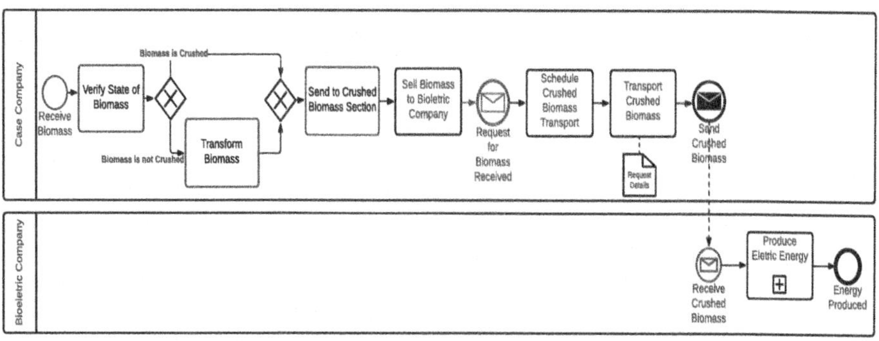

Fig. 3 Biomass business process model using BPMN (excerpt)

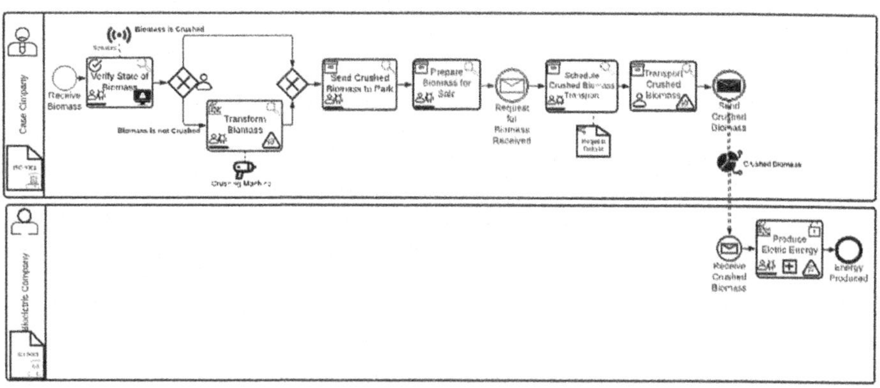

Fig. 4 Biomass business process model using IOBP 4.0 extension

The BPMN extension in Fig. 4 allows more details on the digital elements and information sharing, which cannot be represented with the standard BPMN notation used in Fig. 3. The process model built while using the extension is more accurate in representing the roles of the process participants: the Case Company is the business process coordinator and is ISO-9001 certified. The other process participants are also certified by ISO-9001. New digital elements are integrated into the model produced with the extension (e.g., the crushing machine used to transform the biomass, sensors used to verify the state of the biomass). The Bioelectric Company can monitor the transport of the crushed biomass from the Case Company to their facilities and access information on the scheduled delivery of the biomass. The Case Company also retrieves and analyses data from their tasks (e.g., verifying biomass, transforming biomass). Several documents are shared between the business partners (e.g., request details). Most of the tasks performed are classified as logistics tasks (e.g., transport crushed biomass) and production tasks (e.g., transform biomass). Robots partially automate some tasks (e.g., transform biomass, schedule delivery of biomass), while human actors perform others (e.g., transport biomass). Some tasks have an environmental risk associated (e.g., transport biomass, produce electric energy) and others a technological risk (e.g., verify the state of biomass).

6 Evaluation

The proposed IOBP 4.0 extension, now updated with risk analysis, shares the same principles of the standard BPMN and provides an answer to the need to represent inter-organizational business processes in increasingly digitalized manufacturing contexts. In addition, model intelligibility and detail are improved.

Model completeness is one of the most immediate advantages of IOBP 4.0 over the classic BPMN. First, the proposed extension introduces representative elements of the private/shared data and activities (e.g., produce electric energy is a private task, the transport details document is shared among the partners). Second, the new elements, aligned with the core BPMN standard, represent the key manufacturing stages (e.g., transform biomass is a production task, schedule delivery of biomass is a logistics task). Third, the technology strategy on Industry 4.0 becomes visible (e.g., verify state of biomass is executed by humans and robots). Fourth, the entire business process is integrated into a single model instead of disjoint models from different partners, using different notations, pointing to specific areas of risk in the model. The IOBP 4.0 process model can be used as a tool for joint innovation efforts, enabling identifying internal and external improvement opportunities by any involved organizations. Fifth, the IOBP 4.0 process models can be leveraged to train and onboard new staff (e.g., making IT experts aware of the existing infrastructure, and assisting operators in their contacts with third-party entities). Lastly, the process models can be adopted in internal audits, increasing transparency of the responsibilities, activities, internal/external interactions, and technology investments. Therefore, IOBP 4.0 contributes to an enhanced perception of each partner's contribution and risk elements requiring particular attention for monitoring activities and mitigation actions.

Although there are some similarities with UML activity diagrams, UML is an object-oriented notation primarily focused on modeling and documenting software systems (e.g., web applications, database architecture). Therefore, BPMN extensions may be more accessible to different organizational domain experts (e.g., business analysts, manufacturing technicians) interested in the design of "as-is" and "to-be" risk-aware business processes. In addition, IOBP 4.0 can be helpful in process improvement initiatives that require a descriptive notation of the domain.

Our evaluation over two DSR cycles also revealed weaknesses in our IOBP 4.0 proposal. First, the additional information increases the complexity and readability of the process models compared to the standard BPMN elements. The absence of clear guidelines regarding what to include may result in overloaded models, more challenging to understand by the practitioners. The problem is not so severe when dealing with quality experts (used to ISO 9001 process models and risk-based thinking), but other stakeholders (e.g., operators) may face increased difficulties. Second, the current version of IOBP 4.0 does not identify the state of process transformation. For example, if the specific technology (e.g., IoT infrastructure, app, machine learning model used to support decision making) used in activity X is already deployed or under development. Industry 4.0 adoption is dynamic, so it would be essential to identify the maturity of specific elements (e.g., a task executed by a human but might be executed by a robot in the future). Moreover, the risk evaluation is also inexistent in the model, restricted to disclosing the type of risk.

The team identified three main avenues that could lead to overcoming the limitations—first, inspired in the enterprise architecture field and the ArchiMate [47], separating the process model in views (e.g., digital transformation view for showing only the technology, omitting the IOBP-related data; IOBP view hiding the technology layer; risk analysis view). Testing the complete process's visualization or only a part of its layers will be interesting. Second, the Industry 4.0 maturity level could be represented by a number (e.g., maturity stage ranging from 1-Explorer to 4-Expert) in each element of IOBP 4.0. Several maturity models could be experimented with to improve IOBP 4.0 (e.g. [48]). Finally, risks can be represented quantitatively (e.g., risk matrix result) or using colors to represent the hazardous points.

7 Conclusion

This paper reports the second DSR cycle in a paper pulp company aiming at creating and evaluating a BPMN extension to model inter-organizational business processes in the context of Industry 4.0. This cycle included reviewing relevant literature at the intersection of Industry 4.0, IOBP, and risks, and the proposal of a BPMN extension. The contributions include (1) a domain ontology of IOBP 4.0, (2) the graphical representation of the IOBP 4.0 extension concepts, and (3) a demonstration of the use of the proposed extension in practice.

IOBP 4.0 can be helpful for standards-certified companies adopting a process approach to management and risk-based thinking, like ISO 9001, to disclose their processes and third-party collaborations. IOBP 4.0 may also help coordinate distributed manufacturing processes that are at the core of Industry 4.0 transformation. In the future, the IOBP 4.0 models can be attached to contractual agreements and become a central tool to design, change, and promote shared innovation collaboratively.

There are also limitations in our DSR that we need to state. First, the artifacts produced in this cycle are essential to model IOBP 4.0, but we do not yet have evidence about the proposed approach's benefits to model IOBP 4.0 for the entire collaborative network. Second, the companies that participated in our work are not representative of the entire industry. Future DSR cycles need to integrate more companies adopting Industry 4.0. Third, the main target of this DSR cycle was manufacturing-related IOBP 4.0. However, the model can be extended or adapted to IOBP executed in other relevant sectors and other digital transformation strategies (e.g., health 4.0). Fourth, the proposed approach does not include detailed guidelines for using the IOBP 4.0 extension in modeling activities. Defining a set of design principles to model with the IOBP 4.0 BPMN extension will be important. Finally, the domain concepts and ontology were identified based on a literature review and process documentation analysis in selected companies. In the future, it would be interesting to conduct industrial surveys and assess the social implications of using IOBP 4.0 for different partners.

Acknowledgements This work is funded by national funds through the FCT-Foundation for Science and Technology, I.P., within the scope of the project CISUC-UID/CEC/00326/2020 and by European Social Fund, through the Regional Operational Program Centro 2020.

Appendix A: Examples of IOBP 4.0 Use Cases

The use case (a) presents a private maintenance task executed by a robot with an IT risk. Use case (b) shows a traceable maintenance task executed by a human with a risk for the environment. Use case (c) (in the middle) presents a touchpoint production task executed entirely by hand. Use case (d) introduces a traceable logistics task executed by a co-bot. The output is a shared production plan document. Use case (e) illustrates a traceable logistics task executed by humans. The partnership manager may intervene during task execution by requesting the change of the order details. Therefore, the production plan is changed in a private production task performed by a worker. Finally, use case (f) depicts a priority decision made by the partnership manager (Fig. 5).

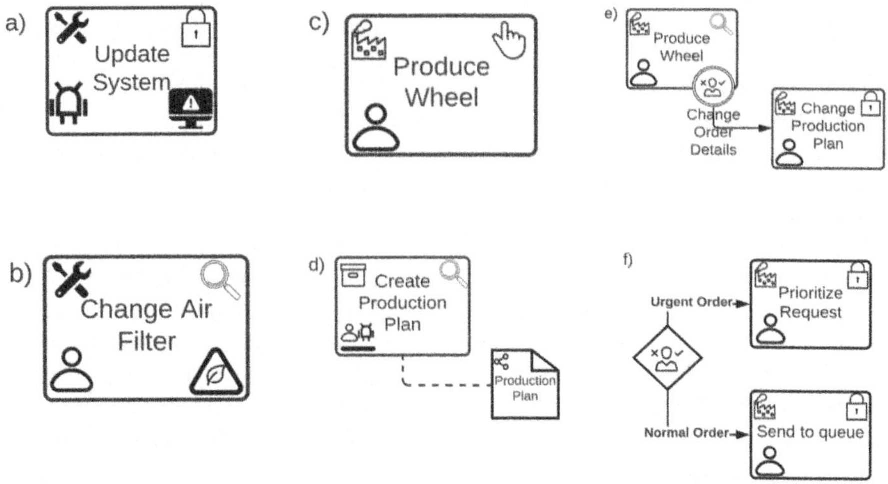

Fig. 5 Examples of IOBP 4.0 use cases

References

1. Baiyere, A., Salmela, H., Tapanainen, T.: Digital transformation and the new logics of business process management. Eur. J. Inf. Syst. **29**, 238–259 (2020). https://doi.org/10.1080/0960085X.2020.1718007
2. Kagermann, H., Wahlster, W., Helbig, J.: Securing the future of German manufacturing industry: recommendations for implementing the strategic initiative INDUSTRIE 4.0. Final Rep. Ind. 4.0 Work. Gr, pp 1–84 (2013)
3. Petrasch, R., Hentschke, R.: Process modeling for industry 4.0 applications: towards an industry 4.0 process modeling language and method. In: 2016 13th International Joint Conference on Computer Science and Software Engineering (JCSSE 2016), pp 1–5 (2016). https://doi.org/10.1109/JCSSE.2016.7748885
4. Bocciarelli, P., D'Ambrogio, A., Giglio, A., Paglia, E.: A BPMN extension for modeling cyber-physical-production-systems in the context of Industry 4.0. In: IEEE 14th International Conference on Networking, Sensing and Control, pp 599–604 (2017). https://doi.org/10.1109/ICNSC.2017.8000159
5. Zur Mühlen, M., Rosemann, M.: Integrating risks in business process models. In: Proceedings of ACIS, pp. 62–72 (2005)
6. Barata, J., da Cunha, P.R., Abrantes, L.: Dealing with risks and workarounds: a guiding framework. In: Ralyté, J., España, S., Pastor, Ó. (eds.) The Practice of Enterprise Modeling, pp. 141–155. Springer International Publishing, Cham (2015)
7. Patrucco, A., Ciccullo, F., Pero, M.: Industry 4.0 and supply chain process re-engineering: a coproduction study of materials management in construction. Bus. Process Manag. J. **26**, 1093–1119 (2020). https://doi.org/10.1108/BPMJ-04-2019-0147
8. Legner, C., Wende, K.: The challenges of inter-organizational business process design-a research agenda. In: Proceedings of the15th European Conference on Information Systems (ECIS 2007), pp 106–118 (2007)
9. Bouchbout, K., Alimazighi, Z.: Inter-organizational business processes modelling framework. CEUR Workshop Proc. **789**, 45–54 (2011)
10. Carnaghan, C.: Business process modeling approaches in the context of process level audit risk assessment: an analysis and comparison. Int. J. Account. Inf. Syst. **7**, 170–204 (2006)

11. Marcinkowski, B., Kuciapski, M.: A business process modeling notation extension for risk handling. Lecture Notes Computer Science (including Subser. Lecture Notes on Artificial Intelligence Lecture Notes Bioinformatics). 7564 LNCS, pp. 374–381 (2012). https://doi.org/10.1007/978-3-642-33260-9_32
12. Dalenogare, L.S., Benitez, G.B., Ayala, N.F., Frank, A.G.: The expected contribution of Industry 4.0 technologies for industrial performance. Int. J. Prod. Econ. **204**, 383–394 (2018). https://doi.org/10.1016/j.ijpe.2018.08.019
13. Lee, E.A.: Cyber physical systems: design challenges. In: Proceedings of the 11th IEEE Symposium Object/Component/Service-Oriented Real-Time Distributed Computing, pp. 363–369 (2008). https://doi.org/10.1109/ISORC.2008.25
14. Keller, M., Rosenberg, M., Brettel, M., Friederichsen, N.: How virtualization, decentrazliation and network building change the manufacturing landscape: an Industry 4.0 perspective. Int. J. Mech. Aerospace, Ind. Mechatron. Manuf. Eng. **8**, 37–44 (2014)
15. Queiroz, M.M., Fosso Wamba, S., Machado, M.C., Telles, R.: Smart production systems drivers for business process management improvement: An integrative framework. Bus. Process Manag. J. 26, 1075–1092 (2020). https://doi.org/10.1108/BPMJ-03-2019-0134
16. Bala, H., Venkatesh, V.: Assimilation of interorganizational business process standards. Inf. Syst. Res. **18**, 340–362 (2007). https://doi.org/10.1287/isre.1070.0134
17. Stahnke, S., Shumaiev, K., Cuellar, J., Kasinathan, P.: Enforcing a cross-organizational workflow: an experience report. Springer International Publishing (2020). https://doi.org/10.1007/978-3-030-49418-6_6
18. Kunchala, J., Yu, J., Yongchareon, S., Liu, C.: An approach to merge collaborating processes of an inter-organizational business process for artifact lifecycle synthesis. Computing **102**, 951–976 (2020). https://doi.org/10.1007/s00607-019-00770-z
19. Liu, D.-R., Shen, M.: Workflow modeling for virtual processes: an order-preserving process-view approach. Inf. Syst. **28**, 505–532 (2003). https://doi.org/10.1016/S0306-4379(02)00028-5
20. Aalst, W.M.P.V.D.: Loosely coupled interorganizational workflows: modeling and analyzing workflows crossing organizational boundaries. Inf. Manag. **37**, 67–75 (2000). https://doi.org/10.1016/S0378-7206(99)00038-5
21. Schoenthaler, F., Augenstein, D., Karle, T., Draghici, A., Popescu, A.-D., Gogan, L.M.: Design and governance of collaborative business processes in Industry 4.0. Procedia—Soc. Behav. Sci. **i**, 544–551 (2015)
22. Breu, R., Dustdar, S., Eder, J., Huemer, C., Kappel, G., Kopke, J., Langer, P., Mangler, J., Mendling, J., Neumann, G., Rinderle-Ma, S., Schulte, S., Sobernig, S., Weber, B.: Towards living inter-organizational processes. In: 2013 IEEE International Conference on Business Informatics, pp 363–366 (2013). https://doi.org/10.1109/CBI.2013.59
23. ISACA: CISA. Review Manual 27th edition. Information Systems Audit and Control Association (2019)
24. Holton, G.A., Knight, F.: Defining risk. Financ. Anal. J. **60**, 19–25 (2006)
25. World Economic Forum: The Global Risks Report 2021: 16th Edition. (2021)
26. Kaplan, R.S.: Risk management and the strategy execution system. Balanc. Scorec. Rep. **11**, 1–6 (2009)
27. Aguilar-Savén, R.S.: Business process modelling: Review and framework. Int. J. Prod. Econ. 90, 129–149 (2004). https://doi.org/10.1016/S0925-5273(03)00102-6
28. Chinosi, M., Trombetta, A.: BPMN: an introduction to the standard. Comput. Stand. Interfaces. **34**, 124–134 (2012). https://doi.org/10.1016/j.csi.2011.06.002
29. Braun, R., Schlieter, H., Burwitz, M., Esswein, W.: BPMN4CP: design and implementation of a BPMN extension for clinical pathways. Proceedings—2014 IEEE International Conference on Bioinformatics and Biomedicine (BIBM 2014). IEEE, pp. 9–16 (2014). https://doi.org/10.1109/BIBM.2014.6999261
30. Stroppi, L.J.R., Chiotti, O., Villarreal, P.D.: Extending BPMN 2.0: method and tool support. In: Dijkman, R., Hofstetter, J., Koehler, J. (eds.) LNBIP Proceedings. Springer Berlin Heidelberg, Berlin, Heidelberg, pp. 59–73 (2011). https://doi.org/10.1007/978-3-642-25160-3_5
31. Object Management Group, I.: Business Process Model and Notation (BPMN) v2.0.2. (2014)

32. Zarour, K., Benmerzoug, D., Guermouche, N., Drira, K.: A systematic literature review on BPMN extensions. Bus. Process Manag. J. **26**, 1473–1503 (2019). https://doi.org/10.1108/BPMJ-01-2019-0040
33. Engels, G., Strothmann, T., Teetz, A.: Adapt cases 4 BPM—a modeling framework for process flexibility in IIoT. In: Proceedings—IEEE International Enterprise Distributed Object Computing Workshop, EDOCW, pp. 59–68 (2018). https://doi.org/10.1109/EDOCW.2018.00020
34. Erasmus, J., Vanderfeesten, I., Traganos, K., Grefen, P.: Using business process models for the specification of manufacturing operations. Comput. Ind. **123**, 103297 (2020). https://doi.org/10.1016/j.compind.2020.103297
35. Yousfi, A., Bauer, C., Saidi, R., Dey, A.K.: UBPMN: a BPMN extension for modeling ubiquitous business processes. Inf. Softw. Technol. **74**, 55–68 (2016). https://doi.org/10.1016/j.infsof.2016.02.002
36. Zor, S., Schumm, D., Leymann, F.: A proposal of BPMN extensions for the manufacturing domain. In: ICMS Proceedings, pp. 1–6 (2011)
37. Fedorowicz, J., Gelinas, U.J., Gogan, J.L., Howard, M., Markus, M.L., Usoff, C., Vidgen, R.: Business process modeling for successful implementation of interorganizational systems. AMCIS 2005 (2005)
38. Amdah, L., Anwar, A.: A DSL for collaborative business process. In: 2020 International Conference on Intelligent Systems and Computer Vision (ISCV 2020), pp. 1–6 (2020). https://doi.org/10.1109/ISCV49265.2020.9204044
39. Polderdijk, M., Vanderfeesten, I., Erasmus, J., Traganos, K., Bosch, T., van Rhijn, G., Fahland, D.: A visualization of human physical risks in manufacturing processes using BPMN. In: Teniente, E., Weidlich, M. (eds.) Business Process Management Workshops, pp. 732–743. Springer International Publishing, Cham (2018)
40. Cardoso, P., Respício, A., Domingos, D.: RiskaBPMN—a BPMN extension for risk assessment. Procedia Comput. Sci. **181**, 1247–1254 (2021). https://doi.org/10.1016/j.procs.2021.01.324
41. Hevner, A.R., March, S.T., Park, J., Ram, S.: Design science in information systems research. MIS Q. **28**, 75–105 (2004)
42. Peffers, K., Tuunanen, T., Rothenberger, M.A., Chatterjee, S.: A design science research methodology for information systems research. J. Manag. Inf. Syst. **24**, 45–77 (2007)
43. Braun, R.: BPMN Extension profiles—adapting the profile mechanism for integrated BPMN Extensibility. In: 17th IEEE Conference on Business Informatics, vol. 1, pp. 133–142 (2015). https://doi.org/10.1109/CBI.2015.41
44. vom Brocke, J., Maedche, A.: The DSR grid: six core dimensions for effectively planning and communicating design science research projects. Electron. Mark. **29**, 379–385 (2019). https://doi.org/10.1007/s12525-019-00358-7
45. Aspridou, M.: Extending BPMN for modeling manufacturing processes Master of Science (2017)
46. Lucidchart: Lucidchart: Online Diagram Software & Visual Solution, https://lucid.app/documents#/dashboard. Accessed 16 Feb 2021
47. The Open Group: ArchiMate® 3.1 Specification (2018)
48. Siedler, C., Dupont, S., Zavareh, M.T., Zeihsel, F., Ehemann, T., Sinnwell, C., Göbel, J.C., Zink, K.J., Aurich, J.C.: Maturity model for determining digitalization levels within different product lifecycle phases. Prod. Eng. 1–20 (2021)

Paving the Way for Smart Community Composting

A Design Science Research Project in Estrela UNESCO Global Geopark

José Monteiro, João Barata, Hugo Gomes, and Emanuel Castro

Abstract Community composting is an essential facet of circular economy and sustainable food production. Our contribution based on design science research presents the development of a regional composting network in Estrela UNESCO Global Geopark. The community composting model uses mobile technologies and geographic information systems. This paper details the instantiation of the mobile solution layer and proposes a plan to scale-up the model to the entire region. The theoretical contribution of this paper is the concept of smart community composting inspired by the 5.0 movement expanding in societies, cities, and industries. For practice, our work presents a mobile information system customized for UNESCO Geoparks and their recently created GEOfood brand to promote sustainable production practices.

Keywords Smart region · Smart community composting · Geopark · Circular economy

A prior version of this paper has been published in the ISD2021 Proceedings (http://aisel.aisnet.org/isd2014/proceedings2021).

J. Monteiro (✉) · J. Barata
University of Coimbra, CISUC, Coimbra, DEI, Portugal
e-mail: jose.monteiro@student.uc.pt

J. Barata
e-mail: barata@dei.uc.pt

H. Gomes · E. Castro
Associação Geopark Estrela, Guarda, Portugal
e-mail: hugogomes@geoparkestrela.pt

E. Castro
e-mail: emanuelcastro@geoparkestrela.pt

E. Insfran Pelozo et al. (eds.), *Advances in Information Systems Development*, Lecture Notes in Information Systems and Organisation 55,
https://doi.org/10.1007/978-3-030-95354-6_10

1 Introduction

Circular economy (CE) is becoming a popular research area in information systems (IS) [1]. The interest is justified by the critical role of information to achieve transparency in material flows, since "*isolated windows of data availability only lead to local optimization of process efficiency for individual actors but fail at realising CE's full potential*" [1]. New digital platforms connecting different stakeholders of sustainable supply chains will be a priority [2].

Sustainable food supply chains will need to implement circular practices. Over 30% of the food is lost, and food production will need to increase by 60% in 2050 [3]. Composting is a possible solution to reduce waste while simultaneously improving the soil and society's response to climate changes [4, 5]. This circular practice can be adopted at homes but also in specific communities [6].

Digital transformation is shifting to the "5.0" era in cities [7] and industry. For example, the priorities established by the European Commission in 2021 include sustainability, human-centric development, and resilience with a "*focus from shareholder to stakeholder value, with benefits for all concerned*" [8]. This vision is inspired in the Society 5.0 proposed by Japan, and also aligned with the recent City 5.0 concept defined by [7] as "*a liveable city that is (re)modelled with the aim of eliminating restriction for its citizens by using digitalization for the provision of public goods and services*". The traditional agriculture sector is also shifting to digitalization for sustainability, as detailed in the report presented by the Food and Agriculture of Organization of the United Nations [9]. Technologies like the Internet of Things (IoT), cloud, and mobile solutions may be adopted in individual smart composting systems [10, 11, 12]. However, there is a lack of research in smart composting at a regional scale. Therefore, smart community composting is the challenge addressed in this paper.

Our Design Science Research (DSR) [13, 14] started in cooperation with Estrela UNESCO Global Geopark (Estrela Geopark) [15]. UNESCO recognized this region's geological relevance in 2020, and their association's strategy puts sustainability at the top of the priorities. They aim to incorporate a circular economy in local food production supported by information technologies (IT). Accordingly, the following research objective was formulated: (RO1) *deploy a smart community composting platform to support Estrela Geopark's circular economy*. Additionally, inspired by the concept of projectability presented by [16], "*to understand how design theories and design principles, as prescriptive constructs, imply intentionality for operation in other places or times*", an additional research objective (RO2) is to "*project smart community composting at the regional scale of Estrela Geopark*".

The remainder of this paper is organized as follows. Section 2 presents the research approach. Next, a review of relevant literature on CE, IS, and smart composting is offered. Section 4 details the design, development, evaluation, and projection of the smart community composting platform. Subsequently, we state the conclusions, limitations, and future work opportunities.

2 Research Approach

DSR [13, 14] is the selected research approach. The resulting IT artifact aims to assist Estrela UNESCO Global Geopark in adopting circular economy practices at a regional level. Figure 1 summarizes the research according to the DSR grid [17].

The work presented in this paper corresponds to DSR-cycle encompassing the phases from the idea conception to the design, development, and deployment of the smart community composting prototype in a natural environment but still under supervised conditions. Additionally, we followed the concept of projectability in DSR [16] to create a possible roadmap for expanding community composting to the entire Geopark region.

2.1 Regional Setting for DSR

Estrela Geopark is a territory in the Iberian central region with geological heritage, "*a rich biodiversity and long history of human presence with strong cultural and economic links to the mountain*" [15]. Geoparks recently launched the GEOfood brand worldwide to distinguish and help producers in protected regions [18]. The GEOfood manifesto fosters sustainability (maximizing local materials; minimizing transport impact), cooperation, and preservation of regional food heritage.

Problem	**Research process**	**Solution description**
A digital platform is necessary to deploy community composting. Existing proposals were not made for regional scale.	Steps of problem formulation, design and development, evaluation, and communication [26]. Future orientation of the artifact [1].	IT artifact with web/mobile interface.
Input knowledge	**Concepts**	**Output knowledge**
GEOfood; Smart Regions; Smart composting systems.	Information systems; Circular economy; Composting; Geographic Information Systems.	Design requirements and a guiding model for community composting in smart regions; Roadmap.

Fig. 1 DSR grid for the development of smart community composting

Estrela Geopark's territory is vast: 2216 km^2 and nine municipalities. Their association intends to include community composting as part of their overall strategy for sustainable local food production.

Composting organic material (e.g., food scrap, weeds, dry leaves, or fruits) is not yet disseminated in the Estrela Geopark community. The transformation of food waste compost can reduce their footprint while informing the population about this critical priority for the coming years. Estrela Geopark also wishes to strengthen the links between different zones in the territory. Notably, they plan to create a network of (1) urban food waste producers and (2) rural food waste recyclers (the local food producers).

At this research stage, Estrela Geopark is interested in modelling the circular economy network for smart composting, deploying the IT solution that supports their circular economy strategy, and draft a regional scale-up of smart community composting. The following section reviews relevant literature on the circular economy, information systems, and smart composting.

3 Literature Review

The selection of papers included in this section was made in Web of Science (WoS) and Scopus. Using specific keywords, we started with a bibliometric analysis and identified crucial clusters and concepts with the VOSviewer tool [19]. Subsequently, we have assessed related work to identify trends in this line of research.

3.1 Information Systems for Circular Economy

Figure 2 presents the results of a search in WoS (all records: 41 results) and Scopus (title, abstract, and keywords: 88 results) using the keyword combination "information systems" + "circular economy".

WoS (at the top) presents four main clusters: the red cluster (on the right) associated with specific products (e.g., nitrogen, fertilizers, nutrients); the central blue cluster for circular economy and the close relation with managerial aspects, reverse logistics, barriers, uncertainty, and emissions; the more "IS-related" green cluster (e.g., model, network, supply chain); and the yellow cluster including transportation and urban development (e.g., solid waste, city). Scopus reveals more clusters, with the red (products, nutrients) and green (IS-related) aligned with WoS, but also included specific clusters of papers about agriculture (blue cluster, aggregating geographic information systems, food waste, biomass). In both cases, it is clear (1) the important role of geographic information systems in circular economy development, (2) the need to create networks within the supply chain, and (3) the significance of food systems in circular economy developments.

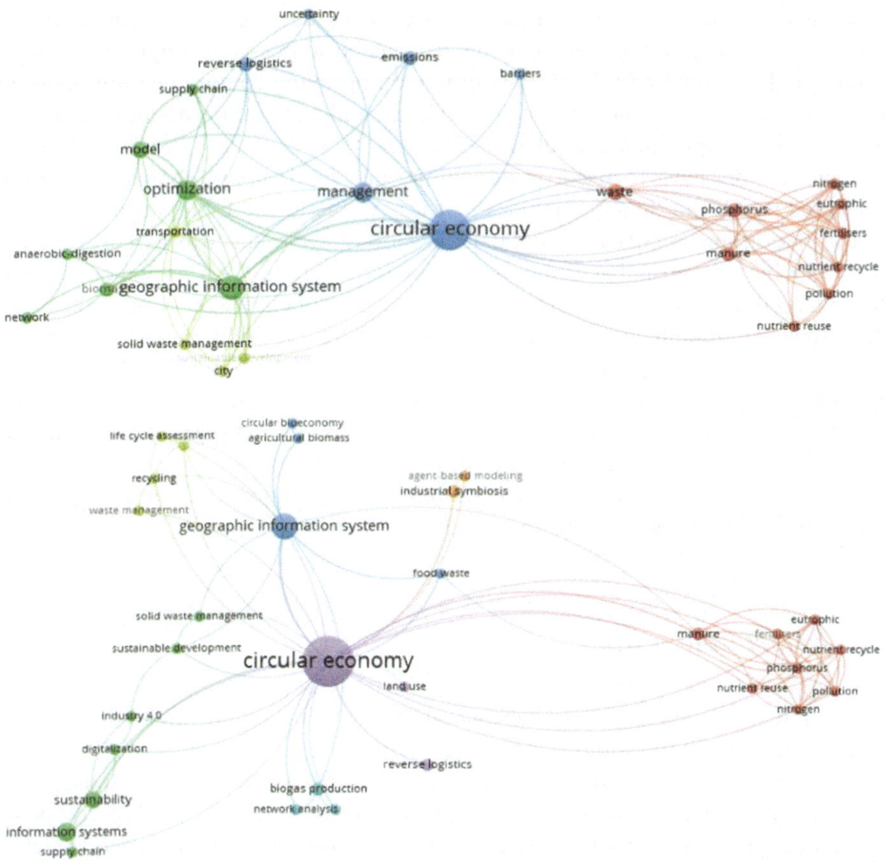

Fig. 2 Information systems and circular economy: bibliometric analysis

The circular economy has entered in IS agenda. The recent papers published by [1] with the purpose to mobilize the IS community for this "grand challenge" reveals two important lines for future research: "[f]*irst, in consideration of recent advances in tracking technologies, we invite discussions on the issue of representational faithfulness of complex product systems in circular material flows. Second, in acknowledgement of the dynamic and often unpredictable nature of circular material flows, we invite discussions on issues of data sharing in large and complex social systems*". An example of a study in this area is [20] for industrial parks' perspective. The main IS elements are (1) the information about companies in the network, (2) material flow, (3) key flow traces, (4) regulations and standards, and (5) industrial symbiosis [20]. Another recent example using geographic information systems is the web-based interface developed for solid waste management in England [21].

Real-time monitoring of supply chains as a whole will enable a clearer understanding of material flows [1], leading to more efficient control, reducing costs and waste, and, where possible re-introducing them back into the chain. Product traceability is currently a significant challenge that can be addressed through information systems and blockchain [22, 23]. In addition to improving communication between stakeholders [24], information systems bring the links of circularity and the ability to balance the supply–demand relation [25].

Some authors have focused on agriculture and food supply chains. The study conducted by [26] in Spain concludes that it is viable to use food waste (collected in distribution and retail) for animal feed. Different organic wastes can be used for producing compost that is important for fertilization, such as wineries [27]. Blockchain is a possible solution to test in the creation of circular economy networks [23]. However, digitalization in general, using different technologies (e.g., IoT, big data, data analytics) can create a more innovative circular economy [28]. Information is crucial to (1) monitor the production of waste, (2) support the creation of networks of stakeholders to reuse waste, as happens in the case of compost, and (3) explore the potential of data to optimize the process.

The following section details the potential of digital transformation for the issue of food waste and smart composting systems.

3.2 *Smart Composting*

Geographic information systems have an essential role in composting digitalization, but there are other opportunities, as shown in Fig. 3.

Only 20 papers were found in Scopus using the keyword "smart compost", and one in WoS. The latter is presented by [29], creating an Arduino-based prototype to monitor temperature, humidity, moisture, and gases. Therefore, we searched all fields

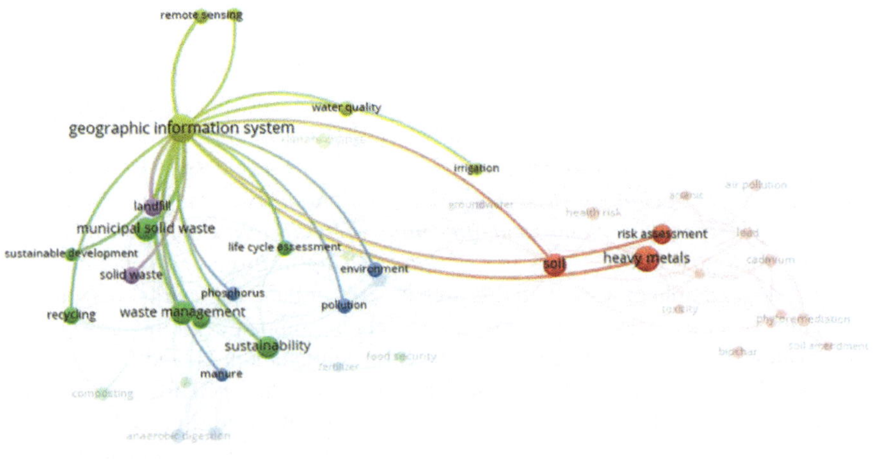

Fig. 3 Information systems and composting: bibliometric analysis in scopus

in Scopus using the keyword (compost OR composting) AND "information system", returning 1724 hits represented in Fig. 3. The yellow cluster highlighted in the figure reveals the importance of remote sensing. An interesting example using wireless sensor networks is presented by [11], illustrating the details of sensing temperature and moisture, and communication infrastructure.

Sensing devices can be used for on-farm composting [30], and several studies present prototypes for smart composting systems. For example, the smart composting systems built by [10] using an Arduino or the IoT-based solution created by [31]. Another example of a smart composting machine is presented by [32], including a mobile app for real-time management of the system parameters. However, these studies are for a single composting unit, and when multiple composting units exist, it is necessary to add the potential of the cloud [12].

Composting is also evolving to a community scale, aiming at more sustainable consumption. New technologies can contribute to this goal, as presented by the study of [33]. Community composting can be implemented in urban areas [5], and its benefits are already reported in the literature, for example, the study made in Chicago [6]. Rural composting is also possible [34]. However, information systems development of urban and regional areas (e.g., UNESCO Global Geoparks) with multiple composting sites is still understudied.

4 Results

This section details the DSR phases of design, development and instantiation, evaluation made by researchers and practitioners, and projectability of system scale-up.

4.1 Smart Community Composting Design

Figure 4 presents a C4 model [35], which systematizes the actors and components involved in the digital twin for community composting in the Estrela Geopark region. C4 modelling includes creating a hierarchical collection of diagrams with four levels of increasing abstraction, namely, *context, container, component, and code* [35]. Figure 4 presents the level 2 diagram (container) summarizing the IT artifact.

The system consists of three essential software elements: (1) a mobile application that will allow the entire community (i.e., GEOfood producers and local population) to interact with the regional community composting network, (2) a network of IoT-enabled composters strategically placed in specific locations of the Estrela Geopark region, and (3) a web platform where Geopark experts will be able to monitor in real-time the status of each of the composters in the network, as well as consult their or GEOfood producers' usage history. All these components are described in detail in the next section. The system also includes a non-relational database (MongoDB)

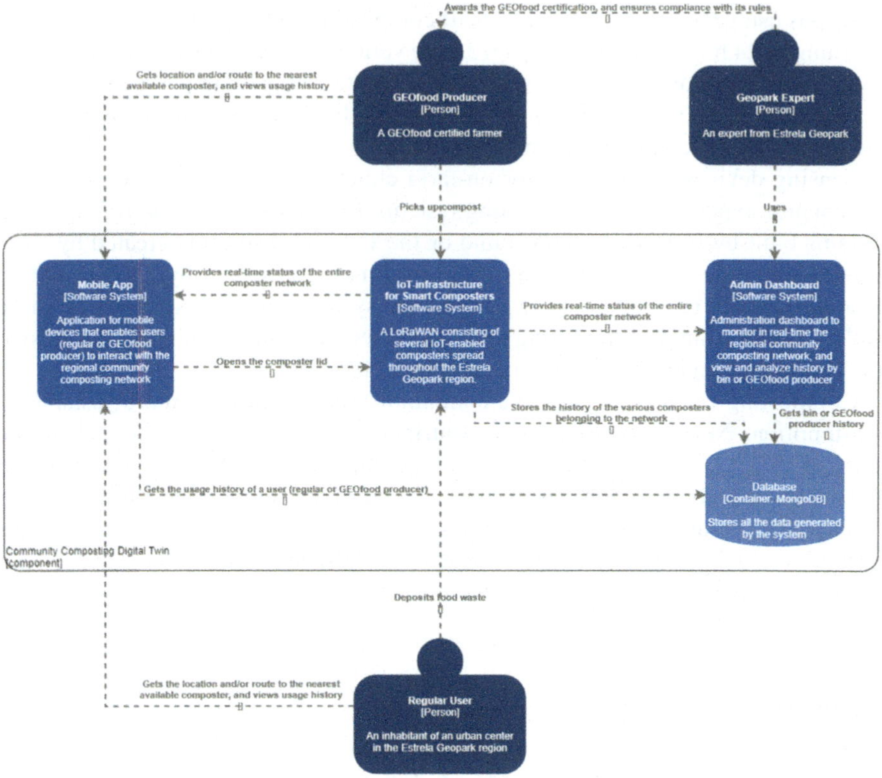

Fig. 4 Container diagram for smart community composting digital twin

that will store all the data generated by the system. This data will be essential to the future adoption of intelligent data analysis and artificial intelligence techniques that provide simulation and prediction capabilities to the digital twin.

Three types of users will interact with the initial version of the system: (1) Geopark experts, (2) GEOfood producers, and (3) local population. GEOfood producers (certified farmers) will use the system to obtain free natural fertilizer to integrate into their agricultural production. GEOfood producers need to comply to different regulations to maintain their GEOfood label. For example, the preference for natural fertilizer on their crops. The local population wants to "recycle" part of their food waste and contribute to regional sustainability. It will be necessary for this type of user to carry out awareness-raising action to make them aware of the importance and impact of adopting circular economy practices for the environment and the local economy. Additionally, municipal policies may provide incentives for community composting. Finally, the Geopark experts will use the system to manage the regional community composting network and verify that the GEOfood producers meet the guidelines for GEOfood certification.

Information systems can enable circular economy practices with the deployment of smart community composting. The next section details the development and instantiation of the mobile components of the system.

4.2 *Artifact Development and Instantiation*

The smart community composting system has three main components: (1) IoT infrastructure for smart composters; (2) web platform for Estrela Geopark supervision; and (3) application for mobile devices.

The IoT infrastructure consists of an extended network of smart composters placed at various points in the Estrela Geopark territory's urban centers. Each smart composter is IoT-enabled, allowing monitoring the compost heap size and the main parameters characterizing the composting process's state (namely, temperature, humidity, and methane) and access control to the bin content (through an electromagnetic lock attacked to the bin lid). The various smart composters are connected via a Low Power Wide Area Network (LPWAN) [36] to communicate with the application server.

Figure 5 displays the real-scale prototype of the smart composter currently being tested.

The physical twin of each composter (the cover was removed to show the interior) maximizes the use of local materials (e.g., wood) and is equipped with an LPWAN device using LoRa [36] and sensors to monitor the most relevant composting process parameters—circuit represented on the right.

The digital twin web platform will allow Estrela Geopark's team to monitor the smart composter network's real-time status. Figure 6 presents the administration dashboard graphical user interface (GUI).

On the left side of Fig. 6, the three-dimensional replica of the composting unit shows the amount of fertilizer. It is also possible to identify the smart

Fig. 5 Smart community composter unit and IoT diagram

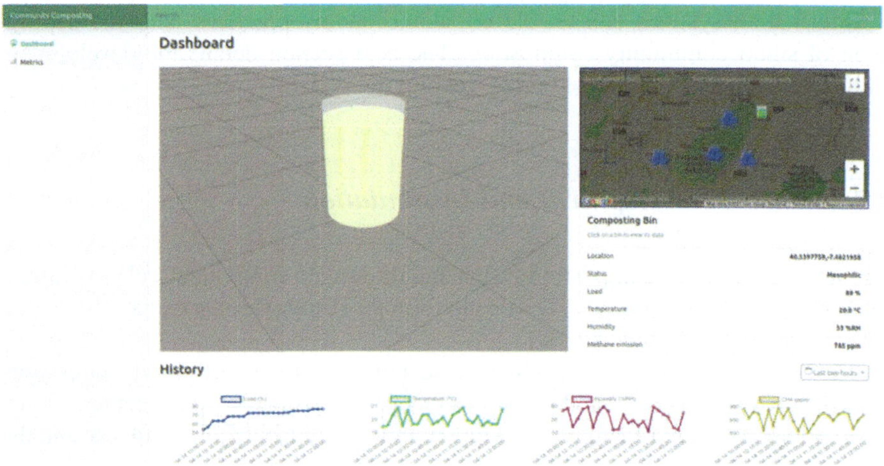

Fig. 6 Administration dashboard of the digital twin

composting network devices' location (on the top-right), the parameters, warnings (e.g., composter waiting for picking), and activity log on the bottom of the screen.

The mobile application is used by GEOfood producers and end-consumers of the food supply chain to connect with the community composting system. The mobile app is optional for the general local population—may assist in locating composting bins but is unnecessary for depositing food waste because that part will be unlocked for improved accessibility. Figure 7 depicts the mobile app GUIs.

The first image (Fig. 7a) presents the system access and registration. The mobile app integrates Google and Facebook authorization mechanisms to facilitate both tasks. Personal data will be required from the users: name, date of birth, the municipality where they live, and their role in the system (Fig. 7b). The producer's database (network of companies adopting the GEOfood brand) is restricted and managed by Estrela Geopark.

The mobile app identifies the nearest available composter according to the user's location and suggests the route to take (Fig. 7c–e). Identifying the nearest available composter will depend on the user's role. On the end-consumer side, the suggested route points to the nearest composter that is not yet a few weeks) (Fig. 7g). On the producer side, the app will point to the composter containing natural fertilizer resulting from the composting process, ready for pick up (Fig. 7f). We assume that the user will only play one of the application roles. According to the association experts, end-consumers are more associated with urban areas since local farmers usually recycle their food waste.

To ensure the integrity of the compost heap during the composting process and consequently the quality of the compost produced, we have equipped the system with mechanisms that prevent users from disturbing the process (by not allowing the lid of the bin to be opened after detecting that it is full) and redirecting them to the nearest available composter (Fig. 7h).

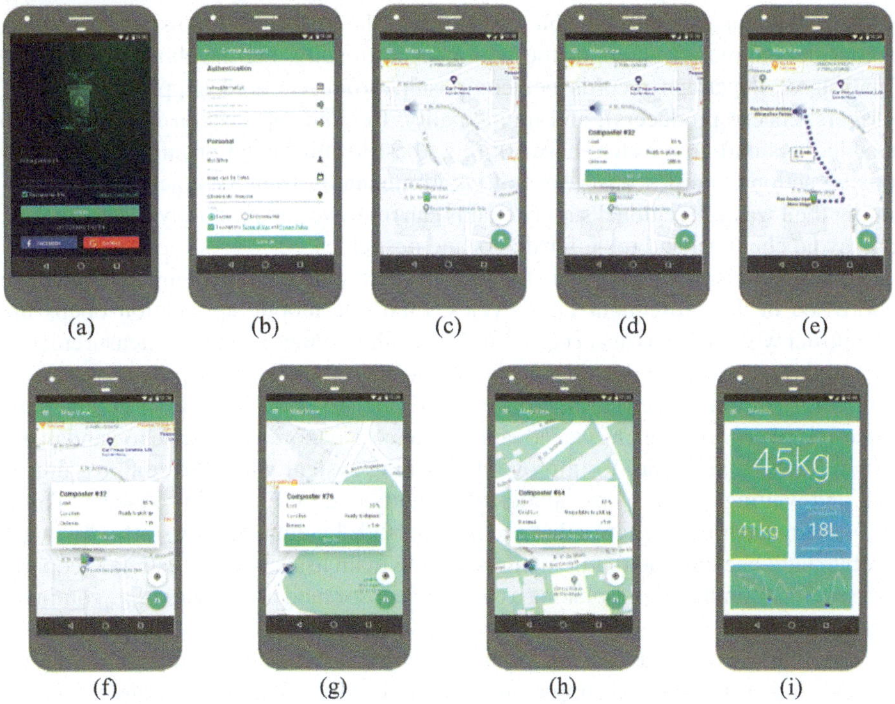

Fig. 7 Mobile application GUI's high-fidelity prototypes

The mobile app also enables users to view metrics related to their interactions with the community composting system. On the one hand, the end-consumer will see how much food waste is reintroduced into the food supply chain and to what extent this contributes to reducing their carbon footprint (Fig. 7i). On the other hand, the GEOfood producer will see the amount of fertilizer introduced into his production and check if they meet the environmental standards to keep GEOfood's certification.

4.3 Evaluation

The real-scale prototype received positive feedback from Estrela Geopark. According to the association experts, the system will be able to generate valuable data to quantify the amount of fertilizer each GEOfood producer picks up to support Estrela Geopark goals. Moreover, the data could be used to conduct quantitative studies to represent the users' behaviors regarding community composting and, finally, understand how community composting can nurture territorial cohesion between urban and rural spaces. Data will be handed in compliance with European Commission directives relating to data protection and privacy.

Estrela Geopark will be able to monitor the real-time status of the smart composters spread throughout the region. Additionally, the dashboard allows the analysis of the usage records per composter, producer, food supply chain (e.g., farmers, cheese producers), and municipality. Remote supervision is necessary to enable the smart composters network (e.g., best location) and promote awareness-raising actions in cities less aware of environmentally friendly practices. Incorporating food waste in regional supply chains can improve soil productivity and quality, and avoid chemical and toxic fertilizers and pesticides.

There are also challenges in the smart community composting that must be addressed in the subsequent DSR cycles. First, the mobile application opens the composter when a user is near (i.e., ~1 to 2 m to allow some error in the measurement). The mobile device requires GPS location and Internet access for proper operation, which is a current system limitation. Second, the structure is made of endogenous materials like wood, which is an advantage but is also more vulnerable to vandalism. Future work is necessary to improve the locking system when the compost unit is full and waiting for pick up—unlocked by authorized GEOfood producers. Third, the system needs maintenance that needs to be made by municipality staff. This is not problematic because the municipalities are the main associates of Estrela Geopark, but specific training (e.g., replacing a damaged sensor) and procedures (e.g., routinely checking if the composter is used correctly) will be required.

This DSR cycle was an essential step toward developing smart community composting in the region, supported by digital twins. However, "*projectability is a quality that one can find in design theories, principles, and artifacts*" [16], as we explore in the next section (RO2).

4.4 Projecting an Iterative Deployment of the Regional Community Composting Network

After evaluating the smart community composting system, preparing a comprehensive process to deploy the IT artifact (i.e., the digital twin) in the entire Estrela Geopark region is vital. However, notwithstanding the interest revealed by local entities, awareness campaigns are crucial to promote adherence of end-consumers to the system. Moreover, younger generations should be included in this process because they (1) will be the future end-consumers and (2) may have a positive influence on the circular economy practices of their family.

The potential of DSR projectability [16] is explored in this section. To do so, we envisioned a "best world": the deployment of composting digital twins covering several sites in all urban centers of the Estrela Geopark region with a significant adhesion by the whole community (i.e., GEOfood producers and local population), starting with the younger population. Therefore, the path to a more circular food supply chain will require a multidisciplinary approach and a sociotechnical

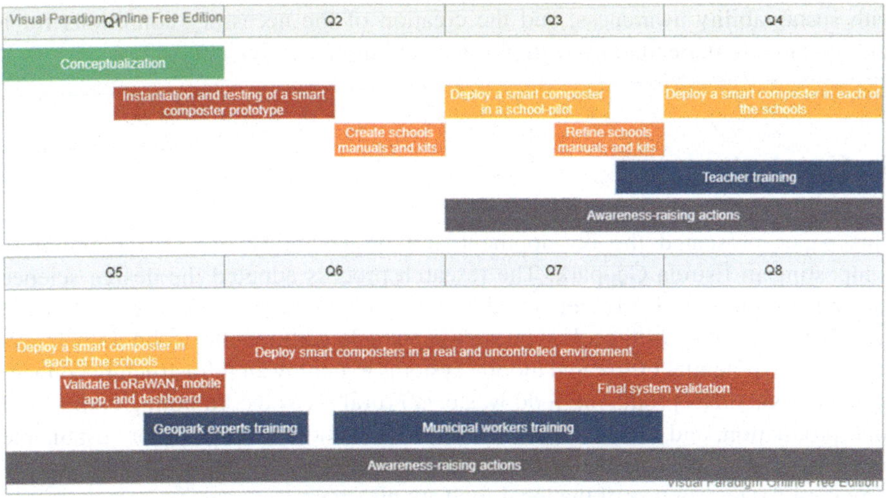

Fig. 8 Smart community composting roadmap for estrela geopark

strategy involving the younger generations in the region, more familiar with mobile technologies.

Figure 8 presents a roadmap for deploying the regional community composting network with the collaboration of secondary and vocational schools. On the one hand, reaching the younger population will promote circular economy awareness. On the other hand, the school network will validate all the system's functionalities before it is extended to the entire community.

Figure 8 suggests a sequence of steps to involve educational institutions, in all municipalities in the region, in the digital twin scale-up. After deploying an individual unit, the scale-up of the composting network needs to evolve gradually, and its success will be heavily dependent on population adherence.

Estrela Geopark already has an educational program (EstrelaEduca) that could be extended to support this roadmap. Training is required to key entities in the "best world", including the students and their parents, producers (via GEOFood certification), and municipalities responsible for the infrastructure. The teachers (e.g., informatics, environment, citizenship) may also receive training to assist the students in assembling and maintaining the smart composter. After the final system validation, the scale-up to the whole community may be more manageable. During this stage, training will be given to municipal workers to maintain the IoT-enabled bins and compost heap and to Geopark experts to manage the system. Several awareness-raising actions should be carried out throughout this process to show how community composting can be relevant for the environment and the regional economy.

Projecting the smart community composting at a regional scale is a complex endeavor, and this is only the first step. However, we found benefits in extending the DSR evaluation, envisioning an opportunity to align technology innovation with sustainability awareness, and the creation of the necessary conditions for a widespread circular economy with physical and digital components.

5 Conclusion

This paper presented the development and projectability of smart community composting in Estrela Geopark. The research process adopted the design science research paradigm [13, 14] and aimed to incorporate circular economy practices in a UNESCO territory with geological significance. In addition, the technology layers explored the potential of IoT and mobile systems to deploy an infrastructure connection (1) urban areas producing food waste, (2) rural areas incorporating compost in food production, and (3) the recently created GEOfood brand [18] for sustainable food and agriculture. A roadmap for digital-twin-enabled community composting is suggested for the context of the local food supply chain.

Some limitations must be stated. First, although Estrela Geopark association confirmed the suitability of the developed artifacts for their community composting strategy, the system is not yet deployed in the entire region. A real-scale prototype is under evaluation before replicating the composting devices in the nine municipalities. Therefore, a roadmap is proposed. Second, transferability to other Geoparks adopting the GEOfood brand is also unconfirmed at this stage. Moreover, each Geopark presents a different combination of urban and rural areas. Only some of them may perhaps share the exact characteristics of Estrela Geopark, with a wide area of urban users and the production of endogenous food products able to incorporate compost in their local supply chain. Currently, there are 161 Geoparks in 44 countries, and 24 are integrating the GEOfood initiative. Third, producers' adherence to the smart composting system can be ensured via GEOfood requirements for using the brand and economic incentives for using compost. However, urban users composting practices are only now beginning in some regions like Estrela Geopark. Some municipalities already support home composting (which may streamline the transition to community composting), but many end-users will need more time to adhere to a circular economy. Nevertheless, the experts participating in this project believe that the system may contribute to this goal, showing the importance of circular economy to the entire region and simplifying compost pick up even in cases where home composting is not common practice.

Substantial opportunities for future work are also identified. First, departing from the DSR limitations found, it will be necessary to scale-up the municipality level platform. A gradual deployment to increase region awareness for circular economy, simultaneously supporting their endogenous food production and external image, is considered the best approach by Estrela Geopark. Second, data analytics and artificial intelligence capabilities are still immature. The data collected can be used to create a circular economy index for the region and identify patterns of compost production in each area of the Geopark. Third, smart community composting is only a part of the circular economy potential. Information systems will be essential to improve sustainability in smart regions, increasing cohesion between urban and rural areas while contributing to the competitiveness of the local economy. DRR projectability [16] is a good starting point to envisioning more sustainable futures.

Acknowledgements This work is funded by national funds through the FCT-Foundation for Science and Technology, I.P., within the scope of the project CISUC-UID/CEC/00326/2020 and by European Social Fund, through the Regional Operational Program Centro 2020.

References

1. Zeiss, R., Ixmeier, A., Recker, J., Kranz, J.: Mobilising information systems scholarship for a circular economy: review, synthesis, and directions for future research. Inf. Syst. J. **31**(1), 148–183 (2021)
2. Chiappetta Jabbour, C.J., Fiorini, P.D.C., Ndubisi, N.O., Queiroz, M.M., Piato, É.L.: Digitally-enabled sustainable supply chains in the 21st century: a review and a research agenda. Sci. Total Environ. **725**, 138177 (2020)
3. Hofmann, T.: Integrating Nature, people, and technology to tackle the global agri-food challenge. J. Agric. Food Chem. **65**(20), 4007–4008 (2017)
4. Bradford, A., Sundby, J., Truelove, A., Andre, A.: Composting in America—A Path to Eliminate Waste, Revitalize Soil and Tackle Global Warming (2019)
5. Dsouza, A., Price, G.W., Dixon, M., Graham, T.: A conceptual framework for incorporation of composting in closed-loop urban controlled environment agriculture. Sustain. **13**(5), 1–28 (2021)
6. Pai, S., Ai, N., Zheng, J.: Decentralized community composting feasibility analysis for residential food waste: a Chicago case study. Sustain. Cities Soc. **50** (March), 101683 (2019)
7. Rosemann, M., Becker, J., Chasin, F.: City 5.0. Bus. Inf. Syst. Eng. **63**(1), 71–77 (2021)
8. European Commission: Industry 5.0 (2021)
9. Santiago Santos Valle, Kienzle, J.: Agriculture 4.0: agricultural robotics and automated equipment for sustainable crop production (FAO) (2020)
10. Bhoir, R., Thakur, R., Tambe, P., Borase, R., Pawar, S.: Design and implementation of smart compost system using IOT. In: 2020 IEEE Interantional Conference for Innovation in Technology (INOCON 2020), pp. 5–9 (2020)
11. Casas, O., López, M., Quílez, M., Martinez-Farre, X., Hornero, G., Rovira, C., Pinilla, M.R., Ramos, P.M., Borges, B., Marques, H., Girão, P.S.: Wireless sensor network for smart composting monitoring and control. Meas. J. Int. Meas. Confed. **47**(1), 483–495 (2014)
12. Nikoloudakis, Y., Panagiotakis, S., Markakis, E., Atsali, G., Manios, T.: Cloud composting: a centralised approach. In: 2016 International Conference on Telecommunications and Multimedia (TEMU 2016), pp. 206–211 (2016)
13. Hevner, A.R., March, S.T., Park, J., Ram, S.: Design science in information systems research. MIS Q. **28**(1), 75–105 (2004)
14. March, S.T., Smith, G.F.: Design and natural science research on information technology. Decis. Support Syst. **15**(4), 251–266 (1995)
15. Vieira, G., de Castro, E., Gomes, H., Loureiro, F., Fernandes, M., Patrocínio, F., Firmino, G., Forte, J.: The Estrela Geopark—from planation surfaces to glacial erosion. In: Landscapes and Landforms of Portugal. pp. 341–357 (2020)
16. Baskerville, R., Pries-Heje, J.: Projectability in design science research. J. Inf. Technol. Theory Appl. **20**(1), 3 (2019)
17. vom Brocke, J., Maedche, A.: The DSR grid: six core dimensions for effectively planning and communicating design science research projects. Electron. Mark. **29**(3), 379–385 (2019)

18. UNESCO Geoparks: GEOFood Manifesto (2021)
19. van Eck, N.J., Waltman, L.: Software survey: VOSviewer, a computer program for bibliometric mapping. Scientometrics **84**(2), 523–538 (2010)
20. Wang, T., Zhang, M., Springer, C.H., Yang, C.: How to promote industrial park recycling transformation in China: an analytic framework based on critical material flow. Environ. Impact Assess. Rev. **87**(January), 106550 (2021)
21. Paul, M., Bussemaker, M.J.: A web-based geographic interface system to support decision making for municipal solid waste management in England. J. Clean. Prod. **263**, 121461 (2020)
22. Gupta, H., Kumar, A., Wasan, P.: Industry 4.0, cleaner production and circular economy: an integrative framework for evaluating ethical and sustainable business performance of manufacturing organizations. J. Clean. Prod. **295**, 126253 (2021)
23. Shojaei, A., Ketabi, R., Razkenari, M., Hakim, H., Wang, J.: Enabling a circular economy in the built environment sector through blockchain technology. J. Clean. Prod. **294**, 126352 (2021)
24. Zeiß, R.: Contribution of information systems to the circular economy in the digital age. In: Smart Cities/Smart Regions—Technische, wirtschaftliche und gesellschaftliche Innovationen, pp. 765–778. Springer Fachmedien Wiesbaden, Wiesbaden (2019)
25. Sarkis, J., Zhu, H.: Information technology and systems in China's circular economy. J. Syst. Inf. Technol. **10**(3), 202–217 (2008)
26. San Martin, D., Orive, M., Martínez, E., Iñarra, B., Ramos, S., González, N., Guinea de Salas, A., Vázquez, L.A., Zufía, J.: Multi-criteria assessment of the viability of valorising vegetable by-products from the distribution as secondary raw material for animal feed. Environ. Sci. Pollut. Res. **28**(13), 15716–15730 (2021)
27. Manniello, C., Statuto, D., Di Pasquale, A., Picuno, P.: Planning the flows of residual biomass produced by wineries for their valorization in the framework of a circular bioeconomy. Lect. Notes Civ. Eng. **67**, 295–303 (2020)
28. Kristoffersen, E., Blomsma, F., Mikalef, P., Li, J.: The smart circular economy: a digital-enabled circular strategies framework for manufacturing companies. J. Bus. Res. **120** (August 2019), 241–261 (2020)
29. Pansari, N.B., Deosarkar, S.B., Nandgaonkar, A.B.: Smart compost system. In: Proceedings of 2nd International Conference on Intelligent Computing and Control Systems (ICICCS 2018), ICICCS, pp. 597–600 (2019)
30. De Corato, U.: Agricultural waste recycling in horticultural intensive farming systems by on-farm composting and compost-based tea application improves soil quality and plant health: a review under the perspective of a circular economy. Sci. Total Environ. **738**, 139840 (2020)
31. Siswoyo Jo, R., Lu, M., Raman, V., Hanghui Then, P.: Design and implementation of iot-enabled compost monitoring system. ISCAIE 2019 - 2019 IEEE Symposium on Computer Applications and Industrial Electronics, pp. 23–28 (2019)
32. Elalami, M., Baskoun, Y., Zahra Beraich, F., Arouch, M., Taouzari, M., Qanadli, S.D.: Design and test of the smart composter controlled by sensors. In: Proceedings of 2019 7th International Renewable and Sustainainable Energy Conference (IRSEC 2019), no. 4, pp. 1–6 (2019)
33. Dantas, T.E.T., de-Souza, E.D., Destro, I.R., Hammes, G., Rodriguez, C.M.T., Soares, S.R.: How the combination of circular economy and Industry 4.0 can contribute towards achieving the sustainable development goals. Sustain. Prod. Consum. **26**, 213–227 (2021)
34. Mohee, R.: Waste management opportunities for rural communities. Agric. Food Eng. Work. Doc. 1–90 (2007)
35. Brown, S.: The C4 model for visualising software architecture. https://c4model.com/. Accessed 27 Oct 2021
36. Mekki, K., Bajic, E., Chaxel, F., Meyer, F.: Overview of cellular LPWAN technologies for IoT deployment: sigfox, LoRaWAN, and NB-IoT. In: 2018 IEEE International Conference on Pervasive Computing and Communications Work, pp. 197–202 (2018)

Reducing Cognitive Load in Learning to Model UML Sequence Diagrams

Sohail Alhazmi, Charles Thevathayan, and Margaret Hamilton

Abstract This paper demonstrates how cognitive load theory can be used to improve learning outcomes by presenting a tool capable of assisting novices to learn to model sequence diagrams effectively. Learning sequence diagrams is known to lead to heavy cognitive load as they must be consistent with the class diagram, while discharging all the responsibilities specified in the underlying use case. Moreover, novices must also consider the various design options and their impact on the qualitative aspects of the model. Our tool allows cognitive load to be better managed by using a 'divide and conquer' approach. In the initial stage, only consistency with the class diagram is enforced. In the second stage, invalid messages are disallowed by tracking the active entity and the current knowledge state in entities. In the third stage, students will not be allowed to submit a diagram until the stated use case goals are met. In the final stage, qualitative feedback and marks are awarded based on established metrics, and students are allowed to improve their scores by resubmitting the model. Students' performance and feedback on the tool show that our novel framework combining scaffolding with a form of gamification has helped to improve the learning outcomes in modelling substantially, especially among stragglers. One benefit of our approach is that it can be adapted to other areas where students may be cognitively challenged.

Keywords Cognitive load theory · Interaction diagrams · e-learning tool · UML modelling · Sequence diagrams

---

A prior version of this paper has been published in the ISD2021 Proceedings (http://aisel.aisnet.org/isd2014/proceedings2021).

S. Alhazmi (✉) · C. Thevathayan · M. Hamilton
RMIT University, Melbourne, Australia
e-mail: s3513690@student.rmit.edu.au

C. Thevathayan
e-mail: charles.thevathayan@rmit.edu.au

M. Hamilton
e-mail: margaret.hamilton@rmit.edu.au

E. Insfran Pelozo et al. (eds.), *Advances in Information Systems Development*,
Lecture Notes in Information Systems and Organisation 55,
https://doi.org/10.1007/978-3-030-95354-6_11

1 Introduction

One of the key responsibilities of a systems analyst is to develop analysis models that identify the architecture of an information system. The Unified Modelling Language (UML) is the most common notation used to describe these models. UML has evolved into a standard object-oriented (OO) modelling notation for designing conceptual models of software systems [21]. Students are exposed to UML early in their study as it plays a crucial role in specifying, visualizing, constructing, and documenting OO software system [15]. Students use UML models to validate design decisions and to examine their influence on quality. With UML as the standard modelling notation in industry, proficiency in UML is a valuable asset for every information system developer novice.

Developing good modelling skills is cognitively demanding and students are expected to acquire them as they progress through various courses. Despite design and UML being a core element in IS and CS degrees, a previous multi-institutional study with 314 participants found that the majority of graduating students were unable to design a software system [11]. A number of early studies investigating student performance in modelling revealed students face the greatest difficulties in modelling interaction diagrams [4, 23], affirming our own experiences working with novices in software engineering (SE) projects. The problem is exacerbated for sequence diagrams (SDs), as the high number of aspects that must be analyzed concurrently in working memory greatly increases the cognitive load [24].

For learning to be effective, formative feedback on heavy cognitive tasks such as modelling becomes necessary for good learning outcomes in subsequent years [22]. With diverse students, ongoing diagnosis is needed for each individual student facing difficulties. However, educators teaching software engineering modelling are facing many challenges as massive class sizes and post-COVID classes make meaningful one-to-one interaction and feedback in the early formative stages difficult. Providing timely feedback to increasingly diverse student cohorts therefore relies on developing learning tools able to guide and provide immediate feedback when students are learning to model.

The cognitive load theory (CLT) postulates that the cognitive load resulting from a task may potentially hamper learning [27]. Any strategy that involves more cognitive load than available working memory can deteriorate performance by overwhelming the learner [29]. Modelling sequence diagrams overwhelms many learners as it involves a high number of constraints that must be concurrently handled in the working memory such as the messages that can initiate other messages, the objects that can receive the messages and the type of messages that can be sent [24]. Only the active object that currently has the control can initiate sending a message. The object to which a message can be directed depends on whether there is an existing association, parameter or local link. Novices find it difficult to understand how interactions are constrained by the type of associations in the class diagrams. For example, a novice may not realize that when the source and destination classes form a one-to-many or many-to-many association, the source object must obtain or be passed a reference to the recipient object. The types of elements that can be sent as part of the message are determined based on the method signature in the class diagram.

Many have asserted the need to develop techniques to reduce the high cognitive load required for learning SDs [25, 29], which stems from the need to consider constraints and requirements imposed by multiple other models, qualitative aspects and the current state of the model. Research has shown cognitive load during modelling can be lowered by subdividing the problem into meaningful parts thereby reducing the number of interacting elements that must be considered concurrently [24]. However, none of the educational modelling tools surveyed have the ability to diagnose and nudge students towards a valid solution or to reduce the cognitive load. To the best of our knowledge, no pedagogy-based tool has been devised for teaching modelling SDs, though many novices are known to face severe difficulties in learning this multifaceted and important modelling artifact.

These problems have led to the research question which we address in this paper:

- How can an e-learning tool be devised to reduce the high cognitive load many novices face when learning to model sequence diagrams?

The rest of the sections are described as follows. Section 2 presents the related work of this study. Section 3 details our methodology. We briefly explain the proposed tool in Sect. 4. Section 5 presents the results which are followed by discussion, limitations and conclusion.

2 Related Work

2.1 Cognitive Load Theory (CLT)

The vast majority of research on CLT is concerned with reducing the cognitive load by managing the design of instructional materials [14, 18], known as the extraneous load. Research has identified several effects that can reduce the extraneous load. Some of these include goal-free effect, worked example effect, completion problem effect, split-attention effect, modality effect, and redundancy effect [28, 30], most of which are intended to deal with the presentation of instructions. Since the UML standard dictates the presentation of the SD, the extraneous load is considered irrelevant.

Recent studies have attempted to reduce the cognitive load inherent in the task by reducing the number of interacting elements involved in the task [8, 30], known as the intrinsic load. One method of reducing intrinsic load is to subdivide the complex task into meaningful modules that can be handled and learned separately [12]. Since the working memory treats each part as a single unit of information, the modular approach can significantly reduce the cognitive load. It is possible to follow this modular approach in SD modelling because some activities such as modelling SDs consistent with class diagrams can be handled separately from other activities. Similarly, identifying the final goal (completeness) for each SD model can be defined by interpreting all the responsibilities specified in the underlying use case. This essentially reduces the number of interacting elements involved in SD modelling by reducing the intrinsic load, leading to reduced cognitive load on working memory.

A few studies have emphasized the need to develop approaches to reduce the high cognitive load required for learning SDs [25, 29], which stems from the need to consider constraints and requirements imposed by multiple other models, qualitative aspects and the current state of the model. Research has shown cognitive load during modelling can be lowered by subdividing the problem into meaningful parts thereby reducing the number of interacting elements that must be considered concurrently [24].

2.2 Existing UML Modelling Tools

Several UML modelling tools were designed in the past for various demands and user profiles with varying levels of complexity. Most of these were intended primarily for practising engineers [19]. Such tools with many advanced characteristics and functionalities (e.g. forward or reverse engineering) aided company designers to model large complex systems. Visual tools have been developed for multi-domain modeling (e.g. computational modeling) including MagicDraw, Modelio2, UMLet, QuickUML and minimUML2 [1]. Several studies have highlighted problems when industrial tools are used in education [1, 2, 20]. Being designed for experts they are often unduly complex, difficult to learn, and distracting for students. In addition, these tools do not provide any useful feedback on the design aspects. Moreover, these tools often do not consider the novices' difficulties and challenges that can alleviate the cognitive loads on novices' modelers [20]. Therefore, some of the important educational aspects such as consistency checking, inter-model dependency and ongoing diagnoses are absent in industrial tools as these tools were targeted for experts and not for novices.

In the recent past, a few non-commercial UML tools have been designed specifically for the educational context [5, 6, 10, 16]. In our previous study [3], we surveyed tools developed for the educational context and summarized the strengths and weaknesses of the existing educational UML tools. The results showed, (1) no past attempts to provide instant feedback on design tasks considering CLT for reducing high cognitive load in modelling task, (2) none of the tools surveyed were able to give qualitative feedback using metrics such as coupling and cohesion, and (3) none of the educational modelling tools surveyed have the ability to diagnose and nudge students towards a valid solution or to reduce the cognitive load.

Employers are increasingly demanding that graduates come with Higher Order Thinking Skills (HOTS) associated with an inherently high cognitive load, while institutions are relying more on online teaching. We therefore posit, more research must be undertaken to effectively facilitate CLT infused e-learning techniques.

3 Methodology

The purpose of this study was to reduce the cognitive load for novices learning modelling SDs by developing an e-learning tool based on the CLT recommendations for managing the cognitive load complexity of modelling SDs.

To evaluate the effectiveness of the e-learning tool, multiple sources of data were collected, including pre-tests and post-tests, a survey gathering the effectiveness of the tool from students' perspectives and data collected through the tool (such as the number of attempts, the number of error messages and the time taken). The participants for this study consisted of a broader variety of undergraduate (UG) and post-graduate (PG) students who enrolled in the Software Engineering Fundamentals (SEF) courses from three different Universities in different countries: Australia, Vietnam, and Saudi Arabia. The SEF course where this e-learning tool was trialed is a core course for all students taking a degree in Computer Science, IT, IS or Software Engineering. The SEF enrolment varies from 100 to 300 students each semester with increasingly diverse cohorts. However, the number of students has dramatically declined due to COVID'19. The SEF course covers many abstract software engineering concepts, including UML design, patterns and principles. Most incoming students having little or no prior experience with object-oriented programming skills find UML design difficult and abstract. Each student was asked to undertake a pre-test before interacting with the tool, followed by a post-test and a survey.

Pre- and post-tests were designed to measure the performance 'improvement' after using the new tool. These questions were designed to cover various levels of the Bloom's taxonomy [9] up to analysis level. These tests focused on UML design concepts, specifically SDs as these were the main learning objectives for our proposed approach. Some questions are designed mainly to test whether students have understood; (1) the interdependencies between domain models (class diagram) and interaction models (SDs), (2) the impact of post-conditions stated in use case on modelling SD, and (3) the importance of qualitative aspects for modelling optimal quality of SDs. Figure 1 shows a sample question from the pre/post-test question bank designed to measure whether students have understood the interdependencies between the class diagram and SD after using the tool.

Statistical techniques were used to measure whether the tool helped to improve learning outcomes among our diverse student cohort. Multiple use-case scenarios of varying difficulty levels were presented for students in the tool. The improvement in performance was determined based on the difference between pre- and post-test scores.

Student perceptions were measured using students' feedback related to the tool through a specially designed survey. A questionnaire was designed to identify how they perceived the effectiveness of the tool in improving their design skills and how the feedback can be improved in the subsequent iteration. We designed a range of Likert-scale type questions and open-ended questions. Some items were used in these questionnaire to measure cognitive complexity and adapted from existing instruments [24].

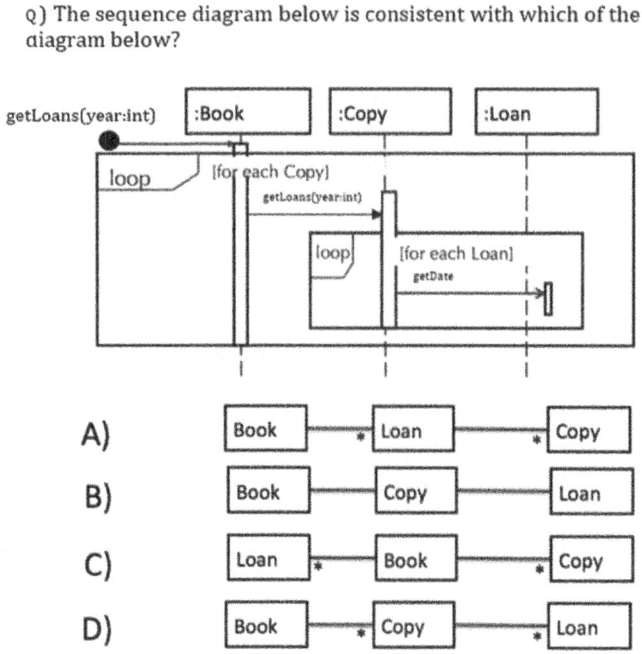

Fig. 1 A sample pre/post-test question designed to measure student understanding of SD concepts

3.1 Managing Cognitive Complexity of Sequence Diagram Modelling in the New E-Learning Modelling Tool

In our previous work [3], we have conducted an exploratory study to identify the most common difficulties facing novice modelling SDs. Several main difficulties were identified and classified as root causes of novices' difficulties with SDs. Table 1 shows a summary of our findings for novice modelling difficulties.

These difficulties suggest high intrinsic load as the main reason why novices were overwhelmed by modelling SDs. Students had to track the current state while ensuring consistency with class diagrams, meet goals stated in use cases, adhere to implicit constraints inherent in the domain as well as come up with an optimal design considering qualitative aspects. These challenges led us to find novel ways to reduce the cognitive load in active memory by decomposing the modelling tasks.

Stage 1: Managing the Most Fundamental Difficulty (Model Consistency Verification)

Our framework provided a way to reduce the cognitive load on novices by requiring them to focus firstly on structural consistency (the most fundamental pressing problem that novices faced when modelling SDs) through consistency checks and instant feedback. For each message, the student specifies the target object as well as

Table 1 Difficulties with modelling sequence diagrams

	Identified novice difficulties	Difficulty classification
1	Students do not realize messages and message elements dispatched in sequence diagrams must be consistent with class diagrams	Consistency verification
2	Students have difficulty detecting when a sequence-diagram is complete as post-conditions stated in use cases can be difficult to interpret	Poorly defined goals. (completeness verification)
3	When deciding which message can be dispatched, students often fail to consider parameter links, local links and links returned earlier as well as the attributes returned by the local and external methods	Difficulty tracking current knowledge state
4	Poor quality of designs mostly resulting in highly coupled and centralized designs	Lack of feedback on qualitative aspects

the list of parameters. If the message is valid the system updates the state of interaction, visually depicts the message and allows the student to proceed, otherwise appropriate diagnostic messages are displayed to guide the novices. Consistency checking against the class diagram is performed based on the class of the message target object and the type of message elements. Figure 2 shows an example of instant error feedback provided after adding an inconsistent message with the class diagram.

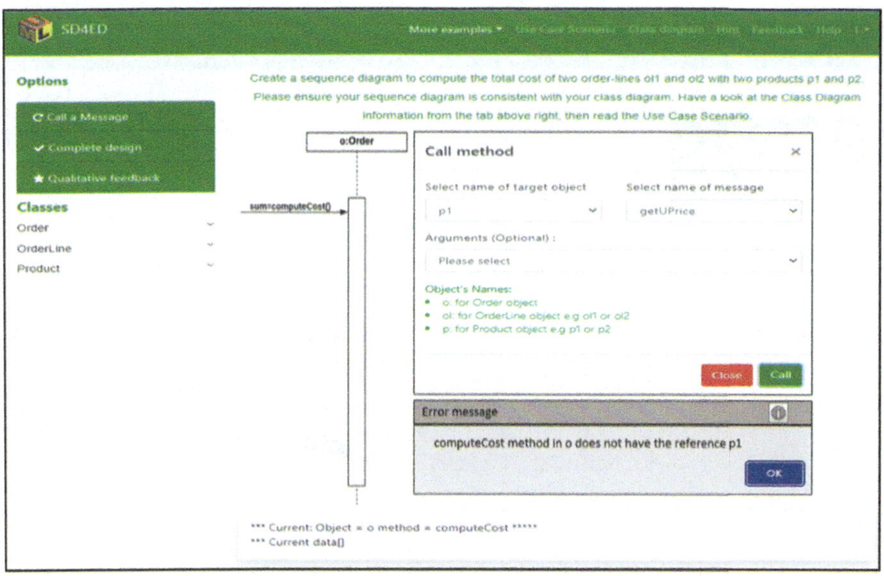

Fig. 2 Example of instant error message generated by tool if consistency constraints are violated

Stage 2: Managing the Difficulty of Tracking Current Knowledge State

For a message to be valid, the knowledge elements at the source entities must be a superset of the message elements dispatched and must contain a link to the target object. When deciding which message can be dispatched students often fail to consider parameter links, local links and links returned earlier as well as attributes returned by local and external methods. Therefore, our tool tracks the knowledge elements at each entity, which combines existing attributes with data and links received or created. These knowledge elements are combined with existing attributes to determine whether a specific message can be dispatched or returned to the caller. Appropriate diagnostic messages are displayed when invalid attempts are made as shown is Fig. 3.

Stage 3: Model Completeness Verification

In the third stage, when students are aware of how SDs are constrained by the underlying class diagram, students will not be allowed to submit a diagram until the stated use case goals are met. So, novices are provided with pre-created objects whose references are explicitly captured in the tool. Students need to meet all the use case post-conditions before submission. By updating all knowledge acquired in objects as messages are exchanged, the framework provides appropriate feedback when some post-conditions are not met.

Figure 4 shows an example of the feedback provided when checking the model meets all the post-conditions and students can view the details of post-conditions yet

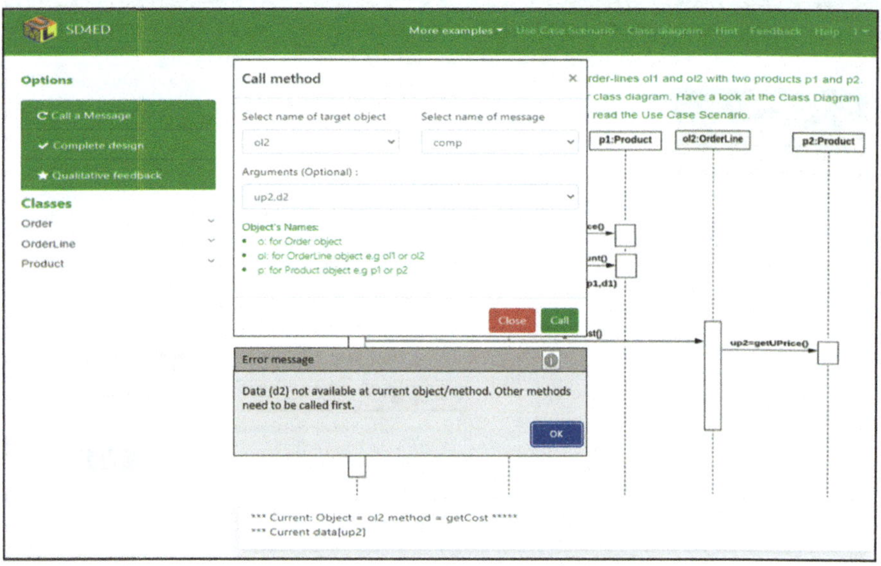

Fig. 3 Diagnostic feedback is displayed when an invalid attempts of sending a message without receiving the required data

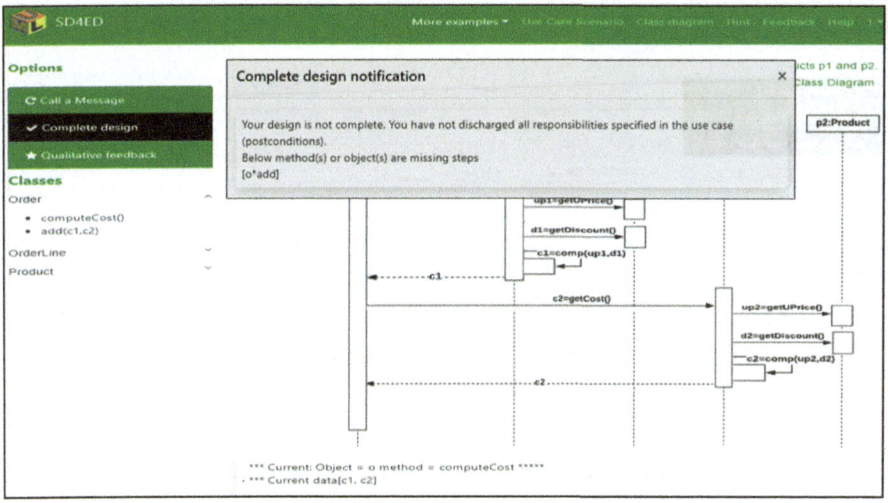

Fig. 4 Example of feedback given if SD submitted without meeting all post-conditions specified in the use case

to be met. Hint buttons are incorporated to allow students to step through towards the goal state one step at a time.

Stage 4: Devising Metrics for Measuring the Quality of the Model

In the final stage, qualitative feedback and scores are given based on devised quality metrics. Students are allowed to improve their scores by resubmitting the design. The holistic feedback on design quality focused on 3 key aspects including maintainability, reusability and performance. To measure the extent of distribution (capturing maintainability), the extent of variation in the number of messages initiated by each interacting object is computed. When all the entities dispatch equal numbers of messages, the extent of distribution is considered the highest. To compute the level of coupling/cohesion (capturing reusability) the metrics devised require computing the ratio of internal and external messages. The coupling/cohesion score decreases as the ratio of external messages over internal messages increases. To measure the performance, the ratio of redundant messages to total messages is computed. The performance is considered the highest, when no redundant message exists. A gamification strategy was used for motivation and engagement. Most students come up with poor designs initially, but are allowed to see their design scores and feedback before redesigning and resubmitting. Such an approach allowed novices to improve their learning outcomes in modelling concepts using a constructivist approach. An example of qualitative holistic feedback and scores provided to novices using our tool is shown in Fig. 5, where a student had designed a centralized design with low cohesion. The details of qualitative holistic feedback generated for the design submitted (Fig. 5) is shown in Table 2.

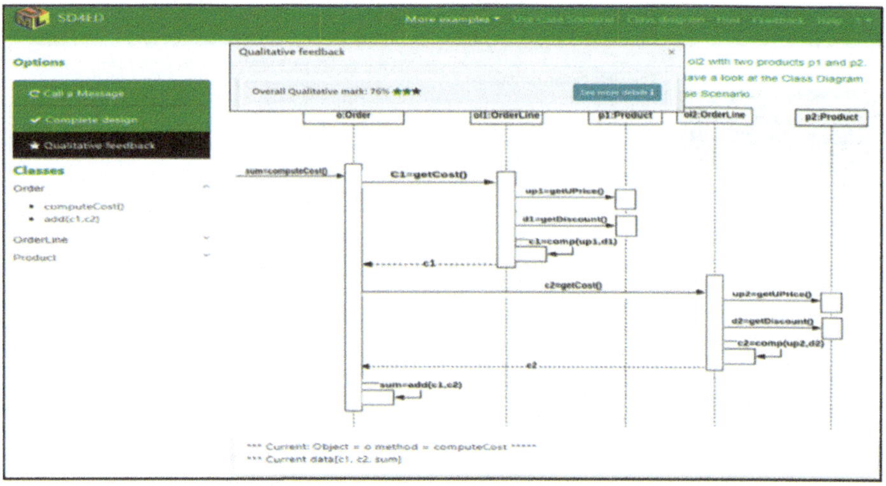

Fig. 5 Example of qualitative feedback generated in the tool

Table 2 Details of qualitative feedback given in the tool for the design submitted in Fig. 5

Quality metrics	Measure	Marks (%)	Goal (min/max)
1. Redundant messages (measuring the performance)	0	100	0 (min)
2. Coupling cohesion ratio (measuring reusability)	7/3	73	5/3 (max)
3. Extent of distribution (measuring maintainability)	1.35	55	0.75 (max)
Overall quality mark		76	

4 Designing of E-Learning Modelling Environment with CLT

The CLT assumes that learning and performance are impaired by overload on human working memory [27]. Modelling SDs is one of the most cognitively demanding tasks among all the UML modelling as it involves a high number of interacting items that must be concurrently handled in the working memory. High cognitive loads for modelling SDs also stem from the need to consider the presence of links (association, local or parameter), availability of knowledge elements at the source object at current state, and possible paths to the goal state by constantly checking the interdependencies with class and use case diagrams. When qualitative measures are used, students also must consider how responsibilities can be delegated effectively by choosing appropriate pathways.

Our e-learning modelling tool for SDs followed CLT recommendations. One such recommendation we followed was to break down the complex task into meaningful parts or modules that can be processed and learned separately [12, 29]. Since the working memory treats each module as a single unit of information, our 'divide-and-conquer' approach has reduced the cognitive load. The problem space was subdivided into meaningful parts, reducing the number of interacting elements to be considered concurrently. Our framework permits the cognitive load to be managed by requiring students to focus only on consistency and constraints aspects before they consider post-conditions (completeness) in use case and qualitative aspects.

Poor usability of e-learning tools can negatively impact educational outcomes, especially when the material to be learnt is complex [26]. Poor usability also limits the potential advantage achieved from e-learning environments [31] by imposing an extraneous cognitive load, as learners struggle with the interface and challenges of the content presented. Some researchers have found significant learning effects from optimising the usability of learning materials [7]. This is most likely to be seen with novice modellers who experience the content as presenting a high intrinsic cognitive load and would therefore be more sensitive to any extraneous load imposed by poor usability [28]. Other researchers have reported improvements in efficiency, satisfaction or motivation [13, 31]. One of the main principles of good interface design suggested [17] is to keep the learners informed through timely appropriate feedback and they also should always know where they are, which actions can be taken and how these actions can be performed. Thus, these factors have been addressed in our tool to help novices achieve better learning outcomes.

4.1 The Design and Development of Our Modelling Environment

Our tool is a web-based environment developed using an agile approach in each stage of development of the tool. Such an iterative approach can help us develop a better environment with an appropriate graphical user interface for novices.

In the first iteration, user interfaces were addressed as the tool's main aspects which needed improvement. Students faced difficulties when first learning to use the interface in the tool developed. Students struggled to draw message lines between source and target objects. The next iteration of the tool development therefore focused on improving the user interface.

The user interface in the second iteration has been fixed to improve student learning the tool. For each message, the student needs to type the name of the target object, the name of the message, and the list of parameters. If the message is valid, the system updates the state of interaction, visually depicts the message and allows the student to proceed. Although most responses about the developed tool were advantages at this stage, students having to type the method name and arguments correctly without any spelling mistakes led to some frustration. Therefore, the usability of the tool should reduce the amount of text the user has to type.

In the final iteration, the user interface has been completely overhauled. We allow students to select from pre-created messages instead of drawing the lines and typing the list of arguments manually without any spelling mistakes. We also added a Hint feature in the tool to reveal possible next steps at any given state. This feature is useful for stragglers who are unable to proceed for a specific time. Most students' responses were positive for the questions related to the user interface after the improvements, which helped them achieve better learning outcomes.

5 Results

This section reports on our results collected from the participants of our longitudinal studies carried out for more than four years on the use of our tool. Each year, we trialed our tool with different cohorts of students who enrolled in the same SEF course. In the second and fourth year, each student was asked to conduct a pre-test before interacting with the tool, followed by a post-test and a survey.

The pre-and post-tests revealed substantial improvement in learning outcomes and student satisfaction for all groups generally, and the improvement was mainly at the higher levels of the Bloom's taxonomy, in the application and analysis types of questions. Table 3 shows the impact by comparing the average marks for pre- and post-test results as well as the percentage gained in three groups. The first group was made up of undergraduate and postgraduate students in the second year of our trial. The second group consisted of postgraduate students converting from other disciplines, and the third group was made up of undergraduate students. In group 1, 68 of the 243 students enrolled in the course, volunteered to trial the tool and complete both tests and the survey were used in the analysis. Table 3 also shows the average pre-test mark was 46.25%, while the average for post-test was 61.25%, resulting in 32% improvement. In group 2, 32 of the 94 students enrolled in the course volunteered to trial the tool. The percentage improvements were higher at 57% as the average mark went up from 35 to 55. In group 3, out of 58 students who enrolled in the SEF course, only 21 students volunteered to trial the tool. The percentage gains were slightly improved at 26.3% as the average result went up from 40 to 51.

Higher cognitive loads have been shown to negatively affect time to complete tasks. Therefore, the time taken to complete pre-and post-tests was analysed to measure whether such an approach can reduce cognitive loads faced by novices

Table 3 Summary of overall results from three different groups, noting the percentage gained between the pre- and post-tests in both groups used

Data	Number of students	Pre-test Av (%)	Post-test Av (%)	Gain (%)	Pre-test Av. completion time(min)	Post-test Av. completion time (min)
Group 1	68 (both)	46.25	61.25	32	13.26	10.25
Group 2	32 (PG)	35	55	57	14.10	12.18
Group 3	21 (UG)	40.38	51	26.3	21.50	11.15

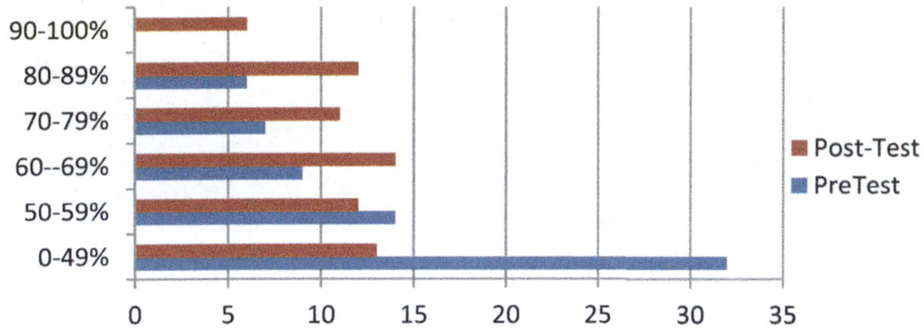

Fig. 6 Marks distribution in pre/post-tests for group 1

learning to model SDs. The results indicated that novices completed their post-tests in less time than pre-tests for all three groups, as shown in Table 3. Although percentage improvements of the tests scores were more noted earlier for the first and second groups than the third group, the average completion time dramatically decreased from 21.50 to 11.15 min for group 3 compared with the other two groups.

To understand the tool's effectiveness on students with different grades, we also analysed the distribution of student marks in pre-and post-tests for group 1 (the large number of different cohorts of students who trailed the tool). We found that the number of students in the 90–100% range went up from 0 to 6 after using the tool while the number of students scoring in the range 0–49 declined by nearly 60% from 32 to 13 students (as showing in Fig. 6). Based on these values, we reject the null hypothesis "No significant improvement after using the tool" as the Chi-square P-value of 0.000269 is less than 0.01. These findings suggest such modelling tools can significantly improve the performance of stragglers in the exam.

We have also analysed the students' individual log files in the tool to identify how students learn the SD concepts during their interaction with the tool. Students were presented with multiple use cases in the tool. Figure 7 illustrates the average number of error messages provided when students violate the specified constraints, number of attempts to reach the final goal, consistency error messages, number of hints used, and qualitative design marks awarded in each attempt. Overall, the results show a regular decrease as the average marks for each of these aspects decreased over many attempts. Note that the qualitative design marks improved over many attempts, increasing from 30 to nearly 69%. Such an approach allowed novices to improve their learning outcomes in modelling concepts using a constructivist approach.

Table 4 also shows the average completion time for the tasks in the tool. The data indicated a consistent decrease in time taken to complete tasks over many attempts as the average time taken declined dramatically.

Overall, participant performance in modeling SDs improved in tests especially for the straggler modelers, who were the main target group in our study. The improvement was specifically in understanding the relationship between modelling task use-cases, class diagrams and SDs. Students also found prompts and fading buttons increased interaction while allowing enough cognitive conflicts necessary for learning. Therefore, the CLT approach used in our tool allowed the cognitive load on novices to be

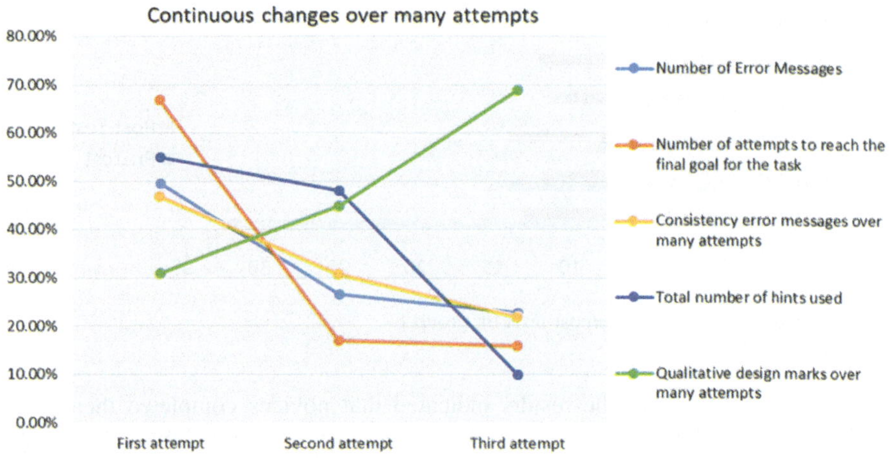

Fig. 7 Overall results from analysing tool log files for students

Table 4 Summary of completion time for tasks from analysing tool log files for all students

Average	First attempt (min)	Second attempt (min)	Third attempt (min)
Completion time for tasks	14.03	8.17	6.9

reduced by requiring them to focus only on consistency constraints at each intermediate stage, before they ensure all use case post-conditions and qualitative aspects were met in their design.

5.1 *Student Perception and Feedback*

Student perceptions were measured using their feedback related to the tool through a specially designed survey. A questionnaire was designed to study the effectiveness of the e-learning tool from students' perspectives.

In the analysis of the results we combine the "Strongly Disagree" and "Disagree" responses under SD/D category, and "Strongly Agree" and "Agree" responses into an SA/A category, respectively. The results show approximately 82% of students confirmed SDs are harder than most other UML diagrams. Responses to the questions are given in Table 5 and reveal that the tool was particularly effective in helping novices identify and correct their misconceptions. Specifically, they found the immediate feedback based on the class diagram and uses case post-conditions supplied beneficial for learning UML design. Over 72% of students had a better understanding of interdependencies between classes and SDs after using the tool and receiving immediate feedback on their SD design. Over 81% of students had

Table 5 The results of the questionnaire

#	Questions	SD/D (%)	N (%)	SA/A (%)
1	The example scenarios presented were easy to follow	9.09	27.27	63.6
2	I find sequence diagrams harder than most other UML diagrams	9.09	9.09	81.82
3	The feedback given using the tool made me confident with SDs	9.09	18.18	72.7
4	The feedback feature on the overall design was useful	0	27.27	72.7
5	The comments were easy to follow	18.18	27.27	54.5
6	The incrementally complex design activities helped me to learn	0	18.18	81.8
7	The system was intuitive and easy to use	18.18	9.09	72.7
8	After using the tool I have a better understanding of SDs	9.09	27.27	63.63
9	After using the tool I am better aware of interdependencies between class and sequence diagrams	18.18	9.09	72.7
10	After using the tool I am better aware of how post-conditions in use cases impact on sequence diagrams	9.1	9.1	81.8
11	The system was responsive	0	36.36	63.63
12	The Hint Features were useful	27.27	27.27	45.4
13	Such a tool should be made available early in the semester	0	27.27	72.7

better awareness of how post-conditions in use cases can impact sequence diagrams. The positive response to the three questions related to student confidence, understanding and awareness suggests the e-learning tool can play a key role in improving the self-efficacy of students.

Students were also surveyed with open-ended questions. Overall, the responses showed students had a better understanding of sequence diagrams, as shown in Table 6. Responses to the question asked in Table 6 show that most students found the feedback mechanism provided at each stage helped them to grasp the design skills and correct their invalid mental models. Moreover, the majority of the students doing the survey found incremental complex design activities improved their understanding of SD.

6 Discussion

Modelling SDs has been shown to be one of the most cognitively demanding tasks among all the UML modelling suite capturing different perspectives [24]. High cognitive loads for modelling SDs stem from the need to consider the presence of links (association, local or parameter), availability of knowledge elements at the source object at current state, and possible paths to the goal state by constantly checking the consistency with class and completeness with use case post-conditions. When

Table 6 Written feedback from the open-ended survey question

Q. What aspects of the tool did you like?	"It was pretty intuitive for the most part. The different levels of complexity were useful"
	"The current object and methods and what current data are exist in each stage"
	"The selection list, the prompt of the current object and method"
	"The quick and immediate feedback we got for several aspects"
	"It was very responsive, it showed visually what "call a method" looks like"
	"I can practice in my own time and get feedback"
	"We can practice with examples and mistakes can be immediately corrected by the tool"
	"I really like the feature where I can check my sequence diagram is complete or not"

qualitative measures are used, students also must consider how responsibilities can be delegated effectively by choosing appropriate pathways. Our model has provided a way to structure the cognitive loads to suit diverse students by requiring students to focus only on consistency and constraints aspects through instant feedback at any stage by aggregating all past interactions before they consider post-conditions (completeness) and qualitative aspects. The model provides tasks at multiple levels starting from the simplest tasks and allowing students to build their self-efficacy with only one type of constraint before moving to more difficult tasks with multiple types of constraints and goals (data, links, valid-termination, goals and qualitative aspects). These decomposition features together with cohort-specific prompting, diagnostic feedback messages and the ability to move to the goal states in steps provide a level of support closer to human tutors.

The lack of resources for teaching and learning as well as ever increasing class sizes have substantially reduced the opportunities for formative feedback, resulting in a high number of invalid and poor-quality student designs. These problems have been made worse by increasing reliance on online learning in recent years and the current lockdowns introduced in response to COVID'19. Lack of resources and limited face-to-face interaction, therefore, have made development of pedagogical tools inevitable. These problems are exacerbated for software engineering courses where increasing numbers of students come from many different disciplines. Most of these students, especially those lacking experience with object-oriented programming find UML modelling and different UML diagrams very abstract. In the initial stage, our pedagogical tools therefore aimed to reduce the high cognitive load in modelling SDs by giving feedback on consistency with class diagrams and then whether responsibilities in use-case diagram are correctly discharged. Our knowledge-based approach guiding students to create consistent and complete UML diagrams has helped stragglers overcome their initial mental blocks.

Though developing the e-learning tool required understanding CLT and running a longitudinal study, our pre- and post-tests with different groups of students reveal that such an approach can help improve the learning outcomes, especially for the strugglers. Our feedback shows that the high cognitive load caused by having to consider various aspects of sequence diagrams concurrently had been one of the main reasons for past student difficulties. Sequence diagrams play a key role with modern software development which requires modelling the interaction between objects using a number of different frameworks as with full stack development. Moreover, the design patterns promoting qualitative attributes such as re maintainability, reusability and performance are expressed mainly through SDs. Hence, we believe more research is needed to develop pedagogical frameworks that can lower the reliance on human tutors for novices. The context of our research, however, is not to replace the existing modelling tools, but to supplement them. Our research is focused on finding ways of helping novice designers to get over the initial learning barriers before proceeding to use tools improving productivity in subsequent courses.

7 Limitations of the Study

Our e-learning tool incorporating CLT has shown substantial improvement in SD design related learning outcomes. However, there are a number of other factors that may have influenced the results. The numbers of students volunteering to take part in these activities remain relatively small as the data collection period usually coincide with students' peak periods. The self-selecting students in any study may not be reflective of the actual cohort, but the grade distribution of participants and non-participants was broadly similar in terms of average and standard deviation, in the mid-semester test prior to the study. The poor usability of the versions used in the first group trialled may have caused some students not to proceed with the post-test and the survey, but usability of the agent for version 3 has greatly improved. Though students perform better when cognitive load is reduced by problem decomposition and scaffolding, it is not clear to what extent students will be able to solve complex modelling problems when no support is provided.

8 Conclusions

Modelling SDs poses a heavy cognitive load on students as constraints and rules imposed by other UML models must be analyzed concurrently, making it the most poorly understood UML artefact. Our approach better manages cognitive load by subdividing a complex problem into independent meaningful parts with a reduced number of interacting elements. In the initial stages, students have to focus only on one or two aspects. Our e-learning modelling tool automatically enforces consistency checking, checks for completeness and gives qualitative feedback based on domain models, use cases and quality metrics specified by the instructor. The theoretical design and pedagogy for the proposed tool is based on CLT.

The extensive automated feedback enables large diverse groups of students to learn to model sequence diagrams. The e-learning tool manages cognitive load by varying the type and amount of help as a student progresses in modelling tasks. In the first stage, inconsistent messages are prevented from being dispatched while giving immediate feedback. In the second stage, invalid messages are disallowed by tracking the active entity and the current knowledge state in entities. In the next stage, submission is disabled until the design itself is valid, and if invalid, feedback is given on constraints violated or unmet. In the final stage, qualitative feedback on the submitted design is provided based on specified metrics. The longitudinal study allowed data collected from experienced tutors, lecturers and participants to evolve a more personalized teaching approach better suited to our increasingly diverse student cohorts. The e-learning modelling tool developed has shown substantial improvements in learning outcomes and student satisfaction. One main benefit of our approach is that it can be easily replicated for other complex modelling tasks. In our future work, we plan to trial our tool with different cohorts of students and other UML models.

Acknowledgements Sohail Alhazmi is supported by a scholarship from the Islamic University in Medina, Saudi Arabia.

References

1. Agner, L.T., Lethbridge, T.C., Soares, I.W.: Student experience with software modeling tools. Softw. Syst. Model. **18**(5), 3025–3047 (2019)
2. Agner, L.T., T.C. Lethbridge.: A survey of tool use in modeling education. In: 2017 ACM/IEEE 20th International Conference on Model Driven Engineering Languages and Systems (MODELS). IEEE (2017)
3. Alhazmi, S., Thevathayan, C., Hamilton, M.: Learning UML sequence diagrams with a new constructivist pedagogical tool: SD4ED. In: Proceedings of the 52nd ACM Technical Symposium on Computer Science Education (2021)
4. Alhazmi, S., Thevathayan, C., Hamilton, M.: Interactive pedagogical agents for learning sequence diagrams. In: International Conference on Artificial Intelligence in Education. Springer (2020)
5. Alphonce, C., Ventura, P.: QuickUML: a tool to support iterative design and code development. In: Companion of the 18th Annual ACM SIGPLAN Conference on Object-Oriented Programming, Systems, Languages, and Applications (2003)
6. Auer, M., Tschurtschenthaler, T., Biffl, S.: A flyweight UML modelling tool for software development in heterogeneous environments. IEEE (2003)
7. Avouris, N.M., Dimitracopoulou, A., Daskalaki, S., Tselios, N.K.: Evaluation of distance-learning environments: Impact of usability on student performance. Int. J. Educ. Telecommun. **7**(4), 355–378 (2001)
8. Bannert, M.: Managing cognitive load—recent trends in cognitive load theory. Learn. Instruct. **12**(1), 139–146 (2002)
9. Bloom, B.S.: Taxonomy of educational objectives. Vol. 1: Cognitive domain, vol. 20, p. 24. McKay, New York (1956)

10. Dranidis, D., Stamatopoulou, I., Ntika, M.: Learning and practicing systems analysis and design with StudentUML. In: Proceedings of the 7th Balkan Conference on Informatics Conference (2015)
11. Eckerdal, A., McCartney, R., Moström, J.E., Ratcliffe, M., Zander, C.: Can graduating students design software systems? ACM SIGCSE Bulletin. **38**(1), 403–407 (2006)
12. Gerjets, P., Scheiter, K., Catrambone, R.: Designing instructional examples to reduce intrinsic cognitive load: molar versus modular presentation of solution procedures. Instr. Sci. **32**(1), 33–58 (2004)
13. Hancock, P.A., Pepe, A.A., Murphy, L.L.: Hedonomics: the power of positive and pleasurable ergonomics. Ergon. Des. **13**(1), 8–14 (2005)
14. Kirschner, P.A.: Cognitive load theory: implications of cognitive load theory on the design of learning. Elsevier (2002)
15. LeBlanc, R.J., Sobel, A., Diaz-Herrera, J.L., Hilburn, T.B.: Software engineering 2004: curriculum guidelines for undergraduate degree programs in software engineering. IEEE Computer Society (2006)
16. Lethbridge, T.C.: Teaching modeling using Umple: principles for the development of an effective tool. In: 2014 IEEE 27th Conference on Software Engineering Education and Training (CSEE&T). IEEE (2014)
17. Nielsen, J.: Ten usability heuristics, http://www.nngroup.com/articles/ten-usability-heuristics. Accessed 17 June 2021
18. Paas, F., Renkl, A., Sweller, J.: Cognitive load theory: instructional implications of the interaction between information structures and cognitive architecture. Instr. Sci. **32**(1/2), 1–8 (2004)
19. Pourali, P., Atlee, J.M.: An experimental investigation on understanding the difficulties and challenges of software modellers when using modelling tools, Technical Report CS-2018–03. David R. Cheriton School of Computer Science (2018)
20. Pourali, P., Atlee, J.M.: An empirical investigation to understand the difficulties and challenges of software modellers when using modelling tools. In: Proceedings of the 21th ACM/IEEE International Conference on Model Driven Engineering Languages and Systems (2018)
21. Rayner, M., Hockey, B.A., Chatzichrisafis, N., Farrell, K.: OMG unified modeling language specification. In: Version 1.3,© 1999 Object Management Group, Inc. Citeseer (2005)
22. Schaffer, H.E., Young, K.R., Ligon, E.W., Chapman, D.D.: Automating individualized formative feedback in large classes based on a directed concept graph. Front. Psychol.. **8**, 260 (2017)
23. Sien, V.Y.: An investigation of difficulties experienced by students developing unified modelling language (UML) class and sequence diagrams. Comput. Sci. Educ. **21**(4), 317–342 (2011)
24. Sin, T.: Improving novice analyst performance in modeling the sequence diagram in systems analysis: a cognitive complexity approach, Florida International University (2009)
25. Song, I.-Y., Khare, R., An, Y., Hilsbos, M.: A multi-level methodology for developing UML sequence diagrams. In: International Conference on Conceptual Modeling. Springer (2008)
26. Sweller, J.: Cognitive load theory, learning difficulty, and instructional design. Learn. instruct. **4**(4), 295–312 (1994)
27. Sweller, J.: Cognitive load during problem solving: effects on learning. Cognit. Sci. **12**(2), 257–285 (1988)
28. Sweller, J., Van Merrienboer, J.J., Paas, F.G.: Cognitive architecture and instructional design. Educ. Psychol. Rev. **10**(3), 251–296 (1998)
29. Syn, T., Batra, D.: Improving sequence diagram modeling performance: a technique based on chunking, ordering, and patterning. J. Database Manage. (JDM). **24**(4), 1–25 (2013)
30. Van Merrienboer, J.J., Sweller, J.: Cognitive load theory and complex learning: recent developments and future directions. Educ. Psychol. Rev. **17**(2), 147–177 (2005)
31. Zaharias, P.: Usability in the context of e-learning: a framework augmenting 'traditional' usability constructs with instructional design and motivation to learn. Int. J. Technol. Human Interact. (IJTHI) **5**(4), 37–59 (2009)

Studying the Influence of Empathy Maps on Brainstorming for Requirements Elicitation: A Quasi-Experiment

Ezequiel Kahan, Emilio Insfran, Marcela Genero, and Alejandro Oliveros

Abstract There is currently a trend that highlights the interest in the use of Design Thinking techniques for the elicitation of requirements. The evidence concerning the effectiveness of these techniques is, however, still scarce, which has consequently led us to carry out a quasi-experiment in order to evaluate the effectiveness of one of the most frequently used DT techniques: Empathy Maps. Empathy Maps were employed by students enrolled on a Bachelor's degree in Computer to understand their influence on the effectiveness of Brainstorming sessions. The students perceived a slightly positive influence as regards the use of the Empathy Maps as part of a requirements elicitation, despite not finding statistically positive results. We obtained several insights that may be useful for practitioners, researchers and lecturers interested in using this type of techniques to improve the requirements elicitation practices, although this preliminary result is not conclusive and should be corroborated in further studies.

Keywords Requirement elicitation · Design thinking · Empathy map · Quasi-experiment

---

A prior version of this paper has been published in the ISD2021 Proceedings (http://aisel.aisnet.org/isd2014/proceedings2021).

E. Kahan (✉) · A. Oliveros
Universidad Nacional de 3 de Febrero, Buenos Aires, Argentina
e-mail: ekahan@untref.edu.ar

A. Oliveros
e-mail: aoliveros@untref.com.ar

E. Insfran
IUMTI—Universitat Politècnica de València, Valencia, Spain
e-mail: einsfran@dsic.upv.es

M. Genero
University of Castilla-La Mancha, Ciudad Real, Spain
e-mail: marcela.genero@uclm.es

E. Insfran Pelozo et al. (eds.), *Advances in Information Systems Development*,
Lecture Notes in Information Systems and Organisation 55,
https://doi.org/10.1007/978-3-030-95354-6_12

1 Introduction

The first work that linked Design Thinking (DT) to Requirements Engineering (RE) appeared more than 8 years ago [27] and since then, the interest in this topic has been increasing. Nowadays there is a solid body of studies demonstrating the potential of applying DT in synergy with RE, in particular with the requirements elicitation phase [8, 11, 14, 15]. DT is considered to be a "*way of finding human needs and creating new solutions using the tools and mindsets of design practitioners*" [16]. DT can be integrated into business and other activities of society, and individuals and teams can use it to generate innovative and implementable ideas that, that have an impact [3]. It is consistent with the initial elicitation goals and practices of RE, including also the agile development methods [27]. The DT process, which is complemented by design tools and techniques, can provide a supportive framework for information system (IS) development by enabling teams to invent new constructs and artefacts [12].

In the field of IS, research efforts related to DT take two principal directions: (1) how IT and IS can support DT practices by generating new tools, and (2) how DT can support problem-solving in the IS context [12]. With regard to this second direction, DT has the potential to solve RE challenges [13, 20], including the discovery of the fuzzy needs and volatile requirements of the multiple stakeholders involved in socio-technical system projects [10]. Evidence shows that it would be possible to improve the application of DT in RE [12], and this can specifically be seen in the elicitation of requirements to which a fragmented perspective of DT is applied, and in which the emphasis is more on techniques than on its integrative perspective. Furthermore, the evidence that exists on its specific techniques is generic, that is, the empirical evidence regarding which of the techniques that are part of the DT process are more appropriate or have better results when the aforementioned problems are confronted. This provides the possibility of conducting experiments with which to evaluate the relevance of a process based on DT in order to incorporate it into requirement elicitation, and the different techniques that form part of it.

This paper, therefore, presents the results of a quasi-experiment carried out in order to investigate whether the use of Empathy Maps in combination with Personas improves the performance of Brainstorming sessions. The improvement was measured in terms of the quantity of requirements obtained in the ideation sessions. We decided to begin by carrying out an evaluation in an academic context. As indicated in [5], experiments with student participants must be considered state of the art for evaluation in RE as a prior and necessary step before carrying out evaluations in industry. The quasi-experiment was conducted with a group of 72 students enrolled on a Bachelor's degree in Computer Engineering at the Universitat Politècnica de València in Spain.

The remaining of this paper is structured as follows. Section 2 introduces a process that incorporates DT techniques for requirements elicitation, while Sect. 3 provides an overview of the related work. Section 4 introduces a definition of the quasi-experiment, along with its planning and execution while Sect. 5 presents the analysis and interpretation of the data collected in the quasi-experiment, and Sect. 6 discusses the threats to validity. Finally, Sect. 7 presents our conclusions and outlines our future work.

2 Requirements Elicitation Process Based on Design Thinking

We propose to use our previous experience [14] as a basis on which to incorporate a process based on the Design Thinking Stanford approach (empathize, define, ideate, prototype, test), which is one of the approaches most frequently used by practitioners [21], into the requirements elicitation phase. Our proposal is based on that of Hehn et al. [9], who introduce multiple strategies for the integration of DT into RE. Of the 5 stages in this approach, we consider the first 3, since we consider that they are the most closely connected with the requirements elicitation phase [15] (see Fig. 1). We consider that *empathy* is a key feature of requirements elicitation and also of DT [23]. Empathy is a concept that includes both the involuntary act of feeling sympathy for someone else and the cognitive act of placing oneself in someone else's position and adopting their perspective [17]. It is the attempt to reconstruct the specific perspective of the other and how he or she perceives the situation. For example, employing empathy techniques can foster software engineers' empathy practices and skills, and help identify requirements that are strongly focused on people, such as privacy requirements [18]. It can be viewed as a form of knowledge construction [17], which is a central aspect of requirements elicitation [19].

Although empathy development occurs in all stages of DT, it is particularly relevant during the "Empathise" stage, which is usually the first stage of the process. Nonetheless, empathy occurs in the entire requirements elicitation process.

As shown in Fig. 1, we propose to use a specific technique in each stage: an Empathy Map, Personas and Brainstorming, respectively. According to the existing literature [15], there are at least 70 DT techniques, although several of them are similar to each other, and it is common to use a small group of them [15]. Our initial

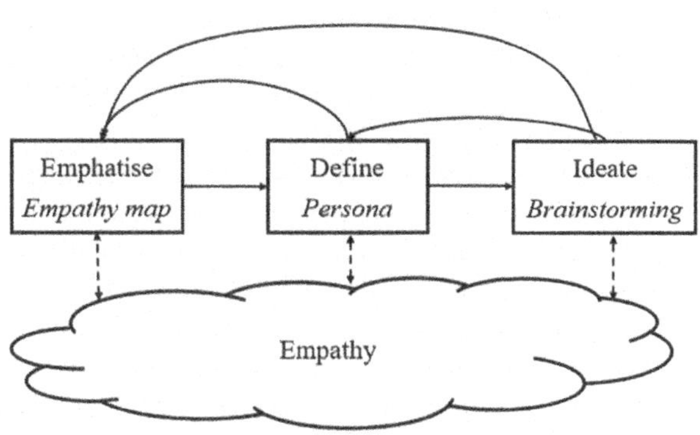

Fig. 1 A process for requirement elicitation based on DT

view is that of empathising using an Empathy map, after which synthesising/defining information using Personas could improve the ideation process, which is carried out by means of Brainstorming. These techniques were chosen on the basis of an exhaustive review of the related literature [14, 15, 25] and the experience of the first author, who has been applying DT as a practitioner in the software industry in Argentina since 2012. We consider that the incorporation of the Empathise stage is a key aspect of an elicitation process based on DT, which is not necessarily present in the more classical requirements elicitation process, or when DT techniques are used individually. Although other authors have referenced several DT techniques, such as Personas and Customer Journey Maps, as effective means for requirements elicitation, they have not addressed the users' emotional and cognitive aspects, but rather the functional requirements and goal aspects of the system [18]. These emotional and cognitive aspects could, in our opinion, be in part achieved by incorporating techniques frequently used during the empathy stage, such as Empathy Maps. Despite the fact that the template for Personas development has, in some cases, included Empathy map attributes [7], these elements, which are a fundamental part of empathy, have not been covered in any depth.

The requirement elicitation process based on DT illustrated in Fig. 1 consists of the following stages and techniques:

- Empathise: During this stage, the goal is to explore the problem space and attempt to understand it by carrying out different activities that include research, consulting domain experts, observing, engaging, and empathising with people. Some of the techniques most frequently employed during this stage are interviews, focus groups, observations, documentary analysis and Empathy Maps. The technique selected for this stage was that of an Empathy Map, since it would make it possible to integrate learning and generate valuable "insights" about the user. An Empathy Map is a simple and easy-to-understand visual representation that allows the knowledge regarding the behaviour and attitudes of one or a group of users to be captured, thus generating empathy. The exercise of creating the map helps participants to consider things from the user's perspective, along with his/her goals and challenges. The map provides four central areas on which to focus: what the user (s) said, did, thought or felt in relation to the problem to be solved.
- Define: During the define stage, the information gathered during the empathise stage converges on the definition of a specific problem. This stage is also denominated as synthesis, because it involves reframing the problem for a specific group of users, environment, or situation. The technique selected for this stage was that of Personas. Personas are fictional characters, which are created on the basis of previous research in order to represent the different types of users that might use a solution. Creating personas helps to understand one's users' needs, experiences, behaviour and goals. The Personas method is used in the design of digital environments, but is also employed in many other contexts, including product development, marketing, communication planning and service design.
- Ideate: This is the stage in which solutions are generated and proposed, in our case, in the form of ideas of requirements. The technique selected for this stage

was that of Brainstorming. Brainstorming is a group creativity technique in which solutions to a specific problem are proposed by gathering a list of ideas spontaneously contributed by the group's members. Inhibitions as regards participation are removed by encouraging people to think more freely and to suggest as many spontaneous new ideas as possible without criticism. Note that we prefer to use the term *idea of requirements* rather than *requirements* when referring to the result of the Brainstorming technique, since it represents raw ideas of requirements that still need to be introduced to and validated with the stakeholders if they are to be considered as the requirements of the information system to be developed.

In addition to these stages and specific techniques, we also consider that DT, as an holistic approach, provides additional enrichment based on empathy building, focusing on user needs and the frequent validation of ideas through the use of prototypes [27].

3 Related Work

The interest in employing DT techniques for requirements elicitation has grown in the IS field in recent years [8, 15]. We, therefore, used the empirical studies found in the two aforementioned SMSs, which cover papers published until 2018, as a basis for our research. Scopus was subsequently used to extend this search until December 2020, which enabled us to discover 5 more empirical studies published from 2017 onwards that show evidence of the use of specific DT techniques in requirements elicitation. All of the studies found are described below. Three of the studies were carried out in an academic context at Brazilian universities [4, 7, 26]:

- Costa et al. [4] carried out an exploratory case study with 17 undergraduate Computer Science students with the aim of discovering: "What are the perceptions of students regarding learning Design Thinking?". Projects using individual techniques (Personas, Empathy Maps) and team techniques (Brainstorming and co-creation workshop) were then employed for the development of the authors' mobile application. The students considered that the techniques used were very useful but stated that more training time was required to carry out the case study.
- Souza et al. [26] presented exploratory case studies performed with 32 and 21 undergraduate students, respectively. The authors selected 15 techniques with which to teach their students that they should elicit the requirements of a specific system of their own choosing. The techniques selected were grouped according to their purpose function: (1) Collection, registration, and organisation of information: exploratory research, rapid ethnography, fly on the wall, interviews, questionnaires, insight cards, Empathy Map, Personas and motivation matrix; (2) Group use: Brainstorming and bodystorming; (3) Stimulating the generation of ideas and representing possible solutions: storytelling, storyboards, prototyping and try it yourself. In both experiences, the students reduced the number of techniques

used: 6 in the first and 12 in the second, with Personas and Brainstorming being those most frequently used, followed by Empathy Maps.

- Ferreira et al. [7] presents a controlled experiment carried out with 37 Computer Science undergraduates in order to compare two Personas-related techniques: traditional Personas and PATHY, which is the traditional Personas technique enriched with some concepts of Empathy Maps. The controlled experiments assessed which of the two techniques helped to generate descriptions of personas that are more focused on potential requirements to be considered in the design of the application. The authors analysed the efficiency of the techniques and the participants' perceptions of their use. PATHY generated more relevant characteristics for the application design than did the technique that followed the traditional description. PATHY was also more efficient as regards creating personas.

Three studies were performed in an industrial context with practitioners [10, 22, 24]:

- Hehn and Uebernickel [10] performed an exploratory case study, carried out by interviewing 18 practitioners. Their findings suggest that DT has the potential to support current RE practices and vice versa. The authors in question believe that an integration of both approaches leverages a symbiotic relationship. As both topics, DT and RE, are broad-ranging, multiple opportunities for further research can be identified. DT provides a structured process for requirements elicitation for complex problems.
- Ruchira et al. [24] performed a case study within the development of agile software projects in the Sri Lankan Software Development Industry. After carrying out 15 interviews with project stakeholders who practice DT in agile projects, they identified that DT practices, such as the human-centred approach, thinking by doing, visualising, the synthesis of diverging and converging, and a collaborative work style, are helpful as regards enhancing the customer's expectations. The most suitable methods by which to identify customers' needs were determined to be: customer journey, story mapping, prototypes, proof of concept and customer profiling.
- Prestes et al. [22] carried out a survey of 127 practitioners on the use of DT in agile software development in Brazil, with the aim of answering the following research question: "How to apply DT practices to improve customer expectations in agile practices?". The results show that a great variety of techniques (more than 50) and different variants of the DT process are employed, with Brainstorming, Personas and Empathy Maps being those most frequently used.

As stated above, the number of publications showing some type of evidence of the use of DT in requirements elicitation has increased in recent years. Studies conducted in academic contexts show that the DT techniques for which there is the most empirical evidence of their use are Personas, Brainstorming and Empathy Maps. The main use of DT is for the ideation stage and the exploration of innovative solutions. The studies focus on the application of DT to elicit requirements without an integrative perspective of them. In these studies, there were no proposals for requirements elicitation processes based on DT. Instead, DT techniques are used individually with greater orientation to creativity than empathy. The studies carried out in an industrial context are more generic, i.e., they do not focus on specific techniques, although the evidence is not very rigorous, since controlled experiments are not carried out or different techniques are not compared but simply used and some type of subjective feedback based on surveys or interviews is collected. It is, therefore, necessary to collect evidence regarding which specific techniques are the most appropriate for each of the stages related to requirement elicitation within the DT requirement elicitation process. This led us to propose a process based on DT as described in Sect. 2 (see Fig. 1), together with specific techniques for each of its phases and to validate it empirically.

4 Quasi-Experiment Description

The quasi-experiment was carried out at the Universitat Politècnica de València (Spain) in October 2019. A quasi-experiment was carried out rather than a "true" experiment because the random assignment of the treatments to the participants was not possible. This quasi-experiment was designed and reported by following the recommendations provided in [28]. The experimental material is available at: https://tinyurl.com/js4m2xj7, and the principal characteristics of the quasi-experiment are described in the following subsections.

4.1 Goal

The main goal of this quasi-experiment was to investigate whether a sequence of *elicitation techniques* influences the effectiveness of subjects when eliciting requirements. The Goal Question Metrics template [1] was employed, and the goal of this quasi-experiment was, therefore, **to analyse** Elicitation Techniques **for the purpose of** comparing them **with respect to** their effectiveness, perceived ease of use, and perceived utility **from the point of view** of requirements analysts **in the context** of students enrolled on a Bachelor's degree in Computer Engineering at the Universitat Politècnica de València in Spain.

4.2 Variables and Hypotheses

The independent variable of interest is the *elicitation technique* used (Empathy Map + Personas + Brainstorming or Personas + Brainstorming); i.e., two treatments were considered ($EM + P + B$ *and* $P + B$).

The dependent variable was *Effectiveness*, which was measured as being the quantity of ideas of requirements (QIR) generated by the students. These QIR were grouped into the following categories:

- People-centred ideas. This category included all the ideas that impact on or are impacted on by people. They include ideas in which people are the central component. For example: "The application will be accessible to all users, including those with functional diversity".
- Business-oriented ideas. This category included all the ideas that describe or propose aspects related to an animal protection centre (the domain chosen for use in this quasi-experiment, as explained below). For example: "Include an inventory that shows the food and medicines available for both purchase and donation".
- Technology-oriented ideas: This category included all the ideas that establish technological requirements. For example, "The public part of the application must be a website".
- Others: Ideas of requirements that do not connect directly with the software application itself. For example, "Creation of tutorials on how to properly care for animals".

The sum of the number of ideas of requirements in each category was, therefore, considered as a measure of *Effectiveness* (QIR = QIR-P + QIR-B + QIR-T + QIR-O). We formulated the following hypotheses:

- H1-0: There is no significant difference between the subjects' effectiveness when using $P + EM + B$ *or* $P + B$ / H1-a: $\neg$ H1-0.

The goal of the statistical analysis is to reject the null hypothesis and possibly accept the alternative ones. The hypothesis presented herein is two-sided, because we did not postulate any effect arising.

4.3 Sample and Participants

We took a convenience sample of two groups of undergraduate students enrolled on a Bachelor's degree in Computer Engineering at the Universitat Politècnica de València (UPV) in Spain (Group A composed of 35 participants and Group B composed of 37 participants). The students attended a course on Requirements Engineering during the academic year 2019–2020. This course included an introduction to and examples of the use of the techniques employed in the quasi-experiment, i.e. Personas, Empathy Maps and Brainstorming. The participants had no prior experience in the use of any of these three techniques. Finally, considering that the main purpose of the quasi-experiment was to study the improvement to the quantity of ideas of requirements generated during the Brainstorming session when using Empathy Maps, and that Brainstorming is a group-based technique, we defined several working groups with which to run the quasi-experiment. Each of the working groups, almost all of which were composed of 5 students, was randomly assigned by the course professor. Only two working groups in Group B had 6 students owing to the number of students enrolled on the course, signifying that there were 7 working groups in Group A (35 students) and 7 working groups in Group B (37 students).

4.4 Experimental Objects and Tasks

The object of the experiment was to describe the characteristics and main needs of an Animal Adoption Centre, called MODEPRAN, which is in the city of Valencia in Spain. This description provided the participants with an overview of and context in which to begin identifying the main stakeholders, and the scope in which to propose the ideas for the software system requirements during the Brainstorming session. This domain was chosen because it was possible that most of the participants would be familiar with the process of adopting animals, which might motivate and inspire interaction among them.

The experimental task included the generation of ideas of requirements by means of a Brainstorming session using only Personas, in the case of Group B (P + B treatment), or using the Personas together with the Empathy Maps, in the case of Group A (*EM + P + B treatment*). The rationale behind this task configuration was that using Personas together with the Empathy Maps might improve empathy with the stakeholders and consequently improve the quantity of ideas of requirements generated during the Brainstorming session. Multiple documents were defined as instrumentation. The documentation included: (i) a description of the MODEPRAN Animal Adoption Centre; (ii) an introduction to the Personas technique with examples; (iii) an introduction to the Empathy Maps technique with examples; (iv) guidelines on how to run a Brainstorming session and the format required in order to report the ideas of requirements generated; and (v) the post-experiment survey, which included both closed questions in order to analyse the perception-based variables of this study (PEOU, PU and MT) and one open question that would enable the participants to express their opinion about the use of the techniques. Table 1 shows the closed questions in the post-experiment survey.

The questionnaire contained three questions related to the students perceptions of the material and training they had received, while the remaining questions were related to the students perceptions when performing the experimental tasks using each treatment. These questions were based on an adaptation of the *Technology Acceptance Model* (TAM) [6], and measured the Perceived ease of use (PEOU) and Perceived utility (PU) using a five-point Likert scale. The number of questions related to PEOU and PU were different for each group because Group A used the Empathy Map technique, and specific questions related to this technique were, therefore, added to the questionnaire.

Table 1 Post-experiment questionnaire

ID	Classification	Group A	Group B
Q1	Material and training (MT1)	The support material used in the exercise was adequate to be able to understand and use each of the techniques (Personas, Empathy Map, Brainstorming)	The support material used in the exercise was adequate to be able to understand and use each of the techniques (Personas, Brainstorming)
Q2	Material and training (MT2)	The explanation received was adequate in order to apply each of the techniques (Personas, Empathy Map, Brainstorming)	The explanation received was adequate in order to apply each of the techniques (Personas, Brainstorming)
Q3	Material and training (MT3)	I now have the knowledge required to be able to use the techniques learned (Personas, Empathy Map, Brainstorming) in real situations	I now have the knowledge required to be able to use the techniques learned (Personas, Brainstorming) in real situations
Q4	Perceived utility (PU1)	The Personas technique was useful for characterising the different stakeholders	The Personas technique was useful for characterising the different stakeholders
Q5	Perceived utility (PU2)	The Brainstorming technique was useful for identifying requirements ideas	The Brainstorming technique was useful for identifying requirements ideas
Q6	Perceived ease of use (PEOU1)	There was a good connection between the different techniques used (Personas, Empathy Map, Brainstorming)	There was a good connection between the different techniques used (Personas, Brainstorming)
Q7	Perceived ease of use (PEOU2)	The sequence in which the techniques were applied (Personas, Empathy Map, Brainstorming) was appropriate	The sequence in which the techniques were applied (Personas, Brainstorming) was appropriate
Q8	Perceived ease of use (PEOU3)	It was easy to construct the Empathy Map	n/a
Q9	Perceived ease of use (PEOU4)	The construction of the Empathy Map did not require a great effort	n/a
Q10	Perceived ease of use (PEOU)	It was easy to separate the information into the 4 quadrants of the Empathy Map	n/a
Q11	Perceived utility (PU3)	The Empathy Map technique was useful for exploring stakeholder goals and motivations	n/a
Q12	Perceived utility (PU4)	Constructing the Empathy Map was beneficial for the Brainstorming session	n/a

(continued)

Table 1 (continued)

ID	Classification	Group A	Group B
Q1	Material and training (MT1)	The support material used in the exercise was adequate to be able to understand and use each of the techniques (Personas, Empathy Map, Brainstorming)	The support material used in the exercise was adequate to be able to understand and use each of the techniques (Personas, Brainstorming)

4.5 Design and Execution

We used a between-subject design, meaning that the participants (i.e., working groups) in the quasi-experiment were assigned to different treatments, with each working group experiencing only one of the treatments. The students were not aware that they were participating in a quasi-experiment and were under the impression that it was just another exercise in the context of the RE course on which they were enrolled. Since the RE course is a weekly course of three hours per week, the training and quasi-experiment were performed in two sessions throughout two weeks. The first week was the training session, whose purpose was to introduce the concepts, examples and small exercises concerning the techniques that would be applied in the quasi-experiment: Personas, Empathy Maps, and Brainstorming in Group A and Personas and Brainstorming in Group B. The quasi-experiment took place in the second week. The quasi-experiment was controlled, meaning that no interactions took place between the working groups. The experimental session lasted approximately three hours. Once the quasi-experiment had finished, in order to prepare the data for the analysis, two of the authors of this paper classified the ideas of requirements obtained by each of the working groups according to the classification introduced in Sect. 4.2 (i.e. people-centred, business-oriented, technology-oriented, others). Each idea of requirements was analysed and classified into one or more category, with the authors reaching a consensus when necessary.

4.6 Analysis Procedure

The data analysis was carried out by considering two phases:

- Analysis of Effectiveness measured through number of QIR attained
  - We first carried out a descriptive study of the measure of the dependent variable, i.e. QIR, in order to obtain a general overview of the data obtained in the quasi-experiment.
  - We performed a Kolmogorov–Smirnov test [29] to determine the normality of distributions.

  - The results of the afore mentioned test were employed as a basis on which to test the hypothesis formulated, using the non-parametric Mann Whitney test [37] for the data collected in the quasi-experiment.

- Analysis of the post-experiment survey

  - The perception-based measures collected from this survey were analysed using descriptive statistics illustrated by box-plots. The analysis was grouped into PEOU, PU and MT questions.

5 Data Analysis and Interpretation

In this section, we present the data analysis and interpretation of the results obtained in the quasi-experiment following the analysis procedure detailed above.

5.1 Analysis of the Effectiveness

Table 2 reports the descriptive statistics of the ideas of requirements classified.

The descriptive statistics show that fewer technology-orientated ideas were generated by the groups in the Empathy Map treatment. One possible explanation for this is that the use of an Empathy Map influences the number of ideas linked to non-functional requirements, thus reducing their number. In order to test the hypothesis formulated, we analyzed the effect of the main factor (Empathy Map) on the measures considered (QIR, QIR-P, QIR-B, QIR-T) using the non- parametric Mann–Whitney test. Table 3 shows the results obtained for each measure employed in the Mann–Whitney U tests, in which the Origin column describes the independent variable, p-value is the statistical significance obtained, op is the estimated observed power of the test, es is the effect size, and r represents the possibility of rejecting the null hypothesis with the data obtained. All these values were calculated using a standard configuration of SPSS. The results obtained do not allow us to reject H1-0, i.e. it would appear that the Empathy Map had no effect on the QIR. Similar results were

Table 2 Descriptive statistics of the ideas of requirements classified

	Treatment EM + P + B (Group A)					Treatment P + B (Group B)				
	Media	Median	SD	Min	Max	Media	Median	SD	Min	Max
QIR	30.86	28	10.792	20	47	31.43	28	11.013	18	48
QIR- P	4.43	4	3.409	1	11	4.43	4	2.37	1	8
QIR-B	22.43	18	8.182	15	36	21	20	9.661	11	36
QIR-T	4	4	2.38	2	9	6	6	3.416	1	11

Table 3 Mann–Whitney test results for QIR

Origin	Requirement elicitation technique			
	p-value	op	es	R
QIR	0.798	<0.051	−0.098	NO
QIF-P	0.846	<0.050	0	NO
QIF-N	0.608	<0.059	0.299	NO
QIF-T	0.221	< 0.216	−1.271	NO

obtained after repeating the test for each individual variable (QIR-P, QIR-B and QIR-T), i.e. it was not possible to reject H1-0 in any of the cases.

5.2 *Analysis of the Post-Experiment Survey*

Figure 2 show the box-plots generated with data obtained from the post-experiment survey. The contents of these figures are analysed separately for each question as follows.

- Q1—Upon evaluating the answers, it would appear that the material used is perceived as adequate, although the use of the Empathy Map generates a slightly lower average value.
- Q2—Upon evaluating the second answer, it follows that the explanation of the techniques provided by the teacher was adequate. There is more dispersion in the answers obtained for this question than in the case of Q1. A possible explanation

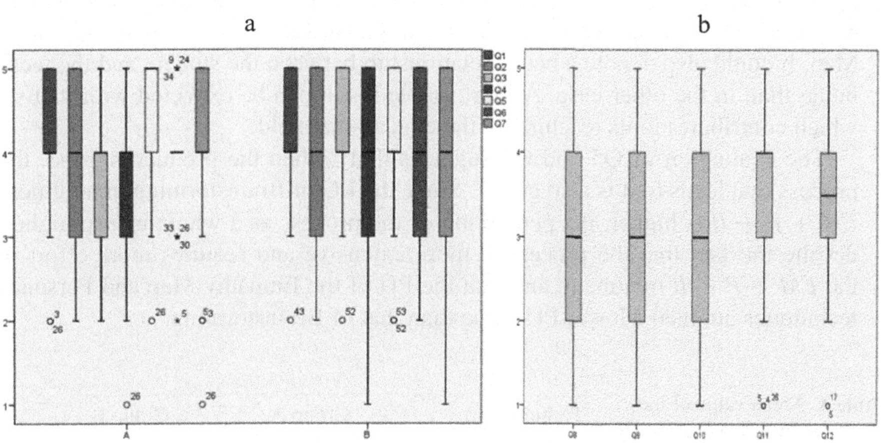

Fig. 2 Box-plots of questions of the post experiment-survey. **a** Questions 1 to 7. **b** Questions 8 to 12 (applied to Group A only)

for this greater dispersion could be the difference in the students' preferences as regards the learning modality. The evaluation of Q1 and Q2 suggests that the teacher's explanation is consistent, since there were no differences between the explanations given to both groups.

- Q3—The perception of the level of knowledge is lower in the Empathy Map treatment. This suggests that the Empathy Map, by requiring more dedication and effort (see specific questions in the next section), allowed the students to attain a more in-depth idea about their knowledge (they were more aware that they did not know as much).
- Q4—The students perceived the Personas technique to be less useful in the Empathy Map treatment. This suggests a certain level of redundancy between both techniques, signifying that the Persona technique was perceived as less useful in the Empathy Map treatment than in that in which it was not employed. It might also suggest that it is not necessary to apply both techniques. In order to discover more about this aspect, in the future, a third treatment could be incorporated in which only the Empathy Map and the Brainstorming session are carried out so as to compare whether there is a variation in the results.
- Q5—The perception of the utility of the use of Brainstorming attained a higher value in the EM + P + B treatment, with a similar distribution of percentiles for the 2 treatments. Upon comparing the mean values attained by the two groups, it will be noted that the students who used the Empathy Map had a better perception of Brainstorming.

  Although the PU of the Empathy Map is the lowest of the 3 techniques (see Fig. 2), it would appear that its use improves the PU of Brainstorming. This suggests that the Empathy Map could help to order the Brainstorming session by providing a prior "qualitative" analysis of the stakeholders (Table 4).
- Q6—A comparison of both conditions shows that there is a lower standard deviation for the perception of connection between the techniques when the Empathy Map treatment is employed. This is indicates an advantage of using the Empathy Map. It could also denote a better relationship between the student and the technique than in the other case. A more stable result can be expected with its use, which contributes to its teaching in the educational field.

The evaluation of Q5 and Q6 suggests that "when the product is good, the process that leads to it is also good". Since the PU of Brainstorming in treatment $EM + P + B$ is higher, the perception of the process as a whole is also higher, despite the fact that the process is more extensive and requires more effort in the $EM + P + B$ treatment, and that the PU of the Empathy Map and Personas techniques attained a lower PU value than that of Brainstorming.

Table 4 Mean value of the PU of the different techniques per Group/treatment

Technique	Group A	Group B
Brainstorming	4.55	4.18
Empathy map	3.36	–
Personas	3.67	3.96

- Q7—Upon comparing both treatments, we discovered that those students who used the Empathy Map perceived the sequences in which the techniques were used in the Empathy Map treatment to be the same, but that a lower standard deviation was attained for the $EM + P + B$ treatment. Again, a more stable result could contribute to its teaching in the educational field.

The results obtained for the specific questions regarding the $EM + P + B$ treatment are detailed below:

- Q11—The perception of utility of the empathy technique is lower than that of Personas and Brainstorming techniques. This is consistent with questions Q9, Q10 and Q11.
- Q8, Q9 and Q11—The median value of the PEOU for the specific questions concerning the EM + P + B treatment show that lower values were attained than for the PEOU concerning People and Brainstorming, which is consistent with a lower PU. There is much more dispersion when compared to the previous answers. One hypothesis is that, as the technique was difficult, it required more effort, and it was complicated to separate the 4 quadrants of the Empathy Map (says, does, thinks and feels), which could have had a positive influence at the time of applying the Brainstorming.

6 Threats to Validity

It is necessary consider certain issues that may have threatened the validity of the experiment:

- External validity may be threatened when experiments are performed with students, as doubts have been raised regarding the representativeness of the subjects with respect to software professionals. Despite this, the tasks to be performed did not require real world experience, and we are, therefore, of the opinion that this quasi-experiment could be considered appropriate, as suggested in literature [2]. There are no threats related to the material used, as to the real systems were employed.
- Threats to internal validity are mitigated by the design of the quasi-experiment. In our case, both the support material and the exercise were the same under both conditions, but an additional technique was presented to one of the groups.
- Conclusion validity concerns the data collection, the reliability of the measurement and the validity of the statistical tests. Statistical tests were used to reject the null hypotheses. We have explicitly mentioned and discussed when non-significant differences were present. It is also necessary to state that the conclusion validity could be also affected by the number of observations. Further replications with larger datasets are, therefore, required to confirm or contradict the results shown herein.
- Construct validity may be influenced by the measures used to attain a quantitative evaluation of the ideas generated, the comprehension of the techniques explained,

the experimentation tasks and the post-experiment questionnaire. We measured the number of ideas in order to avoid subjectivity regarding the way in which they were written, but not having proposed a template could have negatively influenced the classification process. The post-experiment questionnaire was designed using standard forms and scales.

7 Conclusions

This paper describes a quasi-experiment carried out to investigate whether the use of Empathy Maps improves the performance of the Brainstorming technique when used in the context of a requirements elicitation process. The quasi-experiment was carried out with 72 undergraduate students enrolled on a Bachelor's degree in Computer Engineering at the Universitat Politècnica de València (UPV) in Spain. The main findings obtained are the following:

- The total number of ideas does not differ significantly between treatments, and the descriptive analysis shows that the number of ideas of requirements (technological) was lower in Group A, to which the $EM + P + B$ treatment was applied. This gives rise to the theory that the Empathy Map helped the participants to be more aware of functional requirements than non-functional ones. This result was not, however, sufficiently significant to confirm the hypothesis, perhaps because the number of groups involved in the quasi-experiment were not sufficiently large.
- The descriptive analysis of the post-experiment survey shows some promising findings: despite the fact that the PU of the Empathy Map was lower than for the other techniques, the PU of the Brainstorming technique was higher in the $EM + P + B$ treatment. This suggests that, by incorporating the evaluation of emotional and cognitive factors, the Empathy Map helped the students to carry out Brainstorming sessions that were perceived to be more useful. However, the PU results obtained for Personas and Brainstorming had a lower standard deviation when using the Empathy Map. This could be a significant contribution for the requirements community in terms of the stability of the process that we are defining. It is also interesting that the PU was similar when the perception of effort was greater in the $EM + P + B$ treatment, which would imply that the product is valued over the effort required to carry it out.
- With regard to the sequence and connection of the techniques, although the median coincides in both treatments, the standard deviation of the results is lower for the $EM + P + B$ treatment. This again is an indication of the advantage of using the Empathy Map, because it shows that there was a better relationship between the students and the technique, which contributes to the impact of its teaching in the educational field.
- We learned that not having defined a specific measure with which to evaluate the Personas technique prevented us from discovering whether the Empathy Map had any influence on it. The post-experiment survey analysis allowed us to discover that the PU of Persona technique is lower in the Empathy Map treatment, which

could be interpreted as a certain level of overlapping between the two techniques such that the students found it to be redundant and, therefore, not so useful. It might, therefore, be worth comparing the two techniques in the future.

Finally, we are aware that the results obtained from this quasi-experiment are preliminary and that a further replication is required to obtain more conclusive results. We consequently plan to carry out new studies by, for example, using either Empathy Maps or Personas before the brainstorming session in different groups. Moreover, in order to avoid disparity as regards the writing of the ideas of requirements, we plan to use User stories with a common template, which are widely employed in Agile development environments. Our long-term research goal is to continue investigating the synergy of DT methods, practices, techniques and activities with the elicitation of requirements so as to provide a more solid knowledge base with empirical data that will improve the current practices of the Information Systems requirements elicitation.

Acknowledgements The research work presented in this paper is framed within the following projects: GEMA (JCCM, Spain, SBPLY/17/180501/000293), UX-Adapt (Generalitat Valenciana, Spain, AICO/2020/113), AETHER-UCLM (MICINN, Spain, PID2020-112540RB-C42), Adapt@Cloud (MICINN, Spain, TIN2017-84550-R) and Software Development Process Research Project (Requirement Engineering research line, UNTREF, Argentina).

References

1. Basili, V., Rombach, H.D.: Towards a comprehensive framework for reuse: a reuse-enabling software evolution environment.Technical Report CS-TR-2158, University of Maryland, Maryland (1988)
2. Basili, V., Weiss, D.: A methodology for collecting valid software engineering data. IEEE Trans. Softw. Eng. SE-10 728–738 (1984)
3. Brown, T.: Design thinking. Harvard Bus. Rev. https://hbr.org/2008/06/design-thinking (2008). Accessed 22 Sep 2017
4. Costa Valentim, N.M., Silva, W., Conte, T.: The students' perspectives on applying design thinking for the design of mobile applications. In: Proceedings of 2017 IEEE/ACM 39th International Conference on Software Engineering: Software Engineering Education and Training Track (ICSE-SEET), pp. 77–86. IEEE, Buenos Aires (2017)
5. Daun, M., Hübscher, C., Weyer, T.: Controlled experiments with student participants in software engineering: preliminary results from a systematic mapping study (2017)
6. Davis, F.D.: Perceived usefulness, perceived ease of use, and user acceptance of information technology. MIS Q. **13**(3), 319–340 (1989)
7. Ferreira, B., Silva, W., Barbosa, S.D.J., Conte, T.: Technique for representing requirements using personas: a controlled experiment. IET Softw. **12**(3), 280–290 (2018)
8. Ferreira Martins, H., Carvalho de Oliveira Junior, A., Dias Canedo, E., Dias Kosloski, R.A., Ávila Paldês, R., Costa Oliveira, E.: Design thinking: challenges for software requirements elicitation. Information **10**(12), 371 (2019)
9. Hehn, J., Mendez, D., Uebernickel, F., Brenner, W., Broy, M.: On integrating design thinking for human-centered requirements engineering. IEEE Softw. **37**(2), 25–31 (2020)

10. Hehn, J., Uebernickel, F.: The use of design thinking for requirements engineering—an ongoing case study in the field of innovative software-intensive systems. In: Proceedings of 26th IEEE International Requirements Engineering Conference (RE'18). Banff, Alberta, Canada (2018)
11. Hehn, J., Uebernickel, F., Mendez Fernandez, D.: DT4RE: design thinking for requirements engineering: a tutorial on human-centered and structured requirements elicitation. In: Proceedings of 2018 IEEE 26th International Requirements Engineering Conference (RE), pp. 504–505. IEEE, Banff, AB (2018)
12. Hehn, J., Uebernickel, F., Stoeckli, E., Brenner, W.: Designing human-centric information systems: towards an understanding of challenges in specifying requirements within design thinking projects. Multikonferenz für Wirtschaftsinformatik (MKWI) (2018)
13. Jarke, M., Loucopoulos, P., Lyytinen, K., Mylopoulos, J., Robinson, W.: The brave new world of design requirements: four key principles. In: Proceedings of International Conference on Advanced Information Systems Engineering, pp. 470–482. Springer (2010)
14. Kahan, E., Genero, M., Oliveros, A.: Challenges in requirement engineering: could design thinking help? In: Piattini, M., Rupino da Cunha, P., García Rodríguez de Guzmán, I., Pérez-Castillo, R. (eds.) Quality of Information and Communications Technology, pp. 79–86. Springer International Publishing, Cham (2019)
15. Kahan, E., Oliveros, A., Genero, M.: A systematic mapping study on the application of design thinking in requirement engineering. Submitted to Journal of Universal Computer Science (2021)
16. Kelley, T., Kelley, D.: Creative confidence: unleashing the creative potential within us all. Currency, New York (2013)
17. Köppen, E., Meinel, C.: Empathy via design thinking: creation of sense and knowledge. In: Plattner, H., Meinel, C., Leifer, L. (eds.) Design thinking research: building innovators, pp. 15–28. Springer International Publishing, Cham (2015)
18. Levy, M., Hadar, I.: The importance of empathy for analyzing privacy requirements. In: Proceedings of 2018 IEEE 5th International Workshop on Evolving Security & Privacy Requirements Engineering (ESPRE), pp. 9–13. IEEE, Banff, AB (2018)
19. Loucopoulos, P., Karakostas, V.: System requirements engineering. McGraw-Hill Inc., New York, NY, USA (1995)
20. Lyytinen, K., Loucopoulos, P., Mylopoulos, J., Robinson, W.N. (eds.): Design requirements engineering: A ten-year perspective: design requirements Workshop, Cleveland, OH, USA. Revised and Invited Papers. Springer-Verlag, Berlin Heidelberg (2009)
21. Micheli, P., Wilner, S.J.S., Bhatti, S.H., Mura, M., Beverland, M.B.: Doing design thinking: conceptual review, synthesis, and research agenda: doing design thinking. J. Prod. Innov. Manag. **36**(2), 124–148 (2019)
22. Prestes, M., Parizi, R., Marczak, S., Conte, T.: On the use of design thinking: a survey of the Brazilian agile software development community. In: Stray, V., Hoda, R., Paasivaara, M., Kruchten, P. (eds.) Agile Processes in Software Engineering and Extreme Programming, pp. 73–86. Springer International Publishing, Cham (2020)
23. Rozante de Paula, T., Santana Amancio, T., Nonato Flores, J.A.: Design thinking in industry. IEEE Softw. **37**(2), 492–51 (2020)
24. Ruchira Prasad, W.M.D., Perera, G.I.U.S., Jeeva Padmini, K.V., Dilum Bandara, H.M.N.: Adopting design thinking practices to satisfy customer expectations in agile practices: a case from Sri Lankan software development industry. In: Proceedings of 2018 Moratuwa Engineering Research Conference (MERCon), pp. 471–476. IEEE, Moratuwa (2018)
25. Souza, A., Ferreira, B., Valentim, N., Correa, L., Marczak, S., Conte, T.: Supporting the teaching of design thinking techniques for requirements elicitation through a recommendation tool. IET Softw. **14**(6), 693–701 (2020)
26. Souza, A.F., Ferreira, B., Valentim, N., Conte, T.: An experience report on teaching multiple design thinking techniques to software engineering students. In: Proceedings of the XXXII Brazilian Symposium on Software Engineering (SBES 2018), pp. 220–229. ACM Press, Sao Carlos, Brazil (2018)

27. Vetterli, C., Brenner, W., Uebernickel, F., Petrie, C.: From palaces to yurts: why requirements engineering needs design thinking. IEEE Internet Comput. **17**(2), 91–94 (2013)
28. Wohlin, C., Runeson, P., Höst, M., Ohlsson, M., Regnell, B., Wesslén, A.: Experimentation in software engineering. Springer (2012)

Supporting a Bottom-Up Evolution of Microservice Compositions Based on the Choreography of BPMN Fragments

Jesús Ortiz, Victoria Torres, and Pedro Valderas

Abstract Microservices need to be composed in order to provide their customers with valuable services. To do so, event-based choreographies are used many times since they help to maintain a lower coupling among microservices. In a previous work, we presented an approach that proposed creating the big picture of the composition in a BPMN model, splitting in into BPMN fragments and distributing these fragments among microservices. In this way, we implemented a microservice composition as an event-based choreography of BPMN fragments. Based on this approach, this work focuses on supporting the evolution of a microservice composition. We pay special attention to how a microservice composition can be evolved from the local perspective of a microservice, since changes performed locally can affect to the communication among microservices and as a result in the integrity of the whole composition. We present an evolution protocol that allows a microservice composition implemented as an event-based choreography of BPMN fragments to evolve from the local perspective of the composed microservices.

Keywords Microservice · Composition · Evolution · Protocol · Bottom-up

---

A prior version of this paper has been published in the ISD2021 Proceedings (http://aisel.aisnet.org/isd2014/proceedings2021).

J. Ortiz (✉) · V. Torres · P. Valderas
Universitat Poltècnica de València, Valencia, Spain
e-mail: jortiz@pros.upv.es

V. Torres
e-mail: vtorres@pros.upv.es

P. Valderas
e-mail: pvalderas@pros.upv.es

E. Insfran Pelozo et al. (eds.), *Advances in Information Systems Development*, Lecture Notes in Information Systems and Organisation 55,
https://doi.org/10.1007/978-3-030-95354-6_13

1 Introduction

Microservice architectures [3] propose the decomposition of applications into small independent building blocks. Each of these blocks focuses on a single business capability and constitutes a microservice. Microservices should be deployed and evolved independently to facilitate agile development and continuous delivery and integration [4].

However, to provide value-added services to users, microservices need to be composed. This composition can be achieved by means of two options inherited from traditional SOA [14]: orchestration and choreography. In an orchestration, composed microservices are controlled by a central microservice, which monitors the entire application process and invokes the rest of microservices through synchronous calls (usually supported by a REST API). In a choreography, microservices complete their tasks independently. There is not a central microservice controlling the composition, and microservices communicate with each other by asynchronous events. In this sense, choreographies introduce a lower degree of coupling among microservices than orchestration, increasing the independency among them for deployment and evolution.

Although choreographies are encouraged to improved microservices decoupling, they are usually hard to analyze and understand. Choreographies rise the composition complexity since the control flow is distributed across microservices. We faced this problem in a previous work [12, 17]. We proposed a microservice composition approach based on the choreography of BPMN fragments. According to this approach, business process engineers create the big picture of the microservice composition through a BPMN model. Then, this model is split into BPMN fragments which are distributed among microservices. Finally, BPMN fragments are composed through an event-based choreography. This solution introduced two main benefits regarding the microservice composition. On the one hand, it facilitates business engineers to analyze the control flow if composition's requirements need to be modified, since they have the big picture of the composition in a BPMN model. On the other hand, the proposed approach provides a high level of independence and decoupling among microservices since they are composed through an event-based choreography of BPMN fragments.

In this paper, we focus on supporting the evolution of microservice composition considering that both, the big picture and the split one, coexist in the same system. In particular, we pay special attention to how a microservice composition can be evolved from the local perspective of a microservice. This type of evolution introduces significant challenges since changes performed locally by a microservice in a BPMN fragment can affect to the communication among microservices, and impact on the integrity of the whole composition. Although a preliminary characterization of this evolution was presented in [12], our current work goes a step further by presenting an evolution protocol that allows a microservice composition to evolve from the local perspective of the composed microservices. In addition, an extension of the previous characterization is also proposed.

Thus, the main contribution of this work is twofold. First, a protocol that allows us to propagate and communicate local modifications within a microservice composition in order to automate, when possible, compensation actions that maintain the composition integrity. Second, the characterization of changes that can occur from the particular view of a microservice, analyzing the impact that each change has on the global composition and proposing compensation actions that ensure, when possible, the achievement of the global composition goal.

The rest of the paper is organized as follows: Sect. 2 analyses the related work; Sect. 3 provides an overview of the microservice composition approach upon which this work builds on. Section 4 states the problem addressed by the presented work. Section 5 presents the protocol proposed to support local evolutions in the context of a microservice composition. Section 6 introduces a characterization of local changes that is used by the proposed protocol. Section 7 presents the tool support and finally, conclusions and further work are commented in Sect. 8.

2 Related Work

There are several works [6, 7, 13] that face the problem of defining a composition of microservices at a high level of abstraction. However, they pay little attention to how these high-level specifications can be evolved once they have been deployed into a system. Other works [10, 11, 18] face the problem of composing microservices from an architectural point of view. Again, the evolution of the microservice composition is not considered.

Regarding those works that face the challenge of evolution in the context of microservices, [15] proposes a UML model that is based on dividing the architecture of an application into three layers: the architecture layer, the instance layer and the infrastructure layer. The model is built using information from system logs, infrastructure data, message and inter-service operations. Basing on this model, this work focuses on evolving the system in terms of the required number of microservices, proposing the creation of new ones or the remove of existing ones. However, the evolution of a microservice composition is not faced. Hassan and Bahsoon [8] proposes a self-adaptive model that can evolve in runtime to solve the problem of the optimal size of granularity of a microservices. The model is based on a MAPE-K loop to create a systematic solution that improves the life cycle of a microservice accumulating knowledge and establishing parameters to know when a microservice needs to be divided or merged. This work focuses on the decomposition of a system into microservices but pay little attention to their composition. In [2], authors propose an infrastructure called GRU, which uses self-adaptive techniques based on agents to manage large-scale distributed systems. This works focuses on the automatic adaptation of microservices to manage resource consumption, in such a way aspect such as scalability, fault tolerance and performance can be improved. Again, this work does not consider the composition of microservices. Finally, [5] proposes the use of UML sequence diagram to represent a choreography and a refinement process to obtain a definition of this choreography based on AIOCJ. This work allows the evolution of the microservice composition from a top-down perspective. However, a bottom-up evolution that allows local changes from a microservice is not supported.

In the area of web service compositions, Cornax et al. [1] proposes an abstract model defined in UML that can be used to build a choreography of services from two perspectives: top-down and bottom-up. However, the presented solution does not include mechanisms to support the evolution of the proposed model. In [9], authors present a model that extends BPEL4WS to automate the dynamic linking of web services in the context of a composition. The work proposes the creation of a service that integrates new services into the composition, following a bottom-up strategy. This solution allows the evolution of the composition from a bottom-up perspective, but it is based on an orchestration to implement the composition. This limits the independence among composed services that is demanded in microservice architectures.

3 A Composition Microservice Approach Based on BPMN Fragments

In this section, we provide an overview of the approach presented in [17] to compose microservices based on the choreography of BPMN fragments. The steps that this approach proposes to create a microservice composition are the following (see Fig. 1):

Step 1. The first step of our approach consists in the definition of a single BPMN model describing the big picture of the microservice composition. Some modelling guidelines to create this model must be followed in order to clearly indicate the tasks that each microservice must perform. They are presented in [17].

Step 2. Then, the big picture of a microservice composition is split into several BPMN fragments. Each fragment includes the tasks that each microservice is responsible of. In addition, the BPMN fragment is extended with catching and throw message events that define the communication among BPMN fragments each time the logic of the composition requires that the task flow is transferred from one microservice to another. The message events are configured to use a particular event bus at runtime.

Step 3. Once the BPMN fragments of a microservice composition have been obtained, each of them must be deployed into the microservice that is responsible for executing it. Microservices just need to use a BPMN engine to execute these fragments. Each microservice oversees executing its corresponding process fragment and informing the other participants about it through the event bus. In this way, the microservice composition is executed by means of an event-based choreography of BPMN fragments in which microservices waits for an event to execute its corresponding piece of work. Note that this event includes the data that each microservice needs to do so. Note also that the event bus used as communication channel among

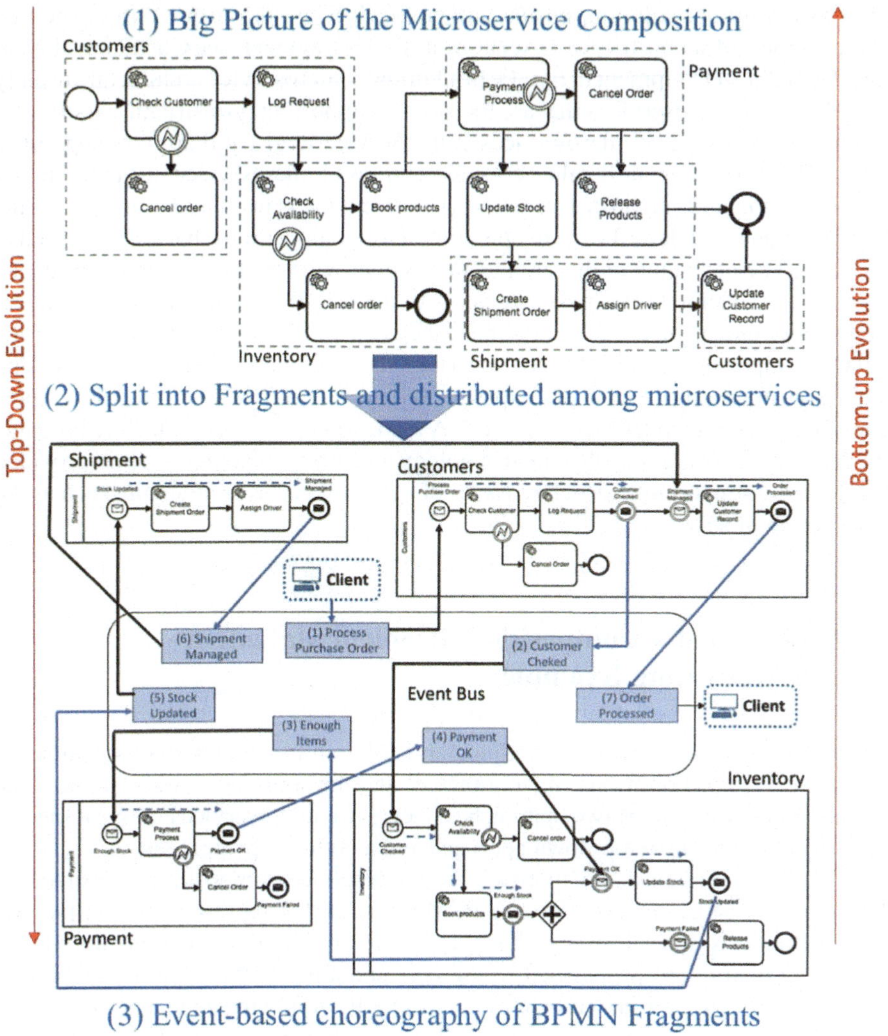

Fig. 1 A composition microservice approach based on BPMN fragments

microservices supports an asynchronous communication. This means that microservices register to the event bus in order to publish or receive events without the need of directly interacting among them in a synchronous fashion. This provides a high degree of decoupling among microservices, which is one of the most demanded characteristics in this type of architectural solution.

Finally, it is worth to remark that this composition approach is supported by a microservice architecture developed to achieve that both descriptions of a composition (big picture and split one) coexist in the same system. A microservice architecture is made up of a set of business microservices that implement the business capabilities of a system. In our solution, business microservices are those that participate in a composition and are in charge of executing a BPMN fragment (see Customers, Inventory, Payment and Shipment in Fig. 1). In addition, a microservice architecture usually includes other microservices that are focused on supporting infrastructure issues. An example of this type of microservices is the Service Registry that gives support to service discovery, containing the network locations of microservice instances. In our solution, we include an infrastructure microservice that is in charge of managing the BPMN models that describe the big pictures of the compositions that are supported in a system. The main goal of this architecture is to provide the two benefits introduced above: (1) to facilitate business engineers to analyze the control flow if composition's requirements need to be modified (they can work with the big picture of the BPMN composition); and (2) to provide a high level of independence and decoupling among the microservices that participate in a composition (microservice's developers can manage their own BPMN fragment). A realization[1] of this architecture has been implemented by using Java/Spring technology and the open-source support provided by Netflix to support infrastructure issues of a microservices architecture such as the discovering of services.[2]

4 Evolution of a Composition. Problem Statement and Motivating Example

Our previous work proposes an architectural solution in which two descriptions of a microservice compositions (the big picture and the split one) coexist in the same system. Thus, we support two approaches to evolve a microservice composition (see red arrows in Fig. 1): a top-down approach and a bottom-up approach.

By following a top-down approach the microservice composition is evolved by business process engineers from the BPMN model that represent the big picture. The evolution is done from a global perspective and the modifications introduced in the big picture are propagated to the corresponding BPMN fragments of each microservice. This top-down evolution is done by following the same process as when a new composition is created, and it is natively supported by the composition approach presented above and introduce in detail in [17].

By following a top-down approach the microservice composition is evolved by business process engineers from the BPMN model that represent the big picture. The evolution is done from a global perspective and the modifications introduced in the big picture are propagated to the corresponding BPMN fragments of each microservice. This top-down evolution is done by following the same process as when a new composition is created, and it is natively supported by the composition approach presented above and introduce in detail in [17].

[1] It can be found in the following GitHub site: https://github.com/pvalderas/microservices-composition-example.

[2] https://github.com/Netflix/eureka.

By following a bottom-up approach the microservice composition evolves from the BPMN fragments of individual microservices. In this case, the evolution is done from the local responsibilities of a specific microservice. This means that developers of a microservice can modify the BPMN fragment under its responsibility as long as they integrate the changes with the rest of the system, i.e., the BPMN fragments of the rest of participant microservices and the BPMN model of the big picture microservice. Note that allowing local changes in a microservice composition reinforce the independence among developments teams that is demanded by this type of architecture, but at the same time may compromise the integrity of the whole composition.

In order to properly understand this problem, let's consider the business process presented in Fig. 1 as a motivating example. This process describes the purchase order in an online shop. Let's focus on the actions that the first two microservices must do. When a client requests to process a purchase, the Customers microservice checks the customer data and logs the request. If the customer data is not valid then the order is cancelled. These actions are represented by the corresponding service tasks in the BPMN fragment of the microservice (see bottom side in Fig. 1). On the contrary, if customer data is valid the control flow is transferred to the Inventory microservice. This flow transfer is represented by a Message Throwing Event in Customers and a Message Catch Event in Inventory. At runtime, this communication is supported by the event bus which allows the execution of an event-based choreography of BPMN fragments. When the Inventory microservice receives the flow control, it checks the availability of the ordered items. If there is not enough stock to satisfy the order, the process of the order is cancelled. On the contrary, the items are booked, and the control flow of the process is transferred to the next microservice. The execution of the composition continues until the "Shipment Managed" event is published in the bus and the control is passed again to the Customers microservice which updates the customer record and informs the client throwing the "Order Processed" event.

Let's consider, for instance, that developers of the Customers microservice decide modifying its BPMN fragment in such a way that the event "Customer Checked" is not published anymore. Then, the microservice Inventory, which is waiting for it, will never start and execute its tasks, and therefore, the microservice composition will never continue. Thus, a local modification in a BPMN fragment has produced that the global composition fails. Next sections elaborate on the approach we propose to face this challenge.

5 A Bottom-Up Approach Protocol to Evolve a Microservice Composition

In this section, we propose a protocol to support local modifications in the context of a microservice composition based on BPMN fragments. The main goal of this protocol is to achieve maximum automation in the synchronization of the local changes of

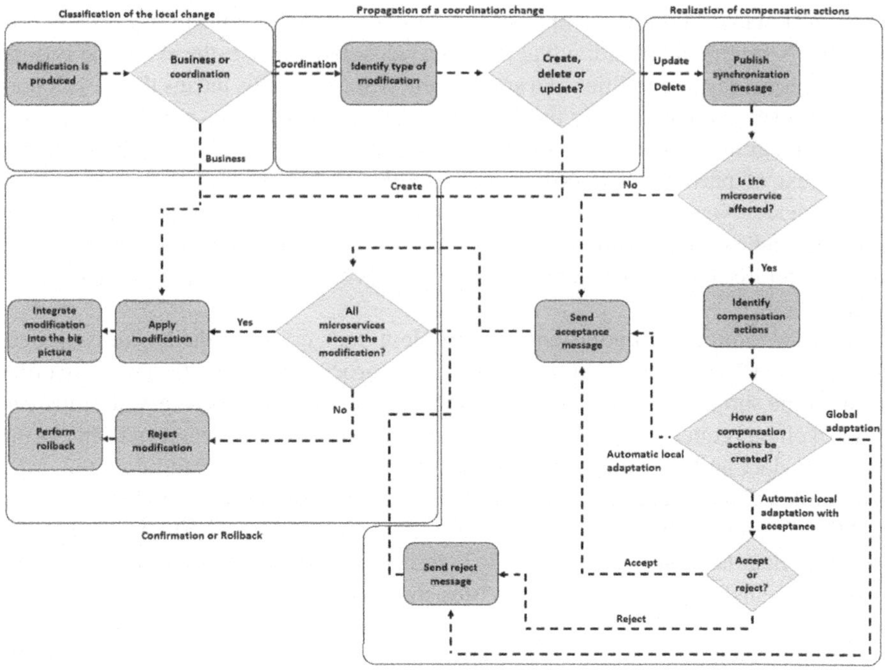

Fig. 2 Protocol for a bottom-up evolution of a microservice composition

a microservice with the rest of the participants in a composition. It is graphically described in Fig. 2.

Note that this protocol implies, in some cases, a communication among microservices during the evolution activity. Following the same publish/subscribe communication strategy followed to support the choreography of BPMN fragments at runtime, this communication is done asynchronously through the publication of messages in the event-bus (see Fig. 2). When a microservice evolves its BPMN fragment with a local change, it publishes a synchronization message in the event bus so the affected participants can react consequently. The proposed protocol is divided into three main phases:

Phase 1. Classification of the local change. A BPMN fragment describes two types of requirements: business and coordination requirements. Thus, the first phase in the proposed protocol includes several steps to classify the local change into any of these two types of requirements. These steps are done by the microservice that perform the local changes.

On the one hand, business requirements are represented by the BPMN tasks that are defined in the fragment of each microservice. They define the actions that each microservice does in the context of a composition but independently from the rest of microservices. Changes in these requirements imply isolated changes in the business responsibilities of the microservice. For instance, in the Customer microservice of the running example, removing the task that logs a request and adding a new task that sends an email confirmation do not affect the rest of microservices. This type of local changes can be applied without any synchronization action with the rest of microservices. They just need to be integrated in the big picture of the composition [17].

On the other hand, coordination requirements define how two or more microservices communicate among them. These requirements are represented by the elements of a BPMN fragment that define an event-based communication, i.e., throwing/catching events. Changes in these requirements imply coordinated modifications in two or more microservices and if they are not controlled, they can have an impact on the integrity of the composition, even forcing the stop the composition flow. Consider, for instance, the example presented above in which the event "Customer Checked" is removed. In these cases, additional efforts may be required to synchronize these local changes with the rest of participants, which are managed in the following two phases of the proposed protocol.

Thus, when a BPMN fragment is modified in a microservice, the BPMN elements are analyzed according to what we explained above in order to classified it as a business or coordination change. This is automatically done by a tool that we present in Sect. 7.

Phase 2. Propagation of a coordination change. If a local modification is classified as a change on coordination requirements it must be precisely characterized in order to create a propagation action. Propagation actions are those that are made by the participant that changes its BPMN fragment from a local perspective. The objective of propagation actions is to inform the rest of microservice about the changes done. To do so, the microservice that perform the local change must publish a message that identifies the modification done over the event-based communication BPMN elements. This modification can be of three types: (1) add, (2) delete, and (3) update an event-based communication element in a BPMN fragment.

Adding a new event-based communication element does not produce any inconsistency in the global composition since coordination requirements are not changed but extended. In fact, this type of change introduces new coordination possibilities among microservices. Thus, the microservice that perform the local changes just need to perform two synchronization actions: (1) integrate changes with the big picture microservice; and (2) publish changes to inform the rest of participants about the new coordination possibilities.

On the contrary, deleting and updating an event-based communication element may produce inconsistencies in the composition since some events required by other microservices may not be produced. In these situations, inspired by the two-phase commit protocol used in distributed database transactions [16], the microservice that performs the local changes in its BPMN fragment cannot confirm them until the affected participants react (either positively or negatively) to them. To allow this reaction, a synchronization message describing the changes must be published in the event bus.

Phase 3. Realization of compensation actions. When a synchronization message with a delete or update action is published in the bus, the microservices that participate in a composition must analyze it in order to decide if compensation actions are needed or not. Compensation actions are those that are made to maintain the integrity of the composition by the microservices that are affected by the local changes of others. If compensation actions are not needed, an automatic acceptance message can be published. On the contrary, affected microservices must react properly. In order to automate as much as possible this reacting behavior we have created a characterization of the inconsistencies that local actions of a microservice produce in the rest of participants as well as the compensation actions that are required to support them. In [12] we presented an initial version of this characterization that is extended in Sect. 6. Depending on the compensation actions required to solve the inconsistencies generated by a local change, a microservice can react as follows:

(1) *Automatic local adaptation.* Compensation actions to maintain the integrity of the composition can be automatically created in an affected microservice since business and coordination requirements are both maintained. For instance, if a microservice just updates the name of a published event (e.g., the event "Payment Ok" is replaced by "Available Credit"), the microservices that were waiting for this event can automatically adapt its BPMN fragment in order to update the new name. Thus, an automatic acceptance of the requested local evolution can be done. This type of adaptation was studied in [12].
(2) *Automatic local adaptation with acceptance.* Compensation actions can be automatically built in the affected microservices in order to support the business requirements. However, the coordination among some microservices may change. For instance, a compensation action may imply changing the execution order of two microservices from sequential to parallel. In this case, business requirements are kept (i.e., all the tasks remain after the change) but the flow of these tasks change, and some data may be missed for some microservices. Thus, a manual acceptance by the developers of the affected microservices is required to confirm the requested local evolution.
(3) *Global adaptation.* Compensation actions to maintain the integrity of the composition imply important modifications in both coordination and business requirements. In this case, a further analysis of the whole composition is needed. Thus, affected microservices automatically reject the requested local evolution and an acceptance or rejection must be done by business engineers from the global perspective of the composition.

Note that a microservice that is affected by the local change of other may need the global vision of the composition in order to decide how reacting to it. This problem is solved in our proposal since our microservice architecture includes the infrastructure big picture microservice which can provide any microservice this information.

Phase 4. Confirmation or Rollback. If all the participants of a composition accept the local changes done by a microservice they can be confirmed and integrated into the big picture. If some rejection message is received, local changes must be rollbacked. Note that participants of a choreographed composition only have the local vision of themselves, which makes it difficult to know how many microservices participate in the composition. This is a challenge when a participant needs an answer of all the other participants, as we propose in our protocol. This problem is solved in our proposal since the infrastructure big picture microservice can provide a locally evolved microservice with this data.

6 Characterization of Reactive Behavior in Affected Microservices

One of the main goals in the protocol presented above is that microservices affected by the local evolution of others can react, as much automatically as possible, to maintain the integrity of the composition when local changes in coordination requirements are produced. In [12], we characterize this reactive behaviour considering local changes that only affect event-based communication without data interchange. In this section, we focus on the impact that changes in event-based communication elements have when they carry data that need to be interchanged among microservices. Due to space problems, we focus here just on characterizing delete actions (cf. phase 2 in Sect. 5) and analysing the generated inconsistencies as well as the compensation actions that are required to correct them and guarantee a functional composition (update actions can be characterized analogously; however, they are left for further work; add actions do not generate inconsistencies, see Phase 2 in the previous section). To properly perform this characterization, we first need to differentiate two types of events:

1. *Status events:* These events are generated by microservices to notify the success or the failure of a piece of work. They allow to define the flow in which microservices must be choreographed to perform their actions. They are events without data. For instance, see the event "Payment OK" of the running example.
2. *Data events:* These events are generated to define the flow of the choreographed microservice composition, but they also carry data that some microservice generates in order to be processed by others. For instance, see the event "Customer Checked" of the running example, which may include customer data such as preferred shipment address or VIP client discounts that are obtained by the Customer microservice when checking its identification credentials.

Considering these two types of events, we characterize next all delete actions that can take place in an event-based communication element (Message Throwing and Catch Event) in a BPMN fragment, as well as the reactive behavior that can be done to compensate them.

#1 Deleting throwing event-based elements that send a status event. This change implies the removal of a BPMN element that sends an event to just inform that a piece of work has been done, without data interchange.

- *Generated inconsistency*: Some microservices will never start or continue since their execution depend on the triggering of the event being just deleted.
- Compensation actions: Change the coordination requirements of the microservices waiting for the removed event. In general, the change will imply waiting

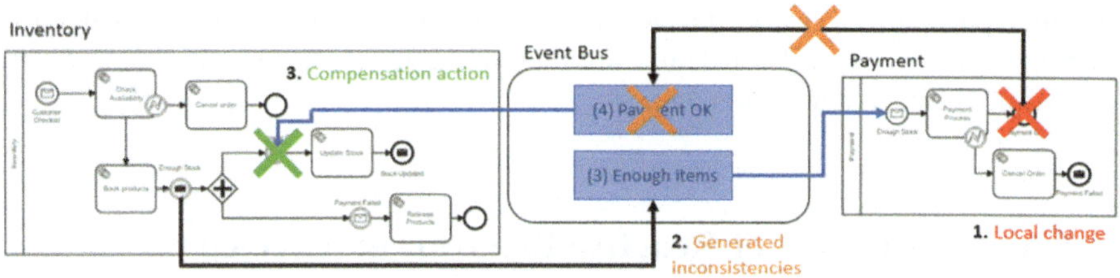

Fig. 3 Graphical example of modification #1

for the previous event that triggered the modified microservice (general case). However, when the previous event is triggered by the own modified microservice the compensation action is to delete the receive element that is waiting for the removed event (exceptional case).

- *Example*: To illustrate the general case with an example, we will assume that the event "Customer Checked" is a status event. In this scenario, an example of the general case is removing the BPMN Message Intermediate Throwing Event "Customer Checked" of the Customers microservice (see lower side in Fig. 1). As a result, the microservice Inventory will never start and execute its tasks, and therefore, the microservice composition will never continue. To allow the execution of the microservice Inventory and maintain its participation in the composition we search for a different event to wait for, for example an event that was triggered previously in the composition, such as the "Process Purchase Order" event. This change produces in turn a change in the execution order of these two microservices (Customers and Inventory microservices), i.e., switching from sequential to parallel execution. This compensation actions are analogous to the ones explained graphically in the characterization of the modification #2 presented below.
- An example of the exception introduced above is removing the BPMN Message End Throwing Event "Payment OK" of the Payment microservice (see Fig. 3). If this case, the Inventory microservice, which is waiting for it, will never continue its tasks (i.e., update the stock), and therefore, the microservice composition will never continue. To solve this, the Inventory microservice can be modified by deleting the Message Intermediate Catching Event that receives the event "Payment OK" in such a way it can update the stock at the same time the payment is processed.
- *Impact of the modification and the compensation actions*: In both the general situation and the exceptional one, business requirements are maintained since the tasks of the microservices are all performed. However, the flow of these tasks changed. In the general situation, two microservices that initially performed their tasks in a sequential way (e.g., first Customers and later Inventory) result in performing their tasks in a parallel way (e.g., after the modification, both Customers and Inventory microservices are executed when the "Process Purchase Order" event is triggered). In the exceptional situation, some tasks of a microservice (e.g., update stock of the Inventory microservice) are performed in parallel with the

tasks of other microservice (e.g., the tasks of the Payment microservice) when initially they were conceived to be executed sequentially.
- Reaction type of the microservice: Automatic local adaptation with acceptance.

#2 Deleting end or intermediate throwing events with propagated data. This change implies the removal of a BPMN element that sends an event that carries data produced previously in the composition and that is required by other microservices to be properly executed.

- *Generated inconsistency*: Some microservices will never start or continue since their execution depend on the data attached to the event being just deleted.
- Compensation actions: The microservices that were waiting for the removed event can be modified to obtain the required data from a previous event.
- *Example*: An example of this modification is removing the BPMN Message Intermediate Throwing Event "Customer Checked" of the Customer microservice (see Fig. 4). Note that this event carries the purchase data that is required by the Inventory microservice and that was initially introduced in the composition by the client application. To allow the Inventory microservice to perform its tasks and maintain its participation in the composition, it can be modified to wait for an event that is triggered previously in the composition, and that contains the data that the Inventory microservice needs. In particular, the Inventory microservice can be modified to wait for the previous "Process Purchase Order" that also contains the data it requires.

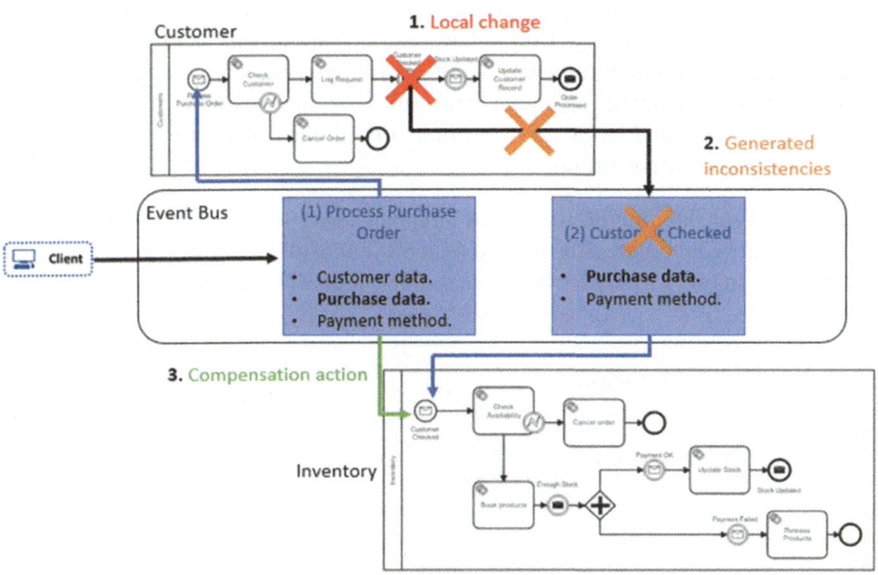

Fig. 4 Graphical example of modification #2

- *Impact of the modification and the compensation actions*: Business requirements are maintained since the tasks of the microservices are all performed. However, as happened in modification #1, coordination requirements change since the tasks of some microservices are performed in parallel when they were initially defined as a sequence. In the previous example, Customer and Inventory were initially executed in a sequential way, but after the modification, they were executed in a parallel way.
- Reaction type of the microservice: Automatic local adaptation with acceptance.

#3 Deleting end or intermediate throwing events with newly introduced data. This change implies the removal of a BPMN element that sends an event with data that other microservice needs to complete its tasks. The data is newly introduced by the deleted event, and it does not exist in previous events.

- *Generated inconsistency*: Some microservices will never start or continue since their execution depend on the data attached to the event being just delete.
- Compensation actions: No compensation actions can be made in the microservices that were waiting for the removed event to obtain the data. Thus, it is required to redesign the microservice composition from a global perspective.
- *Example*: An example of this modification is removing the BPMN Message End Throwing Event "Shipment Managed" of the Shipment microservice (see Fig. 5). If this event is not sent, the Customer microservice will no longer continue its execution and will not participate in the composition. In this example, the Shipment microservice introduces new data in the composition through the event "Shipment Managed". This event contains the details about the shipment order (i.e. shipment company, delivery date, etc.). Without this data, the Customer microservice cannot continue its execution. In this case there are no other events that contains specifically this data. Thus, to allow the Customer microservice to perform its tasks and maintain its participation in the composition, it is required to re-design the composition.

- *Impact of the modification and the compensation actions:* No compensation actions can be automatically applied to achieve that all the microservices perform their tasks in order to satisfy business requirements. Thus, a global redefinition is needed.

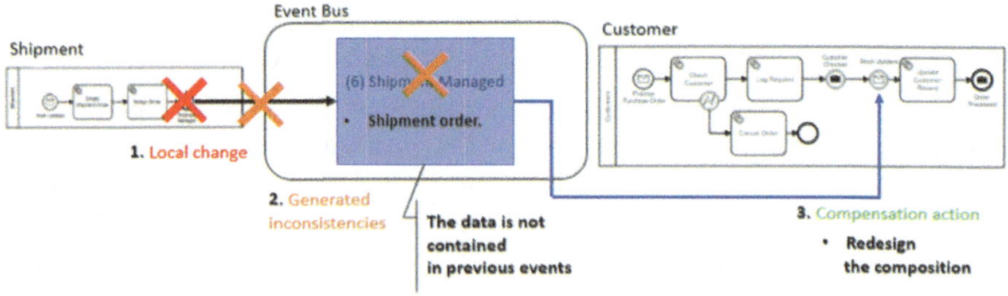

Fig. 5 Graphical example of modification #3

- *Reaction type of the microservice:* Global adaptation.

#4 Deleting start or intermediate catching status events or event with data. This change implies the removal of a BPMN element that defines the event that a microservice must listen to in order to execute some tasks. The event may be a status or a data event.

- *Generated inconsistency:* The modified microservice will no longer participate in the microservice composition. As a consequence, the rest of microservices that were waiting for completion of its tasks will not participate in the composition either.
- *Compensation actions:* In order to maintain the participation of the affected microservices the compensation actions that can be applied are the same that those that could be applied if the throwing events of the modified microservice were deleted.
- *Example*: An example of this modification is removing the BPMN Message Start Event "Enough Items" of the Payment microservice. As we can see in the lower side in Fig. 1 this modification avoids the participation of the Payment microservice and then the status event "Payment OK" will not be triggered. This implies that the Inventory microservice cannot continue its execution. To solve this problem the compensation actions presented in modification #1 can be applied. However, other situations can require applying the compensation actions of modifications #2 or #3.
- Impact of the modification and the compensation actions: Depending on the affected throwing events the impact will be the same of previous modifications.
- *Reaction type of the microservice:* Automatic local adaptation with acceptance or Global adaptation.

7 Tool Support

In order to support microservice developers with tools that facilitate the application of the proposed bottom-up evolution approach we are developing an extended version of the BPMN.io editor. The current version of this tool applies the protocol presented above considering the modification characterization presented in this work and in [12]. In this way, each time a microservice developer modify a BMN fragment, this tool analyses the changes done and publish the corresponding messages in the event bus to inform the others microservices. In addition, it provides developers with information about the modification state.

Figure 6 shows some snapshots of this tool. Figure 6a shows how the tool provides microservice developers with the list of operations published by the microservice in order to be associated to a service task. Figure 6b shows how the tool alert developers that changes done affect coordination requirements and need to be synchronized with the other microservices that participate in the composition. Figure 6c shows a version of the Customers fragment that has been modified and changes need to be accepted by

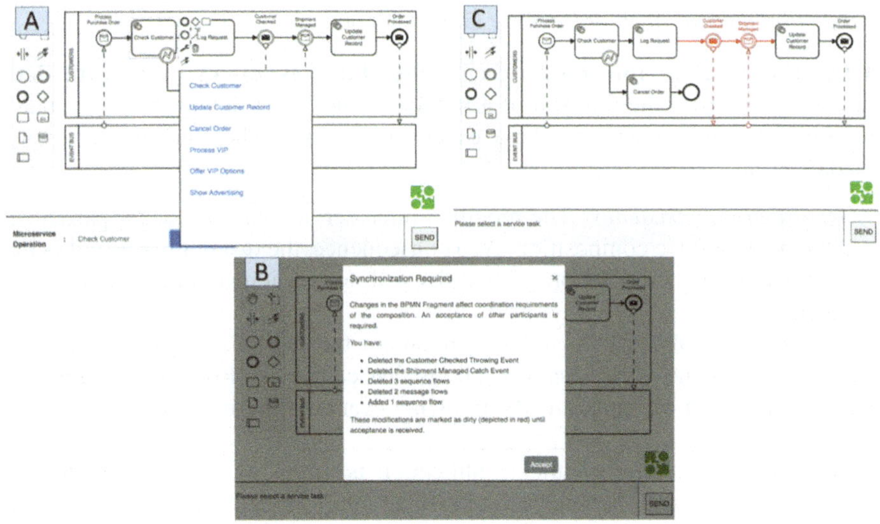

Fig. 6 Extended version of BPMN.io that supports the proposed protocol

the other microservices. The Customer Checked Throwing Event and the Shipment Managed Catch Event have been deleted and need to be accepted. They are depicted in red until the acceptance of the rest of microservice is received.

8 Conclusions and Further Work

In this work, we have presented a protocol that allow us to manage local modifications within a microservice composition based on the choreography of BPMN fragments. The protocol supports the evolution of the composition considering that both representation of a microservice composition, i.e. the big one and the split one, coexist in the same system. This allows us to support a bottom-up evolution in order to allow microservices to perform local changes and synchronize them with both the local view of the rest of microservices and the big picture of the composition. The proposed protocol propagates the local changes to the rest of participants allowing them to generate compensation actions to maintain the composition integrity.

Additionally, we have presented a characterization of changes that can occur from the particular view of a microservice, analyzing the impact that each change has on the global composition and proposing compensation actions that ensure, when possible, the achievement of the global composition goal. Specifically, we have analyzed the impact of deleting event-based communication elements from a BPMN fragment. This complements an initial characterization done in [12].

This work has been initially validated through a case study and the implementation of the required tool support. However, further experiments are needed. In particular, we are currently preparing an experiment with developers to get their feedback on the evolution proposal. In addition, our further work includes expand the proposed protocol to allow the evolution of the microservice composition in runtime. To do so, we want to introduce new components in the architecture composition such as a *Knowledge Registry,* that will act like a database to store logs generated by microservices. Then, these logs will be used to automatically adapt the composition in runtime. To implement this characteristic, we also want to introduce a Mape-K loop, that will compare the logs to identify modifications. Then, the modifications will be characterized to afterwards, plan the compensation actions required to maintain the composition integrity and finally, execute them.

References

1. Cornax, M.C., Dupuy-Chessa, S., Rieu, D.: Bridging the gap between business processes and service composition through service choreographies. In: Working Conference on Method Engineering, pp. 190–203. Springer, Berlin (2011)
2. Florio, L.: Decentralized self-adaptation in large-scale distributed systems. In: Proceedings of the 2015 10th Joint Meeting on Foundations of Software Engineering, pp. 1022–1025 (2015)
3. Fowler, M., Lewis, J.: Microservices. ThoughtWorks (2014)
4. Fowler, M.: Microservices trade-offs. http://martinfowler.com/articles/microservice-trade-offs.html(2015)
5. Giallorenzo, S., Lanese, I., Russo, D.: ChIP: a choreographic integration process. In: OTM Confederated International Conferences" On the Move to Meaningful Internet Systems", pp. 22–40. Springer, Cham (2018)
6. Guidi, C., Lanese, I., Mazzara, M., Montesi, F.: Microservices: a language-based approach. In Present and Ulterior Software Engineering, pp. 217–225. Springer, Cham (2017)
7. Gutiérrez–Fernández, A.M., Resinas, M., Ruiz–Cortés, A.: Redefining a process engine as a microservice platform. In: International Conference on Business Process Management, pp. 252–263. Springer, Cham (2016)
8. Hassan, S., Bahsoon, R.: Microservices and their design trade-offs: a self-adaptive roadmap. In: 2016 IEEE International Conference on Services Computing (SCC), pp. 813–818. IEEE (2016)
9. Mandell, D.J., McIlraith, S.A.: Adapting BPEL4WS for the semantic web: the bottom-up approach to web service interoperation. In: International Semantic Web Conference, pp. 227–241. Springer, Berlin, Heidelberg (2003)
10. Monteiro, D., Gadelha, R., Maia, P.H.M., Rocha, L.S., Mendonça, N.C.: Beethoven: an event-driven lightweight platform for microservice orchestration. In: European Conference on Software Architecture, pp. 191–199. Springer, Cham (2018)
11. Oberhauser, R.: Microflows: lightweight automated planning and enactment of workflows comprising semantically annotated microservices. In: Proceedings of the Sixth International Symposium on Business Modelling and Software Design (BMSD 2016), pp. 134–143 (2016)
12. Ortiz, J., Torres, V., Valderas, P.: Characterization of Bottom-up Microservice Composition Evolution. An Approach Based on the Choreography of BPMN Fragments (2020)
13. Petrasch, R.: Model-based engineering for microservice architectures using enterprise integration patterns for inter-service communication. In: 2017 14th International Joint Conference on Computer Science and Software Engineering (JCSSE), pp. 1–4. IEEE (2017)
14. Rosen, M., Lublinsky, B., Smith, K.T., Balcer, M.J.: Applied SOA: service-oriented architecture and design strategies. Wiley (2012)

15. Sampaio, A.R., Kadiyala, H., Hu, B., Steinbacher, J., Erwin, T., Rosa, N., Beschastnikh, I., Rubin, J.: Supporting microservice evolution. In: 2017 IEEE International Conference on Software Maintenance and Evolution (ICSME), pp. 539–543 (2017)
16. Skeen, D.: Nonblocking commit protocols. In: Proceedings of the 1981 ACM SIGMOD international conference on Management of data, pp. 133–142 (1981)
17. Valderas, P., Torres, V., Pelechano, V.: A microservice composition approach based on the choreography of BPMN fragments. Inf. Softw. Technol. **127**, 106370 (2020)
18. Yahia, E.B.H., Réveillere, L., Bromberg, Y.D., Chevalier, R., Cadot, A.: Medley: an event-driven lightweight platform for service composition. In: International Conference on Web Engineering, pp. 3–20. Springer, Cham (2016)

Team Performance in Large-Scale Agile Software Development

Tomas Gustavsson

Abstract Agile ways of working are nowadays used in many software development departments in larger organizations. When scaling up agile ways of working, new practices for coordinating teams become necessary, and many organizations are implementing the Scaled Agile Framework. The added practices for coordinating teams could have an impact on team performance, but they have not been much studied. In this study, data were obtained by means of a survey questionnaire that was answered by 201 employees from three organizations: one from the automotive industry, one government agency, and a business bank. The study suggests that efficient inter-team coordination does not have a positive relationship to team performance, which is contrary to previous studies. However, results suggests that a high level of psychological safety has a significant positive correlation to team performance.

Keywords Agile software development · Psychological safety · Scaled agile framework · Inter-team coordination

1 Introduction

In software development, there is an industry trend towards adopting large-scale agile ways of working [1]. Although research into the agile approach to software development has matured in the past years, agile ways of working in large-scale settings are not as much explored [19]. One of the fundamental principles in the agile way of working is to allow autonomy to the team [17]. This autonomy is a major reason for success in agile development, and research in other industries also confirms that autonomous and empowered teams are more productive and proactive [14].

A prior version of this paper has been published in the ISD2021 Proceedings (http://aisel.aisnet.org/isd2014/proceedings2021).

T. Gustavsson (✉)
Karlstad University, Karlstad, Sweden
e-mail: tomas.gustavsson@kau.se

E. Insfran Pelozo et al. (eds.), *Advances in Information Systems Development*, Lecture Notes in Information Systems and Organisation 55,
https://doi.org/10.1007/978-3-030-95354-6_14

The balance between the benefits of autonomous teams versus alignment towards a common goal is, therefore, an essential issue for the software industry [19]. Therefore, large-scale practices for coordinating teams have been proposed to reduce negative impacts while maintaining the positive impacts of agile ways of working in the teams. According to an annually recurring industry survey [1], the most commonly adopted framework today for large-scale agile ways of working is the Scaled Agile Framework (SAFe) which prescribes a number of inter-team coordination practices to be used by the organization. The authors of SAFe, Leffingwell et al. [16], make several claims regarding expected beneficial impacts by implementing SAFe based on case studies written by end-users. The claimed benefits include increased team performance due to better coordination and more motivated employees. No drawbacks are mentioned.

But SAFe has been criticized by agile practitioners in several ways, such as being too top-down and inflexible [21], taking away the benefits of autonomy to the team. Schwaber [21] argues that it is more critical for performance to build autonomous teams than to "suffocate" the teams with coordination practices between groups.

A study by Hoegl et al. [12] shows that inter-team coordination has a positive effect on team performance in the individual team, but only to some extent. Their study showed a positive impact on schedule performance but did not show a positive impact on quality or budget, which were the three areas investigated. The positive effects on team performance from inter-team coordination has also been confirmed by Bond-Barnard et al. [5].

In the study by Hoegl et al. [12], the team performance construct included schedule performance, budget and quality. In this study, the team performance construct used in Edmondson [6] will instead be applied to investigate team performance. The construct consists of four items (statements) inquiring the perceived team performance from the individual team members' perspective. This team performance construct suits this study better since the other two constructs used in this study are also based on the perceived experience from the individual team member.

Regarding efficiency in autonomous teams, Edmondson [6] shows that psychological safety is an important mechanism that influences behavioral and performance outcomes. Edmondson defines team psychological safety as a shared belief that the team is safe for interpersonal risk-taking. In a team where members trust each other, dare to seek help from each other, ask questions, and tolerate mistakes, the learning improves. This, in turn, has a positive effect on team performance [6]. Also, the trending values of Modern Agile suggests that agile organizations should stand on four guiding principles, of which one is "Make Safety a Prerequisite" [18].

The question is whether positive effects on team performance is evident in an organization working according to SAFe and if the effect has a stronger impact on team performance than inter-team coordination? The purpose of this study is, therefore, to investigate the correlation between team performance and inter-team coordination in a large-scale agile environment, where organizations have implemented the SAFe framework. This research aims at developing our understanding of the impacts of additional coordinating practices on team performance. Specifically, the following research questions are examined: (1) Is there a positive correlation between inter-team cooperation and team performance in large-scale agile software development?

(2) Is there a positive correlation between psychological safety and team performance in large-scale agile software development?

First, a number of possible impacts on teamwork will be examined to understand if they are perceived as being improved by the implementation of SAFe. Secondly, the derived hypotheses regarding inter-team coordination and psychological safety constructs relating to team performance will be examined in further detail to be able to answer the research questions. The hypotheses are tested by using data from a survey study conducted at three large-scale development environments; one in the automotive industry (24 development teams), one at a government agency (7 teams), and one department in a business bank (7 development teams).

The rest of the paper is organized as follows: Sect. 2 describes large-scale agile software development in more detail. In Sect. 3, constructs and hypotheses are explained. Section 4 shows the research methods used in the study, and Sect. 5 describes the results. Discussions of the results are presented in Sect. 6 as well as limitations to the study.

2 Large-Scale Agile Software Development and Modern Agile

Agile Software Development (ASD) is often defined by the values and principles as described in the "Manifesto for Agile Software Development" [17] which mostly explain what is important for team members, working together in one team. The same goes for Scrum, the most commonly implemented agile framework [1]. But neither the Agile Manifesto [17] nor Scrum is enough to explain how to most efficiently organize multiple teams working together towards a common goal where teams need to coordinate their work. Therefore, several new frameworks designed for large-scale agile adoptions have emerged, of which SAFe is the most commonly adopted today [1].

2.1 The Scaled Agile Framework

SAFe was introduced in August of 2013 and has been further developed, and is now in version 5.1. SAFe describes agile ways of working on different levels, starting from the team level to the program level, portfolio level, and organizational level. SAFe prescribes several practices for coordination between teams, Product Owners and other roles in the organization. On team level, several practices are suggested to manage inter-team coordination of which two of the most important practices [16] are described here.

PI planning is a two-day PI planning workshop to create a joint plan eight to twelve weeks into the future for several cooperating teams. The two-day workshop has a detailed standardized schedule created to involve all team members as well as stakeholders in performing and committing to a comprehensive plan. The final plan is visualized by the use of a program board where committed work and dependencies between teams are highlighted. According to Leffingwell et al. [16] this is the most important coordination practice. The authors even emphasize that if you are not doing PI planning, you are not doing SAFe.

The second coordination practice is called Scrum of Scrums and is a face-to-face coordination meeting between representatives from every team. Scrum of Scrums is suggested to be performed one or two times per week and to be divided into two parts: (1) a short meeting for everybody attending and (2) problem solving for representatives that need to sort out dependency issues not resolved during the first part of the meeting. SAFe suggests following a meeting agenda to focus on what problems that are of importance to the other teams regarding what has been done, what will be done and obstacles to reach the current goal of the iteration.

The critique against SAFe, being too top-down and inflexible [21], is that it seems like an underlying assumption that high performance in the teamwork is obtained by having detailed practices for inter-team coordination.

2.2 Modern Agile

The trending concept Modern Agile [18] focuses on what values are important instead of stressing specific practices or artifacts to be used. Modern Agile focuses on describing important values to be shared in the whole organization to become effective from a single team to top management. Four guiding principles are put forth: (1) Make People Awesome, (2) Make Safety a Prerequisite, (3) Experiment and Learn Rapidly, and (4) Deliver Value Continuously. Regarding the second principle, the following statement clarifies the importance: "Safety is both a basic human need and a key to unlocking high performance" [18]. For Modern Agile, an underlying assumption is that psychological safety will produce high team performance.

3 Constructs and Hypotheses

The conceptualization of team performance as a multidimensional construct is widely acknowledged in the literature [6, 12] but with different views on its content. In Sect. 3.1, team performance and its relation to inter-team coordination, according to Hoegl et al. [12], will be discussed. The view on team performance and its relationship to psychological safety, according to Edmondson [6], will thereafter be presented in Sect. 3.2.

3.1 Inter-Team Coordination and Team Performance

According to Hoegl et al. [12], team performance can be defined as the extent to which a team can meet established objectives. For a development team responsible for developing specific parts of a larger system, several properties may be important, including adherence to predefined quality, a schedule where certain deliverables are expected at predefined times, and costs associated with the team's development activities [12].

In the paper by Hoegl et al. [12], earlier work in defining the latent construct teamwork quality is explained. In a study of software development teams, the within-team collaboration process was conceptualized and empirically validated as a multifaceted higher-order construct. The construct consists of six facets: communication, coordination, the balance of member contributions, mutual support, effort, and cohesion. These facets embrace elements of both task-related and social interaction within teams, and the underlying proposition is that highly collaborative teams display behaviors related to all six teamwork quality facets. The results of the study showed that teamwork quality, to some extent, has a positive influence on team performance [12].

Regarding inter-team coordination, as a team depend on input from another team for accomplishing their task, the work in one team has implications for the work and progress of other teams. There are mainly two forces that create coordination needs between teams in multi-team projects: (1) task interdependencies and (2) changes occurring during the development process [12]. While some coordination needs are possible to plan in advance, software development is always characterized by changes, which often affect the work of several teams. The complexity and uncertainty of development processes, based on interdependencies between teams and frequent changes, can only be dealt with if the information is exchanged between the teams [12].

Hoegl et al. [12] showed that although coordination with other teams might take time and resources, it has, to some degree, a positive effect on team performance. As previously described, Hoegl et al. [12] measured team performance as a combination of schedule performance (delivering on time), adherence to budget, and quality. In their study, inter-team coordination showed a significant positive relationship to schedule performance but not to quality and a negative relationship to adherence to budget.

The positive effects of coordination on performance is also confirmed in later studies. Bond-Barnard et al. [5], for example, conclude that project management success becomes more likely as the degree of coordination improves.

Hypothesis 1. Coordination with other teams is positively associated with team performance.

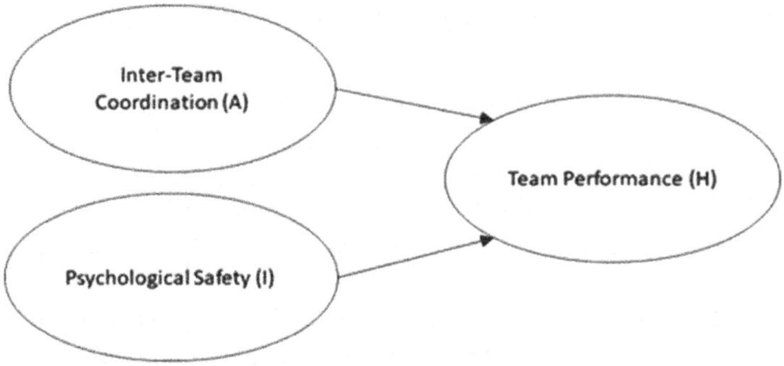

Fig. 1 A model of impact on team performance

3.2 Psychological Safety and Team Performance

Asking for help, admitting errors, and seeking feedback are examples of behaviors that pose a threat to face [6]. Therefore, people in organizations are often reluctant to disclose their errors or are unwilling to ask for help, even when doing so would provide benefits for the team or organization. Edmondson's [6] study shows that high levels of psychological safety have a positive effect on team performance, or rather that learning behavior mediates between team psychological safety and team performance. In her study, team performance is measured by using the scale invented by Hackman [10] to obtain self-report measures of team performance. Edmondson [6] also developed a similar scale to be used by observers who rated team performance.

Hypothesis 2. Psychological safety is positively associated with team performance.

Figure 1 shows the two hypotheses tested in this study.

4 Method

The research setting is first described in this Sect. 4.1, followed by how data was collected from the three case organizations (4.2). Measures and scales are thereafter presented (4.3), followed by descriptions of how data was prepared and analyzed (4.4).

4.1 Research Setting

Two inclusion criteria were used to find cases for this study. First, the case organizations should not be new to agile ways of working, i.e. the study was not indented to compare waterfall and agile. The second criterion was that they should have implemented the same large-scale agile team coordination practices in order to make analysis relevant. To be able to find relevant cases to meet these criteria, a request was sent out to an agile community who organize annual conferences in Sweden. The agile community provided names to a number of possible organizations and after having been in contact with several of them, three different case organizations met the criteria. The actual names of the organizations have been anonymized but will be referred to as Motor, Agency, and Bank. The organizations have used agile ways of working for four to six years, with self-organized autonomous teams working side by side. All three organizations decided to adopt practices for team coordination from the framework SAFe. They all started implementing SAFe during the beginning of 2017. Motor was first, starting in January, while Agency began in March and Bank in April. The development organizations are divided into a number of teams with one Scrum Master per team and almost one Product Owner per team (some are responsible for two teams).

Motor is a department in an organization within the automotive industry that mainly develops software but, to some extent, hardware as well. The observed department, when the survey was conducted, was organized into 24 cross-functional teams, divided into three different set of teams or Agile Release Trains (ART) to use SAFe terminology [16]. Roughly 80 percent of the product development is software development and 20% hardware development. Some of the teams are rather small, so the total amount of people working in the teams is 141, which means an average of 5.9 people per team. The average age in the department is 36.9 years old, with an average of 9.5 years working at Motor.

The Agency project is a SAFe implementation that started as a pilot project in a large Swedish government agency (more than 13 000 employees). Large-scale agile processes were implemented with the aim of finding best practices to be used for the whole organization. Agency consists of seven teams working together in one ART. The total amount of employees in this software development organization is 70 people. This means that the average team consisted of 8.75 people which is the largest average team size of the three investigated organizations. The average age at Agency is 44.9 years, with an average of 10.5 years working at Agency.

Bank is a software development department in one of the major business banks in Sweden (more than 15 000 employees) consisting of seven teams that work together in one ART. Bank decided to implement large-scale agile practices because a new software platform was being developed. This project would increase the number of dependencies between all teams in the department, hence the increased need for coordination practices. The department consists of 7 teams with 42 team members, which means that the average team consists of 6 people. The average age in the department is 38.9 years old with an average of 9.6 years working at Bank.

4.2 Data Collection and Sample

The data was collected using a paper-based questionnaire which was handed out and collected during a two-day planning workshop known as PI planning in SAFe [16]. After a brief introduction of the study, the questionnaire was handed to the respondent to complete by reading it himself or herself.

The survey was conducted in February 2018 at Motor and Agency and in April 2018 at Bank, which means that the organizations had used team coordination practices from SAFe for roughly one year.

For descriptive statistics, 201 survey responses could be used: 109 from Motor, 56 from Agency and 36 from Bank which represents a 78,5 percent (201/256) response rate. This involved questions on opinions on working according to the SAFe framework and perceived differences between the previous way of working and current way of working. One hundred fifty of these responses came from team members. Missing value analysis was conducted on all survey responses. No patterns emerged, and only eight observations were removed due to excessive missing data.

For structural equation modeling (i.e. questions regarding inter-team coordination, team performance, and psychological safety), only responses from employees working in teams were used. Unfortunately, most responses from Agency on these areas were left blank. There are several possible reasons for why the respondents left many statements blank: (1) Agency did not implement all SAFe practices on team-level [8], (2) out of the three cases, most negative voices were raised from employees at Agency [8], and (3) the questionnaire was handed out at the end of the first day of PI planning, and many employees wanted to leave work and go home.

Whatever the reason, with such excessive missing data, it was decided to better exclude all responses from Agency. Rather than risking biased results due to replacing too much missing data with an algorithm method, all 56 responses from Agency were therefore excluded in this part of the analysis. Thus, a total of 80 survey responses could be used from Motor and 31 from Bank, leading up to an overall total of 111 responses, which represents a 61% (111/183) response rate from these two organizations. At Motor, 60 responses came from developers, 14 from Scrum Masters, and six from Product Owners. At Bank, 25 responses came from developers, four from Scrum Masters, and only two from Product Owners.

The low response rate from Product Owners is because some of them did not see themselves as part of the team. As Bass and Haxby explains [4], Product Owners in a large-scale agile context undertake a range of challenging and varied activities beyond those conventionally associated with the role. Some Product Owners work very closely with the team, while some only meet the team on an irregular basis and spend most of their time working with other stakeholders. The latter tend not to see themselves as actual team members, and they chose not to answer the questions regarding inter-team coordination, psychological safety, or team performance in this survey.

4.3 Measures and Scales

The questionnaire consisted of multiple sections: (1) background (e.g., organizational unit), (2) agile role and experience, (3) opinions on working according to the SAFe framework, (4) perceived differences between the previous way of working and current way of working, (5) inter-team collaboration in agile development, (6) teamwork quality and team performance, and (7) psychological safety.

Also, both open questions and multi-choice questions were included in the questionnaire, providing possibilities for both qualitative and quantitative data analysis. In this paper, only the quantitative data from Sects. 3, 4, 5, 6, and 7 are used. A mix of negatively and positively worded items was used to mitigate response set bias. The questionnaire was administered in Swedish at Agency and Bank and in English at Motor since the organization has offices in several countries and use English as the official corporate language.

To understand the overall attitudes towards SAFe practices, five questions were asked inspired by the questionnaire invented by Laanti et al. [15] presented in Table 2. For teamwork quality, one item per facet was used, as presented in Table 3. The questions were invented by the author attempting to capture the perceived difference in impacts during the time of the survey collection compared to before the implementation of SAFe. The measurement scale for inter-team coordination (Cronbach's alpha = 0.705) consists of four items. The items used are described in Hoegl et al. [12], who partly adapted them from scales used by Mott [20], who evaluated coordination, communication, and cooperation between different occupational groups in hospitals.

For psychological safety (Cronbach's alpha = 0.729), the measurement scale consists of four items used in the measurement scale invented by Edmondson [6]. The measurement scale for team performance (Cronbach's alpha = 0.712) consists of four items described in Edmondson [6], who used the scale invented by Hackman [10] to obtain self-report measures of team performance. Due to low communalities and low factor loading on one item in the construct (item H3), only three items were used in the analysis.

Exploratory factor analyses were conducted with the items of inter-team coordination, psychological safety, and team performance, respectively, to confirm the internal consistency of the three scales. Using the Kaiser criterion, the factor analyses resulted in one-factor solutions for all three constructs. Questionnaire items are displayed in Table 1.

The first part of the analysis, with all respondents (N = 201), was done in SPSS. The second part of the analysis was conducted with structural equation modeling in LISREL [13]. The analyses in LISREL are performed at the individual level, with survey responses from employees working in development teams only (N = 111). With such a small group in LISREL, the reliability of the estimates is negatively affected, and the power is low for significance tests.

Following Anderson and Gerbing's [2] two-step approach, construct validity was assessed (convergent and discriminant validity) and nomological validity in the

Table 1 Questionnaire items. Reversed items are shown as (R)

Construct	#	Statement
Inter-team coordination	A1 A2	Processes and activities are well coordinated with other teams Duplicated and overlapping activities are avoided
	A3	Discussions with other teams are conducted constructively
	A4	Conflicts with other teams are settled quickly
Team performance	H1 H2	Recently, this team seems to be "slipping" a bit in its level of performance. (R) Those who receive or use the work this team does often have complaints about our work. (R)
	H3	The quality of work provided by this team is improving over time
	H4	Critical quality errors occur frequently in this team. (R)
Psychological safety	I1 I2	If you make a mistake on this team, it is often held against you. (R) Members of this team are able to bring up problems and tough issues
	I3	People on this team sometimes reject others for being different. (R)
	I4	It is safe to take a risk on this team

Table 2 Opinions statements and descriptive statistics

Statements (Sect. 3 in the questionnaire)	*N*	Mean	Variance	Std. Dev
(1) The PI planning gives me a good overview of our work	201	3.91	0.758	0.871
- Team members	150	3.78	0.710	0.843
- Stakeholders	51	4.25	0.872	0.934
(2) The program board is very helpful for coordination between teams	201	3.20	0.966	0.983
- Team members	150	3.18	0.945	0.972
- Stakeholders	51	3.30	1.087	1.043
(3) The Scrum of Scrums (SoS) meetings solve inter-team coordination problems	201	3.33	0.962	0.981
- Team members	150	3.28	1.037	1.018
- Stakeholders	51	3.54	0.520	0.721
(4) There are many problems with working in a large-scale setting like ours, using SAFe	201	3.48	1.020	1.010
- Team members	150	3.48	0.989	0.994
- Stakeholders	51	3.57	0.995	0.998
(5) I would like to go back to the old way of working (instead of working according to SAFe)	201	2.13	1.404	1.185
- Team members	150	2.27	1.409	1.187
- Stakeholders	51	1.74	1.147	1.071

Table 3 Attitudes towards perceived impacts on teamwork

Statements (Sect. 4 in the questionnaire)	*N*	Mean	Variance	Std. Dev
How does coordination *with other teams* work now, compared to one year ago (before implementing SAFe)?	150	3.50	1.041	1.020
How does communication *within the team* work now, compared to one year ago (before implementing SAFe)?	150	2.92	1.497	1.224
How is the *balance* between member contributions within the team now, compared to one year ago (before implementing SAFe)?	150	2.93	1.206	1.098
How does coordination *within the team* work now, compared to one year ago (before implementing SAFe)?	150	3.09	1.196	1.094
How does *support* within the team (helping each other) work now, compared to one year ago (before implementing SAFe)?	150	3.01	1.437	1.199
How is the *cohesion* within the team now, compared to one year ago (before implementing SAFe)?	150	3.12	1.395	1.181
How does the personal *effort* to achieve goals differ now, compared to one year ago (before implementing SAFe), within the team?	150	3.11	1.270	1.127
How does your *team performance* differ now, compared to one year ago (before implementing SAFe)?	150	3.04	1.144	1.070
In what way has *trust* and sense of personal security changed within the team compared to one year ago (before implementing SAFe)?	150	2.75	1.408	1.187

measurement model before considering the structural model. The rationale is that this alleviates the interaction of the measurement and structural models, allowing for a more accurate assessment of validity and reliability [3].

5 Results

In this section, research data is presented and analyzed to evaluate findings in the descriptive data (Sect. 5.1), and thereafter, a model estimation using LISREL is presented (Sect. 5.2).

5.1 Measures and Scales

The perceptions of the respondents regarding large-scale agile development work according to SAFe were captured in the "opinions" section of the survey. Firstly, three specific statements were presented to evaluate the respondents' view of three inter-team coordination practices. The fourth statement read: "There are many problems with working in a large-scale setting like ours, using SAFe" and the fifth statement asked whether the respondent wanted to go back to the old way of working before SAFe. These questions/statements were answered by all employees (N = 201).

A Likert scale from 1 to 5 was used to collect the responses: 1 = totally disagree, 3 = neutral, and 5 = totally agree. The data distribution to each of the questions was symmetric and normal. In Table 2, descriptive statistics regarding the five statements are presented in three ways. First, the whole population (N = 201), second, employees working in teams (N = 150), and third, the stakeholders who are all respondents not working in a team (N = 51).

As can be seen, responses to the three statements regarding the benefits of coordination practices (PI planning, program board, and Scrum of Scrums) were all above average. In all three statements, stakeholders are more positive than team members. According to the fifth statement ("I would like to go back to the old way of working (instead of working according to SAFe)"), the average is closer to "agree" than "disagree" for both groups. These numbers show that most respondents do not want to go back to the former way of working, before SAFe, especially not the stakeholders.

After having conducted an analysis of variance test between the two groups, using ANOVA, with a p-value threshold of 0.05, the null hypothesis could only be rejected for the first and fifth statements. Hence, there is a significant difference between the two groups regarding the value of PI planning and whether to go back to the old way of working before SAFe.

The next section of survey questions was aimed at team members only. Nine attitude questions were presented to evaluate the respondents' overall attitude toward the perceived impacts on teamwork, based on the areas suggested by Hoegl et al. [12] and Edmondson [6]. A Likert-like scale from 1 to 5 was used to collect the responses: 1 = worse, 3 = same, and 5 = better. The data distribution to each of the questions was symmetric and normal (Table 3).

As can be seen, the highest positive response was inter-team coordination with an average of 3.50, and the lowest was the statement regarding psychological safety with an average of 2.75, which is below neutral. In other words, the employees perceive an impact of better inter-team coordination but a lowered perceived psychological safety on average. For the seven other statements, they were all close to neutral, with two statements below neutral and five slightly above.

5.2 Model Estimation

Table 4 shows descriptive statistics for the three constructs used for hypothesis testing. The skewness and kurtosis statistics indicate that most of the indicators are normally distributed, with some exceptions. Because of these exceptions, raw data was used in LISREL since it is not dependent on a normal distribution.

Convergent validity is achieved if the model fits the data well, t-values associated with the individual items are significant, and if the measures are reliable [7].

Table 4 Scale statistics

Scales (Sects. 5, 6, and 7 in the questionnaire)	Item	Mean	Std. Dev	Skewness	Kurtosis
Inter-team coordination	A1	3.54	0.850	−0.580	−0.030
	A2	3.67	0.800	−0.322	−0.234
	A3	4.04	0.713	−0.513	0.433
	A4	4.01	0.803	−0.874	1.359
Team performance	H1	3.64	1.034	−0.483	−0.333
	H2	4.14	0.720	−0.655	0.602
	H4	4.13	0.832	−0.916	1.064
Psychological safety	I1	4.61	0.649	−1.648	2.289
	I2	4.45	0.599	−0.581	−0.573
	I3	4.58	0.793	−2.209	5.137
	I4	3.91	0.880	−0.557	0.110

Table 5 presents the measurement model statistics. The model fits the data well, and all t-statistics for indicator loadings are significant, which indicates convergent validity [7]. However, the variance extracted for the constructs is not above 0.5, and composite reliability is not above 0.7, so the measured constructs are not entirely reliable [7]. Nomological validity was assessed through the normed Satorra-Bentler scaled x^2 and degrees of freedom, which measures the distance between data and model. The ratio of the x^2 divided by the degrees of freedom should be below 2 [13]. Unfortunately, the p-value which provides an additional measure should be above 0.05 for significance at the 5% level but is only 0.028. However, the root mean square error of approximation of 0.065 is well below 0.08 [13].

Table 5 Measurement model statistics

Scale	Item	Standardized loading	*t*-value	Error	Composite reliability	Variance extracted
Inter-team coordination	A1	0.66	Fixed	0.57	0.67	0.34
	A2	0.60	4.14	0.64		
	A3	0.53	3.89	0.72		
	A4	0.53	3.90	0.72		
Team performance	H1	0.46	3.56	0.79	0.63	0.40
	H2	0.92	Fixed	0.15		
	H4	0.38	3.15	0.86		
Psychological safety	I1	0.70	Fixed	0.51	0.65	0.33
	I2	0.46	3.82	0.79		
	I3	0.60	4.64	0.64		
	I4	0.49	4.03	0.76		

Notes $x^2 = 59.98$, df = 41, p = 0.028, RMSEA = 0.065

The test of discriminant validity was conducted to estimate a confidence interval (±2 standard errors) around the standardized correlations between latent constructs (off-diagonal of the Φ matrix in LISREL). The interval should not include 1 [19]. In Table 6 displaying correlations between latent constructs, none of the confidence intervals around the standardized correlations between latent variables include one. The three constructs all passed this test.

In the structural model, there is the added component of causal relationships between constructs. Table 7 shows the result of the hypotheses tested in the study.

With a t-value below two (1.17), H1 is not supported. This means that inter-team coordination is not significantly correlated to team performance. H2, with a t-value of 4.17, is supported. Psychological safety is significantly correlated to team performance. The statistics of the structural model are also displayed in Fig. 2.

Table 6 Correlations between latent constructs

Correlations			Confidence interval
	Psychological safety (PS)	Inter-team coordination	PS-ITC: 0.31 + 2(0.04) = 0.31
Inter-team coordination (ITC)	0.31 (0.04)		PS-TP: 0.65 + 2(0.05) = 0.75
Team performance (TP)	0.65 (0.05)	0.33 (0.05)	ITC-TP: 0.33 + 2(0.05) = 0.43

Table 7 Structural model statistics

Hypothesis	Standardized loading	*t*-value	Error	Outcome
H1: Inter-team coordination - >Team performance	0.14	1.17	0.14	Fails to reject H_0
H2: Psychological safety - >Team performance	0.60	4.17	0.21	Reject H_0

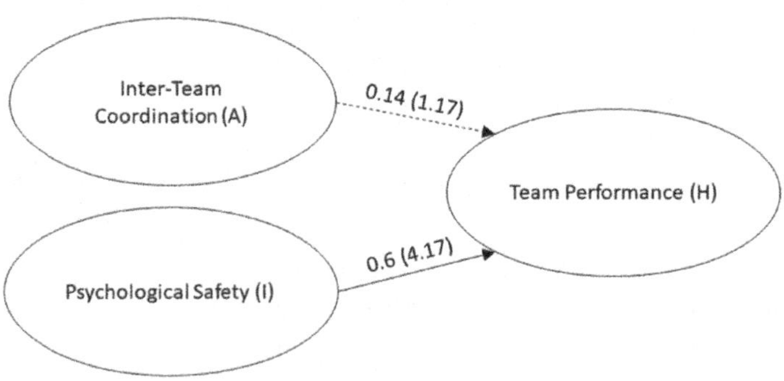

Fig. 2 Structural model

In order to clarify the results, we need to elaborate and discuss the correlations as well as the descriptive statistics on attitudes towards working according to SAFe. This is done in the next section.

6 Discussion

The descriptive statistics show that most respondents do not want to go back to the old way of working as it was before implementing SAFe. That was especially evident for the stakeholders. The answers to the following statement showed a statistically significant difference between stakeholders and team members: "The PI planning gives me a good overview of our work". Although the average was above 3 for both groups (4.25 for stakeholders and 3.78 for team members), this suggests that coordination practices are more appreciated by stakeholders than team members.

The result of investigating the perceived impacts of different aspects of teamwork was somewhat surprising. The six facets of teamwork quality [12] (communication, coordination, balance of member contributions, mutual support, effort, and cohesion) were all close to neutral, with four averages above three and two below three. A high average for increased inter-team coordination was expected (3.5) since the added practices are intended for coordination. Surprisingly, psychological safety was on average perceived as lower (2.75) than before the implementation of SAFe. A possible reason to the decreased psychological safety could be that some people are shy or afraid of speaking up in front of an audience [9]. Several practices, such as PI planning and system demos, requires people to speak up in front of a large number of people. Mistakes could then be highlighted for the whole ART, not just in the single team, which might induce a sense of insecurity for the individual team member.

The results of the structured equation modeling indicate that successful inter-team coordination in large-scale agile software development does not correlate to high team performance. Although this result is contrary to Hoegl et al. [12], one must remember that their study only confirmed a positive relationship with schedule performance (delivering on time), not with quality or adherence to budget. Also, team performance in this study is based on self-reflecting answers, i.e., how the individuals perceived the performance of the team. However, although research shows a positive relationship between inter-team coordination and the overall project success (e. g. [11]), maybe inter-team coordination is not as important for the performance of the individual team. Perhaps it should rather be seen as a teamwork skill on its own, not specifically important for team performance but rather for the performance of a whole project, consisting of several teams.

The study confirms a positive correlation between psychological safety and perceived team performance for teams using SAFe practices for team coordination. This correlation has been proven in other areas as well [6] and does not come as a surprise. The result somewhat confirms the assumption of Modern Agile, which declares psychological safety as a "key to unlocking high performance" [18].

7 Conclusion

When larger organizations scale up their agile ways of working, new practices for coordinating teams becomes necessary. The implemented practices for coordinating teams could have an impact on team performance, but they have so far not been much studied. This study suggests a positive correlation between psychological safety and perceived team performance for teams working in a large-scale setting. However, successful inter-team coordination does not correlate to high team performance, which is contrary to previous studies [12].

The managerial implication of this result is that inter-team coordination does not seem important for team performance, per se. Although originators of SAFe [21] claim increased productivity and more motivated employees, this study does not support that the claimed benefits stem from the added inter-team coordination practices. This does not mean that inter-team coordination is of low importance. It only suggests that improving inter-team coordination will not increase team performance for the individual team. The results do, however, support the second hypothesis, that psychological safety correlates with team performance in a large-scale agile software development setting, where the organization has implemented SAFe team coordination practices.

Regarding managerial implications, this means that large-scale agile software development organizations will benefit from helping teams to increase their level of psychological safety to raise team performance. This confirms previous studies on the impact of high levels of psychological safety [6]. Also, it is important for managers to be aware of the potential decrease of psychological safety. This study shows the average of perceived psychological safety now, compared to before implementing SAFe, was only 2.75 (where three is neutral).

Some limitations needs to be discussed. The results of the descriptive statistics on attitudes towards team coordination practices and perceived impacts could be seen as indicators and are of low explanatory value. For each teamwork quality aspect, only one item has been used per construct, which was not the case in Hoegl et al. [12], where several items per construct were used. But in this study, the constructs were not used for hypothesis testing, only as a way of understanding overall attitudes and perceived impacts. This understanding was important to decide on further analysis in the study. For the structural equation modeling, these results need to be further confirmed since the reliability of the constructs is questionable with low variance extracted as well as composite reliability.

For each investigated factor, only four items were used, which is rather low, and due to low communalities and low factor loading on one item in the team performance construct (item H3), only three items were used for that factor. The argument for not using more than four items per factor was that this was only a part of the survey, which in total consisted of 53 questions. With too many questions, there might be an increased risk of getting few filled out or only partially filled out survey responses.

Fortunately, the number of questions did not seem to discourage participation since the response rate reached as high as 78.5% in total (201/256) and 61% (111/183) useful for hypotheses testing.

Future research needs to be done to confirm these findings on team performance, e.g. by investigating more organizations using SAFe or with similar team coordination practices since the number of participant responses used for hypotheses testing was somewhat low (N = 111).

References

1. 14th Annual State of Agile™ Report, http://stateofagile.versionone.com. Accessed 18 Dec 2020
2. Anderson, J.C., Gerbing, D.W.: Structural equation modeling in practice: a review and recommended two-step approach. Psychol. Bull. **103**(3), 411–423 (1988)
3. Anderson, J.C., Gerbing, D.W.: Assumptions and comparative strengths of the two-step approach: comment on Fornell and Yi. Sociol. Methods Res. **20**(3), 321–333 (1992)
4. Bass, J.M., Haxby, A.: Tailoring product ownership in large-scale agile. IEEE Softw. (2018)
5. Bond-Barnard, T.J., Fletcher, L., Steyn, H.: Linking trust and collaboration in project teams to project management success. Int. J. Managing Projects Bus. **11**(2), 432–457 (2018)
6. Edmondson, A.: Psychological safety and learning behavior in work teams. Adm. Sci. Q. **44**(2), 350–383 (1999)
7. Fornell, C., Larcker, D.F.: Evaluating structural equation models with unobservable variables and measurement error. J. Mark. Res. **18**(1), 39–50 (1981)
8. Gustavsson, T.: Changes over time in a planned inter-team coordination routine. In: Proceedings of the XP2019 Scientific Workshops, May 21–25, Montreal, Canada (2019)
9. Gustavsson, T.: Voices from the teams—impacts on autonomy in large-scale agile software development settings. In: Proceedings of the XP2019 Scientific Workshops, May 21–25, Montreal, Canada (2019)
10. Hackman, J.R.: Groups that Work (and Those That Don't). Jossey-Bass, San Fransisco (1990)
11. Hise, R.T., O'Neal, L., Parasuraman, A., McNeal, J.U.: Marketing/R&D interaction in new product development: implications for new product success rates. J. Prod. Innov. Manage. **7**, 142–155 (1990)
12. Hoegl, M., Weinkauf, K., Gemuenden, H.G.: Interteam coordination, project commitment, and teamwork in multi-team R&D projects: a longitudinal study. Organ. Sci. **15**(1), 38–55 (2004)
13. Joreskog, K., Sorbom, D.: Lisrel 8: Structural Equation Modeling with the Simplis Command Language. Lawrence Erlbaum Associates, Hillsdale (1993)
14. Kirkman, B.L., Rosen, B.: Beyond self-management: antecedents and consequences of team empowerment. Acad. Manag. J. **42**(1), 58–74 (1999)
15. Laanti, M., Salo, O., Abrahamsson, P.: Agile methods rapidly replacing traditional methods at Nokia: a survey of opinions on agile transformation. Inf. Softw. Technol. **53**(3), 276–290 (2011)
16. Leffingwell, D., Yakyama, A., Knaster, R., Jemilo, D., Oren, I.: SAFe reference guide: Scaled Agile Framework for Lean Software and Systems Engineering. Addison Wesley, USA (2017)
17. Manifesto for Agile Software Development (2001). http://agilemanifesto.org. Accessed 15 March 2021
18. Modern Agile. http://modernagile.org. Accessed 11 Jan 2021

19. Moe, N.B., Olsson, H.H., Dingsøyr, T.: Trends in large-scale agile development: a summary of the 4th workshop at XP2016. In: Proceedings of the Scientific Workshop Proceedings of XP2016 (2016)
20. Mott, P.E.: The Characteristics of Effective Organizations. Harper & Row, New York (1972)
21. UnSAFe at any speed. http://kenschwaber.wordpress.com/2013/08/06/unsafe-at-any-speed/. Accessed 12 Jan 2019

Towards Conceptual and Logical Modelling of NoSQL Databases

Jaroslav Pokorný and Karel Richta

Abstract NoSQL databases (DB) support the ability to handle large volumes of data in the absence of an explicit data schema. On the other hand, schema information is sometimes essential for applications during data retrieval. Consequently, there are approaches to schema construction, e.g., in the JSON DB and graph DB communities. The difference between a conceptual and database schema is often vague in this case. We use functional constructs—typed attributes for a conceptual view of DB that provide a sufficiently structured approach for expressing semantics of document and graph data. Attribute names are natural language expressions. Such typed functional data objects can be manipulated by terms of a typed λ-calculus, providing powerful nonprocedural query features for considered data structures. The calculus is extendible. Logical, arithmetic operations, and aggregation functions can be included there. Really, conceptual and database modelling merge in this case. The paper focuses on conceptual/database schemas for JSON and graph NoSQL data models.

Keywords Typed lambda calculus · Functional data objects · NoSQL databases · Relational databases · Database integration

A prior version of this paper has been published in the ISD2021 Proceedings (http://aisel.aisnet.org/isd2014/proceedings2021).

J. Pokorný (✉)
Charles University, Faculty of Mathematics and Physics, Prague, Czech Republic
e-mail: jaroslav.pokorny@matfyz.cuni.cz

K. Richta
University College of Polytechnics, Jihlava, Czech Republic
e-mail: karel.richta@vspj.cz

E. Insfran Pelozo et al. (eds.), *Advances in Information Systems Development*,
Lecture Notes in Information Systems and Organisation 55,
https://doi.org/10.1007/978-3-030-95354-6_15

1 Introduction

Systems that store and process Big Data have become a common component of data management architectures. NoSQL databases (DBs) are often used for storing Big Data today. Generally, Big Data can be a combination of structured, unstructured, and semi-structured data, i.e.

- structured data in DBs and data warehouses based on SQL,
- unstructured data, such as text and document files held in Hadoop clusters or in NoSQL DBs, and
- semi-structured data, such as web server logs or streaming data from sensors.

To deal with such data in a meaningful way, its users must have a detailed understanding of the available data and possess some semantics of what answers they are looking for to make sure the information they get is valid and up to date.

In relational DBs, the user has a relational database schema at disposal and, mostly, a conceptual schema as well. On the other hand, no predefined schema is enforced before writing data into a NoSQL DB. NoSQL DBs are mostly schema-less. This type of data handling is more flexible in the case of Big Data. Similarly, the situation is known in in the case of DBs with unstructured data, or DBs with frequent schema changes. Emphasize that this does not mean that NoSQL DBs do not have a schema. As opposed to statically typed schemas in SQL DB, a schema-less DB contains rather dynamically typed schema. A schema is here required for reading and understanding data and not for optimizing storage. On the other hand, people working with Big Data are making the typical mistake. They want to access data in the NoSQL DB without any knowledge of its schema, and then often find that their queries do not work, that they do not know the keys for identifying subsets of the required data. In this scenario, the data comes without a schema and its multiple data models coexist. Therefore, there is a gap between data modelling and physical data aspects of NoSQL DBs.

Traditionally, data projects that start with data models and data schemas usually behave better than those that do not. That observation remains true in the NoSQL world. However, the big difference with NoSQL is that, because the DB often has no conceptual/database view at disposal, it is more likely developers will just throw data in and solve problems with its semantics later on. The situation becomes even more complicated in the case when the DB is multi-model, i.e., more NoSQL DBs of different categories are integrated in one database system (DBS). This case was simpler when the integrated DBs were relational and equipped with a conceptual/database schema.

There are approaches documenting that conceptual/database data modelling is possible also in NoSQL world. A systematic literature review of the current state of research regarding database design methods in the new database era is performed in [21]. Some NoSQL DBs are based on a Model-Driven Architecture (MDA), i.e., on transformation rules starting from UML diagrams and generating a NoSQL physical data [1]. A generic logical model that describes data according to the common features of the three types of NoSQL systems: column-oriented, document-oriented, and graph-oriented is used here as an intermediate link. Of the newer ones, let us mention the NoAM (NoSQL Abstract Model) [2] presenting a novel abstract data model for NoSQL DB, which exploits the commonalities of various NoSQL systems. NoAM describes in a uniform way the features of many NoSQL systems, and so can be effectively used for an intermediate representation in a NoSQL DB design methodology. A favourite in this area is the Concept and Object Modelling Notation (COMN) [7] enabling to cover the full spectrum of analysis and design, i.e. to represent the objects and concepts in a problem space, logical data design, and concrete NoSQL and SQL DBs implementation.

The traditional problem in the database world is querying. Usual approaches based on SQL and integrated non-relational data types are imported there in some way. Only a few attempts exist enabling to query a database through E-R schemas, e.g., [11]. However, strong means for querying NoSQL database data are still missing. Here we use functional constructs—attributes for a conceptual view of a DB and sufficiently structured approach for expressing semantics of NoSQL data considered in such architecture. Conceptual structures have a database role in this approach and can serve as the basis of a query language. In other words, conceptual/database modelling and querying merge in this case. We will introduce a formal apparatus for typing attributes and languages of terms based on a typed lambda calculus. Consequently, we obtain a tool covering all NoSQL data models in a unified way, i.e., also a possibility of querying multi-model data in a unified way. Even any relational database can be a member of such multi-model architecture.

The rest of the paper is organized as follows. Section 2 illustrates the features of the main categories of NoSQL DB. In Sect. 3, we briefly present a history of conceptual modelling. Section 4 is focused on conceptual/databases schemas for some NoSQL data models, particularly JSON (JavaScript Object Notation) and database graphs. In Sect. 5, we describe a functional type system appropriate for typing conceptual constructs. We also introduce a version of a typed λ-calculus for manipulating these constructs in a query style. Section 6 introduces a variant of conceptual/database schemas for JSON and graph NoSQL data models. Section 7 concludes the paper.

2 Categories of NoSQL DB

NoSQL database management systems (DBMS) are usually classified into four basic categories in terms of the supported data model: key-value stores, document-based stores, column-based stores, and graph-based stores. Due to the vague semantics of the name NoSQL, XML DB, JSON DB, object stores, and multi-model DB are often considered also as NoSQL categories. Typically, rather low-level tools are used for processing NoSQL data of the first three categories, e.g., a software framework and programming model MapReduce in the Hadoop framework and the architecture style REST (e.g., [14]). As usually we will use often shortly DB instead of DBMS. Moreover, a lot of these software do not contain all usual DBMS features.

(i) *Key-value* stores are the simplest NoSQL DB. The key is a unique identifier associated with a value. The value may have different formats for different key-value systems. In some cases, the value is an array, a JSON structure or a simple string of bytes. However, key-value stores typically abstract from the type of value stored, therefore providing only a simple query functionality rather than using a query language. Searches are performed on keys, not values, and they are restricted to exact matches. Rather, a set of operations usable for application programming is at disposal. Key-value stores are suitable for efficient reading and writing of extensive amounts of data. They store all key-value pairs together in a single namespace, which is analogous to a relational schema.

As examples, an open-source in-memory DB Redis[1] and Amazon DynamoDB[2] can be considered. SQL-like and MapReduce querying are not supported in Redis, REST querying is supported by some APIs. DynamoDB has added support for JSON data to provide document-like data structures that better match with objects in the application code.

(ii) *Document-oriented* or *document-based* NoSQL DB store data as collections of similar documents. Each document reminds a row in relational DB, but in a schema-free context. It is specified as self-describing data. In document-based DB, a record, called a document, has its own internal structure and can be stored as a value for a key (document ID). In a document DB, documents can be nested. The users or processing applications have the schematic responsibility in such database. This may result in some disadvantages, such as the lack of integrity constraints (IC). However, the lack of schema provides high flexibility to store a wide range of data, which makes it suitable for storing Big Data. Documents do not have to be a free text, may be structured in various formats, e.g., XML or (mostly) hierarchically in the JSON format, or BSON (Binary JSON). It is possible to store a set of heterogeneous documents inside the same collection.

The MongoDB[3] is a well-known representative of document-oriented NoSQL DB storing data in BSON. MongoDB offers a rich query language having powerful filtering capabilities. MapReduce and REST querying are also supported by MongoDB. Similarly, Apache CouchDB[4] stores JSON documents and offers optionally MapReduce for data retrieval and REST API.

(iii) *Column-based* DB or *wide-column* DB also utilize the key-value concept. Column-based DBs are designed to address the large number of columns and frequent changes in the schema. Column-based stores use a table form but in a flexible and scalable way. Each row consists of a key and one or more related columns, which are called column families. Each column family has a name that should be declared when the table is created and cannot be changed subsequently. Each column family is associated with column qualifiers which are not predefined but can be dynamically created and inserted into the table. Each column is stored in a separate file or region

---

[1] https://redis.io/ (retrieved on 27.1. 2022).

[2] https://aws.amazon.com/dynamodb/ (retrieved on 27. 1. 2022).

[3] https://www.mongodb.com/ (retrieved on 27. 1. 2022).

[4] https://couchdb.apache.org/ (retrieved on 27. 1. 2022).

in the system's storage. Each row's key-column family can have different numbers of columns and the columns can contain different kinds of data. Data is retrieved using a query language. The column structure is appropriate to fast aggregation queries.

The most famous open-source column-oriented DB are HBase[5] and Hypertable.[6] Both DBs have no SQL-like query language, but MapReduce and REST querying is supported there. On the other hand, Apache Cassandra[7] offers the Cassandra Query Language (CQL) whose query style reminds SQL. Recall that we can meet column-oriented stores also in the relational DB world. For example, Vertica[8] is the main representative of this DB category. However, columns are used here only as the way how the Vertica DB stores data.

Remark. There are some soft differences between basic constructs of (i) and (iii). For example, DynamoDB supports two types of primary keys: partition keys and composite primary keys given by couples (partition key, sort key). Here partition keys and sort keys can contain only one attribute. On the other hand, Cassandra allows including more than one column (attribute) into partition keys and clustering columns.

(iv) *Graph databases* (GDB) are storage systems that use graph structures to represent and store data. Their nodes and edges can be labelled to indicate the types of objects and associations they represent. An edge (or a relationship) connects two nodes and may be directed. When directions are added, the relationships between nodes are identified by the names of the nodes and can be traversed according to these directions. A mixed graph is a graph in which some edges may be directed, and some may be undirected. GDBs therefore focus on relationships, rather than data. Nodes and edges may also contain properties that describe the real data items contained within each object. At the scale of the whole GDB, its data model changes as edges are stored with new kinds of relationship data, and nodes are stored with new kinds of data items. The graphs use the technique, in which each node has explicit references to its adjacent node.

The most popular type of GDB is the open source Neo4j[9] with the query language Cypher. REST querying is supported by Neo4j but MapReduce not.

3 Conceptual Modelling in General

In the history of DBMS, there is typically a focus on so-called *semantic* (*conceptual*, *entity-oriented*, or *object-oriented*) *database models* and associated modelling methodologies. The strength of these models is that they are conceptually oriented. Let us recall the E-R model, which occurs in many variants and is traditionally the

[5] https://hbase.apache.org/ (retrieved on 27. 1. 2022).

[6] https://hypertable.org /(retrieved on 27. 1. 2022).

[7] https://cassandra.apache.org/ (retrieved on 27. 1. 2022).

[8] https://www.vertica.com/overview/ (retrieved on 27. 1. 2022).

[9] https://neo4j.com/ (retrieved on 27. 1. 2022).

basis for the design of most relational databases. It is interesting that the expressive power of a given semantic database model depends on a few number of basic constructs only. But most of the interesting "semantic" constructs in semantic database models are redundant, i.e., they do not increase the expressive power of these models.

The possibility of various ways of modelling the same object system is called *semantic relativism.* The existence of this phenomenon was observed (only as a hypothesis) by Klein and Hirschheim who noted in [9] that the possibilities of all E-R approaches are approximately the same. A fundamental theme arising in semantic database models focuses on the development of formal methods for comparing of the information capabilities of conceptual schemas expressed in these models. For example, the work [16] discusses the possibility how to reach it with a functional approach based on typed functional objects and typed λ-calculus.

Other authors give a similar (but imprecise) opinion [8]: semantic database models distinguish each other in that, how many ICs they absorb into basic constructs and how many of them must be formulated explicitly. Many people mean that with powerful tools for formulation of explicit ICs semantic database models offer practically the same chances for conceptual modelling. Unfortunately, this is not true. Really, explicit ICs only "filter" data coming into a DB. The expressiveness of a database model is given by its basic modelling constructs.

Experiences from the last years show that traditional design techniques, e.g., E-R model and UML, cannot be easily used with new database technologies like NoSQL DB. For example, E-R model assumes that data will ultimately be stored in tables. Or, it is not possible to represent data structures that are interrelated without using keys in E-R model. There are some approaches using, e.g., UML [22]. The MDA-based approach presented in [1] implements the UML conceptual model describing Big Data in column-oriented NoSQL systems. These approaches are rather conservative and not sufficiently general for NoSQL data modelling.

There are also approaches to conceptual modelling document data. For example, the authors of [4] propose a model for the conceptual representation of a document data store based on UML class diagrams and mapping rules for its implementation.

In the era of Big Data, it is essential that we have the tools we need to understand the data coming to a user faster than ever before, and to design DB and data processing systems that can adapt easily to changing data schemas and business requirements. Therefore, new NoSQL data organization techniques must be used in parallel with traditional SQL DB. The COMN model mentioned in Sect. 1 can represent the objects and concepts with simple and familiar graphical notation (boxes and lines). It can be used to describe or define any data that is or will be stored in any SQL or NoSQL form, that is, for example, in in graphs and documents. They enable:

- to think about objects, concepts, types, and classes in the real world, using the ordinary meanings of English words,
- to express logical data designs that are without implementation considerations than is possible in any other notation,

- to understand key-value, document-oriented, column-based, and table-oriented DB design in logical and physical terms,
- COMN is a modelling technique, not just notation. COMN provides a notation to handle all constructs that E-R techniques do not do well, and it steps up to the problem of linking physical and conceptual models.
- to represent new multi-model NoSQL DB.

4 Conceptual/Database Schemas of NoSQL DB

In the NoSQL world, there is a problem for those who are not developers, e.g., of MapReduce programs, to understand the DB content. This is because the schema is hidden in MapReduce program. Therefore, most database administrators and data analysts cannot access and understand these schemas. The user's dependence on developers to understand the code significantly reduces his/her possibility to propose changes and expansions of data in such DB. Therefore, data modelling is the key for the better understanding of enterprise data and some level of DB schema design is inevitable. In other words, NoSQL follows *query-driven design*. In the style *schema-for-read*, data does not follow any internal schema.

Concerning an integration of data from different databases, i.e., in the multi-model case, two approaches based on database schema management occur [18]:

- top-down – starting with a global schema to design schemas for particular data stores,
- bottom-up – through middleware, i.e., to use schema mapping for schemas of data stores in sites with a middleware (e.g., OLE DB,[10] JDBC[11]) and then use a query transformation. Data is loosely integrated and managed by multiple servers.

We remind that the former concerns rather homogenous DB models used in integrated data stores, while the latter supports heterogeneous DB models and consequently heterogeneous DBS, particularly when some of these DB models are NoSQL. The latter variant is more relevant in practice (for detailed discussion, see [18]). Moreover, the relational data model is one of these models. The integration of relational and NoSQL DB is one of the possible ways of bringing them [4]. In the case of NoSQL, even more than one database model is included in one DB architecture. For example, Cassandra combines column-based data model and key-value data model, DynamoDB combines document-oriented and key-value data models. ArangoDB[12] represents also a multi-model approach, meaning that it can even address documents, graphs, and key values.

Often XML and JSON data are also considered in the context of NoSQL DB. Both JSON and XML models are "self-describing" and hierarchical. However, JSON is

---

[10] https://searchsqlserver.techtarget.com/definition/OLE-DB (retrieved on 27. 1. 2022)

[11] https://docs.oracle.com/javase/7/docs/technotes/guides/jdbc/jdbc_41.html (retrieved on 27. 6. 2022).

[12] https://www.arangodb.com/ (retrieved on 27. 1. 2022).

```
{
  "$schema":"http://json-schema.org/draft-04/schema",
  "type":"object",
  "properties":{
     "book":{
        "type":"object",
        "properties":{
           "title":{"type":"string"},
           "authors":{"type":"array",
                   "items":{"type":"string"}},
           "issued_in":{"type":"number"},
                   }  }

           }  }
    }
```

Fig. 1 JSON schema fragment for documents containing book objects

easier to read, less verbose, and brings less constraints than XML. For example, a conceptual model for XML called XSEM is proposed in [13]. It divides the conceptual modelling process into conceptual and structural levels.

Both relational and NoSQL databases offer support for JSON, meaning that hybrid solutions, in the context of the schema, are already at disposal [6]. In Sects. 4.1 and 4.2, we shortly summarize some information about JSON and graph schemas, respectively. The conceptual model behind graphs is a variant of E-R model. Functional conceptual variants for JSON and graph data will be presented in Sect. 6.

4.1 JSON Schemas

To manage JSON data collections, we can rely on several schema languages, like JSON Schema,[13] Mongoose,[14] and Joi.[15] Remark that the JSON Schema specification is somewhat complex and is not widely used in practice. A short overview of these languages can be founded in [3]. A formal approach based on typed functional JSON data objects proposed in [20] will be presented in Sect. 6.1. Figure 1 shows an example of JSON schema expressed in the JSON Schema language describing books with a title, authors, and issue date.

[13] http://json-schema.org (retrieved on 27. 1. 2022).

[14] https://mongoosejs.com (retrieved on 27. 1. 2022).

[15] https://github.com/sideway/joi (retrieved on 27. 1. 2022).

4.2 Graph Schemas

The database model used for GDB can be characterized by the following three features:

- Data and the graph database schema are represented by a graph or by data structures generalizing the notion of graph.
- Manipulation of data is expressed by graph transformations like graph-oriented operations and type constructors.
- ICs enforce data consistency.

The *database graph* is mostly a directed, labelled, attributed multigraph. Database graphs with different sets of attributes for nodes/edges of the same types are accepted. This situation occurs in practice, e.g., when no graph database schema is at disposal, i.e., in a schema-less case, which makes such graphs suitable for semi-structured data storage. This is in line with the NoSQL concept.

In [17] we used a binary E-R model as a variant for graph conceptual modelling. A correct graph conceptual schema may be mapped into an equivalent (or nearly equivalent) graph database schema with the straightforward mapping algorithm but with a weaker notion of a database schema, i.e. some inherent ICs at the conceptual level will be neglected to satisfy the usual notation of directed, labelled, attributed multigraphs. Both nodes and edges are defined by a unique identifier (Id). In Fig. 2a, we present a conceptual schema without attributes of entity and relationship types, where a user submits at most to one journal. Explicit conceptual M:N cardinality between movies and journals is lost in the graph database schema (b). We can see that a difference between conceptual view and database view is rather negligible here.

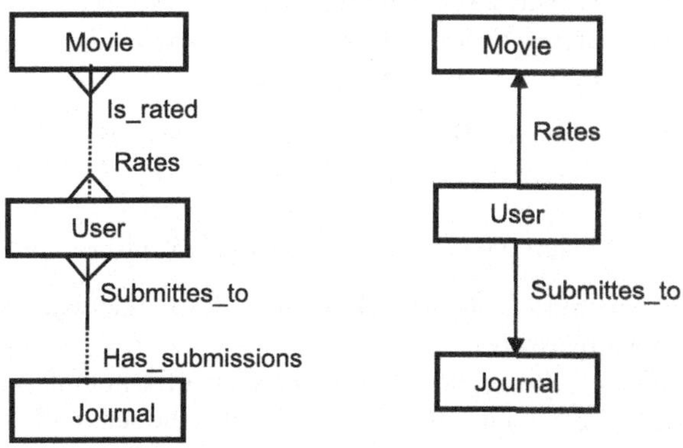

(a) graph conceptual schema (b) graph database schema

Fig. 2 Schemas in graph databases environment

The typed graph model presented in [10] enables using hyper-nodes and hyper-edges, in which a relationship (called a hyper-edge) can connect any number of nodes. This feature better supports graph conceptual modelling.

5 Functional Modelling

Our approach to conceptual/database modelling is based on the notion of function. This notion covers naturally all structures allowed in the recent database models. As a manipulating tool for functions, we have a typed lambda calculus at disposal. At the conceptual level, the approach is inspired by transparent intensional logic, see, e.g., [12, 15], and [5]. Conceptual functions will be named by expressions in a natural language and will be directly used for querying. By using these functions for NoSQL data, we obtain query tools at a conceptual rather than the logical level.

Section 5.1 shortly summarizes functional typing. Attributes are introduced in Sect. 5.2. Section 5.3 describes the traditional manipulation language for functions—typed lambda calculus. The possibility of querying attributes is shortly presented in Sect. 6.2.

5.1 Types

Each conceptual/database model is based on a typing system. For example, in the relational DB model, such a system contains one type—relation. In our basic functional type system, we use functional types and tuple types. In other database models, we will also use types as arrays, sets, and more.

Definition 1. The existence of some (*primitive*) *types* $S_1,\ldots,S_k$ ($k \geq 1$) is assumed. They constitute a base **B**. More complex types are obtained in the following way:

(a) Every member of the base **B** is a (*primitive*) *type over* **B**.
(b) If $S, R_1,\ldots,R_n$ ($n \geq 1$) are types over **B**, then $(S{:}R_1,\ldots,R_n)$ ($n \geq 1$) is a (*functional*) *type over* **B**.
(c) If $R_1,\ldots,R_n$ ($n \geq 1$) are types over **B**, then $(R_1,\ldots,R_n)$ is a (*tuple*) *type over* **B**.

The *functional type system* **T** *over* **B** (or **T** if **B** is assumed) is the least set containing types given by (a)-(c).

For example, *Number*, *String*, *Bool* ∈ **B**. If members of **B** are interpreted as mutually disjoint nonempty sets, then $(S{:}R_1, \ldots, R_n)$ denotes the set of all (total or partial) functions from $R_1 \times \ldots \times R_n$ into S, $(R_1, \ldots, R_n)$ denotes the Cartesian product $R_1 \times \ldots \times R_n$. An object o of the type T is called a *T-object* and can be denoted *as o/T*. $(R_1, \ldots, R_n)$-objects contain an ordered set of respective $R_1, \ldots, R_n$ -objects.

A primitive type *Bool* is defined as the set {TRUE, FALSE}. The type *Bool* allows typing some objects as sets and relations. They will not consider here as separate units. Both can be modelled as unary and n-ary characteristic functions, respectively. Thus, both notions are redundant in **T**.

Mathematical functions may be easily typed. Arithmetic operations $+$, $-$, *, / are examples of (*Number*:*Number*,*Number*)-objects. Logical connectives, quantifiers, and predicates are also typed functions: e.g., **and**/(*Bool*: *Bool*, *Bool*), *R*-identity $=$ *R* is (*Bool*: *R*,*R*)-object, universal *R*-quantifier ΠR, and existential *R*-quantifiers ΣR are (*Bool*:(*Bool*:*R*))—objects. As for our notational convention, we use an infix notation for arithmetic and logical functions. Similarly, we write '∀x…' and '∃x…' for application of the universal and existential quantifier, respectively. With **T**, it is possible to type functions of functions, nested tables, ISA-hierarchies, etc.

Summarizing the notions given above, we will distinguish between object types and objects. Objects are of object types. Because object types are functions, objects are their values. Indeed, the values need mark-up given by the name of the object.

5.2 Attributes

Object structures usable in building a DB can be described by some expressions of a natural language. Each base **B** will consist of descriptive and entity types. Consider **B** $=$ {*User*, *Movie*, *U_ID*, *Name*, *Birth_year*, …, *String*, *Number*}. For example, for GDBs, we can conceive entity types as sets of node IDs. Descriptive types *String*, *Numbers*, etc., serve for domains of properties of entities. Then, e.g., the expression "the movies rated by a given user" (shortly MRU) denotes a ((*Bool*:*Movie*):*User*)-object, i.e. a (partial) function f:*User* → (*Movie* → *Bool*), "the name of a given user" (shortly NU, e.g.) denotes a (*Name*:*User*)-object. Such (named) functions represent attributes. Attribute names are natural language expressions. This fact increases their conceptual features. More formally, *attributes* are functions of type ((*S*:*T*):*W*), where *W* is the logical space (possible worlds), *T* contains time moments, and $S \in$ **T**. Thus, attributes are partial empirical (data) functions. For simplicity, we will not explicitly consider types *W* and *T* for attributes in this paper. Other conceptual constructions are propositions of type *Bool*. Some of them are connected with attributes. Attributes bear a basic information concerning an application domain. We say that attributes generate certain basic propositions. For example, "The name of a given user is Baker" denotes such a proposition. It is generated by the attribute NU.

For database users ICs are also important. Essentially, each IC is a proposition that introduces redundancy into the conceptual/database schema. On the other hand, we need ICs for filtering erroneous data. ICs can be expressed again as simple propositions or, on a more formal level, by a logical language, e.g., by a typed lambda calculus (see Sect. 5.3).

A lot of functions need even no possible world. For example, aggregation functions like COUNT, AVARAGE, and arithmetic operations provide such functions. They have the same behaviour in all possible worlds and time moments. We call such functions *analytical*. On the other hand, attributes are *empirical functions*. Range of these functions are again functions.

Typing system **T** over **B** and a set of attribute specifications enable to consider a *functional conceptual/database schema* as a couple $\mathbf{S}_{\mathrm{LT}} = (\mathbf{A}, \mathbf{I})$, where **A** is a tuple $(A_1, \ldots, A_n)$ of typed variables of LT called *attribute identifiers* and **I** is a tuple of other terms of LT representing ICs. With attributes we can obtain basic true propositions (in an actual world and a given time moment). These propositions form an *information base* for $\mathbf{S}_{\mathrm{LT}}$.

5.3 Typed Lambda Calculus

Our version of the typed lambda calculus (language LT) directly supports manipulating objects typed by **T** introduced in Sect. 5.1. We use it in Sect. 5.4 as a tool for querying a database described as a set of attributes. We also present a syntactic sugar for LT and examples of queries.

Definition 2. We will suppose a collection **Func** of constants, each having a fixed type, and denumerable many variables of each type. Then the *language of* (λ-)*terms* (LT) is defined as follows:

Let types R, S, $R_1, \ldots, R_n$ $(n \geq 1)$ be elements of **T**.

(1) Every variable of type R is a *term* of type R.
(2) Every constant of type R is a *term* of type R.
(3) If M be a term of type $(S{:}R_1, \ldots, R_n)$, and $\mathrm{N}_1, \ldots, \mathrm{N}_n$ are terms of types $R_1, \ldots, R_n$, respectively, then $\mathrm{M}(\mathrm{N}_1, \ldots, \mathrm{N}_n)$ is a *term* of type S. /*application*/
(4) If $x_1, \ldots, x_n$ are different variables of the respective types $R_1, \ldots, R_n$ and M is a term of type S, then $\lambda x_1, \ldots, x_n(\mathrm{M})$ is a term of type $(S{:}R_1, \ldots, R_n)$. /*lambda abstraction*/
(5) If $\mathrm{N}_1, \ldots, \mathrm{N}_n$ are terms of type $R_1, \ldots, R_n$, respectively, then $(\mathrm{N}_1, \ldots, \mathrm{N}_n)$ is a term of type $(R_1, \ldots, R_n)$. /*tuple*/
(6) If M is a term of type $(R_1, \ldots, R_n)$, then $\mathrm{M}[1], \ldots, \mathrm{M}[\mathrm{n}]$ are terms of respective types $R_1, \ldots, R_n$. /*components*/

5.4 Querying with Terms

The language LT with at least applications of functions and lambda abstractions provides a powerful tool for querying database data conceived as functions. A query can be expressed by a term of LT. In Sect. 2, we have mentioned a lot of query languages in particular categories of NoSQL DB. Using LT as a universal query language in this case can be useful in two directions:

(1) increasing the expressive power of querying data in NoSQL DB,
(2) querying data over DBS considered in a multi-model environment.

Regardless of the fact that NoSQL DB are considered schema-less, some explicit database schemas are needed in our approach. Very natural possibilities for the construction of such schemas are offered by GDB. In [11] we used a functional approach in which a property graph is represented by typed partial functions. We were inspired by the HIT Database Model (e.g., [15]), as a functional alternative of a binary E-R model. The functions considered here are of two kinds: *single-valued* and *multivalued*.

Example 5.1: Consider attributes MRU/((*Bool*:*Movie*):*User*) and NU/(*Name*:*User*) from Sect. 5.2 and the query "Give a set of couples associated to each user given by his/her name and the number of movies rated by him/her". An associated LT term providing a relation looks as follows:

λ n, c (c = COUNT(λ m (MRU(u)(m) **and** NU(u) = n))).

or in a more readable version as:

$\lambda\ n^{Name},\ c^{Number}\ (c^{Number} =\ COUNT(\lambda\ m^{Movie}(MRU(u^{User})(m^{Movie})$ **and** $NU(u^{User}) = n^{Name})))$

More structured answers could be achieved by terms like:

λ x, y, … λ u … λ z …(M).

where M/*Bool*. We would get another syntactic sugar, e.g., by introducing the constructs SELECT, WHERE, etc.

We can also suppose that other data models used as typed functions used in LT, e.g., those derived from JSON documents [20]. Then, e.g., comparing to MongoDB querying, LT is more powerful concerning its expressivity due to logical connectives, quantifiers, arithmetic operations, and aggregation functions included in **Func**. LT enables to obtain classical relations, tree structures of *String* values, and even new data as query answers.

Example 5.2: In a multi-model environment integrating NoSQL DB together with a relational DB, we can consider relations as Boolean functions [19], e.g.,

Actors/(*Bool*:*A_ID*, *Name*, *Address*),

Plays/(*Bool*:*Title*, *A_ID*),

Films/(*Bool*:*Title*, *Released*).

A more conceptual approach would take into account an E-R schema in Fig. 3a and the set of associated attributes in Fig. 3b. The straightforward construction of the E-R schema is enabled by the fact that the relations are in 3NF.

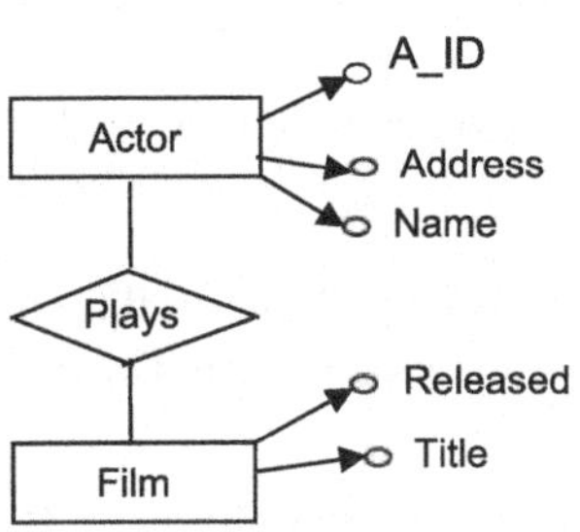

(a) E-R schema

Actor's _A_ID/(*A_ID:Actor*)
Address_of_actor/(*Address:Actor*)
Name_of_actor/(*Name:Actor*)
Released_day_of_the_film/(*Released:Film*)
Title_of_film/(*Title:Film*)
Plays//(*Bool:Title, Actor_ID*)

(b) functional database schema

Fig. 3 Schemas in relational databases environment

These attributes can be used in a multi-model environment together with conceptual structures for JSON data and GDBs which we will present in Sects. 6.1 and 6.3.

6 Functional Conceptual/database Schema Design

Now we focus on the functional approach to two NoSQL models: a document model using JSON objects (Sects. 6.1 and 6.2) and a graph model (Sect. 6.3). We will define functional schemas for both cases. Such schemas can be considered as conceptual schemas, but, on the other hand, they can serve as database schemas with the LT language enabling querying. In a multi-model environment, relational data can be considered too. For each NoSQL model, we must first define an appropriate type system supporting its data structures.

6.1 JSON Functional Schemas

First, we introduce a general functional type system supporting the structure of JSON data. We start with its basic version extending Definition 1. Tuple type is not considered.

Definition 3.

The existence of some (primitive) types $S_1, \ldots, S_k$ ($k \geq 1$) is assumed. They constitute a base **B**. More complex types are obtained in the following way:

(a) Every member of the base **B** is a *(primitive) type over* **B**.
(b) If T_1, T_2 are types over B, then $(T_2{:}T_1)$ is a *(functional) type over* B.
(c) If $T_1, \ldots, T_n$ ($n \geq 1$) are types over **B**, then $\{T_1, \ldots, T_n\}$ is a *set type* over B.
(d) If $T_1, \ldots, T_n$ ($n \geq 1$) are types over **B**, then $[T_1, \ldots, T_n]$ is an *array type* over B.

The *JSON type system* **T** *over* **B** (or **T** if **B** is assumed) is the least set containing types given by (a)–(d).

If members of **B** are interpreted as mutually disjoint nonempty sets, then $\{T_1, \ldots, T_n\}$-objects contain an unordered set of respective $T_1, \ldots, T_n$ objects. $[T_1, \ldots, T_n]$-objects are arrays of respective $T_1, \ldots, T_n$ objects.

For the description of JSON data format we need also a type *Name* in **B** for naming JSON types and regular expressions. Then we define the type system $\mathbf{T}_{reg}$ over **B** as follows.

(e) Let name ∊ *Name*. Then name:*String* is a *named character data over* **B**.
(f) Let T be a set type or named character data. We consider *regular expressions* T^*, $T+$, or $T?$. They can occur in array types, $T?$ can occur in set types.

(g) Let T be a regular expression. Let name $\in$ *Name*. Then name:T is a *named type over* **B**.

A move from character objects to abstract objects is given by the following definition.

Definition 4.

Let $\mathbf{T}_{\text{reg}}$ over **B** be the type system from Definition 3 and **O** be the set of abstract objects. Then the object type system $\mathbf{T}_{\text{O}}$ induced by $\mathbf{T}_{\text{reg}}$ (or $\mathbf{T}_{\text{O}}$ if $\mathbf{T}_{\text{reg}}$ is understood) is the least set containing the object types given by the following rule:

- Let name:T be from $\mathbf{T}_{\text{reg}}$. Replace all names in name:T by their upper-case version. Then NAME:T is a member of $\mathbf{T}_{\text{O}}$.

Example 6.1: Object types from $\mathbf{T}_{\text{O}}$ related to the JSON schema fragment in Fig. 1 include.

TITLE:*String.*
ADDRESS:*String.*
NAME:*String.*
ISSUED:*Number.*
BOOK:{TITLE, AUTHORS, ISSUED?}.
AUTHORS:[AUTHOR*].
AUTHOR:{NAME, ADDRESS?}.

They extend the original JSON schema by a structured author, author's name, and consider more authors including none.

A *JSON-database schema,* $\mathbf{S}_{\text{JSON}}$, is then a set of variables of types from $\mathbf{T}_{\text{O}}$. Given a JSON-database schema $\mathbf{S}_{\text{JSON}}$, a *JSON-database* is any valuation of variables in $\mathbf{S}_{\text{JSON}}$. For convenience, we denote the variables from $\mathbf{S}_{\text{JSON}}$ by the same names as names from $\mathbf{T}_{\text{O}}$, e.g., BOOK, AUTHOR, etc. Then object types in Example 6.1 represent a JSON-database schema. Explicit ICs on the JSON-database are not considered here.

6.2 *Querying JSON Data*

Querying JSON data uses a variation of the LT language from Definition 2. Tuples and components are omitted and sets and arrays are considered.

Let types R, S, R_1, …, R_n ($n \geq 1$) are elements of **T**.

(1) Every variable of type R is a *term* of type R.
(2) Every constant of type R is a *term* of type R.
(3) If M is a term of type (S:R_1, …, R_n), and N_1, …, N_n are terms of types R_1, …, R_n, respectively, then $\text{M}(\text{N}_1, \ldots, \text{N}_n)$ is a *term* of type *S./application/*
(4) If x_1, …, x_n are different variables of the respective types R_1, …, R_n and M is a term of type S, then $\lambda x_1, \ldots, x_n(\text{M})$ is a *term* of type (S:R_1, …, R_n)*/lambda abstraction/*

(5) If M is a term of type $\{T_1, \ldots, T_n\}$ and N is of type $T \in \{T_1, \ldots, T_n\}$, then N(M) is a *term* of type *T*.*/set element/*

(6) If $N_1, \ldots, N_n$ are terms of types $T_1, \ldots, T_n$, respectively, then $[N_1, \ldots, N_n]$ is a *term* of type $[T_1, \ldots, T_n]$.*/array/*

(7) If M is a term of type $[T_1, \ldots, T_n]$, then M[1], ..., M[*n*] are *terms* of types $T_1, \ldots, T_n$, respectively. */elements of array/*

Example 6.2: Then, supposing a book abstract object b, we can specify a selection using a path in a JSON document via composition of functions, e.g.,

NAME(AUTHORS(b)[1]) = 'Gaspar'.

or, in a more friendly way,

b.AUTHORS[1].NAME = 'Gaspar'.

More generally, queries will be expressed by lambda abstractions, similarly as in Example 5.1. Observe also that our LT language allows to consider in a query attributes belonging to different categories of NoSQL databases. Finally, the relational data model can be taken into account, too (see Boolean functions in Example 3.2 or their attribute version in Fig. 3b).

6.3 Graph Functional Schema

The notion of attribute applied in GDBs could be restricted to attributes of types (*R*:*S*), (*Bool*(*R*):*S*), or (*Bool*:*R*,*S*), where *R* and *S* are entity types. This strategy simply covers binary functional types, binary multivalued functional types, and binary relationships described as binary characteristic functions. The last option corresponds to M:N relationship types. For modelling directed graphs, the first two types are sufficient, because M:N relationship types can be expressed by two „inverse " binary multivalued functional types. Here we will consider always one of them, i.e., mixed graphs are not used in our paper. For graphical expressing a graph conceptual schema, we use two types of arrows according to associated binary functional types. Comparing to Fig. 2a, this notation is simpler.

Example 6.3: We describe multivalued functions by double arrows in a conceptual schema graph. Single arrows denote directional functional relationships, e.g., Submits_to. Tuple types with $S_1, \ldots, S_m$ used for properties of edges contain as a last component the entity type of the end node of the given edge, e.g., (Date, Journal) for Submits_to. Then a functional database schema corresponding to the GDB schema in Fig. 4 can look as:

Movie/((*Title*, *Director*, *Released*):*Movie*).

User/((*U_ID*, *U_Name*, *Birth_year*):*User*).

Journal/((*J_name*, *Publisher*, *Address*):*Journal*).

Rates/((*Bool*:*Stars*, *Movie*):*User*).

Submits_to/((*Date*, *Journal*):*User*).

Fig. 4 GDB conceptual schema Movies

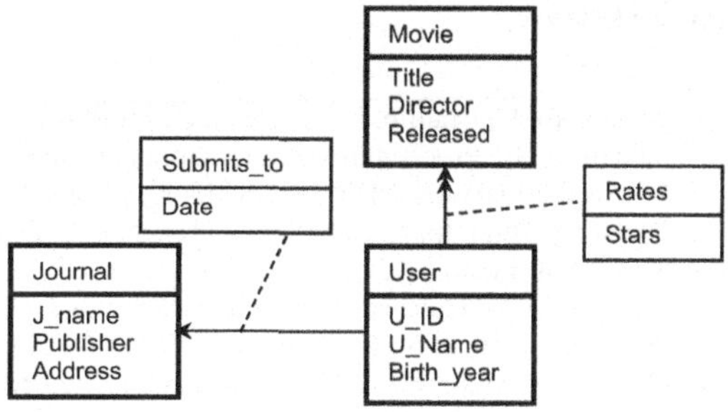

7 Conclusions

In this paper, we have shown a database-oriented view on NoSQL data based on a functional approach to data typing. A conceptual schema can be understood as a set of typed functions. This enables to model the world of relational and NoSQL DB in a more or less unified way. We have also introduced a version of typed λ-calculus, the language LT, which can be used as a formal background for:

- functional data integration from various NoSQL sources with different data models (multi-model environment),
- querying functional data in such integrated environment.

A significant feature of such approach is higher expressive power of query tools based on LT. For example, features supporting constructs of a predicate calculus with arithmetic operations and aggregate functions can be considered in such LT. Moreover, querying over attributes enables to users to see queries more conceptually than querying over a database schema. Clearly, the line between "conceptual" and "logical" is rather blurred in this approach. All depends on the way how attributes are modelled and named. Consequently, the responsibility of developers (programmers) for the optimization of DB is considerably increased.

Some challenges arise for a future research, e.g.:

- how design an adequate user-friendly (maybe extensible) functional query language,
- how to transform LT queries into expressions of NoSQL query languages (e.g., MongoDB, CQL, Neo4j),
- based on LT to specify and formally prove and compare the expressive power of NoSQL query languages.

Acknowledgements This work was supported by the Charles University project Q48.

References

1. Abdelhédi, F., Brahim A.A., Atigui, F., Zurfluh, G.: MDA-based approach for nosql databases modelling. In: Proceedings of International Conference on Big Data Analytics and Knowledge Discovery, DaWAK 2017, LNCS 10440, pp. 88–102 (2017)
2. Atzeni, P., Bugiotti, F., Cabibbo, C., Torlone, R.: Data modelling in the NoSQL world. Comput. Stand. Interfaces, Elsevier, 67, pp.103–149 (2020)
3. Baazizi, M.A., Colazzo, D. Ghelli, G., Sartiani, C.: Schemas and types for JSON data: from theory to practice. In: Proceedings of SIGMOD Conference 2019, pp. 2060–2063 (2019)
4. Chaves, D., Malinowski, E.: Document data modelling: a conceptual perspective. In: Proceedings of ADBIS 2019 Conference, CCIS 1064, pp. 19–27 (2019)
5. Duzi, M., Pokorny, J.: Semantics of general data structures. In: Charrel, P.J., Jaakkola, H., Kangassalo, H. (eds.) Information modelling and knowledge bases IX, pp. 115–130. IOS Press, Amsterdam, Netherlands (1998)
6. Gaspar, D., Coric, I.: Bridging Relational and NoSQL Databases. ADMDM Book Series, IGI Global (2017)
7. Hills, T.: NoSQL and SQL Data Modelling: Bringing Together Data, Semantics, and Software. 1st Edition, Technics Publications (2016)
8. Hull, R., King, R.: Semantic database modelling: survey, applications and research issues. ACM Comp. Survey **19**(3), 201–260 (1987)
9. Klein, H.K., Hirschheim, R.: A comparative framework of data modelling paradigms and approaches. The Comp. Journ. **30**(1), 8–15 (1987)
10. Laux, F.: The typed graph model. In: Proceedings of DBKDA 2020, pp. 13–19. Lisbon, Portugal (2020)
11. Lawley, M., Topor, R.: A query language for EER schemas. In: Proceedings of the 5th Australasian Database Conference, ADC '94, pp. 292–304. Christchurch, New Zealand (1994)
12. Materna, P.: Pokorný, J: Applying the simple theory of types to data bases. Inf. Syst. **6**(4), 283-300 (1981)
13. Nečaský, M.: XSEM—a conceptual model for XML. In: Proceedings of Asia Pacific Conference on Conceptual Modelling, pp. 37–48. Ballarat, Australia. CRPIT, 67 (2007)
14. Pautasso, C., Wilde, E., Alarcon, R.: REST: Advanced Research Topics and Practical Applications, Springer (2014)
15. Pokorný, J.: A function: unifying mechanism for entity-oriented database models. In: Proceedings of ER 1988 Conference, pp. 165–181 (1988)
16. Pokorný, J.: Semantic relativism in conceptual modelling. In: Proceedings of DEXA 1993 Conference, pp. 48–55 (1993)
17. Pokorný, J.: Modelling of graph databases. J. Adv. Eng. Comput. **1**(1), 4–15 (2017)
18. Pokorný, J.: Integration of relational and NoSQL databases. Vietnam J. Comput. Sci. **6**(4), 389–405 (2019)
19. Pokorný, J.: Integration of relational and graph databases functionally. Found. Comput. Decis. Sci. **44**(4), 427–441 (2019)
20. Pokorný, J.: JSON functionally. In: Proceedings of ADBIS 2020 Conference, LNCS 12245, pp. 139–153. Springer Nature Switzerland AG, Cham (2020)
21. Roy-Hubara, N., Sturm, A.: Design methods for the new database era: a systematic literature review. Softw. Syst. Model. **19**, 297–312 (2020)
22. Shin, K., Hwang, Ch., Jung, H.: NoSQL Database design using UML conceptual data model based on peter Chen's framework. Int. J. Appl. Eng. Res. **12**(5), 632–636 (2017)

Towards the Development of a Contingent Use of Systems Development Methodologies Model

Benson Moyo, Magda Huisman, and Lynette Drevin

Abstract Systems development methodologies (SDMs) are divided into two categories: plan-driven SDMs and agile SDMs. Research has shown that no single SDM is suitable for every systems development project situation. This paper aims to present aspects of a study that developed and empirically tested a contingent use of SDMs model to investigate contingent use of SDMs. The developed contingent use of SDMs model is tested using survey data collected from 155 systems development organizations. The findings show that SDMs are adopted and continuously tailored throughout the life cycle of a systems development project. This has theoretical and practical implications for SDM design and deployment. The empirical findings and the model presented in this study can assist researchers to investigate the contingent use of SDMs and improve their implementation in systems development projects. The findings provide insights on how theory and practice co-evolve and inform one another.

Keywords SDM · SDM contingent use model · Plan-driven SDM · Agile SDM · Systems development

---

A prior version of this paper has been published in the ISD2021 Proceedings (http://aisel.aisnet.org/isd2014/proceedings2021).

B. Moyo (✉)
University of Venda, Thohoyandou, South Africa
e-mail: benson.moyo@univen.ac.za

M. Huisman · L. Drevin
North-West University, Potchefstroom, South Africa
e-mail: magda.huisman@nwu.ac.za

L. Drevin
e-mail: lynette.drevin@nwu.ac.za

E. Insfran Pelozo et al. (eds.), *Advances in Information Systems Development*,
Lecture Notes in Information Systems and Organisation 55,
https://doi.org/10.1007/978-3-030-95354-6_16

1 Introduction

Research and practice present two main categories of SDMs namely the plan-driven class and the agile SDM class [23]. The plan-driven SDM class emphasizes the freezing of system development project scope, whereas the agile SDM class emphasizes the freezing of cost, schedule, and quality with the scope considered variable. The systems development project contextual setting consists of a unique set of systems development constraints, characteristics, and concerns that have to be met to achieve optimal interaction between the SDM characteristics and the systems development project contextual factors [23]. These systems' development constraints, characteristics, and concerns are hereafter referred to as contextual stressors. Project contextual stressors such as requirements dynamics [7] and organization culture [14] have been used to compare and contrast the two classes. Both the plan-driven SDM class and the agile SDM class have their strengths and limitations [16, 22] when evaluated on different systems development project contextual stressors.

Research on the agile SDM class has been given extensive attention [1] and some of the studies seek to demonstrate the superiority of the agile SDM class over the plan-driven SDM class [34]. Research and practice have changed this adversarial narrative towards a view in which SDMs coexist and are complementary to each other and that they may be combined to tap into the capabilities of one another in addressing specific systems development project contextual stressors [12, 19]. A common approach to adopting SDMs is to consider agile SDM class instances when the systems development requirements are dynamic and consider plan-driven SDM class instances when the systems development project requirements are stable [2, 17]. According to this viewpoint, adopting an SDM is a one-time conditional decision in which an agile SDM class instance is appropriate when requirements are volatile, and a plan-driven SDM class instance is appropriate when requirements are predictable. This study argues that the interplay between the SDM and systems development project contextual stressors affects requirements dependencies and interdependencies resulting in the need to constantly review and adjust the SDM to fit the systems development project contextual stressors as they evolve. Furthermore, evidence from research and practice suggests that no SDM class is best suited to all possible systems development project contextual stressors [3].

It is argued that each set of systems development project contextual stressors is unique, and therefore should be treated as such [11]. Research has shown that each systems development project is different and it requires a different SDM [3, 5, 11], however, the changes that require the adjustments during the systems development project life cycle have not been extensively investigated. The study views the systems development practitioner's challenge as not only to adopt the most appropriate SDM from among a variety of existing SDMs for each project's contextual stressors but, also to keep the adopted SDM fit with those contextual stressors throughout the project life cycle. Therefore, adopting an SDM for a systems development project is a process rather than a state. The continuous monitoring and evaluation of the fit between the SDM and the systems development project contextual stressors is referred to as the contingent use of SDMs in this study. This concept is defined in the next section.

There is a gap in empirical evidence concerning the state of the contingent use of SDMs. This study's research question is: How can a contingent use of SDMs model be developed to investigate the contingent use of SDMs?

The remainder of the paper is organized as follows. A definition of the contingent use of SDMs is proposed in Sect. 2. The theoretical foundation of the contingent use of SDMs model is presented in Sect. 3. The research design and methodology for the study are described in Sect. 4. Results are presented in Sect. 5. Findings are presented in Sect. 6 and finally, conclusions and recommendations for further study are presented in Sect. 7.

2 Contingent Use of SDMs

Serrador and Pinto [29] point out that systems development practitioners often tailored systems development methodologies to fit the specific circumstances of a systems development project. In practice, each SDM, even the one regarded as the most appropriate, is tailored [16] or adapted [10] to suit systems development project context [8, 10, 16]. The observations made by researchers on the set of activities that are employed to create a fit of systems development methodologies with the systems development contextual stressors [8, 9, 16] led to the formulation of the following definition of contingent use of SDMs: *The contingent use of systems development methodologies is the entire set of activities that are performed to achieve an ideal fit between systems development methodologies and the systems development contextual stressors at any given point in time during the systems development project life cycle.*

The definition suggests that there is a need for context-specific systems development project characterization which may occur preceding systems development (ex-ante), or during systems development (on-the-fly). Therefore, based on the contextual stressors configuration in a specific systems development project, the systems development team has two approaches for adopting an SDM. The first approach entails selecting an existing SDM (choosing from the plan-driven SDM class or the agile SDM class and tailoring the SDM accordingly) [36]. This is referred to as contingency-based SDM selection [36] The second approach entails constructing an SDM (constructing either a hybrid SDM or a new SDM that is fit for purpose using SDM chunks) [16]. This is referred to as situational method engineering [16]. The following two paragraphs describe the two approaches.

The contingency-based SDM selection focuses on the selection of SDM from existing SDMs. The goal is to start from the base SDMs that were designed to encompass a wide spectrum of known systems development project contextual stressors and narrow down to the one that is most appropriate for the contextual stressors at hand. That is the SDM whose underlying assumptions hold for the systems development project contextual stressors at hand, is selected from a repository of SDMs approved by the development team or organization. The fit between the contextual stressors with the candidate SDM is determined by the experience of the members of the systems development team. In cases where the selected SDM is the most appropriate in comparison to the available SDM choices, the selected SDM is tailored to fit the contextual stressors.

The method engineering approach is based on the assumption that each systems development project is unique and should be treated as such. Instead of having a standard SDM prior to a systems development project, the SDM is built around the contextual stressors of the systems development project. The goal is to create SDMs on a systems development project-by-project basis based on specific contextual stressors [16]. The starting point is not a pre-existing SDM, but the contextual stressors of the system's development project. The process entails determining the contextual stressors of the systems development project and constructing the appropriate SDM using SDM components. The SDM components can be derived from a pre-existing repository, theory, or best practice, or they can be created from scratch [16].

The contingent use of SDMs perspectives considers the two approaches as having different starting points and rationale but convergent at the implementation level. An SDM may be constructed from scratch, but it is not common to create an SDM that becomes appropriate to a specific target context without going through some modifications [35]. Therefore, in practice, each constructed SDM goes through evaluation. The evaluation may prove that the SDM is not the best fit in a specific situation due to the emergent properties of contextual stressors and the complex network of dependencies and interdependencies. The constructed SDM would then need to be tailored to achieve an ideal fit for the contextual stressors. This tailoring becomes a transition from situational method engineering to contingency-based SDM selection. The iterative process of creation, evaluation, and improvement of SDMs results in the two approaches being complementary to each other.

The contingent use of SDMs does not consider SDMs to be complete packages for addressing the challenges of systems development projects. It considers SDMs as artifacts that complement one another in a given systems development project. The situational method engineering and the contingency-based SDM selection approaches view the selection of an SDM for a project as a one-time event, when it is actually a continuous process. The contingent use of SDMs approach is based on an understanding of the continuous interplay between the SDM and the contextual stressors, resulting in continuous evaluation of the SDM's ideal fit throughout the systems development project life cycle.

3 Contingent Use of SDMs Model

The study draws on insights from three theoretical models namely the Technology Acceptance Model (TAM) [33], the Task Technology Fit (TTF) [13], and the Diffusion of Innovation (DOI) [26]. The three models provide the appropriate theoretical synergies for the development of the hybrid model for the contingent use of SDMs.

The hybrid model comprises a combination of the determinants from all three models, the TAM, the TTF, and the DOI. These three theoretical models are complementary to each other. The TAM [33] relies on the ex-ante evaluation of an SDM. That is when the adopting units encounter an SDM for the first time, perceived usefulness and perceived ease-of-use (PEOU) influence their decision to adopt it [33]. The benefits of using an SDM are compared with the effort required to use that same SDM. The TAM is concerned with the perceived psychological characteristics of an adopting unit towards adopting an SDM not necessarily the actual characteristics of the SDM. The TTF construct is biased towards investigating the post-ante matching of task characteristics and the functionality offered by an SDM. The TTF has an evidence-oriented focus on how the SDM supports the adopting unit's task accomplishment [13]. The DOI [26] focuses on the learning process about the SDM from adoption to use. It is underpinned by the gradual reduction of ignorance (gaining experience) related to an SDM. The model is presented in Fig. 1. The adoption decision outcome chain is the backbone of the contingent use of SDMs. The adoption decision outcome chain is a three-phased process as shown in Fig. 1. The phases are pre-adoption, adoption, and post-adoption. These three phases entail information-seeking and information-processing activities that an adopting unit goes through.

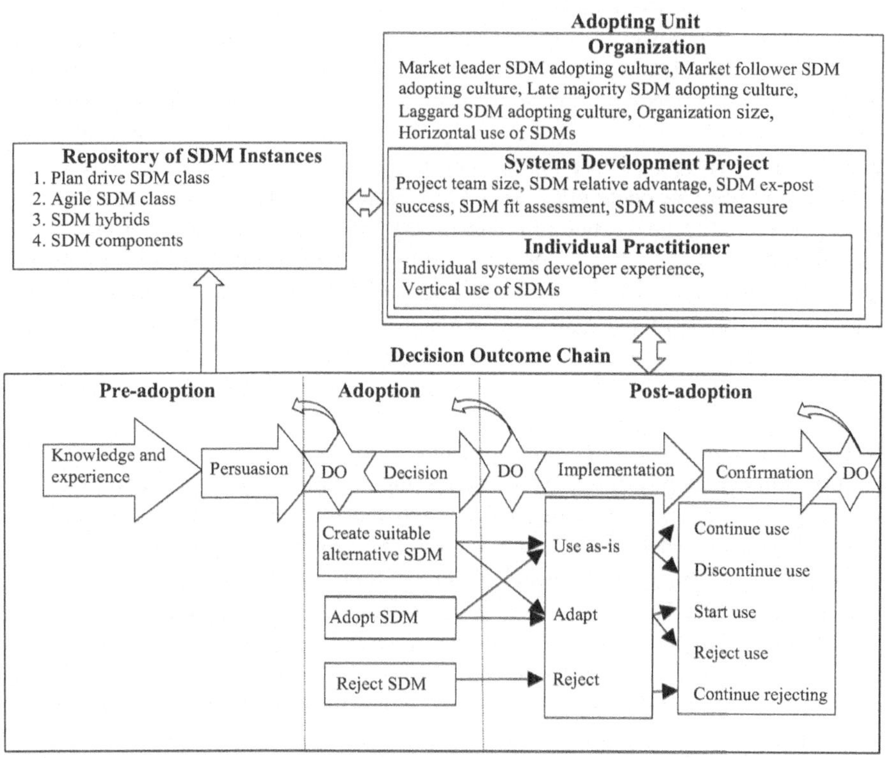

Fig. 1 The contingent use of SDMs model

Each phase consists of a chain of decision outcomes (DOs) on an SDM or its components. The decision outcome chain allows the adopting unit to constantly monitor and evaluate the dynamics of contextual stressors during the systems development project lifecycle and respond accordingly when the need arises.

A set of hypotheses is developed based on the contingent use of SDMs model. The adopting unit is broken down into three levels: the organizational, the system development project, and the individual practitioner. Each hypothesis connects elements from the adopting unit and those in the decision outcome chain.

Following the adoption of an SDM, the adopting unit may begin using it as is. When there are no gaps between the SDM's actual and expected performance, the adopting unit may confirm continued use [30]. If the adopted SDM does not meet the expected task requirements, it may be adapted and further decisions made after the SDM has been reassessed. As a result, the adopting unit will constantly and continuously assess an SDM's fit to the task at hand. Consequently, the following hypothesis is formulated:

H1: The SDM fit assessment positively influences the contingent use of SDMs.

The classification of organizational culture in this study was primarily aimed at an organization's responsiveness in adopting SDMs as contingent innovations. Rogers [26] classified responders to contingent innovation adoption into five adopter classes: innovators, early adopters, early majority, late majority, and laggards. The key trait of the culture of innovators is the acceptance of contingent innovation for its own sake [26]. No organization is expected to adopt an SDM only for its own sake. The market leader category includes innovators and early adopters. Consequently, the study considered the following four categories: market leader, market follower, late majority, and laggards. These correspond to developmental, rational, hierarchical, and group culture respectively. The adopter category into which an organization fits is considered to be a reflection of its SDM adopting culture. The market leader SDM adapting culture is at ease with modifying its behavior in order to capitalize on possibilities without wasting time [26]. The market leader SDM adopting culture is quick and flexible to adopt a new SDM or adapt an already adopted SDM contingently. Consequently, the following hypothesis is formulated:

H2a: There is a positive relationship between the market leader SDM adopting culture and the contingent use of SDMs.

There are several systems development communities to which organizations or team members may pay allegiances, such as the Agile Alliance, the ScrumAlliance, the Project Management Institute (PMI), and the Institute of Electrical and Electronics Engineers (IEEE). It has been found a significant positive relationship between rational (market follower) organizational culture and the deployment of plan-driven SDMs [18]. Consequently, the following hypothesis is formulated:

H2b: There is a negative relationship between the market follower SDM adopting culture and the contingent use of SDMs.

The late majority SDM adopting culture avoids the risks of breaking new ground by pragmatically weighing the costs-benefits ratio experienced by both the market leader SDM adopting culture and the market follower SDM adopting culture organizations. Control and order are important in the market follower SDM adopting culture. A significant positive relationship between hierarchical (late majority) organizational culture and the deployment of plan-driven SDMs have been found [18]. Consequently, the following hypothesis is formulated:

H2c: There is a negative relationship between the late majority SDM adopting culture and the contingent use of SDMs.

The laggard SDM adopting culture trails behind every other SDM adopting culture. They may be affiliated to some systems development communities of practice and take time to embrace change if that change is not coming from their affiliations. Generally, they are slow in adopting new approaches. Consequently, the following hypothesis is formulated:

H2d: There is a negative relationship between the laggard SDM adopting culture and the contingent use of SDMs.

The size of an organization affects the way members interact and share information. The size influences resources, level of specialization, and applicable communication protocols [5, 35]. The larger the organization, the more formal would be the support structures for the systems development activities [5]. Consequently, the following hypothesis is formulated:

H3: The organization size negatively influences the contingent use of SDMs.

The performance of the system development project artifact over a time scale is another measure of the SDM success [31]. The tried and tested SDM may be evaluated by the systems development project artifacts it successfully developed. The success history of an SDM may lead to systems development practitioners resisting changes and adaptation of the SDM in the hope of maintaining the previous success. The success of an SDM (doing it right), is evaluated by the systems development project artifact success (getting it right). Consequently, the following hypothesis is formulated:

H4: The SDM ex-post success negatively influences the contingent use of SDMs.

The systems development project artifact success is interpreted as an indicator of SDM success. It is argued that a systems development project artifact is a result of a successful deployment of an SDM and contingent use of an SDM [10]. Consequently, the following hypotheses are formulated:

H5: The SDM success measure positively influences the contingent use of SDMs.

The experienced systems development practitioner assesses the fit of the SDM to the contextual stressors and adapts it accordingly. With more experience in using various SDMs, a systems development practitioner would know which SDM works, where, when, and why resulting in the systems development practitioner's flexibility in adoption, adaptation, changing, and rejection of SDMs as is necessary [20]. Consequently, the following hypothesis is formulated:

H6: The individual systems development practitioner's experience positively influences the contingent use of SDMs.

The increase in the systems development project team size may lead to an increase in the level of communication formality and development coordination challenges [5, 15]. Consequently, the following hypothesis is formulated:

H7: The systems development project team size negatively influences the contingent use of SDMs.

The SDM knowledge usage is measured in terms of either horizontal use, that is, across projects, or vertical use, which is the intensity of SDM knowledge use. The horizontal use entails the breadth of SDM knowledge use across the development of projects. The vertical use entails the depth of SDM knowledge application on each systems development project [27]. The high level of horizontal and vertical use of SDM knowledge may result in the contingent use of SDMs. Consequently, the following hypotheses are formulated:

H8: The horizontal use of SDM positively influences the contingent use of SDMs.

H9: The vertical use of SDM positively influences the contingent use of SDMs.

The relative advantage of an SDM accounts for the effort needed to tailor the SDM to fit the specific systems development project [32]. When the SDM is fit for purpose then there is the minimum effort required to tailor it to the specific system development contextual stressors. Consequently, the following hypotheses are formulated:

H10: The SDM relative advantage to the systems development project contextual stressors positively influences the contingent use of SDMs.

4 Research Design and Methodology

This research is based on a comprehensive study that uses the Diffusion of Innovation Model, the Task-Technology Fit Model, and the Technology Acceptance Model to investigate the contingent use of systems development methodologies [23]. The research methodology selection is informed by the positivist paradigm and quantitative in nature. The survey was used as the research method [24] and a questionnaire was developed as a survey data-generating instrument, piloted and administered by the researchers. The questionnaire instrument was organized into two main parts. The first part items collected demographic data and the second part consisted of operationalized items that collected data on the contingent use of SDMs. The operationalized items requested the respondents to indicate their level of agreement or disagreement with statements on a six-point Likert-like scale (1-strongly disagree to 6- strongly agree). No neutral point was provided in order for the respondents to express their absolute orientation.

A one-page request letter was sent to organizations explaining the purpose of the survey requesting the prospective respondents to participate. A clause to protect the identities of respondents and their organizations was included in the request letter. The letter also assured strict confidentiality of the data collected and explained the rights of the respondents. To improve the validity and reliability of the responses, the request letter provided core concept definitions as reference points in completing the questionnaire.

The target population was the systems development organizations in South Africa. A random list-based frame sampling technique was used to establish the sample size. Through their web presence, a total of 573 systems development organizations in

South Africa were identified. All the organizations were considered eligible to participate in the survey and were invited to participate. The refusal rate was 35.6%. A questionnaire package consisting of a consent letter and a self-administered questionnaire was sent to each one of the 369 eligible organizations that agreed to participate in the survey. The first preference was the systems development project manager. However, in the case of the manager not being available, other systems development practitioners were co-opted to complete the questionnaire. The unit of analysis is the organizations whereas the unit of inquiry is the systems development practitioners.

A total of 162 questionnaires were completed and returned, giving a response rate of 28.3% which is acceptable [28]. The SPSS version 26 was used for data analysis and the first cycle of data analysis constituted data cleaning. 155 (27.1%) were usable and 1.2% of the received questionnaires were discarded due to missing key data values. The discarded cases were within the acceptable data loss range [4]. The Cronbach's alpha was used to indicate good internal consistency of the items in the scale, in which all the items indicated Cronbach's alpha greater than 0.7. The dimensionality of the scale was determined by the Principal Factor Analysis (PCA) and Promax with Kaiser Normalization rotation. The second cycle of data analysis constitutes descriptive statistics.

5 Results

The following subsections present the empirical results of the study.

5.1 Descriptive Statistics

The size of an organization determines the type and amount of resources available and the communication protocols among other important characteristics. The respondents came from organizations of varying sizes. The majority (42.6%) of the respondents came from organizations with 251 or more employees followed by organizations with 51–250 employees which constituted (33.5%) of organizations and lastly, organizations with 1–50 employees constituted 23.9%.

5.2 Experience of Respondents in the Use of SDMs

The respondents had varying levels of experience in the use of systems development methodologies. The experience of the respondents is associated with the technical knowledge on SDMs acquired over years. The majority (81.3%) of the respondents had the experience of six years and above.

Table 1 Variability in the Use of SDMs

N = 155	Mean	Std. Dev	Frequencies as percentages					
			1	*2*	*3*	*4*	*5*	*6*
Deviation from the SDM prescription was caused by the need to reconfigure some components	4.2	1.34	5.2	6.5	18.7	23.2	30.3	16.1
Deviation from the SDM prescription was caused by the need to remove some irrelevant components	4.0	1.31	3.9	8.4	23.9	25.8	24.5	13.5
Deviation from SDM prescription was caused by the need to address some missing components	3.8	1.39	7.7	9.0	22.6	29.0	19.4	13.3
We created alternative SDMs based on components from existing SDMs	3.8	1.71	12.3	14.8	18.1	14.2	18.1	22.6
No deviation at all from the SDM prescription	3.0	1.70	19.4	31.0	16.8	7.1	12.3	13.5

5.3 Variability in the Use of SDMs

The implementation of SDMs varies from one organization to the other, from one system development project to another and across similar systems development project contexts, and within the same systems development project context over time [3, 6]. The results shown in Table 1 indicate the responses given on a 6-point Likert-like scale on variability in the use of SDMs.

A Cronbach's analysis was conducted on the 5 items and Cronbach's alpha value for the 5 items was 0.71. This indicated that the 5 items had adequate inter-item reliability. Before performing PCA, the suitability of data for factor analysis was assessed. The Kaiser–Meyer–Olkin measure of sampling adequacy (KMO) value was 0.741, which is classified as good [25]. To test whether the variables did not correlate too highly or too lowly with other variables [25] Bartlett's Test of Sphericity was conducted. The Bartlett's Test of Sphericity of $\chi^2(10) = 171.016$, $p < 0.0001$ indicated that the correlations between the items were sufficiently high [25]. The Kaiser criterion revealed that there was only one component with eigenvalues greater than 1 [25] that explained 48,8% of the variance. The component formed the contingent use of SDMs composite variable.

5.4 Contingent Use of SDMs Regression Analysis

Before the application of the standard multiple regression, a preliminary analysis was conducted to ensure no violation of standard linear regression assumptions occurred. The normality of the data was tested by plotting the distributions of the residuals in a histogram of which the bell curve indicated that the data are normally distributed. The independent variables showed that the data points in the Normal Probability Plot (P-P) of the regression standardized residuals followed an approximately straight diagonal line from the bottom left to the top right indicating non-violation of linearity. The largest value of the Mahalanobis' distance was 32.639 with a Cook's Distance of 0.00089, which is far less than 1 indicating the validity of the outlier assumption [25]. The test for multicollinearity was performed by checking the Variance Inflation Factor (VIF) values as indicated in the standardized regression Table 2. The VIF were all less than 10, suggesting that the multicollinearity assumption was not violated.

The assumptions for standard multiple regression were reasonably met to perform standard multiple regression analysis. The standard multiple regression was conducted to test each of the formulated hypotheses for the contingent use of SDMs. The model as a whole explained 44.9% of the variance in the contingent use of SDMs in the data set, $F(13,154) = 10.649$, $p < 0.001$. The contingent use of SDMs regression results are presented in Table 2.

A standard multiple regression analysis was conducted using 13 explanatory variables. The explanatory variables were grouped under three levels of abstraction through which contingent use of SDMs is theorized. These are the organization, the systems development project, and the individual systems development practitioner levels as highlighted in Table 2.

The regression result for assessing the appropriateness of an SDM (SDM fit assessment), throughout a systems development project life cycle indicated a significant and positive relationship with the contingent use of SDMs ($\beta = 0.140$, $p < 0.05$). This supports hypothesis *H1*. The four SDM adopting cultures indicated statistically significant negative associations with the contingent use of SDMs market leader SDM adopting culture ($\beta = -0.279$, $p < 0.05$), market follower SDM adopting culture ($\beta = -0.446$, $p < 0.001$), late majority SDM adopting culture ($\beta = -0.325$, $p < 0.001$) and laggard SDM adopting culture ($\beta = -0.221, p < 0.05$). The hypothesized relationships *H2a, H2b, H2c, H2d* were supported.

The contingent use of SDMs is neither agile nor plan-driven oriented. No culture orientation was favorable for the contingent use of SDMs. These results were unexpected since the market leader SDM adopting culture was hypothesized to have a positive relationship with the contingent use of SDMs. Perhaps this is because the market leader SDM adopting culture embraces the latest innovation and fails to consider specific contextual stressors of a systems development project at hand.

Organization size indicated a significant negative influence on the contingent use of SDMs ($\beta = -0.163$, $p < 0.05$). The finding confirms the hypothesized relationship in hypothesis *H3*. It is also consistent with previous findings on the impact of organizational size in the adoption and use of SDMs [5, 31].

The ex-post success of an SDM indicated a significant negative relationship with the contingent use of SDMs ($\beta = -0.315$, $p < 0.001$). The finding supports hypothesis *H4*. The result is logical, as a history of success of an SDM may result in the users resisting change or adjustment to an SDM that performed successfully on previous occasions.

Table 2 Regression results

Model		Unstandardized coefficients		Standardized coefficients	VIF
		B	Std Error	Beta (β)	
1	Explanatory Variables				
	Intercept	1.130	0.831		
	Organizational level				
	Organization size (number of employees)	−0.121*	0.053	−0.163*	1.452
	Market leader SDM adopting culture	−0.660*	0.267	−0.279*	3.563
	Market follower SDM adopting culture	−1.001***	0.258	−0.446***	3.694
	Late majority SDM adopting culture	−0.829**	0.278	−0.325**	3.341
	Laggard SDM adopting culture	−0.556*	0.274	−0.221*	3.310
	Horizontal use of SDMs	0.103	0.066	0.099	1.132
	Systems development project level				
	Systems development project team size	0.205**	0.066	0.229**	1.515
	SDM success measures	0.242**	0.090	0.180**	1.239
	SDM fit assessment	0.226*	0.104	0.140*	1.162
	SDM ex-post success	−0.557***	0.128	−0.315***	1.477
	SDM relative advantage	0.536***	0.102	0.386***	1.502
	Individual systems development practitioner level				
	Individual systems development practitioner experience in systems development projects	0.200***	0.054	0.247***	1.262
	Vertical use of SDMs	0.158	0.065	0.149	1.039
	R^2	0.495			
	Adjusted R^2	0.449			
	F	10.649****			

Dependent Variable: SDM contingent use $^{*}p < 0.05$, $^{**}p < 0.01$, $^{***}p < 0.001$, $^{****}p < 0.0001$

The SDM success measure significantly and positively influenced the contingent use of the SDMs ($\beta = 0.180$, $p < 0.01$). This supports the hypothesized relationship in hypothesis *H5*.

The individual systems development practitioner experience in systems development projects was significantly and positively related to the contingent use of SDMs ($\beta = 0.247$, $p < 0.001$). That is, respondents who had high levels of experience in systems development projects rated the contingent use of SDMs favorably. The individual systems development practitioner, with high levels of experience in systems development projects, can make a detailed evaluation of an SDM in use. The finding supports the hypothesized relationship in *H6*. The finding is consistent with evidence from the literature that experience is an influential factor in SDM adoption [3, 6, 21].

The systems development team size ($\beta = 0.229$, $p < 0.01$) was significantly and positively related to the contingent use of SDMs. Respondents from larger systems development teams indicated a high propensity towards the contingent use of SDMs. This supports hypothesis *H7,* but in the opposite direction. This is likely because when the team increase in size, the SDM is adapted to meet the requirements of team roles assignment and division of systems development tasks.

There was no statistically significant relationship found between the horizontal use and the contingent use of SDMs. Therefore, the hypothesized relationship in hypothesis *H8* was not supported. The relationship between the vertical use of SDMs and the contingent use of SDMs was non-significant. Thus, there was no credible evidence to support the hypothesized relationship in *H9*.

The SDM relative advantage indicated a statistically significant and positive relationship with contingent use of SDMs ($\beta = 0.386$, $p < 0.01$), and this supported hypothesis *H10*. Respondents indicated that they judged SDMs based on their relative advantage over others given the specific systems development contextual stressors. This finding is consistent with previous studies' findings on adopting the most appropriate SDM based on the project situation [3, 5, 11].

6 Findings

Thirteen hypotheses were formulated and empirically tested using empirical evidence from the systems development industry in South Africa. A standard multiple regression model assessment demonstrated the predictive power of the contingent use of SDMs model based on the empirical evidence for the study. The empirical validation indicated that only eleven hypotheses were supported. A summary of the hypotheses testing results is presented in Table 3. The final model is presented in Fig. 2.

The research question posed for the study was: How can a contingent use of SDMs model be developed? The study first proposed a working definition of the contingent use of SDMs to provide a frame of reference. Based on the Diffusion of Innovation Model, the Task-Technology Fit, and the Acceptance of Technology Model, an initial version of the contingent use of SDMs model was drafted from literature. This initial version of the contingent use of SDMs was then validated against empirical evidence

Table 3 Hypothesis testing results

Hypothesis tested	Results
H1: The SDM fit assessment positively influences the contingent use of SDMs	Supported
H2a: There is a positive relationship between the market leader SDM adopting culture and the contingent use of SDMs	Supported but in the opposite direction
H2b: There is a negative relationship between the market follower SDM adopting culture and the contingent use of SDMs	Supported
H2c: There is a negative relationship between the late majority SDM adopting culture and the contingent use of SDMs	Supported
H2d: There is a negative relationship between the laggard SDM adopting culture and the contingent use of SDMs	Supported
H3: The organization size negatively influences the contingent use of SDMs	Supported
H4: The SDM ex-post success negatively influences the contingent use of SDMs	Supported
H5: The SDM success measure positively influences the contingent use of SDMs	Supported
H6: The individual systems development practitioner's experience negatively influences the contingent use of SDMs	Supported
H7: The systems development project team size negatively influences the contingent use of SDMs	Supported but in the opposite direction
H8: The horizontal use of SDM positively influences the contingent use of SDMs	Not supported
H9: The vertical use of SDM positively influences the contingent use of SDMs	Not supported
H10: The SDM relative advantage to the systems development project contextual stressors positively influences the contingent use of SDMs	Supported

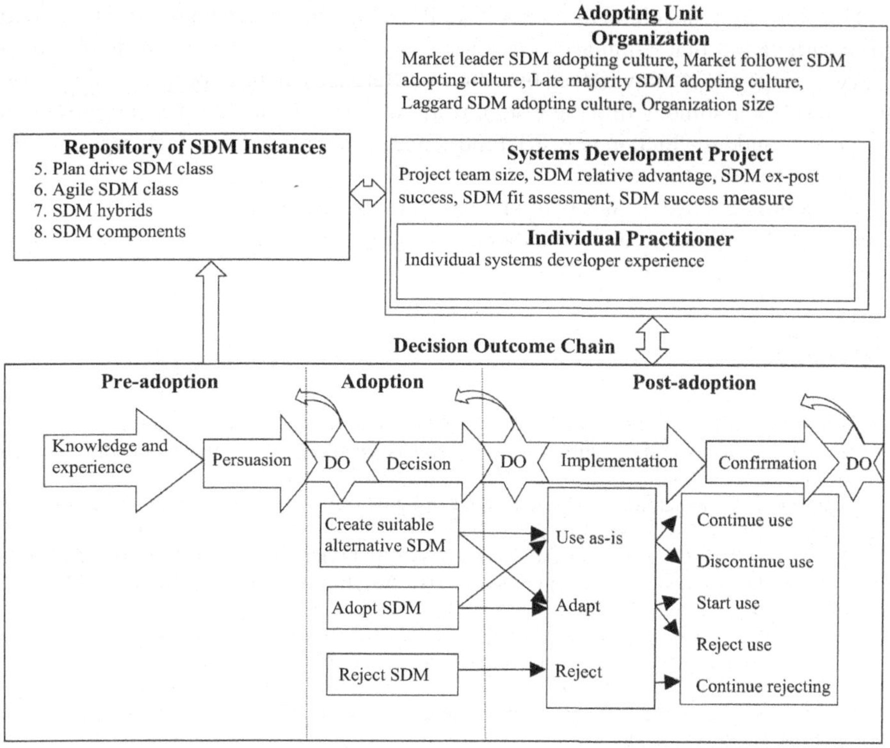

Fig. 2 Final contingent use of SDMs model

from the systems development industry in South Africa. The initial version of the contingent use of SDMs model evolved after validation to the second version of the contingent use of SDMs model which is presented in Fig. 2. The main contribution of this research is the development of a contingent use of SDMs model to describe and explain the contingent use of SDMs in systems development organizations.

7 Conclusions

The study concludes that the two SDM classes are viewed as extreme opposites, but in practice, they complement each other. Some SDMs are combined to create hybrid SDMs or interleaved on the same systems development project. Organizational culture, especially the market follower SDM adopting culture, provides the largest unique contribution to the contingent use of SDMs model. SDMs are used contingently in the South African systems development industry. The contingent use of the SDMs model provides the foundation for future empirical studies investigating the contingent use of SDMs, and it is expected to evolve.

This study does not claim the generalisability of the findings because it is limited to those participants that voluntarily participated from a single country. Furthermore, in a survey, respondents may induce bias due to differences in the experiences they have and roles they assume within their organizations. Each organization was represented by one respondent which may restrict the scope of perspectives of each organization that participated in the survey.

The contingent use of SDMs model is still in its early stages of development and needs further validation and refinement using empirical evidence.

References

1. Abrahamsson, P., Salo, O., Ronkainen, J., and Warsta, J.: Agile software development methods: Review and analysis (2071). https://arxiv.org/ftp/arxiv/papers/1709/1709.08439.pdf. Accessed 25 Aug 2019
2. Agerfalk, P.J., Fitzgerald, B.: Flexible and distributed software processes: old petunias in new bowls? Commun. ACM **49**(10), 27–34 (2006)
3. Aitken, A., Ilango, V.: A comparative analysis of traditional software engineering and agile software development. In: System Sciences (HICSS) 46th Hawaii International Conference, pp. 4751–4760. IEEE (2013)
4. Bannon, W., Jr.: Missing data within a quantitative research study: how to assess it, treat it, and why you should care. J. Am. Assoc. Nurse Practitioners **27**(4), 230–232 (2015)
5. Barlow, J.B., Giboney, J., Keith, M.J., Wilson, D., Schuetzler, R.M., Lowry, P.B., Vance, A.: Overview and guidance on agile development in large organizations. Commun. Assoc. Inf. Syst. **29**(2), 25–44 (2011)
6. Berente, N., Hansen, S.W., Rosenkranz, C.: Rule formation and change in information systems development: how institutional logics shape isd practices and processes. In: 48th Hawaii International Conference on System Sciences, pp. 5104–5113. IEEE (2015)
7. Boehm, B., Turner, R.: Balancing agility and discipline: evaluating and integrating agile and plan-driven methods. In: Proceedings 26th International Conference on Software Engineering, pp. 718–719. IEEE (2004)
8. Brinkkemper, S.: Method engineering: engineering of information systems development methods and tools. Inf. Softw. Technol. **38**(4), 275–280 (1996)
9. Conboy, K., Fitzgerald, B.: Method and developer characteristics for effective agile method tailoring: a study of XP expert opinion. ACM Trans. Softw. Eng. Methodol. **20**(1), 2:1–2:30 (2010)
10. Diebold, P., Ostberg, J.P., Wagner, S., Zendler, U.: What do practitioners vary in using scrum? In: International Conference on Agile Software Development, pp. 40–51. Springer, Cham (2015)
11. Fitzgerald, B., Russo, N.L., O'Kane, T.: Software development method tailoring at Motorola. Commun. ACM **46**(4), 65–70 (2003)
12. Gill, A.Q., Henderson-Sellers, B., Niazi, M.: Scaling for agility: a reference model for hybrid traditional-agile software development methodologies. Inf. Syst. Front.: A J. Res. Innov. **20**(2), 315–341 (2018)
13. Goodhue, D.L.: Understanding user evaluations of information systems. Manage. Sci. **41**(12), 1827–1844 (1995)
14. Gruver, G., Mouser, T.: Leading the transformation: applying agile and devops principles at scale. IT Revolution, Portland (2015)
15. Harb, Y., Noteboom, C., Sarnikar, S.: Evaluating project characteristics for selecting the best-fit agile software development methodology: a teaching case. J. Midwest Assoc. Inf. Syst. (JMWAIS) **1**(1), 33–52 (2015)

16. Henderson-Sellers, B., Ralyte, J., Agerfalk, P.J., Rossi, M.: Situational Method Engineering. Springer, Heidelberg (2014)
17. Highsmith, J.A., Highsmith, J.: Agile Software Development Ecosystems. Addison-Wesley, Boston (2002)
18. Iivari, J., Huisman, M.: The relationship between organisational culture and the deployment of systems development methodologies. MIS Q. **31**(1), 35–58 (2007)
19. Isaias, P., Issa, I.: High Level Models and Methodologies for Information Systems. Springer, New York (2015)
20. Jun, L., Qiuzhen, W., Qingguo, M.: The effects of project uncertainty and risk management on IS development project performance: a vendor perspective. Int. J. Project Manage. **29**(7), 923–933 (2011)
21. Marks, G., O'Connor, R.V., Clarke, P.M.: The impact of situational context on the software development process–a case study of a highly innovative start-up organization. In: International Conference on Software Process Improvement and Capability Determination, pp. 455–466. Springer, Cham (2017)
22. Mirza, M.S., Datta, S.: Strengths and weakness of traditional and agile processes-a systematic review. J. Softw. **14**(5), 209–219 (2019)
23. Moyo, B.: The contingent use of systems development methodologies in South Africa. Northwest University, Potchefstroom (Unpublished doctoral thesis) (2020)
24. Oates, B.: Researching Information Systems and Computing. Sage, London (2006)
25. Pallant, J.: SPSS survival manual: a step by step guide to data analysis using IBM SPSS 6th (edn.) McGraw-Hill, Maidenhead (2016)
26. Rogers, E.M.: Diffusion of Innovations. Simon and Schuster, New York (2003)
27. Russo, N.L., Fitzgerald, G., Shams, S.: Exploring adoption and use of agile methods: a comparative case study. In: Proceedings of the Nineteenth Americas Conference on Information Systems, pp. 1–8. Chicago, Illinois (2013)
28. Sekaran, U., Bougie, R.: Research Methods for Business, A Skill-Building Approach, 5th edn. Wiley, Haddington (2010)
29. Serrador, P., Pinto, J.K.: Does agile work? A quantitative analysis of agile project success. Int. J. Project Manage. **33**(5), 1041–1051 (2015)
30. Sun, H.: A longitudinal study of herd behavior in the adoption and continued use of technology. MIS Q. **37**(4), 1013–1041 (2013)
31. Turner, R., Zolin, R.: Forecasting success on large projects: developing reliable scales to predict multiple perspectives by multiple stakeholders over multiple time frames. Project Manage. J. **43**(5), 87–99 (2012)
32. Vavpotic, D., Hovelja, T.: Improving the evaluation of software development methodology adoption and its impact on enterprise performance. Comput. Sci. Inf. Syst. **9**(1), 165–188 (2012)
33. Venkatesh, V., Davis, F.D.: A model of the antecedents of perceived ease of use: development and test. Decis. Sci. **27**(3), 451–481 (1996)
34. Versionone.: The State of Agile Survey (2018). https://explore.versionone.com/state-of-agile/12th-annual-state-of-agile-report-overview. Accessed 28 Oct 2019
35. Vijayasarathy, L.R., Butler, C.W.: Choice of software development methodologies: Do organizational, project, and team characteristics matter? IEEE Softw. **33**(5), 86–94 (2015)
36. Zhu, Z.: Evaluating contingency approaches to information systems design. Int. J. Inf. Manage. **22**(5), 343–356 (2002)

The manufacturer's authorised representative in the EU is Springer Nature Customer Service Centre GmbH, Europaplatz 3, 69115 Heidelberg, Germany. If you have any concerns regarding our products, please contact ProductSafety@springernature.com

Printed and bound by CPI Group (UK) Ltd, Croydon, CR0 4YY
30/09/2026
02225251-0007